A Woman Styled Bold

A Woman Styled Bold

The Life of
Cornelia Connelly
1809–1879

RADEGUNDE FLAXMAN

Foreword by Rosemary Haughton

Darton, Longman and Todd
London

First published in 1991 by
Darton, Longman and Todd Ltd
89 Lillie Road, London SW6 1UD

Reprinted 1991

British Library Cataloguing in Publication Data
Flaxman, Radegunde
  A woman styled bold: the life of Cornelia Connelly 1809–
1879.
  1. Christianity. Religious orders
  I. Title
  271.97

ISBN 0–232–51935–8

Phototypeset by
Input Typesetting Ltd, London SW19 8DR
Printed and bound in Great Britain by
Courier International Ltd

For Ursula, James and
Elizabeth Mary

Contents

Contents

Part II 1849–1879

Illustrations

Foreword

I first encountered Cornelia when I visited Mayfield in my wartime teens, because my younger sister was at school there. (My non-Catholic mother thought a convent school might have a calming affect on her rebellious daughter!) Mayfield, quintessential English village (now much damaged by being part of the richer 'commuter belt' for Londoners), clearly felt like peace and stability to Cornelia, looking for a place to help the young to grow up humanely. When I first went there it was still – because of wartime simplicities – very much as Cornelia knew it. The place, and the little bit of the story of Cornelia that I learned then, captured my romantic teenage imagination, but my attraction to Cornelia survived the teens and the romance, and she became for me one of the needed signs of how women can deal with tragedy and create hope. (I sent one of my daughters to school at Mayfield too, and that decision had roots in memories of that early experience.)

Over the years I read whatever I could find about Cornelia, in convent libraries or on retreat. For a long time it was not much, and what there was tended to surround her with an aura of conventional piety, which was not difficult because she herself naturally used the conventional spiritual language of her time to express her struggles and suffering and her sense of vocation. But Cornelia's passion could not be stuffed for ever into the narrow categories of what a 'holy' woman should be and do and say. It is now possible to recognise her for the prophet she was, and Radegunde Flaxman's book will allow many more people to do so.

This book matters to women who are trying, with an agony Cornelia would understand, to be true to the God-within, in an era when the official churches seem to have lost their prophetic character and in which women count for not much more than they did when Cornelia fought for her vocation, her Society and her own spiritual survival.

Cornelia was called a 'bold' woman, and it was not intended as a compliment. This was a woman whose passionate inner conviction burned through the polite hypocrisy of so much religion of her time and ours, and through the smothering false piety which demanded she give up her integrity in the name of a spurious concept of obedience. Throughout most of her adult life she had to live under the weight of constant anxiety about the fate of the

xi

children who had been taken from her, and about the future of the Society which she had been called to form. These two 'hostages' were constantly used by the church and by her husband in attempts to manipulate her conscience and possess her achievements. Cornelia strenuously sought to be obedient where she felt obedience was, however painfully, due, yet refused to be manipulated. As a woman of her time she accepted the fact of a woman's subordination, but something bright and unquenchable in her would not let her betray her integrity in return for acceptability or a spurious kind of 'peace'. Her secret, as a woman and a Christian, was that her self was founded in the awareness of God who had called her. She might have adapted the self-epitaph of Thomas More, for she was 'the Church's good servant – but God's first', and it was this which drove officials to incredible depths of deceit and slander to destroy her reputation and her work. She gave her life to the service of the church to which God called her, but she would not put the church – in the persons of its officials – in the place of God. That was her martyrdom and her glory.

We need to reflect on the experience of this extraordinary woman. She was a difficult, faithful, angry woman, a woman whose sense of fun was not extinguished by sorrow, whose tragic motherhood reached out to so many who needed it. This is a story to cry over, to laugh at, a story to enrage and encourage. It seems unlikely that Cornelia, the mould-breaker, will ever be fitted into the mould that canonisation requires, but her prophetic spirit is a light we need on the shadowed path we are called to tread – as women, as Christians, as human beings – in a period of unprecedented and unpredictable change and risk.

ROSEMARY HAUGHTON

Sources

The facts of this extraordinary life story, as told in this book, are to be found in the archives of the Society of the Holy Child Jesus in Rome (SHCJ/R). They consist of 55 volumes of the 'writings' of Cornelia Connelly: that is, 1261 letters (to family, ecclesiastics, business and professional men, pupils, sisters), legal and personal documents, notebooks, directives, account books, constitutions. A second set of 85 volumes consists of copies of 6943 documents found in SHCJ, and 117 other archives, mostly in England, Rome and the USA. These volumes cover family affairs, foundations and apostolates, community and government affairs, dealings with bishops and the Holy See. There are also collections of additional documents, unbound but catalogued. This book is not cluttered with detailed references but most of the original MSS held by the Society are in Rome, and both sets above exist in duplicate in the Society archives in USA (Rosemont, PA), England (Mayfield) and Nigeria (Jos), in all of which they are available.

Also accessible, and in the British Library and the Library of Congress, is the *Positio* (*Documentary Study . . . Cornelia Connelly*, Rome, 1983), required by the Catholic Church for its canonisation process. It is an examination in 3 volumes (1500 pp.) and an introductory volume, the *Informatio* (262 pp.), based on the above sets and very fully noted. The few notes in the present biography add information (largely bibliographical) or give sources not part of SHCJ/R.

In the text of this book 'Bellasis' refers to an unpublished biography of Cornelia Connelly by Mother Mary Francis Bellasis (1842–1927), and 'Buckle' to materials collected for a biography by Mother Maria Joseph Buckle (1822–1902). Spelling is modernised in quotations.

Acknowledgements

I can only record, not measure, the debt I owe to all the Sisters of the Society of the Holy Child Jesus whose previous research has enriched this work. They are in a sense co-authors – the many who wrote in *Source*; Mary Evangelist Stewart and Marie Madeleine Amy, their enormous collection of documents; Caritas McCarthy, her numerous studies, her book, her scholarship; very especially the creators of the *Positio*, that almost inexhaustible source of facts, comment and reference: Ursula Blake, its director and chief author, Annette Dawson her untiring assistant, Maureen Crook, M. Dennis Lynch, Magdalen O'Brien, Pierre Rubeaux, Marie Tierney who all contributed substantially to its learning and excellence; Elizabeth Mary Strub whose *Informatio* inspires and who spent days checking my first draft. Their writings echo through this biography, giving it credibility and colour. I thank each one for whatever of her work has been taken up into mine and regret I cannot possibly footnote my many debts.

I owe a great deal too to Denis Paz's recent book on Pierce Connelly, and as much to John Marmion's far-reaching study of Cornelia and education. Without these two pieces of work mine would have been the more superficial. The Sacred Heart sisters most generously allowed me to live with them where once Cornelia lived, Grand Coteau, and shared with me what they knew of those early days. Useful information has come to me through – among many others – Sr Helen Logan SHCJ, Sean Byrne, Fr Mark Miller, F. J. Turner SJ, Leo Warren. Elizabeth Sweeting gave me good practical advice for the opening chapters. The curator of the Old Swedes' church, Wilmington has allowed me to quote from the Vestrymen's Minutes an early letter of Connelly's. I am grateful particularly to the librarians of the English College and the North American College in Rome, of the MSS department of the Free Library, Philadelphia, and of the Preston Records Office; and, among many archivists, especially to Sr Winnie Wickins SHCJ, and Fr Peter Dennison of the Birmingham Archdiocese. Mrs Molly Wright and then Signora Sharon Risoldi have typed and retyped for me unflaggingly. The long-suffering community in which I live has cheered me with their interest. And without the goodwill of DLT the book would never have survived. Not least I want to thank my religious superiors, Elizabeth Mary Strub and Mary Ann Buckley. They sustained me with their encouragement, provided every facility, and – amazingly – never gave up on me.

RADEGUNDE FLAXMAN SHCJ

Prologue

December. The year 1831. The Philadelphia to Pittsburgh stagecoach bumped along. The passengers jerked to and fro. For three days the horses had clopped on, heaving the vehicle over a road more and more deeply rutted as inhabited land fell behind, a five and half days journey going west for 310 miles across farmland at first and then the forests and mountains of Pennsylvania. The coach had no springs but was slung on great leather straps. It was open-sided. Nine passengers squeezed upon three seats, huddling close in their great coats and shawls, illusory comfort in so draughty a vehicle, and cold air swept them when the leather curtains were pushed aside. Among them were a young man, thin and eagerly alert, and a young woman, small, dark and glowing. The Reverend Pierce Connelly, aged twenty-seven, was an Episcopal minister on his way south to Natchez to take up his first rectorship, and with him was his wife Cornelia who would have her twenty-third birthday when they were on the Mississippi. They had been married less than a month. In the intervals of gazing at the land as it unfolded before them on this first lap they remembered what lay behind, Philadelphia and family farewells at four o'clock in the morning.

By the late afternoon of the third day all that was familiar had receded. Wilderness had replaced farms, forest clearings were rare, settlers' cabins peered from the solitude. Goods wagons went this route between interior and coast. So did travellers and immigrants. The Connellys were part of the tide flowing west, growing fuller and fuller as the century went by, and eventually settling itself in islands of life in the untracked spaces. Most, like themselves, were heading initially for the mountains, the great barricade between the known east and the unknown, beckoning west.

Both Cornelia and Pierce were American-born. Their families reached back into pre-Revolution days and they were young people of the still new republic, alive at a time when the country was pulsing with hope. When Cornelia was born it was only thirty-three years old and patriotism burned high. For a whole people – newly caught up in nationhood and with the space of a vast continent calling them – a new kind of freedom had sprung into being, born of land and dominion. The concept of boundary, edge, limit, of 'thus far and no further' changed. The line had faded. What lay beyond was more important than what was already possessed, the immediate was a springboard into the future, the good a chance for the better. In this sense Americans would always be at a beginning, and as Cornelia and Pierce looked out eagerly from the coach for their first sight of the Alleghenies which they would soon have to cross, they were laying hold of their American inheritance. They were people who did not look back.

On the third day the road began to rise steadily, boring its way through forest. Behind were the darkening lands of the east, ahead, beneath a red sun, ridge upon ridge of mountain.

For the next two days the two Connellys journeyed for ninety miles through the Alleghenies, rumbling up and down a switch-back road increasingly steep and snowy. They stopped each night at an inn where they found a warm fireside, dined on wild turkey and venison, and listened to true stories about wolves. Each morning they set off again at four. On the sixth day the road descended. And in Pittsburgh they boarded a steamboat heading down the Ohio for the Mississippi, a journey of seventeen hundred miles.

Part I

1809–1851

1

Childhood and Youth

Relatively little is known of the lives of Pierce and Cornelia before their journey south began. Mere threads of heredity and knots of circumstance exist, pulled mostly from public records which allow us, like Theseus in the labyrinth, to find our way through the landscape of their youth. That landscape was dominated by the style and fortunes of Philadelphia. Pierce was born there in 1804 and Cornelia five years later.

It was a stimulating environment. Philadelphians still believed in their city's pride of place and looked confidently to the future even though the new republic's government had by then moved to Washington. The commercial prosperity of a large port went hand in hand with a sophisticated polite society and cultural development – an academy of arts, an academy of natural sciences, an Athenaeum 'to disseminate useful knowledge', a medical college, an historical society. There were libraries. The university grew. A school system for both girls and boys developed rapidly. Parents in 1830 were 'earnestly and affectionately recommended to send your offspring and those under your care to these seminaries: they have proved of great value to thousands of our youth'.[1]

On 14 May 1831, about seven months before the Connellys departed for Natchez, a journalist produced a resounding paragraph in the *Philadelphia Album*:

> Philadelphia is truly the Athens of America; in its public institutions, in its benevolent and charitable societies, in its literary reputation – in its site, the beautiful regularity of its streets – its buildings both public and private – in every particular, except in the dust and dirt, the noise and bustle which attends an extensive shipping, we are superior without a doubt to every other City in the Union.

The wealthy merchants who financed the Philadelphia Exchange in that same year had much the same qualities in mind, but expressed them with more elegantly veiled satisfaction: their beautiful building was to be 'proof of the liberal spirit and cultivated taste which in our days distinguish the mercantile community'.[2] It was a centre of vitality and enterprise, of wealth and social grace in which Pierce and Cornelia spent all their young lives and which they must have remembered as the coach lumbered towards Pittsburgh.

PIERCE CONNELLY, 1804–25[3]

Connellys had probably arrived in America in the eighteenth century, immigrants from Northern Ireland, Presbyterian perhaps, escaping from Catholic pressure and British domination. Initially they would have come to Philadelphia hard on the heels of the Palatinate Germans whom William Penn had invited to populate Pennsylvania, his colony of tolerance. Pierce's grandfather George died there in 1773 leaving three sons, and his father Henry and his uncle John lived to be important men in their city. Pierce therefore belonged to a family which successfully bridged the years of the Revolution, and his boyhood home would have echoed with memories of colonial life, of the struggle for independence, and with all the immediate interests of a growing family in a growing young nation.

Pierce's father, Henry Connelly, had distinguished himself in the city's tradition of craftsmanship. In early times Philadelphia had looked for its expression of prosperity to England's élitist culture. We have only to think of the tone set by Penn's lifestyle. He had lived up river at Pennsbury in a spacious country house with formal gardens, his lawns seeded with English grass and laid by English gardeners. He gave fine dinners and came down the Delaware in a twelve-oared barge like an English monarch down the Thames. Others of lesser standing in the home country than Penn – who belonged to a titled family – came to his city to better themselves, aspiring in this New World to what only the aristocracy had in the Old. The flow of immigrant artisans increased, their front-room workshops began to line the downtown alleys by the river and by the time the city was the national capital its own craftsmen could meet the needs of what was a very elegant society. Henry Connelly, cabinet maker, had emerged from among the craftsmen as the best exponent of Sheraton style. Some of his pieces, set with a personal monogram, still grace Philadelphia homes and enrich American museums. At first he both lived and worked at 16 Chestnut Street down near the Delaware front where merchants and shipmen jostled with craftsmen and bankers for ever greater prosperity. Then he moved to a more pretentious house, 44 Spruce Street in Society Hill, and this is probably where Pierce was born, not far from the dockside. Eventually the family home was yet further west up fashionable Spruce, at number 233, and if any of the four boys went to school at the Episcopal Academy, which is possible, it was just along the block.

A frequent visitor in the Henry Connelly home was Pierce's uncle, Colonel John Connelly, twenty years older than his brother. Both were men of philanthropic bent, both firm Presbyterians, pewholders at the First Presbyterian Church on Market Street, elders there and John a trustee. From him the Connelly boys could imbibe a great deal that was formative for the young American. He had served in the Revolutionary war and in the 1812 war against Britain. He had survived the horrors of the yellow fever plague of 1793, when he had tended the sick. He was an early member of the Society for Alleviating the Miseries of Public Prisoners. At one time he was a senator in the Pennsylvania Legislature, at another a member of the House of Representatives. From being only one of many shopkeepers in 1777 with a downtown business on Front Street, their uncle John had risen to some eminence in the city.

In the year 1800 Elizabeth Pierce at the age of twenty-two became Henry Connelly's second wife. No picture of her has been traced, but Thomas Sully painted her husband as a dark-eyed twinkling man with a kind mouth and an alert expression. They had twenty-six years together. When he retired from cabinet-making in 1824 they went to her homeground in Delaware near Mill Creek Hundred where her parents still lived. 'Pierce' was a common Swedish family name thereabouts, evidently treasured by Elizabeth since her eldest son received it.

It is unfortunate that we know so little about Elizabeth Connelly. Three baby daughters died almost at birth but all four sons survived so hers was the only woman's influence on Pierce within the home. Emotional disturbance, pathological in its depth and expression, hidden as a young man but suddenly apparent later at a time of crisis, perhaps had its source in his childhood relationship with her. He was her firstborn, a sensitive child if we judge by the grown man, affectionate and dependent. Years later, as a man of thirty-two, he turned to his mother, still to him in moments of crisis 'dearest, dearest', and wanted to be to her again what he felt he had been long ago when as 'a little boy I used to go up into the big front room to say my prayers after I had come in from school'. When he was forty he wrote wretchedly to his youngest brother, 'Love even of parents does not depend always on merit, yet perhaps if I had deserved more love I should have had it'. No letter of his mother's is extant, but one is briefly quoted by Cornelia:

> . . . remember that the same father and mother that raised you raised them though your advantages [were] much greater than theirs. Your pleasures and pursuits were totally different, you got your knowledge from books & the fashionable world, Harry from men and manners etc., etc. John and George lost their father when they most needed him.

When Henry Connelly died in 1825 he bequeathed all he had to his wife and entrusted her with the maintenance and education of all his children during their minority. Harry, aged twenty, took over his father's cotton mill in nearby Roseville and John, aged seventeen, worked with him for some time; George, thirteen, was sent to university. Pierce, twenty-two, had completed his formal education the previous year at the University of Pennsylvania, but having announced to his Presbyterian family that he wished to be an Episcopal minister he now turned to theological studies.

CORNELIA PEACOCK, 1809–31

Cornelia Augusta Peacock was born on 15 January 1809 at a house on the north-west corner of 8th and Filbert, in those days a fashionable residential area in Philadelphia. The house, numbered 1, 3 and 5, was large enough to hold the family of ten, as it then was, plus any servant they might have had. Possibly Cornelia's arrival in the world coincided with the peak of her father's fortunes. Although American-born like Pierce, her ancestral roots were less fully American than his, her immediate family situation less stable and its members less prominent. In these ways, at least materially, Pierce was more advantaged than she. Yet what little information there is of either conveys the certainty that hers was a happy, secure childhood that formed her to love and trust. Unlike Pierce's it had running through it no vein of rejection or of thwarted hunger for affection to distort her experience of life and people.

Cornelia's father Ralph Peacock was a Yorkshireman who with his brother William had emigrated to America as recently as 1794 or 1795. When his youngest child Cornelia was born Philadelphia had been his home for fourteen years, but the memory of twice as long in the quiet country village of Nunnington in northern England must still have been green. He had lived there, the youngest of six, for twenty-eight years; an uneventful life, that of a remote village perched on a little hill overlooking the Vale of York. Here for centuries his ancestors had tilled the fields[4] and now lay, as did his parents, in the ancient country churchyard. Possibly he stayed for the sake of the mother who survived their father by twenty years. She too had come from a local village, Nawton, and Ralph would record his love of her and his Yorkshire home by giving her family name Dodsworth to his first-born. It had been a life that he left probably without too much regret but nevertheless it slept in the very bones of memory. To what extent Ralph Peacock talked to his little daughter of his native land we do not know but she eventually showed something of a farmer's qualities, the certainty in her heart of goodness and growth, and the abundant capacity to wait and endure with hope having faced year after year the season's calamities. Hot-tempered and untidy little girl as she later described herself to have been, yet in all her portraits, beginning with the first when she was about twenty-two, there is an extraordinary repose, as of one at rest and sure.

We have only one anecdote of Cornelia in childhood, and it is set on her father's farm near Mount Holly in New Jersey. She and her sister were wandering in forbidden fields and found themselves in the middle of a herd of bullocks. Cornelia, aged seven, daringly provoked one but when he rushed at her all bravery evaporated and she fled for safety to a shed. Mary, however, at the great age of eleven, remained calm and determined. She advanced upon the animal and by dint of opening and shutting her red parasol at him, backed him over a bank and he was killed.

The farm was one of Ralph's later acquisitions. Although he is variously listed as 'merchant', 'import merchant grocer', 'distiller', it would seem that he was also caught up in the property boom of the day and was chiefly a speculator in land and houses. In so short a period as 1800–14 he moved house or business or both nine times, a mobility which characterised a fast-growing city but does not necessarily prove the prosperity of the individual. Apparently in 1812 he had taken advantage of the Insolvent Act which suggests that ultimately disaster overtook him. He died at the age of fifty in 1818 in a nursing home in Camden leaving considerable debts behind him.

Cornelia was only nine. There would be no more countryside adventures on the Mount Holly farm. No more drives with Papa in his gig. No more visits to his current merchant store. No more standing tiptoe at the end of Market Street to gaze over the fish stalls below and see if Papa's ferry was churning its way across the Delaware (it had been called 'The Washington' and its special job was carrying horses and wagons over to Camden). There is no reference to her father anywhere in Cornelia's writings but his death was her first experience of loss. Someone familiar and loved was no longer there and the incomprehensible gap had to be closed for her by her loving family: Dodsworth aged twenty, artistic and named for his English grand-mother; Adeline aged eighteen, Cornelia's 'dear Sissy', beautiful and already married to a very wealthy man, Louis Duval; Ralph William, named for the Peacock father and uncle, his little sister's 'dear Ralpho'; George Stein-metz, about fifteen years old, probably called after his maternal great-uncle John. 'Put a cap on George,' Cornelia laughingly wrote many years later to his wife, 'and you will see my picture': he was dark-eyed with curly black hair; Mary Francis, thirteen, she of the bullock and red parasol, 'my best beloved sister and the sweetest friend of my youthful days, even then like a Guardian Angel to me'. More shadowy because we have no portrait, no anecdote, her mother Mary Swope Bowen Peacock. At this time, hurt by

9

the mystery of death, it must have been to her especially that the nine-year-old turned. Years later she wrote to a niece, 'None can ever quite equal a Mother's love.'

It was on Mrs Peacock's side that her daughter was a third-generation American. Her great-grandfather Daniel Steinmetz was one of those German immigrants from Europe early in the eighteenth century, probably from the Palatinate where many of his compatriots were discriminated against for their beliefs. His ship, the *Dragon*, reached dock in the Delaware in 1732 and in the following years he did so well that at his death in 1760 he was able to leave the eight children large properties in the Philadelphia area. In 1768 a daughter Susannah married a doctor Jacob Swope, also from the Palatinate. In the same year she died giving birth to Mary, Cornelia's mother. Members of both these families, Swopes and Steinmetzes, committed themselves to support the struggle for independence.

Mary Swope's first marriage, like her second, was to an Englishman, John Bowen of Bowen Hall, a successful sugar planter in Jamaica. He died in 1794 but she had lived in the West Indies for at least some of that time and had borne him two children, Isabella and John, both of whom were probably living in the Peacock home when Cornelia was born. The lifestyle of the owners on a plantation was more spacious and affluent than that of the Peacocks. The mother was usually mistress of the total establishment, expected to manage many aspects of estate and household. Often she was the educator of her children at least in their younger years, and perhaps also guide to the slaves of which on the Bowen seven-hundred-acre plantation there were more than a hundred, all of which meant that Cornelia's mother was probably a very competent woman. She also had a comfortable Bowen annuity, a city lot and house inherited from her mother and the prospect of further inheritance from the estate of her Steinmetz grandparent. Her two Bowen children were handsomely provided for by their father. When her second husband died and some of his property had to be sold to pay his debts, the family circumstances, though reduced, were not radically so. In addition to this economic security she had acquired a cultural breadth beyond what Philadelphia alone could have given her. This, along with the practical experience of plantation life and the ease that is bred of wealth, became part of Cornelia's own inheritance.

We know nothing of Mrs Peacock's education and little of Cornelia's though it is more easily deducible. Philadelphia in the early nineteenth century had already developed a tradition of serious concern for education, including that of girls. By the eve of the Revolution wealthy parents even in the south and the islands were sending sons and daughters to its schools. The city system was based on the monitorial methods of Lancaster and Bell but by the turn of the century many private establishments for young ladies had appeared up and down the smartest streets, and a choice of boarding schools lay within reach. No doubt they varied in the quality of what was offered and some, with little thought of real education, confined themselves to the three Rs and social graces. But Philadelphia upper class society travelled in Europe, read European books and had French- and German-speaking people in its midst which was an incentive to the genuine study of languages. The freedom with which the sexes mixed encouraged the girls to wish to learn what the boys did, for instance mathematics, classics, philosophy. Young women often therefore supplemented their school curricula with special subject study under tutors because day school hours were very short, only 11.30 to 1.30 p.m., and their programmes too limited.[5] Possibly Cornelia went to school but there is no record to that effect. Whilst she was still young Mrs Peacock may well have taught her, as was a custom of the day. When she was older she certainly had tutors.

The Peacocks occupied a three-storied house in the fashionable Arch Street area. An inventory reveals its degree of comfort: feather beds and curtains for four-posters, looking glasses and pictures, counterpanes and carpets. On the ground floor in the parlours rugs, good tableware, a chintz-covered sofa, 'fancy' chairs, mantel lamps and brass candlesticks, fire screens and bellows, and, delightful for a child, two birdcages with green baize covers to silence the birdsong at night. It was the home of a close-knit family. Years later Cornelia would write, 'the older I grow the more intensely I love you all', and she remembered with joy that she was to all of them 'Nelie' or 'little Ne'. They had known the death at eleven months of the child one ahead of her. 'Little Ne' was God's unexpected gift, bobbing along at the end of the line. And when father, then mother had died, they all stepped in and cherished her.

Mrs Peacock died after a severe and lingering illness on Tuesday, 13 May 1823. *Poulson's Daily Advertizer* 'respectfully invited . . . her friends and . . . the family . . . to attend her funeral from her late dwelling on Tenth above Arch . . . at 9 o'clock'. A subdued young girl clad in mourning rode in one of the carriages to and from the burial ground. In her fourteen years the great human realities had often closed in on her – birth, marriage, sickness, death. The hope-filled weddings of her half-brother John and her own sister Addie had given place to grief when children were painfully born and so soon were dead. Her father and recently her brother Dodsworth had been taken by death, and still more recently she had spent many hours at her mother's bedside watching the ravage of illness till she too died.

The sadness of Cornelia's fourteenth year was crowned by the break-up of the family. It was decided that their home should be disposed of. Ralph and George would set up on their own. Mary, who was eighteen, would go to live further up Arch Street with the Duvals where Addie, now twenty-three, was in need of company as her nursery gradually filled. 'Little Ne' was to be adopted by her half-sister Isabella Bowen Montgomery, a very great change. The Montgomerys were well-to-do and childless. Because Isabella had been married in the year of Cornelia's birth, they did not have the intimacy born of living under the same family roof for even a year, nor had the Montgomery house on Chestnut Street the atmosphere of a home filled with the life and memories of children. Isabella had had the early upbringing of a wealthy childhood in Jamaica and she brought wealth to her marriage, yet in later years Cornelia remembered her as living 'in a most plain and simple way'. Possibly it was a rather strict household. It lacked too the religious unity of the Peacock home. Isabella was Presbyterian, Austin Episcopalian, the religious affiliation generally speaking of Philadelphia's upper class. There were many ways in which at first Cornelia would feel isolated, and times when she must have been thrown back on inner resources and perhaps on religious belief as never before.

But Isabella was generous. No expense was spared in developing Cornelia's talents, we are told. She was 'highly educated at home by Professors and Tutors . . . conversed in several languages . . . was an artist and musician'.

The most crucial of the influences on Cornelia in the Montgomery household proved to be the contact with Protestant Episcopalianism. In childhood days she had attended the second Presbyterian church of Arch Street, sitting each Sunday in the family pew which her mother had continued to rent even after her father died. Two of her sisters were married there. A Peacock baby and recently Dodsworth and then her mother were buried in its churchyard. It can be fairly safely assumed that Cornelia saw herself as a member and had been baptised as a baby, although no record survives. Very possibly she attended Sunday school. Sustained preaching and a catechetical system were part of the Presbyterian organisation, and by the time she was fourteen she could have imbibed a good deal.

But only three months before Cornelia left her home in May 1823 a new church opened, St Stephen's, built to the west of the city in a residential area of handsome houses among trees and open spaces. Bishop White, leader of the American Protestant Episcopal Church, consecrated it and the inaugural homily was given by the high churchman John Henry Hobart of New York. The first rector was a disciple of his and a man of sanctity and eloquence, with the result that the church rapidly became a centre of Episcopalian influence.[6] From the time Cornelia moved to Chestnut Street she must have been drawn into his spiritual orbit, because he was Isabella's brother-in-law. Isabella herself, unlike the rest of the Peacock family, appears, according to Cornelia, to have been religiously indifferent. On the other hand her husband was Episcopalian and it would seem certain that the Revd James Montgomery DD was *persona grata* in Cornelia's new home during the eight years she remained there. The family of her half-brother John Bowen, and then all the Duvals were soon worshipping at St Stephen's, their children's names in the baptismal register. At twenty-two she too took the step. Montgomery baptised her into the Episcopal church on 25 February 1831 and two weeks later her sister Mary followed.

MEETING AND MARRIAGE

Information about Pierce during the years when Cornelia was living with the Montgomerys is thin. Until 1824 he lived in Philadelphia and presumably moved with the family down to the Wilmington area, then known as Christina. In September 1825 he was cited as a candidate by Bishop White at the Episcopal convention, and for the next three years either lived in Philadelphia or visited somewhat frequently for the sake of his studies. Almost certainly he was tutored by Bishop White who, like Montgomery, moved in circles familiar to Cornelia.[7]

Pierce began his life as an Episcopalian minister, with parsonage and a yearly stipend of $500, at Old Trinity, Wilmington. In January 1827 the trustees gave him the call; in June he was ordained deacon at Christ Church, Philadelphia, the Bishop's church: and his name appears on the Old Trinity list of ministers for 1827–8. Trinity was the Old Swedes' church, the history of which he and his brothers will have heard on childhood visits to the Pierce relatives, and no doubt the young man in the pulpit for the first occasion was known to at least some of the congregation. He was tall and thin, aged twenty-three, with a lofty forehead and a little chin, his ears rather high on his head. He was also endowed with a sense of drama and much eloquence. Our first glimpse of his personality appears a year later, however, in the letter of resignation partly preserved in the minutes of a meeting of the trustees:

> [I was] led to this step because I foresee what I deprecate: because I do not choose to expose myself to collision with a party who think themselves fitter to govern than either you or me, who believe their own articles wiser than the Canon of the Church and would have their minister be bound by one rather than the other – with whom I have already remonstrated in the most affectionate manner and because I will never consent to remain where I am not allowed or enabled to pursue uninterruptedly the course which I think my duty prescribes me.[8]

At some date after that Pierce became an assistant minister at the church of St James, Kingsessing and on 5 October 1828 was ordained priest.

Ambitious for better things he applied in 1829 to be rector of Holy Trinity, Boston but was disappointed. Kingsessing, however, was in the Philadelphia orbit and it was probably during these years 1828–31 that he met Cornelia. She and the Duvals, the Montgomerys, the Whites and the Bowens all moved in Episcopalian circles, and, as one of Adeline's daughters later wrote, Pierce 'was an assistant clergyman in one of the Episcopal Churches, very handsome, fascinating. A number of young ladies, friends of C. Peacock, were vying with each other for the attentions of the young minister.' Even so, in the eyes of Mrs Montgomery Pierce did not qualify as a suitor for her ward.

Events make Isabella's opposition interesting. Had Pierce been called to the Boston pulpit she might have felt better about him, income and standing would have been guaranteed. Apparently his university education, his engaging manners, his intelligence and religious sincerity counted for little in the face of socially discreditable origins. Alternatively, her account bears the imprint of the writer's prejudices, not Isabella's. Hindsight suggests that Isabella saw something she did not quite like in Pierce and feared to commit her young sister to him. Or, given her religious indifference, she underestimated a basic cause of Cornelia's love, his ardent belief in the church he served.

Cornelia became an Episcopalian in February 1831 and they were married in December. Whether Pierce's proposal of marriage came before or after that decision is not known. Many years later she said that she renewed her baptismal vows every day of her life. But her love for him, whether acknowledged yet or not, must have influenced her, and when he did propose, Isabella misjudged her young sister's determination to marry him: she arranged to be wedded at Adeline's house instead.

The account by Cornelia's niece is our only source of information about the circumstances which led to the marriage. Its author was seventy-six years old at the time of writing, recording an event which had taken place four years before she was born. Presumably it bears a core of truth that had become a kind of family legend. It tells us:

When Mrs Montgomery . . . discovered the growing attachment of Cornelia, she was much displeased, as she had great ambitions that her beautiful and accomplished sister would make a better match. The young minister was poor and his family had not the social standing of the Peacocks and Montgomerys, young Pierce's father being in trade, furniture business I believe. Mrs Montgomery forbid him the house. He must discontinue his visits. I think Cornelia . . . sang in his church. She had a beautiful and cultivated voice . . . Always possessed of strong will power,

[she] appealed to her eldest sister . . . and arranged to visit her and be married from her house . . . the handsome residence of my mother.

In the custom of the day, the ceremony took place on Thursday evening, 1 December 1831, in the large upstairs drawing room of Adeline's house on Chestnut Street. No doubt it was a very beautiful occasion for Louis Duval was a wealthy man. We have to envision Connellys and Duvals and Bowens and Pierces in a setting of candles and gilt-edged mirrors, of the polished wood surfaces and striped upholstery belonging to elegant contemporary furniture. Pierce was tall and prepossessing. 'Little Ne', dressed by her sister, more than ordinarily lovely. She was at this time, we are told:

. . . rather below than above the middle height, slight in figure, with a profusion of wavy black hair, her face singularly beautiful, her features finely chiselled, her eyes very dark and full of fire and sweetness, and they would quickly fill with tears on hearing of any trouble or sorrow. Her forehead was high and broad and her nose aquiline. Her smile was very sweet . . .

Bishop White married them. Soon after the wedding the young couple left Philadelphia. Pierce, on 17 October 1831, had been offered the charge of Trinity church at Natchez in Mississippi where his family had property. The salary was to be $1000 a year and travel expenses would be paid. They packed their belongings, said their farewells and set out together with a shared enthusiasm for his calling, a young minister and his wife.

2

The Minister and his Wife

NATCHEZ, 1831–5

On the Mississippi. The great river was aptly called by the Indians the Father of Waters. Between its banks the melted snows of distant mountains and the rains and rivers of more than a million square miles poured down to the Gulf. Its waters rolled. Its broad course was treacherous, neither cleared nor dredged, nowhere straightened and scarcely charted. It took the Connellys down to the low, undulating lands of the deep south, out of one world into another. Their steamboat was a kind of floating castle with white ramparts and forward drawbridges always up, travelling at possibly fifteen miles an hour, breathing smoke through tall black chimneys. The journey could take two weeks. The paddlesteamer of 1831 was not yet the queen of the river it would soon become. When the furnace was stoked high, explosion and death threatened.

Cornelia could have been the only woman aboard. Planters, merchants, land speculators; crew; mulattos and Negroes; perhaps a Methodist circuit rider, a transient community floating through a strange domain. Every planter had his footage of land on the bank and the boat answered any hail across the water. Those standing on the deck could catch no glimpse of the plantation homes of which in the north they heard so much. Cultivated land in these lower reaches lay far back to escape flooding. All that met wondering eyes, except for the rare bluffs that rose up at regular intervals on the eastern bank, was a wilderness of low, swampy shore. Who could blame Pierce the Philadelphian, if perhaps fleeting depression touched him as he looked at the dreary landscape and remembered his Boston ambitions? When the boat churned round the great bend and Natchez at last came into view, he and his wife must have gazed intently, for here their home was to be.

Natchez sat high on a bluff of the east bank, a lighthouse overlooking the river curve where the ferry crossed to Louisiana. Wharves and taverns crowded under the bluff and boats stretched for a mile along the shore. Above, Natchez-on-the-Hill stood like a signpost between plantations behind and river below. Perched above the great north-south highway which the river had become, when the Connellys came it was an important cotton port, prosperous and smart. An imposing high esplanade at the end of its main street looked out across the Mississippi. Below was the port. Behind lay a chequerboard of streets, unpaved but tree-lined. Along the sidewalks men hitched their horses. Here and there a white house with a lacy wrought-iron balcony recalled the Spanish past. Already there were two well-built churches, an Episcopalian and a Presbyterian. Blacks were everywhere, many of them free people. It was still a crossroads for adventurers, but the needs of affluent cotton planters and merchants dominated. Their carriages arriving in town with the ladies of distant plantations made a fine sight, each with its gentleman escort astride his mount.

Many travellers of the thirties recorded their impressions of Natchez.[1] A Yankee, Joseph Ingraham, estimated the population at three thousand inhabitants, mostly coloured. He found there what he termed a society of 'refinement and elegance', unsurpassed he thought by any in America. Pierce and Cornelia at once had the entrée to this polite society, probably through his prosperous brother Harry who as a cotton mill owner near Wilmington often took the boat south. A personal friendship was soon established with one of the most wealthy and distinguished planters of the neighbourhood, Dr Newton Mercer of the Laurel Hill.

The town was a mere spot of activity in the midst of the deep quiet of immense surrounding forest. Often in the coming months Pierce, on his way to visit a parishioner and riding along one of the tunnel-like roads that ran in every direction out of Natchez, would be scarcely aware of the plantation homes hidden in the densely wooded scene. A gate would reveal a drive and the drive would wander through trees and cottonfields before the house, probably white and galleried, at last appeared. Near it, framed in the forest greens, there was often a park-like garden, formal and shady but full of colour and fragrance. Laurel Hill was no exception. Dr Mercer's devoted friend Colonel Huntington once wrote to him about planting his park with 'the youthful-looking and tender Jessamine . . . whose delicious fragrance is worth a journey of a hundred miles'.[2] Somewhere on every plantation were the slave quarters, white-washed cabins perhaps set among chinaberry trees. There were all the utilities needed to make the plantation self-sufficient, and a family graveyard made lovely like a garden. Pierce would have conducted burial services in some of these – in the forest swamps death was bred with the seasons. And homes were remote from each other. More often than not 'the guests who came to dinner might stay a week'.

Pierce had been offered salary and travelling expenses but no rectory, and on 4 December 1832 he bought a property about a mile from the town centre and from his church. Ingraham describes it. He was ambling on horseback along the town's southern outskirts and 'passed several neat dwellings of the cottage order, one of which with a gallery in front and surrounded by a smooth green slope was the residence of the Episcopalian clergyman. It was a chaste and pretty mansion.' This 'mansion' the Connellys called Whitecottage. Mansion, compared with the homes of some of the planters at that date, it certainly was not. These had towering pillared porticoes that reached from ground to second floor, encircling galleries on both levels, and many, many rooms. Compared with these Whitecottage was a cottage indeed. Cornelia was pregnant and only two weeks later, on 17 December, gave birth to a son, Mercer. Possibly Merty, as they called the child, was born at Laurel Hill – he was namesake and godchild of Dr Mercer, his black mammy Phoebe had belonged to the doctor and her daughter Sally was his christening gift – but by February they had taken possession of their cottage. Mary Peacock had arrived to live with them, George Connelly was there on a visit. Mercer's baptism by his father on 10 February was the opportunity to entertain for the first time, an occasion for celebration, the birth of a son to the young rector and his wife and the founding of family and home.

The house lay on the Upper Woodville Road, now Homochito Street, and Dr Mercer passed it when he rode the six miles in from Laurel Hill. Owners of plantations lying south and south-east normally came into town that way, and since many of them and their ladies were Episcopalian and some of them Pierce's vestrymen, Whitecottage was well placed as a port of call. As Mary Peacock said, she had seen Pierce 'often entertaining so much company and living so generously'. The planters as a class were cultured, humanitarian, politically often whig, and religiously more often than not Episcopalian. In many ways they cherished the ideals of the English lady and gentleman and for Cornelia and Pierce it was the Mercers, their friends, who exemplified this combination of qualities. Their home, Laurel Hill, was set in the midst of a vast and well-ordered estate. The great house, in its furnishings and library, reflected the educated tastes of those who read and travelled at leisure in Europe. Several hundred slaves worked the plantations and for these, their 'people', they showed the most Christian concern, as the Connellys saw. Dr Mercer is said never to have sold a slave and rarely to have bought one. He gave them leisure time, comfort and medical care. His 'great anxiety', as later expressed in his will, which left money to each one, was 'to provide for that class which was made dependent on me . . . to treat them justly and kindly . . . to prepare them for the great change in their condition which I have long seen was inevitable'.[3] That he provided the Connellys with one of his 'people' to be Mercer's nurse was a sign of trust. Pierce when he left Natchez was working on a special catechism for Negroes and Cornelia loved her slaves. Sally's descendants say that Mrs Connelly not only gave her Christian instruction but even set her free.

Pierce said later how much he enjoyed this 'agreeable and cultivated social circle', but on the other hand his ministry in Natchez in some of its aspects was extraordinarily demanding. It is true that it had something of the stability of an established church in a small place. He visited in the parish, administered the sacraments, met with his vestrymen. Sometimes he gave an address in the town, at for instance the local orphanage to the ladies who ran it; and he preached regularly in his church, Holy Trinity. Ingraham was there one Sunday when Pierce was delivering his homily. The preacher's manner, he noted, was 'engaging and mild' but 'the numbers were few', confined to 'opulent planters, merchants and professional men along with their families'. Pierce must have been well aware of the immense difficulties of enlarging his congregation. The greater part of the population was black, more easily attracted to evangelical styles of worship than to that of his church. Episcopalians were fairly numerous in the district but they were widely scattered. Those on remote plantations kept faith and devotion alive as best they could through morning and evening family prayers, but few were within reach of a church or were ever called on by a clergyman.

Pierce served the church of St Paul at Woodville and Christ's in Jefferson County, both more than thirty miles from Natchez. In addition to parish visiting in the town, he went to whatever outlying plantations he could reach. But as James Otey the Episcopalian bishop of Tennessee wrote, in his Visitation Report of the Diocese of Mississippi, 1835:

> With but one clergy man (the Rev. Mr Connelly) in active employment within the bounds of a large diocese it cannot be expected that the results of his labours, confined as these are to Natchez and its vicinity, will be more than to keep alive some feeling of interest in the church beyond the limits of his own parish.

This episcopal visitation, made at the request of the Revd Connelly and his committee, took place in January 1835, its main purpose to administer the sacrament of confirmation. On arrival Bishop Otey found Pierce 'confined to his room by severe indisposition' – whether brought on by exhaustion or by the religious anxieties to which Cornelia later referred, we cannot know. Only after a week was he sufficiently recovered to accompany the bishop on his visits which were, on the whole, Pierce's normal rounds. The Report thus incidentally presents a picture of his routine experience. They had to brave weather that was 'disagreeably cold and inclement'. They reached hospitality in isolated plantation homes only after long, hard riding. On occasion swamp made roads impassable, and the bishop wrote that 'few . . . will be found ready to encounter the fatigues and dangers of exposure to a southern climate'. It becomes clear that the field for his ministry was in some aspects unusual, hard and depressing. Not the least of the hardship was lack of a fellow minister with whom to share the load.

In such circumstances a wife's support was important. It was gratifying for them both to find him highly praised in the Report when it came: 'The success of Mr Connelly in gathering a large congregation under circumstances of extraordinary depression lays the ground of reasonable calculation to suppose that labours equally faithful will in other places be crowned with similar results.' Statistics show the degree of Pierce's success. In 1832 when they arrived there were fourteen communicants including Cornelia: in 1835 when they left there were sixty-two. In an office Report destined for the eyes not only of Pierce's own committee but also presumably for the House of Bishops, Otey praises the rector's 'faithful labours', the 'pious instructions, the affectionate expostulations, the impressive warnings which marked the character of his addresses to his people'.

At this point in the lives of the Connellys (and Cornelia was expecting their second child in about six weeks time), they had been married for three happy years. Cornelia often sat in the family pew at Holy Trinity, heard her husband preach and knew from experience the truth of the bishop's comment. Their years in the parish had been crowned by his appreciation. Yet in the near future a full congregation again assembled and listened for the last time to their rector:

> . . . the scenes which we have shared together come up again before me. How regularly have I received you at these rails. How often have we knelt beside the bed, and stood around the grave . . . how shall I forget my happy days amongst you . . . how shall I thank you for all your goodness, not only to me personally, but to those dearer than myself.

Pierce had resigned his parish and written to the bishop:

> I know the grief that what I am going to tell you will create . . . my faith is shaken in the Protestant religion. I have resigned my parish . . . to weigh deliberately and devoutly my future duty . . . I pretend not to say where the truth will lead me; I only am persuaded of my present duty, and am determined by the help of God to follow it.

Only six months had passed since the bishop's Report had praised him so highly and publicly. It was a drastic action to take so soon and had incalculable consequences in his own life. And for 'those dearer than myself'.

PIERCE'S STRUGGLE, 1834–5

The Connellys had been deeply affected by the anti-Catholicism of their day. The nineteenth century in the United States saw an enormously increased tide of immigrants, relatively negligible in the early decades but threatening to contemporaries. Generally these poor people arrived destitute. They were a swelling source of cheap labour and they imperilled the livelihood of native poor Americans. They made rapid industrial growth possible and in the east where farmland and countryside had long been the peaceful scene, urban areas began to spread. When Jackson's democrats set out to mobilise the immigrant vote they became a political threat, and for conservatives afraid for traditional institutions and seeing unwanted change on the horizon, they were a foreign menace. Out of this combination of fears nativism grew. The south, and therefore Natchez, had its part in this national experience. Immigrants travelled west across the southern states seeking land and fortune. Many settled there. The population of the states of Mississippi and Arkansas (where Pierce joined in the land speculation) increased steadily.

These same immigrants, in whatever part of the States they settled, were also often Catholic. Through them the Roman church, in earlier days a tiny percentage of the population, became more and more evident. In 1807 there had been only one see, fifteen years later there were ten; and by 1827 at least thirty Protestant papers had been established, all preaching the need to protect the United States from papal power. When in 1829 the Catholic bishops held their first council and made statements (for the guidance of their own flock) about parochial schools and about the use of the Bible, Protestant fears rose. In August 1834 a well-organised mob attacked and burnt a convent near Boston. New periodicals like the *Downfall of Babylon* appeared. Samuel F. B. Morse and Lyman Beecher produced tracts which between them lit the torches of Protestant aggression.

These two propagandists were the chief catalysts of a widespread fear for the nation's liberty. There was an alliance, they said, between the invading immigrants and the Catholic church, its purpose to destroy the American republic and establish popery and despotism. Beecher wrote that the immigrants rolling in were like an enlisted army. Morse, counting on the country's sense of 'manifest destiny', summoned an inflated patriotism: 'It is liberty itself that is in danger . . . the liberty of the world . . . In the agony of its struggles against despotism, the WORLD EXPECTS AMERICA, REPUBLICAN AMERICA, TO DO HER DUTY.'[4] Facts like the existence in the States of European missionary societies and of Catholic schools were presented from a bias of hatred and the inflammatory periodicals of the Protestant propaganda press promptly filled in the imaginary plot with false

21

detail. But they sometimes failed in their purpose. The violence and evident distortion moved Pierce Connelly into 'a laborious study of the controversy', a 'course of reading', he wrote, 'which the miserable fanaticism of the periodicals drove me into'.

The struggle through which Pierce now went is a revelation of the man to whom Cornelia was married.

When the Connellys arrived in Natchez they were already aware of and had shared in anti-Catholic attitudes, in particular those of the Episcopal church. While Pierce was curate at St James's his bishops had issued a pastoral letter in 1829 warning their flocks against papal perils. When he became rector of Holy Trinity he continued to take Episcopalian periodicals and in them, fairly often, were anti-Catholic articles. In Natchez itself discussion among his planter friends would have been in favour generally of the Episcopal church, a body which officially described itself as Protestant. Yet against such continuing anti-Catholic pressure Pierce's own basic attraction to much that was Catholic apparently struggled. He had been, he wrote in 1836 for the *Dublin Review*

> ... in good truth a high churchman ... I *did believe* the 'Church has authority', and without indeed having very definite ideas of what 'the Church' is, I thought all my duty was to keep my vows and 'hear the Church', believing and teaching just what she decreed should be believed and taught. Nor indeed could I, or can I ever, conceive the practicability of acting upon the notion of private judgement.

In Natchez he felt 'in *solitude* as to political, philosophical and theological associations'. He was aware of 'the great armada which is waging in the world with books instead of swords' and he went so far as to refuse to cooperate in distributing propaganda pamphlets, or to have Protestant auxiliary societies in his parish. But he did not allow himself to look closely at his thoughts until he made 'acquaintance with a distinguished foreigner in the winter of thirty-three and thirty-four'.

One winter evening, probably late in 1833, there was in Natchez a social gathering to which the Connellys were invited. In all likelihood it took place at Somerset, the home of the Chotards. Its purpose was to introduce the guest who over the next few years would often come to stay there, the Chevalier Joseph Nicholas Nicollet. Nicollet was a distinguished Frenchman, scholar and scientist, a mathematical geographer. Financial misfortune bred of the 1830 revolution in France had brought him across the Atlantic hoping to make a scientific tour in America and to contribute to the knowledge of its physical geography. Drawn by the thought of the Mississippi he soon moved west and St Louis became his headquarters. He wanted to survey and map the whole river basin and was eventually commissioned by the American government, but meanwhile far-sighted friends gave him hospitality and financed him. Among these was Major Henry Chotard, successful planter and owner of large and beautiful Somerset. On this occasion we can imagine carriages bearing the family's guests up its winding drive, and in its double drawing-rooms Mrs Chotard and her three daughters welcoming them. The Connellys were their personal friends.

Pierce recalled Nicollet for the *Dublin Review*: an impressive man, 'altogether remarkable' who in the midst of his professional labours had also paid wonderful attention to American political and religious institutions. He was also a Catholic. The extraordinary journal[5] of his daily scientific observations, which he compiled in small, neat writing and adorned with little pen and ink maps and vivid drawings, was also lit by belief. The beauty of the vast and lonely prairies led him to commune with his God. His travels had shown him too the truth of what the Catholic bishop, Rosati of St Louis, wrote:

> . . . the war which all Protestant sects in the United States have so openly declared and so powerfully pursued for several years against the Catholic Religion . . . Imaginary stories, facts invented or wrongly presented, calumnies, false interpretations of Catholic doctrine, fanatic and inflammable declamations, all are employed to degrade our Holy Church, vilify her ministers and decry the faithful.

When that evening at Somerset the subject of religion and the current anti-Catholic propaganda was raised, Nicollet spoke up. Rosati, following Pierce, described the moment:

> . . . [he] pointed out clearly the unworthiness of such conduct which no decent man could approve and which a sincerely religious mind would never hesitate to condemn . . . He concluded that a religion which made use of such means to sustain itself and to attack the Catholic Religion could not be animated by the Spirit of God, could not be his work.

Connelly was surprised, the bishop reported, to hear his own thoughts coming from the mouth of this stranger and thereafter 'began himself to reflect of set purpose on the Catholic Religion'. In the following months of that winter 1833–4 he and Pierce discussed 'systems of philosophy and politics'. At Whitecottage he was a frequent visitor and became, as Cornelia said later, 'our great and good friend'.

In January 1835 Nicollet returned from a year of further exploration. In the interval Cornelia had conceived her second child and Pierce had pursued his course of reading, in some of which she must have shared. He too had just returned from travels with Bishop Otey, on visitation. For the first time since coming to Natchez he had had, on the rounds with the bishop, companionship in his ministry and Otey realised he was under great strain (which Cornelia too must have seen). He wrote later that Pierce 'felt most keenly the want of . . . friendly sympathy and countenance'. This the bishop certainly gave him: 'I have seen him weep like a child (it was an amiable weakness) in recounting the sufferings of his spirit from this cause', and Pierce himself wrote, 'the Bishop must well remember how sincerely but vainly I combated the melancholy with which my own experience and my own convictions often overwhelmed me'. It seems that his reading had brought him to the point when he unburdened himself to the bishop, sharing with him his attraction to the Roman church and his horror of the democracy he found rampant outside it and that Otey had tried to steady him with personal encouragement and advice to keep his thoughts to himself – 'silence instead of Martyrdom' as Pierce put it to Nicollet, writing to him immediately upon return. His letter was chiefly on the evils of democracy but it ends with: 'the only object I now have in view is, my dear friend, to give you the reasons why opinions which I honestly and deliberately hold can for the present at least be communicated only confidentially'. Not till August does the meaning of this become clear.

Until then Pierce bore his burden and took no action. He was buoyed up by the approval his vestry showed when they increased his salary by half and backpaid it for a year, and by Otey's public praise in the Visitation Report which was at once printed. His wife gave birth to their second child Adeline; the bishop was in the parish for Easter and stood sponsor for the child at her baptism on Easter Day; and his friend Nicollet was over at Somerset for part of July.

But there was also much to fuel the conflict within him. Beecher and Morse were proclaiming danger to American liberty. Both Connellys were reading such things as 'Miss Read's *Six Months in A Convent*, de Ricci's *Secrets* etc. etc. etc. and sundry periodicals' and neither of them, as Cornelia wrote, was 'much in the dark respecting all that can be urged against Catholicism'. Through spring and early summer 1835 the forces against foreigners and Catholics swelled; in June a Native American Democrat Association was formed in New York, and soon the *Downfall of Babylon* was pressing for an anti-Catholic political party.

Other forces less easy to name were perhaps also at work in Pierce. In March that year he had attended an Episcopalian convention called in New Orleans to decide whom to recommend as bishop for a proposed new south-western diocese. He travelled with Bishop Brownell after preliminary meetings at Natchez.[6] If, having had so much praise in Otey's Report, he thought himself in the running, he was disappointed. He was appointed chairman and Dr Francis L. Hawks was 'unanimously chosen by the clergy and laity'. But it is surprising that he went at all. Although in normal circumstances he would be expected there as the only active clergyman from Mississippi, on this occasion there was a substantial reason for absenting himself. Cornelia was very soon indeed going to give birth to their second child. He departed on 27 February and knew he could not be back before 7 March at the very earliest. Ady was born on the 6th. At that date childbirth was a matter of high risk and we know that Cornelia's health was delicate.

Six months later disillusion indeed possessed his soul. Pierce kept a commonplace book of excerpts and personal notes. One entry refers to a meeting that left him angry and contemptuous, probably the August General Convention[7] in Philadelphia which Hawks and Henry U. Onderdonk attended. Names on the page are barely legible. At the top is written 'Ex[tract] of Letter, Natchez, August 1835', and below:

> D——is all gloriousness without & all emptiness within – Hawk's duplicity – Henry U. Onderdonk's want of moral honesty & affectation of the Greek. D'Lancy's hard amiability & his ignorance so beautifully overlaid – poor Dr——ch——t's coxcombery in the parlour and his trickery in the church. If I turn State Evidence it is not from any fear of being convicted but to atone for all my participation in the Sins of others. The world can see the truth and they may judge of the motives. Let those who protest or deny give equal proof of their sincerity before they expect to have allowed equal claims to belief. Swiss soldiers fight as well as the native troops while they consider their pay as adequate.

There is no more. The passage does not appear in any known letter. The reference to turning State Evidence suggests that the experience precipitated his decision to resign; and so does its arrogant, judgmental tone, and its hint of heroism on a world stage.

On the 20th of the same month a letter of a very different tone did go to Nicollet. The whole text appeared in the 1836 *Dublin Review*. As a result of prolonged study, he says:

> My faith in Protestantism is so shaken, that I am compelled in conscience to lay aside for the present my functions; I begin to think the necessary tendency of Protestantism is revolutionary, immoral, and irreligious . . . My present design is to place myself within reach of full information on the Roman Catholic side. If my doubts are confirmed, I shall not hesitate to seek to be reconciled to the Church of Rome, and place myself under the discipline and at the disposal of their ecclesiastical authority . . . I owe it to truth and to myself, that no precipitancy should lessen the weight of so important a step . . . It is not only giving up the honours and emoluments of my profession and my standing, but it is to be attended

with the rage and malignity, the abuse and the calumny, of the pious public, and the alienation of kindred and friends . . . My first object, of course, is to inform myself fully of the dogmas, discipline, and worship of the Roman Catholic Church as established by received general councils; my next to compare its moral influence with that of the Reformed Faith.

In view of the substance of this correspondence and of Pierce's declared friendship with the Catholic Nicollet, it is difficult to accept as true what Pierce wrote only six days later in his letter of resignation to Bishop Otey (also in the *Dublin Review*): '. . . do not think I have been led to [his present feelings] by any exterior influence . . . I have had no communication on the subject with any clergyman *or laymen* of their church' (emphasis added).

The letter to Bishop Otey, dated 26 August, was thirteen pages long. His farewell sermon, delivered on 6 September, ran to seven. Printed copies were at once available for private circulation and Pierce thereby soon became a public figure, the object of precisely the kind of quasi-martyrdom which he foresaw for himself, and also of much admiration.

In these two documents Pierce has two things to say about the future. Both are significant as much for his wife and family as for himself, one as to his convictions, the other as to his character. The first concerns his office as clergyman. To his bishop he said (and conveyed the same point to his parishioners): 'The intention of my vows I have no doubt about: it is only of where I ought to pay them that I am uncertain. My allegiance as an ecclesiastic, I now fear, may have been mistaken. I will always show it was at least sincere.' Apparently it was essential that he remained a priest, though whether he should become a Catholic was still in doubt and possibly he was hoping that his priesthood would be accepted by Rome. The pronouncement against Anglican orders by Leo XIII lay many years ahead and Nicollet, a learned man but not a canon lawyer, could not have advised him on this.

The second concerns how he should proceed. In a matter of such moment, he had told Nicollet, precipitancy could have no part. To his congregation he spoke in similar vein: his course would be 'long and laboriously and devoutly weighed'. His bishop was told that he intended to examine the whole question, and for Nicollet he outlined what that would involve. 'Trust my faithfulness,' he begs, and 'do not fear my rashness'. Yet without knowing whether he was going to leave the Episcopalians, or whether if he did the Roman Catholic church would allow him to remain a priest, he had burnt his boats. Publicly he had deprived himself of his parish and incidentally of income for his wife and children. If this was indeed heroism for the sake of truth it was also an ill-judged and precipitate action.

The letter and the sermon, along with an address Pierce gave in Baltimore cathedral six years later when he had become a Catholic, reveal how deeply scandalised he was by the effects, as he saw it, of Protestant private judgment. 'I must have some guide to lead me into truth: I must have some power to obey,' he told Otey, and this failure of authority in the Episcopal church he put down to her alliance with Protestantism. The Protestant religion to him was: 'A system of error, insubordination, and excitement: a faction of persons, and opinions, against human nature, civil government, and almighty God.'

He set out for St Louis where he sought out Nicollet to be introduced to Rosati. 'Monseigneur, My friend has just come from Natchez,' Nicollet wrote on 15 September, with evident joy:

> It is done, he has raised his standard in the Holy Cause before leaving his flock. We are very much moved and yet happy for we have been talking together for the last hour. I do not need to tell you the impatience which he sustains until he has the honour of being presented to you. I send you two copies of his declaration, not yet published although printed. Send a copy if you would be so kind, to our dear president of the University [Fr Verhaegen SJ]. Let us meet for a little while this afternoon, all four of us if possible, that I may have the joy of putting my friend in better hands than mine.

'MY DEAR HUSBAND'

While Pierce unburdened his soul in St Louis his wife waited anxiously at home. At this moment in their history Cornelia steps forward from the wings. She speaks through two letters, the earliest that survive and both written at the time of her husband's resignation.

The first is to her sister Addie, dated 1 September 1835. Pierce's letter to Otey has gone but he has not yet preached his farewell sermon, nor yet departed for St Louis. She is at Whitecottage, and her letter is difficult to write. To her sorrow Addie had never been able to visit them at Natchez so care had to go into telling what would be most unwelcome news. The family in Philadelphia would most certainly not like it. Cornelia goes straight to the point and though she is reassuring she makes plain her loyal agreement with her husband's decision and sounds full of cheerful confidence. She had shared to some extent in the progress of Pierce's thinking and had been increasingly aware of the turmoil of his mind and worried to see the effect on his health. But if what he told the bishop, 'nor have I consulted on the step I now take with any human being whatever', is accepted as literally true then she had known for certain for only a week before writing

27

to Addie. The letter is mostly about him and she defends him with loving pride. As to herself she is silent except to express confidence in her husband and her trust in the 'Kind Providence of God':

Dearest Addie

I have put off writing to you for several days past from my unwillingness to tell you what I know will give you great trouble. Pierce has resigned his parish, he has laid aside the active duties of his ministry to examine at leisure and with care the distinctive doctrines of the Roman Catholic religion. The attacks upon the Catholics have led him into laborious study of the controversy and he begins to doubt whether they are not more near the truth than we. His health is considerably injured by his late labours and he is now suffering with a constant pain in his breast, but I trust in God that rest, care and exercise will in a little time restore him. His parish show great regret at his resignation and give him stronger proofs than ever of their confidence and affection, are very anxious for him to continue to live amongst them at any rate. They are going to have a gold cup made to be presented to him. I need scarcely point out to you, dear Addie, the importance of the step he takes, the immense thought and labour he has undergone or the great sacrifice of feeling as well as interest that he makes. His salary is $1500, fees within the last eight months $580 and presents to the family, during that time, I have estimated at upwards of $700.

But, dear Addie, what are these things? He must do his duty and I do not fear, under any circumstances, that God in his Kind Providence will find a way for him to support his family without going back into the world again. He intends preaching his farewell sermon next Sunday and then taking the first boat for St Louis to see Bishop Rosati. Of course he will not take any further step without long and careful deliberation. As our future movements are uncertain we determined it was better he should leave us here. He will return as soon as possible. Our property will probably be sold in five or six weeks. We may possibly go to Europe but everything is at present uncertain. 2 or 3000 dollars spent there will give him the opportunity and leisure to pursue the studies he desires, will be of great service to his health and will still leave us about 8000 dollars from the sale of our little property, every single investment of which God seems most mercifully to have blessed.

Do not be unhappy about us, dear Addie, and do not be too anxious. I have perfect confidence in the piety, integrity and learning of my dear husband, and if you mistrust my judgment recollect that he has the increased confidence and esteem of the best and first men of this parish. I will write soon again. May God bless you, dear Addie. and lead us all into the truth for His dear Son's sake. Mary and Pierce send you all a great deal of love. The children are well. Pierce thinks little Addie is like you. Mercer talks about you and sends kisses to you. I cannot answer for his distinctive ideas of you. Goodbye again, my dear Sissy. How much I wish you could pay us a visit this fall, for let our movements be what they may, it is out of the question for Pierce to think of encountering a northern winter. Keep perfectly quiet about all I have told you. You will before long hear it from other quarters, but at all events the least said about it the better, at present. We are looking anxiously for letters from you. Dear Addie, I have so much to say to you that I can scarcely stop writing, but have no more time to spare.

> Believe me ever,
> your affectionate sister,
> C. Connelly.

The second letter, to Pierce, is different. Both reveal a wife whose all in all is her husband and her husband's affairs, and a mother whose children are rarely far from her thoughts. But together they are something of a paradox. In the first she is a woman of mature self-possession, a shadow of the future. The second is the spontaneous expression of a strong but still dependent love. Cornelia has missed him so much she is overcome with tears and rushes almost at once to talk to him on paper:

> *Whitecottage, Sep. 22, 1835*
>
> Dear love my more than life what a baby I am. I can cry better than write. Your long and anxiously looked for letter I received about an hour since. O my love I have *wished* to be a Catholic in my acts of love but I am afraid in truth & spirit have been but a discontented protestant, but you have now taken me as far as Memphis and until I hear from or see you again I must rest satisfied with your dear letter and keep it as the good Catholic does his Agnus Dei. I sent you two letters of introduction from Dr Mercer the day after you left us and wrote you a few lines in the envelope but they were so gloomy that I tore it up and sent you a blank sheet: the truth was I wandered about the house & looked over your desk & in your drawers for three or four days . . .

There had been other occasions when Pierce was away but never for so long. None had been loaded with such uncertainties for the future, nor with the sure knowledge that this their first home would soon be under the auctioneer's hammer. Moreover Pierce's 'health had been injured by his late labours'. She was rescued from anxiety and gloom by the immediate need to be a loving mother as well as a remembered wife:

> Ady got sick & I was obliged to give her a dose of Cal. She had scarcely

recovered before dear little Mercer was taken with fever which continued nearly a week . . . the Dr assured me there was no cause for uneasiness . . . He has not eaten anything for a week until today when he took some bread and milk . . .

The letter flows on cheerfully about parish business and visits of friends, ideas for the winter, news from his mother. Its loving trust calls to mind what Cornelia's sister Mary who was living with them said, that they were 'the happiest couple that ever breathed'. Several times, too, she speaks as if they were both already Catholic in spirit though not in fact. She has apostolic daydreams, 'a catholic establishment on our lands'. She longs for those dear to her to become Catholic, all passing remarks and nothing to do with institution or dogma, but they reflect her heart's desires.

And the letter is full of support for Pierce. If as the mother of two young children she had had difficulty in trusting an unexpected future, it is evident from this letter that there was also much to strengthen her: her personal growth in understanding the Catholicism which Pierce had set out to explore, and her devotion to her husband. Frequently in it she gives him what her heart tells her he needs, encouragement to believe in himself. He has made an irrevocable decision in which it is now her role to support him:

> My own dear life it seems almost as if you were with me again to send me your 'thoughts'. Dearest love I hope & trust that you will be with us by the time this reaches St Louis & dearest do not distress yourself about the alienation of any of your family. If you should rise they will be ready enough to bow down to you – some specimen already. If you do not, you have that within which they can neither give nor take. G[eorge Connelly] was never more kind & amiable & I do not think I ever saw him show more pride in you than at the present moment & Mr B[ingaman] . . . *regretted deeply* that he had not seen you.

Then, remembering the man to whom she felt they owed so much: 'Give the warmest remembrance from me to our great and good friend Mr Nicollet whom I pray God may be with you. Oh my love make haste back. It seems a year that you have been gone.'

DEPARTURE, 1835

When this loving appeal reached St Louis Pierce was already on his way back. He returned, Mary Peacock wrote, 'after a most delightful trip, his health much improved'. Bishop Rosati reports something of what happened there:

He came and threw himself into my arms bathed in tears. It was in our Cathedral that he assisted for the first time at the celebration of the Holy Mysteries by which he was greatly impressed. We had long conversations . . . he sought enlightenment on various points . . .

He also bought some theological books and decided to go to Rome, for which Rosati undertook to give him introductions. He met many Catholics and returned to Natchez reassured. Rosati 'recognised with joy the purity of intention, his rectitude, his candour in telling me his difficulties' and could not restrain his own 'tears on seeing this generous man' who had sacrificed so much for conscience's sake, 'ready to leave his country and go out to an uncertain future in a strange land'.

This admiration was also strong in Natchez. Most of those who knew him well held him in great affection and esteem, which the step he had taken only increased. His congregation wept when he preached to them for the last time, and organised a parish collection to present him with a costly gold cup. Mary Peacock, who unlike Cornelia was not yet disposed to become a Catholic, said in an adulatory letter to Addie:

They are all very fond of Pierce . . . I do not believe there is another parish in the United States as deeply and sincerely attached as his to him; they are crazy to have him remain among them. All the most intelligent and first men here, publicly make known how much his late, noble and disinterested course has elevated him in their estimation.

The news was not so appreciatively accepted elsewhere. In the public journals, Otey wrote, Pierce's conduct was 'the subject of severe, not to say uncharitable comment', and among the Peacocks and Duvals and Connellys in Philadelphia there was a great stirring. 'We wrote some eight or ten letters', said Addie's husband Lewis Duval, and Addie was blunt:

. . . it certainly is, my dear Neely, a source of great mortification to us that the public generally, not only the Episcopal body, should entertain so unfavourable an opinion of Mr C's judgment, prudence and strength of mind as they are forced into by the publication of his letter to Bishop Otey and his farewell sermon . . . It is the general and, I believe, the freely expressed opinion among the clergy that there is an aberration of mind on the subject of religion.

Harry Connelly set off for Natchez to see for himself what truth there was in what the papers were saying and relieved them all by reporting 'no derangement' and by adding that he himself believed that Pierce had always been inclined to the Catholic faith. For Ralph and George, the two young Peacock brothers in Rio Grande seeking their fortune, Lewis Duval summed up his personal view of Pierce's conduct: 'I have the greatest confidence in his piety and honour, but the course he has taken is much to be deplored and evinces a want of judgment and prudence, that I am fearful will prove seriously detrimental to their happiness.'

One or two others besides the family had their doubts. At the time of his resignation Pierce insisted and Cornelia reiterated that he intended to take ample time for study before deciding whether to join the Roman church. Acquaintances who feared his lack of balance but wished to be fair refrained from expressing their doubts. Otey was one of these. To Pierce, leaving the country still a Protestant *en route* for Rome to study, he showed only his affection. Afterwards when Pierce had all too quickly become a Catholic and had written fervidly pressing him too to conversion, Otey wrote in the *Churchman*, 'The truth is, that poor Connelly's mind is unbalanced. I was unwilling to believe this at first.' Another was Dr Merrill, one of Pierce's vestrymen. When the news reached him he wrote – prophetically – to Dr Mercer: 'Bishop Otey says his mind is unbalanced but I think it never was balanced. I do not believe he will stop where he is. His enthusiasm and want of judgment will lead him into other extravagances, and I fear to abandon his family.'

On 17 October the packet of letters arrived from Philadelphia. One from Addie Cornelia felt obliged to answer at once. 'Pierce is not a Catholic nor could he be a Catholic priest,' she wrote, 'if he desired it while I live.' She made this statement about a week after her husband had returned from St Louis. One of the subjects Rosati and Pierce had discussed (a later letter reveals this as likely) was whether he could be a priest in the Roman Catholic church. He would have learnt that only in very rare cases and under certain conditions which included separation of husband and wife, did Rome allow a married man to become a priest while his wife still lived. Cornelia's very positive denial of the possibility for Pierce suggests that he had told her about it and she, happily married and believing in their marriage, had gaily dismissed it as unthinkable.

She takes up further matters with Addie. As to Pierce's mind, 'it is as sound as ever and [he is] as capable as ever to support his family'. Her sister had painted a gloomy picture of the future and presumed that Cornelia must be extremely worried, but 'Pierce's health has been almost entirely restored by his trip . . . and as to our pecuniary prospects, are they not much fairer now than when we married? Pierce at this moment could realize from 15–17000 dollars', and Addie is upbraided:

> . . . how is it that you have so little confidence in my good husband? You seem really to think he has lost his mind. What do you mean by 'renouncing his faith' and 'committing himself'? Refer to my last letter and you

32

will see that I told you he would examine the subject long and carefully before he makes any decision . . .

She defends the Catholic church with a warmth that reveals how deeply she is herself drawn to it. Like Pierce she cannot see the 'unity of the faith in the bond of peace' in the divided denominations of the Protestant religion: 'Can that be one army whose branches fight against each other rather than the world?' Unlike Pierce, it is not structures and authority but the preaching of Christ crucified that draws her. 'Look at the attacks upon the Catholics,' she says, 'the oldest and most numerous church which is now preaching Christ crucified and whose faithful followers are at this time suffering Martyrdom in Asia as the early Christians did.' One sentence reveals a personal conviction, that the seeking of Christ in his church is sovereign in life, and because Pierce's action has proved this to be his conviction too she loves him yet more: 'Was it to his own honor and glory that Pierce vowed to devote his life or was it to the Church of Christ?' Her love illumines the letter. Pierce is 'all that is estimable and far, far above what your sister ever deserved or looked for in her husband'. If because he is seeking the truth he asks her to step into the unknown she is 'proud to say that against all my prejudices and in spite of the horrors which I have always nurtured for the Catholic faith, I am ready at once to submit to whatever my loved husband believes to be the path of duty'.

The way in which Cornelia here expresses her relationship with her husband calls for comment. By nature she was by no means submissive. Her decision to marry against opposition was an independent choice. She was naturally spontaneous, strong, warm. She was also clear-headed, but the age in which she lived demanded submissiveness from wife to husband. In all things temporal his was the final say. Both law and society agreed with him and the wife had no rights. A girl would be bred to this concept and to a future in which as wife she could not dream otherwise. Cornelia's family was no exception. 'Be a Catholic, or whatever will make you happiest,' Addie wrote to her, 'follow the path of duty strictly. Be advised by your dear good partner, he is your earthly guide', and to their two young brothers she preached the expected submissiveness even more clearly:

I am not at all surprised at the effects of Pierce's influence over her mind, nor would I for a moment wish her to differ with her kind husband. No indeed! I should desire her positively to exercise her strength of mind and endeavour to be congenial. The path of duty will lead her to think as he does, and she ought certainly to view things as he does for their mutual happiness. I do not hesitate in saying that under similar circumstances I should pursue that course.

The nineteenth-century Christian road to fulfilment and happiness for such as Cornelia lay through the cherishing of her husband whatever the circumstances, 'for better, for worse'. At this early stage in their married life her sky was unclouded. She was young. They had a family and enough money. New depths of faith had opened before her. Her husband was admired and she loved him. 'As regards my loved husband, our blessed little ones and myself,' she wrote to Addie, 'I never was happier in my life.'

The day finally came when for the last time they looked round their home and its surroundings. The house was already sold, and so were the cows; everything else was to be auctioned. Memories were put away: musical evenings with Colonel Huntington and his violin, visits from Nicollet – whose weather-beaten face earned him a nickname in the *Dublin Review*:

> Dear old Ebony, I can scarcely now refrain from wandering far off my subject when I think of all the delight and all the affection too, with which, seated around the table or on the gallery of that dear cottage in the warm south-west, we used to read . . . instead of music of an evening.

Two slaves, Phoebe and Sally, they kept: Dr Mercer would care for them. Abraham and Jimmy had been sold. No washing of clothes could be done at sea on the two-month voyage so Cornelia and Mary had made enough basketfuls for a baby and a three-year old. Now, all preparations completed, they went to stay briefly with the Chotards at Somerset and were surrounded by friendship and approval. Finally, the river took them once more on its broad and irreversible current. They embarked at Natchez on Thursday, 19th November 1835, and reached New Orleans on the 21st.

3

Conversion

All along the river levee a curtain of ships' masts edged the horizon. On the other side and below, sheltering from terrible and unpredictable flood, lay New Orleans. Well back from the bank, in the Place d'Armes of the French Quarter and facing out across the square to the Mississippi, lay the old cathedral of St Louis. A church had stood there since 1727, a cathedral since 1795, still the heart of the city. Pierce and Cornelia are unlikely as Protestants to have been inside on former visits but now they planned to go the day after their arrival. New Orleans was French in her origins and both French and Spanish in her religious and cultural traditions. It was a predominantly Catholic city and on Sunday, 22 November there was to be a solemn Catholic ceremony.

The next morning they were part of a packed congregation. 'We were all at the Cathedral to-day to witness the consecration of a bishop,' Harry Connelly wrote to his wife, 'it was a very impressing sight.' The bishop elect was Fr Anthony Blanc, the co-consecrators Bishops Rosati and Purcell of Cincinnati and the homilist Portier of Mobile. The liturgy was enormously long and splendid, all in Latin punctuated with music, but a sermon was in French. The mass was part of it. Pierce had attended mass before but Cornelia almost certainly never had. He would surely have been caught up in the vision of the fullness of priesthood. The Episcopalian Revd Connelly who so desired authority in his priestly calling heard the apostolic commission and the oath of obedience to the Holy See. At a guess he prayed that his own future held some way in which he could remain a minister of the gospel.

When the ceremony was over 'Pierce and myself dined with all the Bishops, Priests and other invited guests,' Harry's letter went on, 'amounting to upwards of seventy at the Cathedral. It was as pleasant and agreeable a dinner party as I ever was at, all lively as crickets and as noisy.' Pierce was thus received with welcome arms into the midst of the assembled Catholic clergy. Rosati found him 'firmer than ever in his resolution'. Blanc and Purcell became his friends. Priests he had met at St Louis greeted him. Others were introduced. He was a centre of attention.

Where the Connellys stayed in New Orleans we do not know. Pierce had to scan the French and English columns of the marine news in *L'Abeille* and not till 30 November did he find: 'For Marseilles. The A no. 1 fast sailing ship *Edwin*, Wilson master, having most part of her freight engaged, will meet with quick despatch. For freight of 200 barrels and passage, apply to Theodore Nicolet & Co., 26 Bienville Street.' During the ten-day wait he found time to put a pamphlet together consisting of his letter of resignation and his farewell sermon with additional notes, see it through the printer's and on 4 December send a hundred copies up river to his sick friend Nicollet for sale and distribution. Because 'ten thousand little matters' had harassed him he had missed an earlier chance to write, but now:

> . . . dear Nicollet be assured that both of us . . . are often with you at St Louis in our affectionate and faithful hearts, and no one on this side of the broad water that separates you from your own France would more carefully or more cheerfully have been your sister and nurse than chérie Nelie. God knows how anxiously I wait for news of you before leaving New Orleans.

For Cornelia too the ceremony at the cathedral meant much. It was a milestone on her personal route into Catholicism. In a legal statement which she later had to make about herself and Pierce she said that 'at New Orleans in the month of November . . . she became unwilling to embark for Europe until she made a formal profession' of the Catholic faith. Presumably she had intended to wait with Pierce till they reached Rome before committing herself, but this great liturgy was both a religious experience and a rich Catholic instruction, her first. The homilist's theme (the adopted theme of her own life) was the place of accepted suffering in the life of the Christian. Whilst Pierce was going about town, she 'forestalled' her husband, as Rosati put it, and asked to be prepared to become a Catholic. Day by day Rosati talked with her and was impressed. He was himself a highly intelligent man, fluent in three languages, one who found time in a life of arduous missionary travel and administration to keep up his literary interests, and who as a priest was sought after for his human sympathy and wisdom. He considered Madame Connelly 'a woman of great intellectual powers', described her as 'cultivated' and 'very carefully educated' and was not alone in his admiration. Bishop Blanc, whom she must often have met at the Residence, wrote, 'Mad. Connelly is a wonderful woman.' Purcell inscribed a book for her: 'Bp Purcell begs to present this little volume with a blessing and prayer, humble, earnest persevering prayer, to Mrs Cornelia Connelly. N.O. 7th Dec. 1835. May *His* Angel watch over thee and thine!'

Cornelia has left us no record of these days, but the significance for Pierce of the episcopal consecration could not have escaped her. In Natchez it had been possible to dismiss the possibility of the priesthood for him from her mind, and to do so almost lightheartedly because their marriage was so happy that the consequences were unthinkable. For one who told Addie she thanked God every day 'for having so blessed me in such a husband & our dear children in such a father' it was inconceivable that Pierce could ever desire what would break up their marriage. Now perhaps she glimpsed why he might. No information that Rosati gave would have been reassuring except that Rome only very rarely granted such a request, and to this likelihood she had to trust. There was no way back.

This was true not only because Pierce had closed the road behind them. A moment had come when Cornelia herself must act. He had not yet committed himself to Roman Catholicism but she had reached the point of personal conviction. If practical wisdom suggested that she waited with Pierce till Rome, the belief in her heart told her otherwise. Out of 'the truth, the blessed truth' she felt compelled to act. And there was too another kind of prompting, the voyage. In Natchez the sea was far away. Here in New Orleans it could not be forgotten: the sight of ships, the heave of water at the wharfside, salt in the air, the stories told. Danger of death would soon be a reality. Now was the time to act. Rosati wrote: 'she did not want to face the dangers of the sea before she had made profession of the Catholic Religion and tasted how sweet and kind God is to those who seek Him'.

We do not know what transpired when she first raised the matter with Pierce, and later he would conveniently ignore what his response had been. It was 'with full sanction and approval of her husband' that she was received into the Catholic church. According to Bishop Blanc 'her happiness was great on the day of her Com[munion] and her husband fully shared it'. No event in Cornelia's future among many that were momentous would be more pivotal than this. By breaking away from her husband's plans in a matter so intimate to their relationship as religion, this nineteenth-century wife made a kind of quantum leap out of dependence into freedom. Henceforth she is more and more herself, and at the same time more and more free for God, whatever her husband may ask of her.

The day after this event Pierce was again writing to Nicollet whom nothing would have pleased more than to know that Mrs Connelly was now a Catholic, yet her husband does not mention it. The letter is worth including here in part, for the light it sheds on the man Cornelia had married. On the very day of embarkation a response from Bishop Otey to his resignation had at last arrived. Pierce wrote:

37

Dear dear Nicollet

We sail to-day. I seize the moment however to give you information . . .
The Bishop has written to me in the kindest and warmest manner. His
affection and his regard are not in the least changed. He still calls me
'dear dear Connelly' and says 'I have loved you with an affection which
I want words adequately . . . to express'. His letter is a long one so full
of tenderness but even now I cannot look it over without my eyes filling
with tears. He thinks there is a marked & palpable incongruity in my
conclusions from the premises laid down in the printed letter & charges
it somewhat to my horror of democracy. But he says, 'the intention of
this letter will be fully answered when it assures you of my undiminished
regard, of the regard I feel for your honesty & candour of purpose, of the
deep sorrow I experience in the clear perception which I have or think I
have of your error & delusion & the causes of them, and of the continuance
of my fervent prayers for the happiness & well-being of you & yours . . .
Let me hear from you by letter.' Do you wonder my dear friend that I
love and honour such a man? And ought I not to be grateful, may I not
feel honoured in his friendship and esteem?

This is two-thirds of the letter. Except for her concern for Nicollet's health,
Cornelia is not mentioned. Her intention was not a secret and there had
been time to communicate with her family. Pierce appears as pathetically
needy of approval and astonishingly forgetful. Sadly, they never saw Nicollet
again.

Thursday, 10 December 1835 found the Connellys on the brink of departure for Europe. According to Rosati Pierce was already 'convinced of the
truth of the Catholic Religion' but did not intend to 'make public profession'
because 'he had his reasons for waiting'. It was known that he had doubts
about miracles and planned further study. What he wanted, it would appear,
was ordination.

Some time during that day they at last got aboard. 'Their farewell to us
all was most moving,' Blanc wrote. Cornelia, the baby, the small Merty
and the nurse found their cramped quarters below deck and stowed the
family baggage. Here in appallingly little space they would make the two
months crossing, and before dawn next day the ship sailed.

TO ROME, 1836

'Jan. 21. We ran up on deck just after sunset – land in sight. 40 days since
we left N.O.' It was Pierce who recorded this moment. They had had a
wearisome and exhausting voyage: contrary winds alternating with calms,

the children sick one after the other, the nurse too ill ever to help. Cornelia had 'suffered sadly', Pierce told Rosati and he was worried about the fatigue of his 'delicate little wife'. But now they stood incredulously gazing. On the horizon lay Spain and Africa. The captain lent them a glass through which they spotted Cape Spartel jutting into the sea. Then Cape Trafalgar loomed up with its tower. When the ship sailed through the straits they could pick out the houses and gardens of Tariffa 'and even a bridge in the town'. On one side were 'the beautiful hills of Spain', Pierce wrote, and 'long shadows through the vallies', and on the other Africa, like 'mountains of coal . . . Never can I forget the gratitude and delight with which we gazed.' On 2 February it was Cornelia who took up the story at Marseilles. For three hours they waited outside the harbour for a pilot. When the little pilot boat appeared she was agog with interest: 'What queer looking fellows with their brown knit caps hanging down over one ear . . .' When the pilot came aboard, 'gabbing French – what shoes!' she exclaimed, 'how can he walk in them! They look like wooden boats!' She was appalled to hear they might be confined to ship for quarantine, 'Oh terrible. Can't we in any way escape five days more in that little cabin?' and then, as so often in her life, her realistic, practical self bobbed up: 'Oh bien! We must make up our minds to endure it cheerfully,' and she turned again to the scene.

The ship was quarantined only briefly after all and on the next day Pierce wrote to his mother: 'we came to-day ashore. Nelie [is] alongside of me before the fire in one of the prettiest little rooms you ever saw and one of the pleasantest parts of the city.' They stayed for three weeks in their comfortable lodgings, and during that time she made her way at least once up through the narrow streets to the ancient cathedral and saw one of the canons. If during the long voyage the thought of Pierce's desire to be a priest and its consequences had haunted her, she may well have gone for advice and support. Rome was now very near.

The Connellys had made their first momentous journey in the New World, travelling two thousand miles to Natchez, and passing through faintly populated lands, the mere fringe to unexplored wilderness. Five years later when the *Edwin* sailed through the Straits of Gibraltar it brought them into a very different and old world. This continent was congested. For centuries peoples had fought for survival or land or prosperity. Now Europe was weighed down, as America as yet was not, by long-established social structures, by extremes of poverty and wealth and by its traditions of government.

Despite stirrings of democracy and a revolution in France, the Europe to which the Connellys came was still largely ruled by absolute monarchs. On the heels of the French Revolution liberty had often degenerated into licence and terror and a reaction had set in to which Pierce, no lover of democracy, was not unsympathetic. And in Rome he would find his ideal: a pope who ruled the Papal States from a throne and at the same time demanded from his flock the obedience of faith. Indeed the combination at that time of spiritual and temporal authority, both seemingly absolute, in the office of pope, might well prove irresistible to a man of Pierce's temperament.

Thursday, 25 February found the Connelly family, a French nanny and all their boxes in a hired carriage driving across the campagna to the Eternal City. As Pierce had already discovered when crossing the Atlantic, 'the troubles and pain attendant upon travelling with little children were far greater' than could be imagined. The baby Adeline was not yet a year old and Mercer, a very delicate little boy and something of a handful, according to his mother who told his aunt he liked to play the master, was only just three. Both of them still had colds and so had Cornelia. The nanny Annette did not speak English, they were all cooped up and the road was bumpy. It was also freezing weather, the Tiber had flooded badly that year, marshes were full and farms were water-logged. The last lap must have seemed disproportionately long.

The Via Aurelia brought them across the campagna from the west and when at last they saw the city on the horizon the winter sun was setting behind them. 'You may suppose,' Pierce wrote to their friend Bishop Purcell, 'we looked out for the first glimpse of the Miraculous City with breathless interest.' The *vettura* rattled on along the ancient paved road. Soon they were keeping company with the arches of Trajan's aqueduct and finally they came up to the city walls, at which they would have gazed with some amazement. Rome at that date was still a walled city. The population was about 200,000. The people lived in a congestion of palazzos, churches and dwelling-houses crammed into the north-west quarter of the whole enclosed area. The rest of the land within the walls was laid out as gardens of beautiful villas or as vineyards owned by old Roman families or monasteries. Some of it was public meadow. Most of the ancient ruins of the early Roman Empire stood amidst fields in the southern part. Cows grazed there and people wandered at will. Gates pierced the walls and travellers coming from Civitavecchia entered by the Porta Cavalleggeri.

As their coach lumbered under the arch an exhausted Cornelia was probably no more than grateful to be nearly there but Pierce was overflowing with religious fervour. He told Bishop Purcell:

A little incident occurred as we entered. Just as a sudden turn brought us right before St Peter's and apparently no more than a square off, a flock of birds rose up from each of the smaller cupolas. They maintained for a moment their separate companies but suddenly they . . . joined themselves together and then continued indistinguishably mixing in all their infinite and graceful evolutions . . . I connected the beautiful sight above me with the sure promises of God that one day there shall be no more traces of all our schisms in the Church than the birds had left behind them [of] tracks in air to show where once they flew in separate bands apart.

Their driver eventually brought them to the Via della Croce, to the Hotel Spillman. 'We are in delightful rooms,' Cornelia wrote: '3 chambers; a dining room, sitting room, anteroom, & our expenses including the table . . . are but $70 per month.' There was no piano so they hired one at 20 cents a day. They would be able to receive visitors in this setting and the three bedrooms allowed ample space for a nursery. Pierce too would have been pleased. The important people to whom he had introductions lived within easy reach. The scene was well set for their Roman stay and next morning the multitudinous church bells, ringing at sunrise, called them into what was for them an amazing world. Papal time was reckoned according to the old Roman usage. The first hour of the twenty-four began with the evening angelus half an hour after sunset, and on 2 March Pierce wrote to Rosati: 'We can hardly believe our identity or the reality of all we see around us in this ancient city. It seems like a dream or the acting of a play that we should have so shifted scenes & changed characters within six short months.'

ADVICE TO PIERCE, 1836

Pierce lost no time in making his contacts. His letter to Rosati was written within a week. He speaks gratefully of 'the incalcuable service you have done us not only in introducing us to such a holy and charming man as Cardinal Odescalchi, but through the amiable and excellent Cardinal Weld to a circle of the highest & most interesting English society in Rome'. Visitors were beginning to call on them and 'Mrs Connelly has already nothing to wish for in the number of kind and agreeable acquaintances of her own sex, some of them distinguished converts.' The unexpected social opportunities seem to have gratified Pierce immensely.

An impressive circle of interested ecclesiastics gathered round him. He made his way down the Piazza di Spagna to present his credentials to the Cardinal Prefect of the Propaganda, that is, the Congregation for the Propagation of the Faith. As an inquirer from the United States, then a mission land in the eyes of Rome, it was correct, as Rosati will have told him, to go there first. It was both administrative centre and international seminary. Over the years ex-students, missionaries and their bishops had kept up a close correspondence with its officials. The knowledge accumulated there about Catholic needs and conditions in many lands beyond

41

Europe endowed its prefect with great influence, not least with the pope. Much depended on this visit when Pierce first bent to kiss Cardinal Fransoni's ring and presented Rosati's letter.

The man whom the cardinal saw before him was by then thirty-one years old. His passport described him: '5ft 10½in, forehead retreating, eyes grey, nose prominent, mouth small, chin long, hair bald, complexion pale, face thin'. In the course of interviews Fransoni was impressed. 'All that you have told me concerning his conduct and the decision which, with the help of God, he has taken, is most satisfactory,' he told Rosati. 'I listened to him with that real interest and concern which his circumstances arouse.'

Also at the Propaganda Pierce met the rector of the college. Mgr Charles von Reisach, only thirty-five, soon to be a bishop then cardinal, had been rector when the present pope was prefect there and they had remained on terms of friendship. Pierce was able to inform Rosati that he had 'just called . . . & had the goodness to pass an hour with us . . . [He] tells me His Holiness had listened with interest to his account of us & that I shall soon have the honour of an audience.'

Then there were the Jesuits. Pierce's personal knowledge of the Society of Jesus when he came to Rome was limited to contacts made in St Louis, but he had soon visited at the Collegio Romano and at the Gesù, and had contacted Fr Anthony Kohlmann SJ. Any of the American bishops who knew him might have provided this introduction, for Kohlmann was well known in their country. In 1804 he had volunteered for the American mission. There he had made legal history by refusing in a court trial to break the seal of confession. He was the pastor who laid the foundation stone of old St Patrick's, New York, had been a president of Georgetown and had spent long periods in Pennsylvania. Such a background must have recommended him to Pierce. When it came to inquiring about procedures for abjuration and about the validity of Anglican sacraments, Kohlmann was qualified to advise because he had been a consultor of the Congregation of the Holy Office (which dealt with matters of faith).

While calling on the Jesuits Pierce had the good fortune to meet Mgr Bruté, a zealous Frenchman and missionary colleague of Rosati, in the States since 1810 and recently made a bishop. He was now in Rome recruiting for his newly constituted and vast mid-west diocese, Vincennes. Later he would recommend the Connellys to the Jesuits in Louisiana. Now he introduced them to John McCloskey, future bishop and cardinal, one of thirteen students from the States at the Propaganda. McCloskey became a Connelly friend, especially of Cornelia who was only a year older than he. The Propaganda, where he lived, was not two hundred yards from their hotel, and a day would come when a troubled Cornelia was glad to have him so near.

Rosati's letters of introduction also took Pierce to the Palazzo Odescalchi,[1] the residence of Gregory XVI's vicar general. On the first occasion it was not the latter who received him, but the English Cardinal Weld whose apartment was in the same palace. The cardinal was very gracious. Having spent an hour with Pierce he asked him to bring the children to visit him. So we can imagine the Connelly family only a day or two after their arrival in Rome coming by carriage into the stately colonnaded court that led off the Piazza SS Apostoli. There was a broad white marble staircase to be walked up, for Merty quite a climb. Next they crossed a big and nearly empty *sala* with benches where messengers and footmen dawdled, and then a handsome room with old carved bookcases all round and a high, coffered ceiling. Here they could sit down and look about them. The cardinal had been a married man. After his wife's death and daughter's marriage he had become a priest and now he had grandchildren. A pleasing picture must have greeted him when he came in. Whatever turns the talk may have taken, he liked his visitors and introduced them to English society through his son-in-law Lord Clifford.

The all-important cardinal vicar, Odescalchi, was likely to sympathise with Pierce's story. For many years he had desired to be a Jesuit. He had first asked in 1814 but Pius VII had refused to release him. The desire was still with him when the Connellys were in Rome, and not long after they had returned to America he asked again and Gregory XVI agreed. When Cornelia met him in 1836 she wrote to her sister: 'I have been presented to Cardinal Odescalchi . . . [He] looks like everybody says he is, a perfect saint on earth.' Such a priest would quickly compassionate any man in whom recognisable vocation was frustrated.

But the cardinal was a wise man, the adviser of three popes. He advised Pierce to remain a layman. This is known from Pierce's own letter to Rosati. He and the latter, one infers, had discussed the matter in America and Pierce very promptly reported back:

> It is with sincere pleasure that I communicate to you that the Cardinal Vicar thinks my prospects of usefulness in embracing the Catholic faith will be greater as a married man than as a priest; & he wisely argues that the example of my conversion will be kept in sight longer & more frequently remembered than if I were to take my place among the clergy and thus retire more completely from the world.

He then expresses his great willingness to accept this advice: 'For my own part I can only say as I trust I do in humbleness and in sincerity, Lord here am I! What wilt thou have me do? & relying on his grace to help me, endeavour to make myself useful in whatever way be my vocation.' What follows suggests that his thoughts have turned, or been turned by either

Weld or Odescalchi, to the causes he has for contentment in his married state:

> My dear wife . . . had a great deal to suffer during the passage . . . & I cannot but look back with wonder at all Mrs Connelly has undergone & with gratitude and thankfulness to God who gave her strength and preserved her health. We feel now as if we were home in our quiet and most comfortable lodgings, and have little disposition to think of further moving about.

Cornelia was filled with relief and joy. A long letter to her sister Mary begun four days later makes no reference to the shadow that had overhung her because she had never admitted its existence to the family. Now she can write of her present life with a transparent happiness about its every aspect. She is 'blessed with a dear husband' she tells Mary and their days are full. The Eternal City rejoices her:

> I have seen nothing of Rome yet though I have been out every day. But seeing it won't do. It must be studied and it will take at least a year to study it with any kind of advantage. At every step you see the most precious works of art. The beautiful obelisks, columns, statues and fountains in every piazza (open space), the magnificent churches and palaces, shops, streets, all is a mass of confusion to me at present.

She is taking music lessons. She and Pierce have begun Italian, and she is trying to improve her French conversation with a daily exercise. The children constantly occupy her: Ady can now 'just get up by a chair alone'; she cannot get Mercer to keep his little spectacles on for even ten minutes at a time. She enjoys the new people they met: Lady Arundell was exactly like 'the widows we have seen on the stage, large and fat with blue eyes and rosy cheeks and wearing a black lace cap trimmed with black ribbon, the ribbon being high in the centre'. Bishop Bruté is 'a most holy man'. She has 'become very sociable' with the daughter of Mother Seton, foundress of the Sisters of Charity. She took the air with her at the foot of Trinità dei Monti, remembering mutual friends in Philadelphia, and later they shared a papal audience.[2] She has hobnobbed with Lord Clifford who is a widower and has six children, about how to tell New Testament stories to a young child.

They have also met the earl of Shrewsbury, John Talbot, with his family at their Roman home – the Palazzo Simonetti on the Corso – and specially enjoyed herself. 'We dined two or three days ago at Lord Shrewsbury's,' she wrote. 'The countess is a most fascinating woman, great dignity of manner, rather tall & very handsome face, and her faith, her piety! Oh it would charm you and she does so much good among the poor.' There are two daughters, she says, the older one Princess Talbot, not yet married, but Gwendaline (to become her personal friend) 'has made a very splendid marriage with the Prince Borghese, of immense wealth and rich too in qualities of heart and mind. The Princess his wife, is beautiful, amiable & clever (English). She speaks four languages and is a splendid musician.' Then mirth overtakes Cornelia at the memory of herself at that dinner. At half past seven, all in full dress, 'Dear Mary, you may imagine poor little American me seated at a table surrounded by Princesses, Earls and Countesses!' But among these people she is at ease and remarks that she and Pierce 'find no difference between the polished society of P[hiladelphia] & the society of the English Nobility excepting that they carry more humility in their politeness'. Lord and Lady Shrewsbury called very soon at Hotel Spillman and there began between the two families an important friendship.

Permeating all this happiness was Cornelia's religious belief. 'I feel my faith, my hope, my happiness increase every day,' she tells her sister; and again, I 'never, never before was so happy in my religion'.

CONSEQUENCES, 1836

Cornelia's joy in her husband's willingness to be a layman was short-lived. On some day in the middle of March she went in great grief to see their friend John McCloskey. As cardinal in New York he still remembered the occasion and described it to Cornelia's niece, Adeline Mack. She states that it took place when he was 'a young priest studying in Rome', that is, between February 1835 and September 1837:

> I can see Mrs Connelly approaching me clasping her hands and her beautiful eyes uplifted to my face. 'Father McCloskey, is it necessary for Pierce Connelly to make this sacrifice and sacrifice me? I love my husband and my darling children. Why must I give them up? I love my religion and why cannot we remain happy, as the Earl of Shrewsbury's family? Why?

It was a cruel reversal. Everything most dear might after all be taken from her.

Between 2 March, when Pierce wrote to Rosati of his willingness to remain a layman, and 28 March after his reception into the Catholic church, we have no comments of his own to illuminate the road he took. Official church records give us the fundamental fact. On 16 March he petitioned not only to be admitted to the church and confirmed, but also to be considered for holy orders.[3] In those two weeks he moved from the mood of contentment and pious acceptance that characterised his letter to Rosati into decisive contrary action.

Pierce was an emotional, impressionable man. He needed to stand well, be noticed, be approved and supported. Cardinal Odescalchi, whose presence he reached on 1 or 2 March, was a man of known holiness and compassion, advising from experience far beyond anything of Pierce's, and who, in addition, would seem to be speaking, however gently, with the voice of authority. It would be very understandable if this neophyte, sincerely desiring to act in accordance with the love of God, unconsciously bent himself beyond what he was able to sustain. That something of the kind may have happened at that first meeting is suggested by the almost adulatory way in which he described the cardinal three weeks later. To Bishop Otey he pictured himself, when he became a Catholic, as 'kneeling before the Saintly and Angelic Odescalchi'. For his mother at the same time, and later to Dr Mercer, he wrote:

> The Cardinal himself is . . . full of unction & most imposing in all his functions, very fluent & graceful in his diction, yet so animated as to seem really to rise from his chair while preaching: a countenance frank & intelligent & full of elegance & dignity, yet of greatest simplicity, and though not fifty years of age with a certain something, perhaps a striking air of piety that gives him all the venerableness of fourscore.

It would be no wonder if, at the word of so impressive a personality, the vision of an apostolic layman in the midst of his Christian family prevailed with Pierce for a few days at least. Conceivably the strength of his desire for ordination reasserted itself as the interview with Odescalchi receded.

The expected papal audience, its date now unknown, was undeniably a factor in Pierce's turnabout. Kohlmann could have told him that a case as unusual as his took time and was eventually decided by the pope himself. Whether he changed his mind before or after seeing the Holy Father we cannot be sure. Perhaps he was wavering beforehand and put in the petition afterwards as a result of whatever it was that the pope said. In that case there was a sudden agony for Cornelia when he returned and told her. The meeting with Gregory XVI, to which she was not invited, was the turning point for both of them and for their children.

Gregory XVI's successor would see the revolutionary forces breach the walls at Porta Pia and have to retreat permanently across the Tiber into the Vatican. But in the Connellys' day Gregory's coach often rumbled through the streets as for hundreds of years before him popes had ridden or been borne across the city. They had issued edicts, heard cases, bestowed blessings. They had held court, set up hospices for pilgrims and the poor, imprisoned or exiled their enemies at will. Each had acted with charity or less than justice according to the limits of his wisdom. Above all they had ruled as autocrats and this tradition Gregory had inherited. He was a monk, a scholar, Dom Mauro Capellari, a member of that very ancient community the Camaldolese. A life of obedience and tradition had been his lot. He had learned to value the past and what should be handed on, to prize religious life as a sign of the church and a source of great good. New ways of doing things, like building railways or allowing lay participation in government, he ignored and the reforms he did effect were not radical enough for the day. The Papal States were believed by many to be the worst governed country in Europe at that date. Instead of pursuing reform he preserved and glorified the Roman past, trusting its long-tried stability to ride the revolutionary storms, and traditional doctrine and practice to hold the faithful true. Museums and libraries were magnificently improved. The ancient forums were excavated. Archaeology and learning prospered. Rome became again a Mecca for artists and scholars.

Rome also became the source of missionary renewal in the church. Because Gregory had been prefect of the Propaganda he knew about Catholic life beyond the confines of Europe. Missions fields, he told his cardinals, were his chief care. For them he wanted priests, sisters, schools, money, and ways to link them closely with Rome. He set up new dioceses and new communities. He encouraged religious vocations. Converts he often received personally. He was interested in the United States and was aware of the growing and needy immigrant church there. Those who had prepared the way for Pierce's audience could count on Gregory's interest in an American convert clergyman who wanted to be ordained. Such an aspiration could conjure up in this pope's mind a vision of missionary fruitfulness.

There were other grounds too for immediate sympathy. Gregory would find in Pierce not only a convert from Protestant republican America but also one whose political views were acceptable to himself. Pierce was seeking religious authority for his own life and he thought as well that his country needed it. Nothing could have fallen more comfortingly on the ears of the beleaguered pope. Although Rome was under fire from liberal thinkers all over Europe, Gregory continued to believe in both papal infallibility and the temporal power.[4] The theocracy of the Papal States, in his view, was not an anachronism but a permanent necessity. In the European battle he plumped for the style of the legitimate monarchies. Nor would he countenance the free church in a free state demanded for peoples by, for example, the Abbé Lammenais. Pierce's Commonplace Book shows he was familiar with these issues. He was sympathetic to the position taken by the pope.

Finally Gregory's personality would have cemented understanding between them. Visitors warmed quickly to this pope. According to Nicholas Wiseman, then rector of the English College in Rome, his manner was fatherly rather than that of a sovereign: 'the function of the throne' at an audience was soon replaced by 'the innocent repartee, the pleasant anecdote, still more the cheery laugh'. He was a man of strong emotion easily betrayed. In prayer tears sometimes ran down his face, and 'often those who have approached him with a tale of distress . . . have seen his features quiver'.[5] Pierce too was a man of sensibilities – and eloquent.

Cornelia, overwhelmed by the volte-face and by the thought of possible separation, must have gone to John McCloskey very soon indeed after the audience. Fransoni's letter to Rosati, already referred to, hoped that Pierce would remain 'steadfast to his holy purpose' and added that 'the Holy Father, when he received him, certainly showed him a very special, fatherly affection'.

Meanwhile Odescalchi, who had made inquiries of the Holy Office about procedure, was simply reminded that whereas baptism could be administered conditionally, neither Anglican confirmation nor ordination was valid, and which sacraments to confer was left in his hands. The case, in such early stages, had presumably not been put formally by the Holy Office to the pope for decision, but Odescalchi as well as Fransoni and von Reisach will have told him about it and the immediate course of action emerged from informal consultation. The upshot, one deduces, was that whereas the cardinal vicar had urged that Pierce remain a layman, Gregory preferred a compromise. The desire for the priesthood should not be rejected outright. Let this generous convert be received and confirmed and time would prove whether he (a married man) would be 'steadfast to his holy purpose'. The door to ordination at a later date should be left open.

One proposal, that Pierce should be ordained in the Greek Rite, possibly emanated from the pope during the audience. Gregory was interested in the new Greek College on the Via del Babuino. Pierce could have studied oriental liturgy there while pursuing the rest of the priestly course at the Propaganda or at the Collegio Romano. But the suggestion came to nothing, perhaps because no Greek church existed at that date in either America or England and Pierce saw no prospect of ministry in either country. On the other hand had he agreed he could have been both priest and family man. What, one wonders, did Cornelia feel if she heard that Pierce had rejected this proposal. He knew the alternative was separation from his wife.

There was little consolation for Fr McCloskey to offer the young wife and mother who came to him in such distress. She now knew definitely that separation and its consequences might be asked of her because her husband's request had not been rebuffed. John McCloskey could have told her the New York story of the Barber family who twenty years before had been permitted to do precisely what Pierce's desire could lead the Connelly family to. Others in Rome knew that Gregory XVI, the Camaldolese monk, was sympathetic to this kind of request, especially from converts. All that she lived for might one day be lost to her, and the matter was now beyond the reach of ordinary domestic decision. It touched the relationship with God that was growing stronger in her every day. It could not be pushed away or promptly settled, as she had done at Whitecottage. It would have to be left lying, lived with, pondered over until conscience and heart could peacefully say Yes or No in case Pierce one day decided to repeat his request. For perhaps years of uncertainty, of waiting on him, her personal haunting question would have to be, What before God should I say if that day ever comes?

Cornelia's sanguine, practical temperament must eventually have come to her rescue. What could not be avoided had to be endured. Better, it could be accepted cheerfully like the five more days in the ship's cabin. She was also still young and still in love. And almost at once a long-desired event created perspective for her. 'You may imagine my joy,' she wrote, 'Pierce has made his abjuration . . . Oh my sisters, what is all that this world can give or take away compared with the joy of feeling yourself in the true way.' She could share the joy of the occasion with her sisters but not its anguish. The good for Pierce in which she so deeply rejoiced made possible also what she most dreaded. For her husband it made possible what he most desired.

It was Holy Week, 1836. Pierce had become a Catholic on 27 March, Palm Sunday. On Maundy Thursday both of them went to the now familiar Palazzo Odescalchi to be confirmed by their friend Cardinal Weld. Pierce's snobbish predilections were given full satisfaction. He was able to tell his mother that no one was present except 'the cardinal's family, and Lord Shrewsbury's . . . who treated us with the greatest kindness & distinction . . . The Earl himself stood Godfather to me & the countess to Cornelia.' Easter day found the Connellys at yet another beginning.

EASTER 1836

Cornelia reached this moment with joy, but she would be staying alone with the children in Rome for more than four months because Lord Shrewsbury had invited her husband to England for the summer.

Pierce reached it in a state of exaltation. The study of Catholicism had been reduced to the experience of an exciting five and a half weeks and he arrived at Easter apparently able to see nothing except his own convictions. At once he was writing with an excessive fervour to his ex-bishop and soon to his mother and his good friend Dr Mercer, hoping to convert them. For Bishop Otey he gives an example of the kind of experience which had

49

influenced him. He had been to the Trinità dei Pellegrini where pilgrims were lodged and fed during Holy Week by the noblest and most learned men and women in the land, anonymously and coarsely clad. 'Dear Bishop,' he exclaims, 'Protestantism has no such examples of charity & humility to offer as I last night witnessed in the dim light of these chambers.' He pours out his feelings:

> Would to God you were here with me at Rome. You would do what I have done, you would not, you could not, resist the power of God, you would be too happy and too grateful to throw yourself into the bosom of that dear and holy mother . . . the neglected, the forsaken, the persecuted Church of Rome.

Beyond this illusory prospect of the general conversion of his friends lay another yet more heady, that he might one day be a priest. Everything had gone Pierce's way. Ordination had become a possibility but he did not yet have to sacrifice his wife and children. Moreover the world, or at least Rome, was now at his feet. The Connellys' conversion was reported with warm acclaim in the *Diario di Roma*. His Natchez letter and sermon were to be translated into Italian. High ecclesiastics and an influential aristocratic laity were his friends. A new horizon, England, with Paris *en route*, lay ahead. Since his family was to be comfortably fixed in an apartment on the Corso in the palazzo where the Shrewsburys rented the *piano nobile*, there was nothing to hold him back. Nelie's love could be taken for granted and she would make herself happy with the children until his return.

In some such state of mind Pierce left Rome for England late in April. He stayed in Paris for about two weeks, and there, briefly, his feet touched ground. On 22 May Cornelia was answering a letter of his, not extant, in which he was full of self-doubt. He was missing her and the children and could see no future for himself. 'Don't give way to depression,' she wrote. In England Pierce would have to carry loneliness and need for her around with him. At the same time experiences across the country would rouse his will to be a priest.

4

Interim

In the England of 1836, behind a façade of immutability, forces of change were gaining momentum. The landscape, rural since time immemorial, was already sprouting mills and smoke stacks. What lay ahead was industrial transformation and democracy. It would no longer be a nation of country poor governed by the tiny majority of landowners who were the aristocratic élite of centuries. When Pierce arrived, fearful of democracy and impressed by high social standing, he viewed England from the socially privileged side of the fence and, at least in what we have of letters, betrayed little interest in the other. The man in England whose guest he was belonged to the tiny majority.

John Talbot, sixteenth Earl of Shrewsbury and Waterford, was a member of that small hierarchical group of about three hundred families who headed the aristocracy. He owned country estates in Staffordshire and Oxfordshire (Alton Towers and Heythrop), property in Torquay where the family sometimes went to find a mild winter, and a town house in the select West End of London. There, to 7 Stanhope Street, the earl came with his family to stay for the London season or to pause *en route* for Alton or the continent. St James's Square, the Palace, clubland and Westminster were all in easy reach, and so was Rotten Row where the fashionable rode. There too came Pierce Connelly. What had so gratified Pierce in Rome, the unexpected acceptance into the 'highest and most interesting English society', as he described it, could now in England with the patronage of the earl be taken for granted. He remained in London until some time in June.

His interests however were not purely social. Lord Shrewsbury belonged, within the aristocratic circle, to a small group whose family tradition was Catholic. His country seat, Alton Towers, was the hospitable centre of Catholic influence. Those most close to him in the Catholic revival were Bishop Walsh, the vicar apostolic of the Midland District in which Alton was situated, and three other younger men: Nicholas Wiseman the rector of the English College in Rome, and two converts, Augustus Welby Pugin

51

and Ambrose Phillipps de Lisle. These three were afire with their own enthusiasms whereas 'Good Earl John' was a practical and pious man. Pierce's conversion he thought a most extraordinary call from God, and his invitation enabled Pierce to consider what openings there might be for him in the country. It also put him into just the kind of milieu most suited to his personality and interests, a Catholic circle of high social standing which saw itself as an influential vanguard.

Of this group in twelve years' time Dr Nicholas Wiseman would find himself centre stage in a Connelly drama, but in May 1836 he had met neither of them. Since July 1835 he had been on a long visit in England acquainting himself with the life of the church there. Now he was in London. So was his good friend the earl and so was Pierce. Shrewsbury thought Connelly's conversion sufficiently important to send copies of his letter of resignation and the farewell sermon to John Lingard, the English Catholic historian. And Wiseman had recently agreed to be joint editor and responsible for the religious content of the new Catholic quarterly, the *Dublin Review*. That the earl introduced Pierce and his story seems very likely. The first issue had just come out and the second, due in July, was in preparation. Before Wiseman left the country to return to the English College in Rome it had appeared and eight of its pages were taken up with the 'Conversion of the Rev. Pierce Connelly A.M.'. The co-editor, M. J. Quin, to whom Wiseman would have passed Pierce's material for editing, said it would cause a sensation.

Certainly these two men met, either now or later in the year in Rome where both were often at Shrewsbury's dinner table – Wiseman aged thirty-four and Connelly thirty-two. The rector was a man of great vitality and most varied interests and learning. He thought and spoke in broad dramatic perspectives. He shone as a conversationalist. He was an advocate of all things Roman and papal. Gregory XVI was his personal friend. He had discussed religion with Lammenais and Montalembert, Newman and Gladstone. He knew everyone. He was (as yet) a success. The Roman Catholic church in its universality and with all its doctrines and devotions and ceremonies was the passion of his life, and the Oxford Movement a 'wonderful phenomenon', a sign that England was moving out of the untruth of Protestantism towards true religion once more. Wherever they first met, Wiseman would have mirrored Pierce's own widening mind and ambitions.

By the third week in June he was near Birmingham at Oscott College, the seminary and preparatory school in the Midland District. When Pierce arrived Pugin's gothic building plans were under discussion, and it was the time of the college end-of-year exhibition, a unique opportunity in general for him to hear about Catholicism in England. Oxford too was near. John Henry Newman was by then a figure in the university community and

influential among the undergraduates. *Tracts for the Times* had been appearing since 1833, and very recently he and Pusey had been accused of 'popery'
because on doctrinal grounds they opposed government appointment to the
Regius Chair of Divinity. Pierce has left no comment on any of this but he
did visit Oxford and must have known. He will have watched with interest
the catholicising movement within the Anglican Church. 'I believe in ONE
church,' he had said to his Natchez parishioners, desiring especially union
between Episcopalians and Romans. Here in England he found others working for the same end.

One of these was George Spencer, a local mission priest he met at Oscott,
younger son of Lord Spencer of Althorp and, like Pierce, a convert Anglican.
He arranged for Pierce to stay with him on his mission at West Bromwich,
one of the villages already caught in the industrial tentacles that reached
out from Birmingham and where he served the most destitute. Spencer
thought nothing of sleeping on the floor, trudging twenty miles a day, being
pelted with stones. His prayer, his parishioners knew, was that he might
become poorer than the poorest. Here was a view of England and a style
of the apostolic life with which Pierce was not personally familiar. If it
moved him, no word to that effect has survived, but the friendship with
Spencer lasted over several years, and for Cornelia he was 'holy Mr Spencer'.

Spencer introduced Pierce to Ambrose Phillipps, also a convert. Phillipps
had remained a layman, and married a niece of Lord Clifford whom Pierce
and Cornelia knew in Rome. Like Spencer he wanted prayer for the conversion of his country organised.[1] At the end of June he welcomed them to
Grace Dieu, his country estate in Leicestershire. Here Pierce found an
English gentleman of his own age, happily married and the father of two
young children, as he was himself, a man content with his lot as a layman
but also enviably provided for – as Pierce was not – with an inherited
income. How he used this was evident. In the locality he had established a
school and a monastery, and had plans to build chapels. In his own chapel
mass was celebrated with full gothic ritual. Conversions apparently abounded. The three men were fervent converts and the recurring theme of
conversation was how to revive the faith. Missioners were needed, they
thought. The Italian Luigi Gentili had already been working in the western
district and in spite of the language difficulty they both wanted another
Italian to come, a mutual friend, the Passionist Dominic Barberi. Even in
this happy family home the shortage of priests in England must have thrust
itself upon the visitor.

Pierce's peregrinations eventually brought him to Alton Towers, the earl's
family seat. Its many acres lay spread around the house, farmed, wooded,
landscaped. A little river, the Churnet, flowed through a quiet valley and
on a rocky cliff the crumbling towers of an ancestor's castle stood, built

there seven hundred years before. On the other bank, overlooking the scene, was the great house. Pierce described it admiringly in the language of the day as 'a noble pile of Gothic building'. His post-chaise turned in through the lodge gate at the foot of the hill and started up the long carriageway. The final sweep brought him through parkland, past a lake, across lawns and up to an entrance flanked with heraldic hounds, talbots in stone. Views opened on every side. Contemporaries described this spot as the Enchanted Valley.

Pierce kept an album in which he preserved souvenirs of the great people he had met, and among its visiting cards and notes and cut-out signatures there is, undated, a delicately drawn ground plan of Alton Towers. He often talked about its grandeur and beauties to his wife and eventually she saw it for herself. In the midst of its splendour he also saw why his patron was known as the Good Earl. The poor among his tenants came regularly to the house and were given food, clothes and medical care. He and his lady visited in the schools which they built and supported. During that summer of Pierce's stay he was arguing with his friend Ambrose Phillipps about the relative usefulness of a Trappist monastery and wrote in September, 'I am apt to think that a society of brothers of Christian Instruction with alms-houses for the poor old people would be more *useful* than a regular monkery.' He thought the new Poor Law system harsh with its 'horrid haunts, the common workhouses' and preferred 'almshouses where the poor forlorn wretches may find a comfortable asylum with the benefits of religion'.[2] Pierce himself, a man earning no income but with wife and children to support, experienced Shrewsbury's great goodness. During this visit the earl undertook to educate Mercer when he was old enough for school.

From Alton there were expeditions. Pierce 'went about much', glimpses of which appear in a letter to his brother. Through the earl he had made 'some invaluable acquaintances . . . I have not been able to accept all the invitations I have had from great people . . . but I have at least seen a good deal of England and learnt something of its Society.' Alton Towers, he says, 'is one of the show houses, and all strangers who come in their own carriages are allowed to see the house as well as the gardens'.[3] The letter was written from Stonyhurst where the Jesuits, prompted by their liaison in Rome, Thomas Glover SJ, received him warmly, put him next to the president at dinner and, according to Pierce, toasted him as a celebrity. He elaborated for his brother's benefit:

I then gave them Lord Shrewsbury's name, which they drank 3 times 3. This you may suppose was gratifying enough to me, for on being wel-comed to England I was in some manner called on to give Lord Shrewsbury, as it is publicly known through himself that I came to England by his invitation on a visit.

Life seems to have been very gratifying to Pierce's ego, yet in this same letter signs of dispiritedness appear again. He is depressed because he does not hear from the family in America: 'I suppose I need not ask why none of you write to us. It seems as if we ought not to look for it, but it would be a great comfort to hear from you all now and then' – the voice of an affectionate and lonely man, longing for approval. He is also missing wife and family. Through the earl's kindness he has spent his time, he says, as delightfully as it would be possible 'anywhere away from dear Nelie and the children. You may be sure I miss them dreadfully and sometimes cannot help being quite low spirited without them.'

Nevertheless the visit to England seems not to have dulled his desire for ordination. Rome had not yet defined its attitude to Anglican orders and very possibly indeed he discussed their validity with George Spencer at this time. And perhaps with others: the July issue of the *Dublin Review*, carrying his account of his conversion, arrived when he was still at Alton. The sympathetic words written by the editor Quin, then his guest at the Towers, were a challenge to discussion among those present: 'It is to be regretted that Mr Connelly's marriage state of necessity precludes him from entering the sacred ministry of our church.'

Not long after this Pierce departed and early in September was on his way back to Cornelia and the children.

CORNELIA IN ROME

Cornelia meantime had spent the four months much less excitingly. For the summer Rome was emptied of all who could afford to escape its heat. She was in the Palazzo Simonetti on the Corso in the heart of Rome, well placed for the winter season and *carnevale* but not for the summer. The Shrewsburys had departed for England and their daughter Gwendaline went out to Frascati with her new baby and her husband, the Prince Marcantonio Borghese. Tradition has it that Cornelia stayed with them at the Villa Aldobrandini but certainly in May she was in Rome 'busy from morning till night'. She was not very well, the children both had whooping cough and she told her sister that she went out 'very seldom, excepting to Church'. She dined out only occasionally, she lent two of Ady's baby dresses for a friend to take a pattern, and copies of Shakespeare and Coleridge to another. The church of St Ignatius was near and at the altar of the boy-saint Aloysius

Gonzaga she prayed regularly for Merty. Little else is known of her doings. It was a quiet existence, an opportunity to take stock of present and future.

One joy had come just before Pierce set off for England, a letter from her own family in Philadelphia, the first since leaving New Orleans. She answered: 'My darling dear sweet Addie, I thank you for ever for your sweet letter. It was like ice-cream on a summer day excepting that it lasted longer. I read and re-read it.' Then with a leap of love she continued: 'Oh Addie you dear little pet, how I could hug you up. I knew you could not be angry with your dear Pierce or little Ne long.' She feared that recent news may have upset them again: Pierce's abjuration and 'the abuse & disgust so plentifully poured out in the *Churchman*' on him. Cornelia's sisters were very dear to her: 'I pray for you all every night and all ways in my thoughts.'

She turned to the subject of Pierce:

Dearest Addie, I thank you a thousand times for your kind feelings towards my dear husband, but how much more you would love him did you know him better, if you did but know him as I do. Oh how often do I think if only I had a heart as full of love and charity I would be too happy.

Gwendaline Borghese had introduced her to her own spiritual director, Mgr von Reisach, and Cornelia went to see him every Saturday evening at the convent of the Sacred Heart on Trinità dei Monti. She now had the prospect of guidance for a prolonged period. No notes have survived of this time but some points are reasonably clear. When at last Pierce became a Catholic she had been overwhelmed, as we have seen, by a realisation that the gift was greater than any other that God and life could give or take. If in these days she thought about the permanent separation that possibly lay ahead it would have been in the context of this awareness. It was now that she wrote to her sister that the gospel must be taken very seriously. Mary was told that one must be '*willing* to be led like a little child in the firm belief in the *words of our Saviour*', and the familiar verse of Matthew 19 (in the Douay version) presumably now began to press themselves upon her: 'Everyone that hath left home, or brethren, or sisters or father or mother or wife or children or lands for My Name's sake, shall receive a hundredfold and shall possess life everlasting.'

She must have thought about her situation, and perhaps with the help of her director reviewed the facts. They were: it was not certain that Pierce would in the end be allowed to be a priest, even if he wanted to be. Were it so for him, she should rejoice because there was no greater call she could desire for him than to be a priest in Christ's church – she had seen his charity and ardour kindling faith in others. But there was their marriage.

They loved each other, and the children were dear. And it was a sacred bond. Were he to become a Catholic priest it had to be God's will, not just his. His wish would have to be authenticated by the church, he must wait to try his heart and so must she, and if eventually he asked it would be the pope's decision not hers or her husband's. Meanwhile she should do all she could to sustain their marriage. When in July Mgr von Reisach was called to the dignity of bishop it was a loss to her: 'I feel much afflicted and indeed desolate when I think of ever losing your holy direction and most consoling advice.'

Towards the end of May a letter (not extant) arrived from Pierce. Her answer is as revealing as her answer to his first letter in absence, less than two years earlier. In some sense their relationship has reversed itself. It is no longer her need of him but his of her that strikes the reader. Pierce is downcast about himself and his prospects in England, wonders if they ought to go back to America, fears she might not want that and is apparently putting his trust more in her than in God. She rallies him:

Rome, Sunday, 22 [May] 1836

Dearest life I received your dear letter from Paris the day before yesterday. Let me kiss you for it, but at the same time give you a good scolding for being so dull. Dear love I knew it would be so. Give it all to the Church, all, all and then I shall have it too for am I not one of its children without a wish that is not connected with it? Oh, petty, don't think about want or any affliction that it may please the Almighty to punish us with. While we have the kingdom of heaven within us will we not be happy in spite of every earthly want, and while we have faith will we not be able to bear all even unto death?

There are no paragraphs and it just flows on:

Oh love think not of me. If I still have too much pride I deserve to be punished for it and to suffer in the *sight of our relatives* for this I believe is my most tender point and where the Almighty could punish me the most severely. But never think of this my love if your duty to God would be better fulfilled by going home . . .

She pours out encouragement:

But I cannot conceive that you could be more useful by going back to America than remaining in Europe for at least 4 or 5 years; and can it be possible that a man of your abilities would not be useful to the catholics of England? I cannot think so. At all events we could but stay in Germany as I told you in my last and live there as I proposed to you. But at all events don't give way to depression. The Almighty will not forsake you after having done so much for you. He will give you faith and give you strength to go on in the good work and be useful in the world, and have you not already increased the faith of some and shaken others?

He is to give himself all, all to the church, in his immediate circumstances, trusting to God in the present moment and not glooming about himself. Cornelia is emerging as the stronger of the two. They were reunited by mid-September and soon Cornelia had conceived their third child, the John Henry who was to be the darling of her heart.

ROME, VIENNA, HOME, 1837

For the next seven months the Connellys lived in Rome absorbing all that it offered. Cornelia continued with music and the training of her singing voice. Art appealed to them both. The many studios of foreign artists, and their haunt, the Caffé Greco near the Piazza di Spagna, were always patronised by *stranieri* including the Americans, and like their compatriots the Connellys would have been fascinated to see the Italian models draped on the Spanish Steps in suitable attitudes as they waited to be hired, here a Magdalene, there a Christ and even a white-bearded old man to serve as God. The great galleries had to be visited, and the Vatican halls to be toured at night by torchlight, a popular way of viewing sculpture. There were too the treasures of Etruscan art so recently discovered and housed by Pope Gregory in a special new museum, and the amazing frescos wherever they went, in churches where they worshipped or palazzos where they dined. They were visitors at the Pontificia Accademia di San Luca and knew its president, Professor Minardi (according to whom, said her husband, Madame Connelly's profile was more perfect than those of Grecian models). Both were especially attracted by the art of painting and both took lessons.

For the time being the Eternal City was home. Their circle of friends and acquaintance grew. Inquiries about the children were made, Pierce's advice was sought – on what to wear at functions, whether he would look over a translation, whether to publish a controversial statement. Personal feast-day greetings came to Cornelia and invitations of every kind went to and fro. Roman society was international. At receptions they met diplomats and cardinals and were invited into the homes of many of the old Roman families. When the time came to leave Pierce was able to write with perfect truth if also some self importance, that 'we have enjoyed the society of some of the most distinguished and delightful people that can be found and received the kindest attention from all the first people'. Cornelia, he said, had been 'a universal favourite and has received enough flattery to have turned even her head'.

Cornelia's chief friend was the nineteen-year-old daughter of the Shrewsburys, Gwendaline Borghese. She was beautiful, devout, simple, and for Cornelia the living example of what a young Catholic wife and mother should be. Her position in society was lofty and demanding because she was the adored wife of the heir in one of Rome's great families. In the huge palazzo by the Porta Ripetta she often had to give four balls a week during the carnival season, yet the Roman populace loved her for her charity to the very poor. Whilst her husband set up a savings bank to help the peasants, she found her way into the worst of the hovels in Rome and herself looked after the sick and destitute who lived in them. Cornelia referred to the 'help and happiness' it had been for her to accompany Gwendaline sometimes on such expeditions, and when she and Pierce left the city she carried the inspiration of that friendship away with her.

Life in Rome followed a yearly rhythm which bore the Connellys along with it. In October came the vintage festival in the Borghese gardens. In December began visits to the Christmas cribs all over the city. Carnival time ended just before Ash Wednesday with the torchlight procession of the Moccoletti in the Corso which the whole Connelly family could watch from the balconies of the Palazzo Simonetti. After that, all through Lent, came mass in the stational churches to be crowned by the solemnities of Holy Week and Easter Day at the Vatican. Through Cardinal Weld Madame Connelly had a special invitation to these in the Sistine chapel where the pope celebrated.

In January 1837 an unparalleled religious opportunity came their way to deepen their understanding of the church and especially of the mystery of the incarnation. The year before, for the first time and with the encouragement of Pope Gregory, Vincent Pallotti had organised a week-long celebration of the Epiphany, the feast of Christ's manifestation to the gentiles. It was envisioned as an annual event and in fact happened for 130 successive years. Clerical colleges and religious orders took part. Oriental rites had their place. A multitude of means was employed, and posters announced events all over the city. In 1837 the solemnities took place in the vast church of San Carlo on the Corso and Gioacchino Ventura produced a booklet of daily readings on the incarnation. The Borghese–Doria circle, including the pious Shrewsburys, would not miss such a happening, and six years later in 1843 Prince Doria sent Cornelia a set of the three volumes of the Epiphany discourses delivered by Ventura after she left Rome. She kept and used them all her life.

The decision to leave Rome in the spring of 1837 was rather sudden. Unexpected news from the Planters' Bank in Natchez may have reached them, rumblings of the American financial panic from Pierce's brother George who had charge of his affairs. To reduce their proposed European stay of several years by beginning a leisurely journey homewards probably seemed wise. Cornelia, expecting her baby in June, would soon be unable to travel, and in the event it proved fortunate that they departed because six weeks later came the news that cholera had broken out in Rome. Before leaving Pierce had important fish to fry. He visited Cardinal Fransoni who was a friend and probably also Cardinal Lambruschini, the pope's secretary of state. One or other of them gave him a letter to deliver personally to the great Metternich in Vienna. That Pierce would yet again find himself among the best people was thus assured.

Before they left the Connellys had an audience on 25 April with the pope. All that is known about it is that it took place in the Vatican Library and Gregory gave them presents. He had seen Pierce at least once before, alone, and both of them about a year previously in a group of Americans. Now as he talked with Cornelia and watched them together he probably speculated on what the future might hold. If the children were present, his memory of the Connellys would be not only of a husband hoping to be a priest, but also of a united family and of a mother who loved her children.

Four days later they left Rome by coach from the Flaminian Gate to travel north. Stops were marked on Pierce's family passport as they moved from Umbria into Tuscany, then across the Legations and on to Venetia. In Florence and Venice they stayed several days to enjoy the sights. Storms delayed them going over the Alps but by the end of May they were settled in the centre of Vienna. Ady had just recovered from measles, Pierce wrote to his brother on 3 June and later, after the birth of the baby on the 22nd, added that Cornelia was 'quite well'. On the 24th the child was baptised in St Augustine's church, Johann Baptist Heinrich Maria Aloysius – soon to become 'Dutch John' in the family and sometimes 'Pretty Boy'.

The remainder, most of what survives of Pierce's letter, is taken up with his interview with Prince Metternich:

> . . . the great man, who may be said for 40 years to have controlled the diplomacy of Europe. My letter of recommendation was from the Cardinal Secretary of State at Rome and you may suppose I was impatient to present it. In the second ante chamber a livery servant shewed me into another through which he said the Prince would pass directly. He bowed inquiringly as I put the letter into his hand, and in a few moments sent for me into the library where he allowed me to remain with him tête-à-tête some twenty minutes when I felt I was abusing his generosity and took my leave without waiting the usual signal from men in high station.

Clearly it afforded Pierce great satisfaction and Cardinal Lambruschini and the Austrian ambassador in Rome conveyed to him through Fransoni their 'interest' that he had been so graciously received. For whatever reason the high Roman diplomats used him as their missive-bearer to one of the church's most powerful allies, Pierce himself was unlikely to have under-estimated the occasion's potential for himself, and who knows what fine dreams of future importance it may have induced.

Relatively little else is known of the Austrian interlude in the lives of the Connellys. Cornelia was recovering from childbirth but Pierce received many invitations from the Viennese Catholic élite. The few surviving letters are notes often preserved in his souvenir book and reveal the admiring affection which he, and Cornelia as his wife, aroused. Partly it was the conversion story that won hearts. To Pierce, for example, who carefully preserved the note in his album, the Archduke Maximilian, uncle to the emperor, wrote:

> Dear Sir,
> It is with the utmost satisfaction, that I go hold of the occasion given me by your letter of the 17 July to testify you my particular esteem grounded upon the non equivocal proofs of truly religious feelings given by you in the most solemn and edifying way.
> May you be sure that I was very glad to make your acquaintance, and that I will be for ever
> your affectionate
> Maximilian.

He was received by the Empress Mother at Schönbrunn. And the duchess of Anhalt-Coethem, ruler with the duke of a small and ancient duchy in the north, invited him to visit. She and her husband, like the Connellys, were both converts. Austrians would have been especially interested to meet American converts because the Leopold Association for missionary work in Ohio and the Mississippi Valley had been founded by a member of the Austrian imperial family.

A few days after the baby was born a letter written in Paris on 13 June arrived from Dr Mercer:

> Intelligence from America is more and more disastrous . . . A general bankruptcy has taken place . . . Some of our friends I fear are ruined and all more or less involved. Our Countrymen are returning in crowds. The packets are crowded to excess . . . The credits of almost all the Americans are stopped . . . I hope that you and Mrs Connelly will not forget that you may both remain *too long abroad*.

They reached Paris some time in August and had to stay till 7 November when at last they obtained berths on a packet from Le Havre. While they waited a letter from a Roman friend caught up with them. The Abbé Augustin Thiener, a professor at the Propaganda, sent messages and news. It brought them the warmth of friendship at a time when their hopes of ever returning must have been low: 'you know my heart, which offers you wishes for all possible happiness . . . Permit me to embrace you very tenderly together with your dear wife and children . . . let me know your address in America.' A final greeting followed for 'your family', described as 'a true glory of our Holy Church'.

The voyage was daunting and the family thus so admiringly described now included a young baby as well as a little boy and a toddler girl. What lay beyond was unknown and the parents faced it rather differently. Pierce's experiences in Europe had by no means prepared him for the immediate poverty that very possibly awaited them. It was understandably in something of a panic that he hoped his brother John could find him a 'clerkship in a bank or a drivership in a plantation, or mastership in a Grammar School . . . any place whatever which will bring in annually a sum somewhat proportioned to our desires as well as our necessities'. Cornelia on the other hand was 'dancing with delight' at the thought of being home.

5

Time of Trial

THE UNEXPECTED

The winter seas were kind and on 7 January 1838 the Connelly family reached New Orleans in safety. Within a few days they took boat up river intending to rebuild their lives in Natchez. Only five months later they were gone again.

They had returned with three little children. They had no home to go to. Their invested money was lost. Pierce considered turning lawyer in Natchez and Cornelia thought about opening a school for young ladies. Eventually a position in a bank was found, and 'music scholars at 10 guineas a quarter thronged' to Cornelia. Their two slaves Phoebe and Sally rejoined them. Ex-parishioners welcomed them back. The Catholics, recently stirred into action by the expected advent of a bishop for Natchez, were especially glad to take into their small number two converts, 'both much loved and respected in the city'. Pierce had scarcely arrived when he was called to chair their meetings and we find him letting it be known that he and his wife intended to reside there. Wherever it was they lived, Cornelia made it a home. There her little daughter had her third birthday, kind Protestant doctors attended her sick baby and did it for friendship's sake, and her husband courted Natchez polite society.

Nothing written by Cornelia about this very brief period in their lives has survived, but a later letter from Pierce to Lord Shrewsbury has. In it, four months after the event, he accounts for their departure. It would appear that for her husband the situation was more humiliating than his self-importance could easily bear:

> . . . not to let the poor Catholics suffer in our humiliation, we received every week some twenty or thirty of the best society of the place at a little soirée, and by making our house somewhat more exclusive than the most exclusive soon made it the most fashionable. And it was quite a ridiculous contrast, the meanness of my morning's occupation and the aristocracy

63

of the evening's society where no one of my *superiors* [in the bank] took offence even that they were never asked.

His humble situation however secured their existence and the decision to move yet again and so soon could not have been anticipated by anyone. Pierce had just agreed to be a church trustee.

It happened that a new colony of Jesuits was about to plant a college at Grand Coteau in Louisiana. They were all French-speaking and a professor for English was needed. Bishop Blanc had suggested the Connellys. Bishop Bruté of Roman days arrived to introduce the idea. Two weeks later, in spring 1838, the Jesuit rector himself appeared:

> What was my surprise on coming home from my clerkly duties in the bank to find the Father Superior installed in his chamber on a visit to us for the purpose of deliberating the projected . . . residence. He very frankly represented their present poverty & the debts that would protract it, and that it could only be the labour of my blessed little wife that would for some time bring in any revenue.

The Religious of the Sacred Heart had a convent and school nearby and Cornelia would teach music for them.

This was matter for discernment. Nicolas Point SJ[1] stayed for three days. That Cornelia would have to be the family's sole support was not the only thing to be pondered. There would be no society for them in so remote a place other than that of religious, and their house 'would be little better than an Indian hut'. Pierce does not tell Shrewsbury that the rector undertook to arrange for the free education of Ady and Mercer at the two schools, but gives as reasons for going that they were 'without priest and chapel' at Natchez and 'without the sympathy of a single Catholic of our own rank'. Ten months later than Point's visit he gave the general of the Jesuits, Fr Roothaan, what may have been a more fundamental motivation: 'After having begun to think that we would, my dear wife and I, be obliged to separate in order to earn our bread, just when we had found great material prosperity, the good God called me to serve the Society of Jesus.'

Of Cornelia's feelings nothing is said. Always they are hidden behind her husband's reiterated 'we', 'my holy little wife', 'my dear wife and I'. On this occasion she may have been in complete agreement. She had, after all, urged Pierce to give his heart 'all to the Church, all, all' and here was a clear way to do it, a lay ministry involving them both.

GRAND COTEAU, 1838

A day towards the end of June, then, found the Connellys once more on the river, going south. Eventually a small steamboat took them up the Bayou Teche for Washington landing. They floated away, Pierce told Lord Shrewsbury, 'through the forests of Louisiana to the lands of the prairie that lie between the river and the Gulf of Mexico'. The Teche, Indian word for 'snake', was one of the immense bayoux of the Mississippi. 'You have no idea,' Pierce went on, 'of the wild beauty of these temporary rivers.' He calls them the gutters of the overflowing Father of Torrents. It was new to the travellers, a flat, lush land of innumerable waterways. Banks slid by where the boughs of trees were draped with grey-green Spanish moss, or in shadowy swamps ancient roots of cypress jutted up like skeleton knees from a watery grave. As the boat pushed further into wilderness signs of human habitation receded. Twilight fell and quickly the dark. In the middle of the night they were put down at a muddy landing, and with three weary little children, ages five, three and one, a French governess who had come with them from Paris, two Negroes and all their worldly goods, Pierce and Cornelia climbed into some sort of wagon from the college and were taken to their new home through the darkness.

Visits from Natchez to New Orleans, a cosmopolitan and seething port, would have prepared the Connellys but little for the world into which they woke the next day. Louisiana was unknown to them. In 1682 an intrepid Frenchman, Sieur de la Salle, had explored right down the river to the Gulf. He claimed the whole great unknown valley for his king, Louis XIV, and named it Louisiana. At the mouth a French fort and then a port grew, the new Orleans, colonial capital of the new France. Gradually the lower banks were settled. Irish and Germans came, and after 1755 hundreds of refugees from what had been French Acadia in the north, violently expelled by the British. Some made homes along the Mississippi. Most went into the forests and prairie of the uncharted interior. In 1838 when the Connellys arrived what was beautiful wilderness once roamed by Indians had belonged to the United States for thirty-three years, a vast wild land.

Settlers dwelt far apart, often owning thousands of acres, and Grand Coteau, a rising in the prairie, was a remote solitude. About nine miles away in the little village of Opelousas a huge scattered parish had a chapel, St Landry. Two zealous parishioners, Mr and Mrs Charles Smith, wealthy settlers from the east, had seen that immigration would increase the Catholic population and built a church of St Charles Borromeo at Grand Coteau. They also gave land for the provision of Catholic education, and in 1821 Mrs Smith established a convent for the Sacred Heart nuns to run a school. When the Connellys came in June 1838 the Jesuits were in the throes of building a college close to the church, and the surroundings of the convent were still more or less as described by Mother Audé RSCJ in 1821: 'The property includes a vast garden [farm] . . . fields, extensive pasture lands and an orchard planted with fig and peach trees, the fruits which thrive best in this region. Cotton, sugar and coffee succeed very well also. One sees immense prairies covered in horses and cattle.'[2]

In this wild place Pierce and Cornelia settled to build their new life. They had expected to have at once a house promised by Fr Point, but a 'litigious old lady', Mrs Mudd, refused to move into the alternative offered and they had to wait for about nine months. Pierce reported to the earl: 'Here we are then with the three children, the little French governess [Mlle Mignard] & two faithful slaves whom we reserved for ourselves, living in what they call our Chateau of Malmaison, being a cabin about 10 feet high & forty long divided into three compartments.' He continues contentedly, perhaps inspired by the Jesuits who with their fifty-six boarders were crammed into even closer quarters until the college was finished. The principal variety of existence was 'going to mass sometimes in the Parish Church which is at the College & sometimes at the Chapel of the Sacré Coeur at the Convent; and the greatest *event* that happens to us is the reception of a letter.' In these conditions they settled again to family life, and there were other challenges too: the monotony of limited contacts; the difficulty of providing a happy home for a growing family in the face of very slender means; and a special challenge to themselves as married people in a place where religious life was the norm and theirs the exception.

In the grounds of the convent stood a cottage which the nuns had provided for the use of the bishop. Anthony Blanc's diocese was about 96,000 square miles, priests few. Since his consecration he had been to Europe to recruit, and a college for boys at St Charles was now beginning because he had personally persuaded the superior general of the Society of Jesus to send men from France. In this first year of its existence, zealous for its success, he appeared twice after the Connellys had arrived and stayed in the cottage. They were his protegées. In a letter full of missionary news to Bishop Purcell he remarked that 'Mr Connelly and Lady are finally settled'. Every morning for two weeks Pierce served his mass, always appearing 'in a *surplice* if you please' and wearing a Protestant soutane. Cornelia he saw in the school, especially on the day of the concert in his honour. They invited him into their home and he told Purcell with satisfaction that they felt 'uncommonly happy in every respect'.

This happiness and their good fortune increased as the months passed. Pierce told the earl, 'My wife . . . is as gay as a bird' and he was 'more desirous than ever' to have the house Mrs Mudd still occupied. Before Christmas Cornelia probably realised she had conceived their fourth child,

and Merty's birthday on 17 December fell at a time of expectation, domestic
as well as liturgical. In February Pierce was asked to teach drawing at the
convent school, thereby increasing their small income, and some time in
March Mrs Mudd gave in and they were able to move. They called the house
'Gracemere'. By degrees Pierce bought it and once again the Connellys put
down roots. Merty was six, Ady four and Pretty Boy nearly two. Mlle
Mignard was still with them.

Gracemere was well placed. A path across fields led to the college in one
direction and the convent in the other. It was right in the middle of the
wild countryside. If Cornelia was afraid for the children when they ran
through the lush prairie grass where rattlesnakes often slept in the sun, she
also rejoiced in the natural beauty around and above them. There were
endless woodlands to be rambled through where in early summer dogwood
and honeysuckle caught the sunlight; tracks to be wandered along where
loops of vine invited them to sit and swing and the strange grey moss
dangled overhead; groves of little palms to negotiate; tall pines and great
live oaks to linger beneath; there were cool stretches of cypress forest, and
swamplands where duck lived in the reeds; bayoux where elephant's ear
hung over the water's edge; if it was September a sudden clump of red-pink
lilies might surprise them; if it was October they heard the wild honking of
geese in the sky, beating their way south to the Louisiana marshes. The
children played outdoors. They picked up pecans for Cornelia's pie. They
tangled the heaps of Spanish moss when Phoebe was stuffing the Gracemere
mattresses; they shouted at papa's new cows and fell over Sally's wooden
bucket and chased the dog round the wood piles. They watched for the red
cardinal darting between the trees and for the whirring wings of the hum-
ming birds.

There were disadvantages. Louisiana was semi-tropical. Rain and heat
were no healthy combination for a young family, none of them very robust,
and they could not have managed without their Negro help. Tub and
washing line for three small children were always full. All water was hand-
pumped, milk was kept in water jars down a pit, the privy had to be well
away from the house. The good God, however, had not placed their home
in New Orleans, 'the wet grave' of thousands, nor in their time did the
deadly fever sweep their corner of the prairie as it so frequently swept the
rest of the State. And Cornelia was blessed with the right temperament. As
she watched Pierce and Merty set out together for school or arranged to
have gumbo for supper and grits for breakfast yet again, it is more likely
that cheerful gratitude prevailed in her than worry. She was never one to
mourn the inevitables of her situation. These had to be cheerfully accommodated.

Her daily walk to the convent school was now a little longer than her husband's to St Charles. On a hot day it might be half an hour before she reached the gateway and the formal French garden that the nuns had made. The path lay straight down the middle and whatever the season there was always colour and fragrance. The little flowerbeds were round or square or octagonal, each with neat brick edges, and between them at regular intervals camellias grew. Beyond lay the school building, white with shuttered windows left and right of the door, narrow wooden galleries on two floors and dormers above. Beside it stood the old community house.

By the time the Connellys came to Grand Coteau the Sacred Heart nuns were at last well established.[3] They had survived nearly eighteen years, slaves worked the plantation for them and the school on the prairie was flourishing. A few of the children rode in by day or arrived by wagon but most of the eighty boarders were from very distant parts of the south-west, the daughters of Louisiana farmers, sometimes of wealthy plantation owners whose sons went north to college. Some, had the school not been opened, would have received no more education than a rare local priest could have given them in his spare time. The nuns offered a very good schooling.

Until now Cornelia had little experience of women's religious life. Here in Grand Coteau she found herself caught up in the concerns of the nuns, gradually learning what were the patterns and springs of their existence. There had been, as she will have heard, lonely years of fidelity to prayer and to the self-giving of their rule amidst great deprivation. Life was still very difficult, but with the recent coming of the Jesuits, and of the rector as their own chaplain, they had at last companionship on their mission and the sustaining joy of daily mass.

Every day she was at the convent for several hours. Nuns became her friends, and their director Nicolas Point her director. Because she taught the children to sing for church she was drawn into devotional practices. In chapel she saw adult Negroes and black babies coming for baptism and sometimes a pupil or alumna to be received as a Catholic. She heard the nuns chanting office, watched aspirants being clothed in the religious habit and novices making their profession of vows. In that same chapel at mass as each liturgical year went by she listened to a procession of homilies. The nuns revered their chaplain. He could reach both hearts and wills, they said, and he inspired Cornelia too. There was also continually before her the witness of the nuns' hard-working charity and of their good influence on the children. It could not have been long before 'Mrs Connelly' admired and loved what she saw, and understood very well the place of religious life in the mission of the church.

'Mr Connelly's' situation was different. He came already knowing and admiring the prestigious Society of Jesus in Europe. Ignatius was his chosen patron. He had met the superior-general. He arrived at St Charles full of high expectation and, as Point later said, with the motives of an apostle. He described himself to Lord Shrewsbury as 'a sort of aide-de-camp to the Superior' and the establishment at Grand Coteau was certainly somewhat camp-like in that first year of its existence: too many pupils for too few Jesuits in half-ready accommodation, communicating in a mixture of English and French, and assailed violently by the Protestant press. His letter to the earl betrays nostalgia for dear Rome and dear England and the 'long halls of dear Alton Towers', but he had – at first – 'little doubt of the success of the institution'. Louisiana was made up of a 'miserable rabble . . . without sentiment, without education, without manners', and the arrival of the Jesuits was 'the only possible blessing' that could befall it.

Three months later he sounded a quite different note. By then this Jesuit college was not setting the standards he thought it should, either in studies or in conduct, and he took it upon himself to pontificate – at great length – to the general. There was division in the Jesuit community about the college programme. Pierce took sides and sent destructive criticism, focusing with personal animosity on the visiting provincial superior. Only one person, Fr Point, the rector and Pierce's close friend, emerges as worthy: he is 'imbued with the spirit of the Society and your own, Father'. Unasked and not a Jesuit, he takes it on himself to inform, judge and advise: 'The eight months I have spent here have given me the chance of studying the situation and of noting facts which I think before God, I should tell you about.' Only part of Roothaan's answer has survived: 'if I were to accept literally all you say and all the implications of your words, then I would have to reply, "Would that the Society had never set foot in the States! Everything it has done there is worthless",' and Pierce is advised, 'Let us try not to see only the bad side of things.' Two years later when Pierce hoped to be a Jesuit himself he wrote very differently. For his support of Point against a superior an abject apology went to the general.[4]

In spite of this discontent with the college Pierce told Roothaan that he was happy. 'We and our small children' have found in the prairie, he said, 'solitude, sanctity and the greatest happiness'. This remained apparently true although sorrows came. At the college there was sickness throughout the summer and a death. At Gracemere in hot July their fourth child, Mary Magdalene, was born. Cornelia, up and about too soon, fell sick, and after seven weeks, in what must have been heavy grief, she lost her baby, the first to die. But there came consolations too: birthdays, Sally's marriage to Nace, a college Negro, visiting priests, school occasions. Cornelia said many years later that this was one of the happiest years of her life. She remembered at the convent the 'bright and happy community', the 'sweet devotion among the children', the 'beautiful French cantiques' they sang and the 'joyous walks and recreations in the garden and forest'. Pierce too wrote of their life. For a friend he described evenings at Gracemere: games with the children and then family prayers. Afterwards when the house was quiet he and Cornelia 'read together, always ending up with a chapter of the *Imitation of Christ*'. As their second Grand Coteau Christmas drew near both were full of special anticipation. For the first time Peacocks and Connellys were coming to stay. It would 'enliven and vary our dear prairie', said Pierce. Also for the first time both had decided to make a retreat before the feast, Pierce with the Jesuits, Cornelia with the nuns. It would begin on 21 December.

THE FIRST SORROW, 1840

Cornelia now stood at the brink of the great spiritual and formative experience of her life. Many had stood unknowingly at the same threshold. Moses, tending sheep in the wilderness, suddenly aware of the living God, I AM WHO I AM, became his servant. The child Samuel 'who did not yet know the Lord' was spoken to as he lay in the dark, and he 'grew and the Lord was with him; and not one of his words fell to the ground'. Paul was struck down on a journey, knew who was present to him and for ever after preached Jesus in word and deed. Until this time in her life Cornelia, like Samuel, was waiting, thinking, wondering, a very good woman giving generously to God whatever seemed due. Her attitude was like Samuel's: 'Speak Lord, thy servant heareth.' It would seem that now, during 1840, God communicated with her in a way so full of power and love that she knew, irrevocably and unforgettably, that God's love alone mattered. Such experiences are impenetrable but they can be validated by the life lived afterwards.

The *Spiritual Exercises* of Ignatius of Loyola to which Pierce and Cornelia were about to be introduced, were an attempt to create for others the dynamics of conversion. Ignatius wanted to be able to guide people drawn by God, and so he noted down reminders of the experiences he had had and of the aids he found for himself. These were his book. Pierce and Cornelia, directed by Théodore de Theux[5] and Point respectively, were to be in retreat using the first part only. What the time meant to Pierce is not recorded. As to Cornelia: 'She used to tell us that her first retreat at Grand Coteau was only one of three days but so thoroughly did she imbibe the spirit of it that her conversion was accomplished in that short space of time.' The 'sketch of her interior life', she said, 'was then drawn', and later retreats only deepened what had already been done.

It began on the evening of 21 December and ended perhaps at noon on Christmas Eve. Each day she attended three talks and saw Fr Point in private. The important early exercises of an Ignatian retreat are a microcosm of the whole. It is not impossible for a retreatant to find herself on the third day already with a lasting desire to give love for love at uncounted cost. Years later, asked about the prayer to suffer with Christ suffering, she answered (emphasis now added), 'I could not help it *from the first*, the prayer came from the depths of my heart *involuntarily*.' More and more compellingly in the next forty years she was motivated by the desire to respond always and with love, 'Your will be done.' In the immediate present the practical steps she at once took at Christmas to redirect her life are simple signs of her seriousness. Soon afterwards came two isolated (as known to us) but significant prayers. Then the call is authenticated astonishingly when a terrible and totally unforeseen suffering did not obliterate her desire but increased it.

On Christmas Day 1839 Fr Point gave her a notebook, and on the day after during some pause in family festivities she carefully set down what she believed she should now do. If the thought of separation sometimes haunted her she was in the present wife and mother, and as such Point knew and directed her. The resolutions, worded as if for the rest of her life, reflect her sense of responsibility to God for children and household as well as herself. 'Never pass one year without making a retreat,' she wrote, and added that at her death she will ask her children to promise the same. She will follow a rule of life: daily morning prayer, midday and evening reflection as Point had taught her; but she will also give some kind of rule to the Negroes, and by implication bring up her family similarly. In her home there was surely a Christmas crib in a quiet corner. There, with husband and children around her, we can imagine Cornelia in the following days often silently renewing her surrender to the God who had become a human being and who was now the source for her of all perspective and action. Very practically and humbly she set out against the obstacles within herself to loving, and chose for the first her 'want of order'.

The days were happy. On 29 December long-expected Peacocks and Connellys joined them – according to the Sacred Heart superior there were '10 persons . . . Imagine the joy!' If in the evening Pierce wanted to write a serious letter he had to be in the living room where games with the children were in progress all round him. Nearly always 'their Mama lends an arm to the medley and sends all dancing, or rather stamping, round and round the piano till some youngster screams for assistance'. Merriment over, all took part in prayers in front of Fra Angelico's Annunciation before the children went to bed. For Cornelia during these days there was a mother's special joy. At last her relatives were seeing all three of her children, Merty just seven, Ady nearly five and John Henry a toddler, the more precious for her for the recent loss of her baby. There was too joy as wife. She saw Pierce the centre of attention talking with characteristic, compelling charm

71

on every possible subject. Family wounds created by doubts about her husband when he resigned good prospects at Natchez could now be healed in the happiness of their new home.

With all this one might suppose that the Connelly marriage had stabilised, but Pierce's comment to his friend when he described that happy family evening early in 1840 reveals a discontent. It did not suit his aspirations: 'how little,' he wrote, 'this looks like walking the Royal Road our Master counselled & set the example of walking'; and when all the visitors except Mary Peacock had gone, some occurrence prompted in Cornelia a prayer filled with premonition and anguish. The prayer is in her notebook and whatever occasioned it was so memorable that she carefully dated her entry. Its cause has to be guessed: that at Christmas the question of ordination had arisen during Pierce's retreat, and de Theux had said Pierce should tell his wife. There had been little quiet between Christmas and the end of the holidays for such a disclosure, and the family visit made it inopportune. No chance came till just before he returned to college for the opening liturgy of the school year on 21 January. It was the 20th, last day of the holidays, when his wife wrote: 'O my God, trim Thy vine, cut it up to the quick, but in Thy great mercy root it not yet up. My God help me in my great weakness, help me to serve Thee with new fervour.' If in fact Pierce had spoken to her about ordination, then from now on the thought of separation will rarely have left her.

Externally all went on at its own even pace. Every day she gave singing classes down at the convent and Pierce taught English to the college boys. At Gracemere she planned meals with the Negroes and taught them their catechism; played with the children, mended their clothes and helped Mlle Mignard with some of their lessons. In the evening she read and talked with her husband and her sister Mary, now once more their permanent guest. And she clung to the rule she made after her retreat, to give time to daily prayer. The days were sunny, the country lovely and she sometimes took the children out. On one such occasion very soon her prayer for 'new fervour' was granted.

The early biographers relate the story as she herself told it, using her own words for what she prayed:

One day towards the end of January 1840, as she was walking with her children she looked upon her peaceful home, surrounded by the beauties of nature and at that moment flooded with glorious sunshine . . . Her children played around her . . . A feeling of intense happiness filled her soul as she gazed. Suddenly, as she afterwards related, impelled by she knew not what, she raised her eyes to heaven and exclaimed, 'Oh my

God! if all this happiness is not for Thy greater glory and the good of my soul, take it from me. I make the sacrifice.

She had – it would seem – since she wrote her prayer on the 20th, seen and struggled against the temptation to love God only conditionally. Not separation! her spirit had cried, anything but that. Her prayer for help was answered when awareness of God's goodness pressed in on her. It overwhelmed her with a presence and a knowledge she could only describe as an 'intense happiness', and freed her spirit – she knew not how – to say, 'I am yours. Take anything.' She was not asking for the separation to happen. No devoted wife and mother could. But she was saying that even that, the most extreme sacrifice conceivable to her, if it seemed to be for God's glory she would not refuse. Now it remained for her to pray (throughout her life) for fidelity, whatever the circumstances, to the unconditional love she had offered her good God.

A peaceful time stretched ahead. Mary and Cornelia had not seen each other since the day after the consecration at New Orleans. During the ten days after the visitors left Cornelia told Mary about her retreat and prayed with her every day. They read scripture and talked about Ignatius' *Exercises* and in the end Mary decided to become a Catholic. Bishop Blanc had arrived and was staying at the cottage, and she asked for instruction. Mary's presence at Gracemere and her conversion were part of Cornelia's total gratitude to God on that sunny afternoon out with the children, and the very next day it was probably she, with her 'almost unvarying cheerfulness of mind', who took charge of the mother's household when an accident shattered all family joy.

With this accident on 31 January suffering came to Cornelia with sudden violence and in a way undreamed of. The next entry in her notebook is on 2 February 1840. It briefly records the death of her youngest child. For details we have to turn again to the early biographers who had them from Cornelia's own account. John Henry was two and a half years old, light-haired and fair-complexioned but with large dark eyes, 'the delight of my heart,' she said. He was playing outside with the Newfoundland dog and was tumbled into a pan of boiling sugar juice. His mother held him in her arms for forty-three hours and he died at dawn on 2 February. The notebook entry is made with deliberate care, words and format significant to the mother who made it. At the top is the date, boxed in with dark hand-drawn lines. Beneath comes a simple, very large M, a symbol of Mary. It floats over all that follows. Then the names of the Holy Family one under the other. Then John Henry's name. Finally a two-line description of what happened: 'Fell a victim on Friday – Suffered 43 hours & was taken "into the temple of the Lord" on the Purification.'

Here is an epitaph, hidden away on a single page in a woman's small notebook. To read it is to stand by a grave and at the same time be warmed to life by the fire of another's faith. In the universal language of scripture and liturgy it records not only the death of the child but also, mysteriously, the experience of the mother, an experience of the transcendental at the core of her personal human anguish. The outsider gazing at the page is led to the edge of some oblation where Cornelia seems to have been drawn into the sacrificial love of both the God incarnate and his mother. The depth of her desire to remain always in that attitude herself appears in her notebook on 9 February, a mere week later. Personal sorrow has not obliterated her readiness to suffer and she is sure the desire is from God. 'I will ask my God,' she wrote, 'without ceasing, and he will give me to drink.' A little prayer is squeezed in immediately below. She will contemplate Jesus in his sufferings, she says, through the eyes of his mother, and begs him to give her a share in Mary's steadfast compassion. This she did constantly until her death, turning to Our Lady of Sorrows at every crisis.

When in after years Cornelia related the circumstances of the accident to others, she did not see it in isolation. She linked its agony with the intense happiness of the day before and with her offering then, which she seems to imply was prompted by God. One is reminded of the advice she later gave the inquirer about the prayer to suffer with Christ. If it comes 'without your seeking it, or wishing it, be sure it is from God and do not resist it'. When, in this light, we consider the order of events and prayers from the conversion retreat until the notebook entry on 9 February, they suggest a single, extraordinary and cumulative experience. Apparently it left her profoundly receptive of God's love and, for that reason and in spite of the final anguish, still reaching out to him and still desiring not to refuse. As she would one day write, 'we are *ourselves* the only obstacle to the overflowing of His Divine love'. That kind of hollowing out takes a lifetime and one wonders how often in the coming painful years Cornelia opened her notebook at this epitaph, to renew her offering. The last word 'Purification' stands by itself in the middle of the bottom line.

THE SECOND SORROW, 1840

Life had to go on. When John Henry had been buried and that same evening Mary had been received into the church, and then next morning Bishop Blank had left, routine was resumed and little by little drew the household out of shock. Ady's fifth birthday came early in March and adult grief had to be hidden. Cornelia clung to her rule of life, Lent passed, Easter came and went. At Pentecost a convent pupil was baptised and Mr and Mrs

Connelly were asked to be her godparents. Both schools were busy. Pierce worked hard to collect information for the Sacred Heart superior about education in America. Perhaps by the end of June when some of his boys spent his feast day at Gracemere surface wounds were healing.

Two events during the summer are recorded in Cornelia's notebook. The first came at the end of three days of prayer made by the nuns in preparation for the feast of the Sacred Heart. The entry must signify something of great importance, and it was in this month – even though, if our hypothesis is correct, Pierce had already warned his wife of the possibility of separation – that their last child was conceived. In her notebook she glued a picture of the hearts of Jesus and Mary. It speaks of burning love and great suffering. Below is the single word 'Memorare', and below that the date 'June 26 1840'. Her child was born on 29 March 1841. Did she hope this conception would deter Pierce from separation? Was this why she said, later, that her religious community was founded on a breaking heart.

The second event was three days of prayer in July, centred on St Joseph. Her notes suggest that Point, who was about to leave Grand Coteau, had been encouraging in her an attitude of confidence in God. She resolves, among other things, 'to fulfil days as imposed by God himself' and chooses Joseph 'for our Protector', thinking in both statements presumably of Pierce and her children and the child she was carrying. After that the notebook falls almost entirely silent for three months.

Point's departure in July, at the beginning of this period, bore hard on both husband and wife. He had gone to the Indian missions. According to Pierce, this man, only five years older than himself, was 'not only un des nôtres but the most distinguished' Jesuit he had met in the United States and 'a brother as well as a Father to us both'. The whole direction of both their lives had been influenced by him. He had arrived in Natchez, a stranger and a Jesuit, to invite them to Grand Coteau, to a leap in the dark. The impression he then made inspired Pierce to say that 'the good God called me to serve the Society of Jesus', and the admiration was mutual. The Jesuit later wrote to his general that Mr Connelly was 'of all Americans the most upright, the most noble, the most devoted to our mission, and at the same time the most simple and the most humble that I know'. He had not been Pierce's director but certainly he was his confidant: Pierce had often told him, he goes on, that were his spiritual director so to advise him, both he and his wife would be willing to embrace the religious life. No decision had yet been reached about this with de Theux when Point left for the Rockies and Pierce was still swinging, supposedly, between desires and doubts. But his friend must have known which way the wind was blowing, even though, as Cornelia states, he knew nothing of the actual plan which her husband eventually put to her.

As to Cornelia, Point was her director from the time she came to Grand Coteau. His daily homilies had led her through the Christian year. He had introduced her to the *Exercises* in her first retreat, supported her through the dark days first of Mary Magdalene's and then John Henry's terrible death. He had seen her regularly throughout months of anxiety and somehow found time to direct her through three days of prayer just when he was about to leave. Looking back after years, she revered him for his apostolic spirit and for having set her foot on the road to unconditional loving.

During the next three months, when nothing of Cornelia's has survived, two letters reveal much of Pierce. The first, written on 15 July 1840, was to Baron Hübner, a diplomat in the entourage of Metternich and a warm friend to Connelly. Its immediate purpose was to send the notes on America and education; but that takes a mere paragraph and quickly Pierce is writing about himself. Nostalgia for Europe, melancholy in loneliness, discontent with present conditions, and an almost ecstatic love for his family succeed one another. The baron's letter had been 'as dearly welcome to my little wife as to myself . . . We are *exiles*.' There have been many sorrows and now had come the departure of Fr Point, 'the only intimate friend and associate I have near me'. He protests that he has never regretted coming to Grand Coteau yet describes himself as 'occupied in teaching the first rudiments to . . . low bred children, & my little wife, with no other companions than the Ladies of the Convent, engaged every day in the drudgery of music lessons'. In these circumstances it is not to be wondered at that 'our hearts wander to where there are so many grateful and delightful associations'. Cornelia and the children are his immeasurable consolation: 'Not a day passes me that I do not tremble in the possession of the great star of happiness that is left me independently of the world, in one of the loveliest families the earth bears in its bosom.'

After this letter and Point's departure in late July, the hot summer still stretched ahead. Cornelia, pregnant, watched and waited. François Abbadie SJ became her director and Pierce remained with de Theux. In mid-September the school holidays began, Pierce decided to make an eight-day retreat and it lay before them, a likely turning point for both. A letter to Shrewsbury, written in October, indicates something of what Pierce already had in mind.

It is long, some sixteen hundred words. Much of it describes a local Negro insurrection and the 'hue and cry' against the Jesuits. There is also flattering encouragement to the earl for all he is doing for Catholicism in England, and something on the church's progress in the United States, but much space is devoted to a particular request and a reminder. Pierce wanted Shrewsbury to oversee the sale of a painting for him. He hopes that if it does not fetch £200, a considerable sum then, it can stay at Alton Towers 'until I or my little boy reclaim it', and then the reminder appears: 'I always look forward to accepting' the offer to educate Mercer in England. These things were written only the day before he began the retreat during which he opted for ordination. Clearly plans were maturing whether or not agreed with Cornelia, and although she too was a friend of the Shrewsburys there is, apart from her 'affectionate regards', no reference to her. Nor to their little girl, nor to the fact that another child is on the way and that Cornelia has not been well.

Next there appears the desire to be in Europe again: 'How many, many grateful recollections do your Lordship's letters bring crowding together: for a moment it is almost impossible for our frail nature not to yearn towards Holy Rome, or beautiful Alton Towers & all their delightful associations.' Then he repeats what he had written to Hübner, that life at Gracemere does not sufficiently challenge his spiritual ambition: 'God forgive us! for here in our wilderness and solitude we have still so much to enjoy & so little to do and suffer that it seems but little like travelling the Royal Road Our Master walked in' – though they had lost two children, one most dreadfully. Finally, behind his expressed abandonment to the will of God, there appears faintly the face of discontent with the *obscurity* of his apostolic lot: 'all that he asks of *us* is a spirit of *Prest accomplir* [the Talbot motto], whatever he calls us to & whenever & wherever, while you dear Lord Shrewsbury are already in the face of England & the world fulfilling . . . glorious duties . . . bringing back . . . the ages of faith.'

Next day, 9 October, Pierce began the second retreat of his life. During it he would decide whether or not to sacrifice his marriage to the priesthood. One argument lay open to him: his call to the ministry pre-dated his marriage, and though the Catholic church had advised him to remain a layman he knew that he could still be a priest if his wife would consent to separation. He lived up at the college, dining in silence with the Jesuits and following the *Exercises* as they did. De Theux directed him. Cornelia remained at home with the children and perhaps saw him in the distance every day at mass. She no longer had illusions that what her husband might decide was unattainable, and on 13 October, the Feast of St Edward the Confessor, he spoke with her.

The *Exercises* are structured to help anyone who wants to decide the state of life in which he can best praise and serve God. Cornelia would have known this, and that in an eight-day retreat a provisional choice might be made at the fifth day. They met after mass. Pierce told her that he was now sure he should seek ordination in the Catholic church and asked her to co-operate. Later she set down what he had said: it was his 'declared wish and intention . . . to take Holy Orders in the Roman Catholic Church' and they should therefore 'live in constant and perfect chastity, abstaining from sexual intercourse with each other in order to the more fully devoting themselves to the service of God'. She told her director, Abbadie, how she answered and he remembered (in French) what she said: 'This is a very grave matter; think about it deeply, and twice over; but if the good God asks the sacrifice, I am prepared to make it & with all my heart.'

We have to note here that Cornelia's consent is not yet definitive. She is fully aware of the gravity of the proposal and speaks warningly. The co-operation she now voices is with God, the actual future not yet certain. In her notebook there appears at the top of a new page the barest of entries: 'St Edward's Day *13th October 1840*', which tells us nothing, but her early biographer, a Holy Child nun who knew her long and personally, wrote that Cornelia had said, 'the Feast of St Edward was the beginning of the Society of the Holy Child Jesus, and that it was founded on a breaking heart'.

ROADS DIVIDING, 1841

The pain of separation now began to thrust itself upon both husband and wife. When after three more days of retreat Pierce returned to his family life they took up their trial agreement to live as celibates, and, according to later statements of both, maintained it steadfastly. They had voluntarily accepted the greatest possible deprivation for themselves, to be poor in what ordinarily endows the happily married with a spiritual and psychological wealth. For the time being only their directors knew of Pierce's hopes and Gracemere remained to all appearances a happy home. On Pierce, with a long-desired future in prospect, the present may not have borne so hardly, but suffering there must have been. Egotistical man as he was, he referred to his wife with admiring affection and much later claimed that he had loved her 'as woman rarely has been loved'. Cornelia, on the other hand, was not the initiator of the situation. In the midst of the suffering which now assailed her she clung to trying to do whatever God wanted, as her reply to Pierce shows. For this reason she had willingly freed her husband to investigate further, but for the same reason husband and children were still to be loved devotedly day by day, and she had to remain ready, which she did, to return to the fullness of their marriage should the priesthood ultimately be denied him.

For the coming months, therefore, the natural duties of Cornelia's daily life had to be met with a loving fortitude. She was not strong and she was pregnant. School began only two days after Pierce spoke to her, and a dear friend, Madame Gareschè, mindful of Cornelia's health now that classes had begun again, wrote and reminded her, 'it is a duty in you to nurse your delicate constitution'. Some time quite soon came tragic news from the Shrewsbury's of the deaths of Gwendaline Borghese and her three little boys. The children's birthdays and Christmas had to be cheerfully celebrated. The first anniversary of John Henry's death came along. On 29 March she bore her last baby, Frank. In the middle of June dearly beloved Mary entered the convent. In July the baby was ill and nearly died. In August Mlle Mignard, who had been with them since Paris, followed Mary to the convent and Cornelia was left with the family at Gracemere, alone except for Sally and Phoebe. During this procession of sadness another letter arrived from Madame Garesché, to revive for Cornelia memories of earlier and happier days:

> . . . how often I commune with you in thought you cannot imagine. I am ever resting my thoughts on the pleasant countenance of my sweet Cornelia when she uttered her final observation of leaving all things to God, & submitting to his divine will in every dispensation; then I get back to the pleasant meal, preceded by Grace, the innocent and mirthful conversation of Mr C. I look back to that little dining room as to the sweetest I ever took a meal in.

In Pierce's letters of the time there are a few references to wife and family. For a friend he calls their life one of 'luxurious domestic happiness' and again mourns it is not the Royal Road of the Cross. The bishop, on being told of the baby's nearness to death, hears that 'we prayed that he might only be left behind if it were *ad majorem Dei gloriam*, not otherwise' and in regard to Mary's and Mlle Mignard's departure to the convent, 'you will be surprised to see how well my little wife manages to get along . . . I tell them the house is just as gay & a great deal quieter without them'. Pierce was well satisfied, apparently, with the way things were going.

Only Cornelia's notebook shows anything of her suffering and that most meagrely. In its privacy there occurs soon after Pierce's proposal an entry which inadvertently reveals the cause of her heartbreak: she believed their end would in fact be the priesthood and religious life. It would be a miracle, she notes, were it to prove otherwise, and writes resolutely that they must 'work out their calling . . . what one is called to do, she is called to do with all her might'. It was with that conviction that she set out to make family life at Gracemere all that it could be in spite of the sexual deprivation she was suffering, and of the bleakness of her prospects and those of the children. Whether she could do this was part of the working out. She also had to decide – which, unlike Pierce, she had not yet done – whether or not God was calling *her* to religious life. Those with whom they had consulted in the United States assumed that a Yes to Pierce would entail this for her. But the empowering was God's, whether for marriage or religion. She had to pray for the heart's knowledge of his will. She arranged to make a private retreat of eight days in January 1841 with de Theux. After it she included a monthly day of reflection in her life as well as the daily prayer she already made. 'Presumption' appears in her notebook. To think one is called to the religious life is not presumption, but it is 'to think there is no fear of ourselves. It is not presumption to have hope & joy & confidence in God's grace. It is presumption to think we do & will always deserve God's grace.' On 1 September there appears a prayer of self-giving: 'O my good Jesus I *do* give myself all to Thee to suffer and die on the cross, poor as Thou wert poor, abandoned as Thou wert abandoned by all but thee O Mary.'

Cornelia was now learning something of what being abandoned could mean. As was to be expected, since October 1840 Pierce had increasingly focused his attention on his own future. Hours were spent in writing long letters to friends in America and old friends in Europe with whom it was now important to re-establish contact. He was in touch with the superior-general of the Jesuits and was hoping to become a member of the Society. He had taken part in ordination ceremonies at the college and more often dined up there with the religious.

On 17 September his wife began a second retreat of the year with de Theux. Through what struggles of the spirit she arrived at the certainty of conscience which now allowed her to consent to their separation – provisionally – is nowhere recorded. In her own words to Pierce, it was 'a very grave matter'. Here was a woman who had taken seriously her marriage vow, who had declared 'I love my husband and my darling children' and whose husband was asking for separation so that he could be a priest. Church law stated that such a request could not be granted without her consent. She understood his apostolic desires and she wanted his greater good but there are questions she must have asked herself. What of his health? It had broken down at Natchez. Could he stay the course of the long Jesuit training, and of the demanding daily pastoral life which would follow? More difficult: if she refused his 'repeated requests', as she called them, what effect would it have on him as husband and father? Above all, ought she to stand in the way of his obvious potential for this ministry in the church? It was not easy: later she once said, 'you see, it is not for nothing I have given him up'. The only thing we know in regard to her responsibilities as mother is that when she consented it was in the belief that her darling children would be 'as much under my eyes as if I had not left the world'. At the end of the eight days she wrote in her notebook: 'Ex[amined] Vocation. Decided.'

With this consent Pierce was free to present his petition in Rome. Cornelia's decision about her own call to religious life remained contingent upon the success of her husband's request, but now there was for both the relief of agreed action. She adopted his proposition as hers and Pierce himself went into retreat with the Jesuits knowing that his way was clear. A little note from her to him is written in her usual, cheerful, practical fashion. It was the last day of her own retreat when she was contemplating the mystery of the ascension:

September 25 [1841]

Dearest

Be sure to send Sally back at ½ past 2 – we will be at the ascension and after going through the sorrows we wont give up the right to the joys you know. I wish you all a merry dinner as a preparation for your retreat. Father said we might relax a little to-day though perhaps he did not mean quite so far as I am doing – but I am not *yet* a religious.

Yours ever in JC.

After his eight days Pierce leapt into action. Newman's *Tract 90* had shaken the Anglican Church in February 1841 and in England a tide of conversions was hoped for. It had roused Pierce's enthusiasm. As an ex-Episcopalian clergyman with a possible future in England were he a Jesuit there, he could envisage for himself a special ministry, and pursued his correspondence with George Spencer on church unity. Europe was undoubtedly where Pierce wished to be. It was the scene of remembered success and of many influential contacts. It was also, in view of his strictures on education in the United States, where he wanted his sons to get their schooling. When he needed to account publicly for his departure from Grand Coteau the half-truth he used was that he was 'forced by what I consider my children's interests'.

Plans for departure were quickly under way. As appears in his November letter to Spencer, he intended to have all his family with him in Europe:

. . . all these things we will talk together when we meet next spring . . . Do you know of any modest little inn or private dwelling near the College where I could board for a short time with my wife & the two little ones that will still be left us when Mercer is with you. Though if I should determine to pass the next winter in Rome I must try to find a convent where they will take her and them.

Spencer was a spiritual director at the seminary of Oscott College and through Shrewsbury's interest the school attached to it was a possibility for Merty. In January Pierce gave notice to the Jesuits that he would be leaving and began negotiations to sell Gracemere to them. But in the end the family did not at once go together. Pierce took Merty and Cornelia was left behind with Ady and the baby.

Two years later Pierce wrote to his brother John:

When I took leave of dear Nelie on Ascension day in 1842 we did not

81

know that we should ever see one another again until we both had on our long gowns. It was thought necessary that we should be tried by a separation of that kind. Moreover, arrangements were to be made about the children but things could not be settled then and . . . I always wished Nelie and the children to be on the same side of the ocean.

What idea of separation did Pierce entertain, one wonders. If he means that Nelie might have become a nun (or novice) while he was away, he forgets – if he yet knew – that were she to have put on her 'long gown' at Grand Coteau she would no longer have been free to go anywhere, let alone cross the ocean, at *his* will. This he certainly expected her to be able to do, and before he had reached Rome he wrote to John (who, like George, corresponded with Cornelia), 'I mean George to take Nelie with him when he goes North next year . . . and I shall meet Nelie in Philadelphia or perhaps Cincinnati.' But the situation was complex, made more so by remoteness from Rome. Evidence is thin, and though Pierce wanted them all on one side of the Atlantic it was not necessarily possible at once. Seemingly they thought the pope, assured by Pierce of his wife's consent, could grant the petition at once and then Pierce would deal with the practical consequences and fetch the family.

No word of Cornelia's survives from this patch of time, not even of any protest she made about Merty's removal to England. Bishop Blanc disapproved. Aged nine, Merty was being removed from his mother, his home, his school – from all that was familiar. It would have been possible for his father, if the pope granted the petition, to return to America to enter the Society of Jesus. A vast field of ministry was opening to the Jesuits there, and even though he was critical of the schooling at Grand Coteau, there was also Georgetown in Washington DC with both a novitiate and a college. Pierce's mind, however, was set on the Society and the priesthood in Europe, and like Hector dragged at the heels of Achilles' chariot, Cornelia and the children appear to be hitched to his ambitions. Practical wisdom perhaps convinced Cornelia she must agree with the pig-headed Pierce. Her husband, she probably realised, had become a burden to the college,[6] and her son's future there was in doubt because the Jesuits were so poor; whereas Shrewsbury's offer to educate him could be counted on. But often agreement does not describe the heart's inclinations. When both were hoping for a visit from Bishop Blanc, Pierce told him she had said: 'I have a great deal in my heart to say to him.'

Somehow the secret was kept. Even their brother George, to whom Pierce often wrote, was left in the dark. He sent Cornelia cheerful, affectionate postscripts. Her letters, he said, were like lumps of sugar. He wanted more because Pierce 'writes to me about the Trappists and what is going on in

Europe but says nothing of what is going on in Gracemere'. What was going on was the dismantling of life together. Phoebe and Sally and Sally's children were transferred to the Jesuits, furniture and pictures were auctioned, books and house sold to the college. Pierce went to stay there with Merty, and Cornelia, in her husband's blithe words, was 'delightfully fixed at the convent'. On 5 May 1842 he and Merty left Grand Coteau for good. Ady had gone to board at the convent school. Cornelia was in Bishop's Cottage very close by. There she made a temporary home for herself and the baby Frank, Bun as he was called, until her husband should send for them.

JOURNEYS, 1842

The further trial of separation, which Pierce called this period, was very different for husband and wife. His was peripatetic, exciting and entirely within his own initiatives. Hers was a time of silent waiting, a life of routine and quiet, its only journey an interior one.

In Philadelphia Pierce had a wait of about three weeks before he and Merty sailed for England, well-filled weeks if his only surviving letter to Cornelia is anything to go by. He gave a series of discourses in Baltimore cathedral in which he spoke of his conversion and of his desire to see the Episcopal church in union with Rome. He relayed a great many details about the boarding accommodation for pupils in the Visitation convent he had been to. Visits to friends and family had taken up time and he reassured her that the Montgomerys, with whom she had lived as a young girl and had defied in order to marry him, were now full of goodwill towards her. Everyone doted on Merty. The boy's education in England would take about seven years, and someone, he said, had remarked that, for so long, a 'mother must be found for the child'. Except for this statement the lengthy letter is merely newsy. There is no sign (but the end page is mutilated) of concern for his wife left behind and no reference to the serious purpose of his journey.

By 4 July he and Merty were in England and it now appears how unsettled, indeed how vague, his prospects though not his intentions really were. In London, desirous to become a Jesuit in England, he discussed his situation with Fr Randall Lythgoe, the Jesuit provincial superior. Then, being a man in a hurry, he wrote to him from Alton Towers (where he was surrounded by old friends, the Shrewsburys, Spencer, Pugin, Phillipps, Bishop Walsh), pressing for an early answer to his questions:

Is it necessary that both should begin their noviceship together? Can the little boy [Frank] remain near his mother during her noviceship? At what age could he be received at Hodder [the Jesuit school for little boys]? In fine the thing is to find out what are the means and when is the soonest time that both may enter a holier state. If it is necessary that the mother should remain for some time longer with the child, would music lessons make provision for them at a convent? And a dispensation be had for the husband in the interim? If the thing is really impracticable for a time is there any way for the family to provide for itself in England during that time?

Lythgoe's answer suggests that he had measured his man. He remarks that further theological studies are '*necessary* in order to acquire the *habit* & *feeling* of a Catholic Priest'. As to what Pierce should do, he has 'weighed all the circumstances': he would not be justified in admitting Pierce to the Society until Cornelia had been admitted to a convent; it would be wiser to return to America for two years to provide for the children rather than attempt it in Europe. *After that* he could begin theological studies in a Jesuit house for one or two years. *Then* his little son could be received at Hodder. *Then* Pierce and Cornelia would be free to follow their own vocations to religious life. In other words, Pierce was told he should wait for three if not four years before doing what he wanted to do at once. Characteristically, he did nothing of the kind, even though he had assured Lythgoe that he would receive whatever he advised as 'the counsels of God'.

In no way was Pierce deflected from his immediate purpose. Mercer could remain at Oscott where Shrewsbury had agreed he should go, and the earl at this juncture was informed of Pierce's purpose in going to Rome. When Shrewsbury received the 'astounding news' he replied: 'What do you want? to break the laws common and Divine? to give up your lovely wife and children? No such sacrifice is demanded of you. You are mad! By ambition the Angels fell! Stop at once, and be a good Catholic husband and father.'

Apparently Pierce talked him round but the earl continued to say it was impractible for the time being and did not, Pierce admitted, do anything to further him in his desires. It was Bishop Walsh who came to his aid, though he may not have known the full story. Through him Pierce acquired a travelling tutorship with young Robert Berkeley of Spetchley Park. 'One of the best families in England,' he wrote to John, 'Belgium, Fribourg, Munich, Milan, Ancona, Loretto to Rome and back, Florence, Genoa and Paris. What a delightful tour if Nelie were along. How much rather would I be at home with the little ones than anywhere else without them . . . Darling Mercer, I have not seen him for nearly two months . . . I shall spend a week at Oscott before going abroad.' He drew a salary of £200 per annum (a very comfortable emolument: a teacher or clerk at that day would have to *live* on £60)[7] plus all expenses paid and a servant when required. He left for the continent with young Berkeley in mid-September.

Cornelia's cottage was very small, two rooms opening on to a wide wooden porch. It was adequate only for a simple life, just large enough for mother and child and whatever trunks and treasures Cornelia had brought from Gracemere – toys and clothes for Ady and Bun, her own wardrobe and jewellery, her music, her little red Bible. A letter of hers to John Connelly fleetingly shows her at home there: 'Frank says Unco Dohn when we talk about you. Ady tells me to tell you she wants to see you very much and sends you many kisses.' Although the letters that passed between Pierce and Cornelia after he left New York for Europe have not survived, we know that they kept in touch. He wrote also to his brothers, and news was passed round among them all. She told John that he was going to 'travel with young Berkeley until spring', heard from him at various places *en route*, and conveyed to the family an apparently cheerful acceptance of the present separation.

She lived in the bishop's cottage for more than a year, dividing her time between making a home and earning their living. Every day she gave music lessons at the convent for most of the morning and in the afternoon was free for her children. But it was also a life in which whatever she was doing she sought with great earnestness to entrust herself entirely and simply to God. Permanent separation now almost certainly lay ahead and this new situation was a kind of trial run of life without Pierce, and of the authenticity of her own vocation to religious life. Especially there was the question of her continuing responsibility for a small son and, less directly, for Ady. Cornelia probably thought, as did Pierce, that soon, while her little son still had need of her, she would have to be a novice. Now she had her first chance to reckon the difficulties.

At this juncture she was only on the outskirts of religious life and independent of the Sacred Heart rule, but the nuns welcomed her. Their superior. Mother Maria Cutts, whom Pierce had told why his wife believed she would one day be a religious, became a good friend. She introduced her to the inner discipline of religious life as understood there, and encouraged her through what was a time of struggle. It would be surprising were there no sense of being abandoned, no temptation to envy and blame her husband and reach out possessively to her children, even to cry out against God, 'Why me?' But what we have in this second notebook (which Mme Cutts gave her) is not that side of the picture. Instead there is the evidence of a sustained generous effort to put herself, come what might, into God's hands.

The notebook is tiny but quite fat and has many entries that belong to a later or unidentifiable date. It would seem that initially Cornelia laid out its pages with deliberate care, as if she knew that again she stood at a beginning. On the inside covers, front and back, she put the foundation virtues of Christian living: 'Faith. Hope. Charity'. On the first leaf appears '*Prayer & Practice*', a characteristic combination, for Cornelia was never one to keep her head in the clouds. On the corresponding last leaf, carefully coloured and gilded, are the Christian's destiny: 'Heaven. Hell. Death. Judgement'. For the journey, on her second page, she asks for help 'to begin now' and reminds herself not to look back having put her hand to the plough. Then at once comes a daily timetable and a list of devotions. After that she has allocated sections for different purposes, heading each with some illuminated word like 'Passion' or 'AMDG'. At the end, tucked in just before the Four Last Things, appears a prayer of Père de la Colombière on confidence in God. The initial letter is carefully painted in red and gold and at the end she added her own 'Amen'. She now stood in great need of this confidence. The presence of her little boy, 'trying to say everything: with pretty curling hair & rosy cheeks & saucy chin', her last child, was a piercing reminder of all that was to be lost to her.

From the many crowded entries a few will show the self-giving direction in which God was drawing her. At the very beginning she writes that every day she will 'give P[ierce], self, children, all' into the care of the Mother of God. On the Feast of the Sacred Heart a line reveals the intensity of her desires: her own heart is to 'be a witness of my love and say to thee without ceasing, "Yes Lord I am all thine" '. When she knew Pierce's travelling plans she began to pray for 'Pierce and M[erty], for Berkeleys and that all may turn to Gl[ory] of God, for Mr Spencer's int[entions] and all at Oscott'. Meditations for Our Lady of Sorrows to whom she had turned regularly since the death of John Henry appear often; so do references to the passion. At the end of the retreat made with the nuns she offers (and deliberately initials and dates) 'to support all kinds of adversities' if that is what God chooses her for. The earnestness with which she strove to respond is evident in the notebook. This is where the '*Practice*' becomes visible. Page after page records whether she had done each day what she undertook; notes and carefully copied extracts; in one place, advice to herself about keeping her rule, which she took from the Lord's words to Francis of Assisi: 'à la lettre, à la lettre, à la lettre, sans glose, sans glose, sans glose', followed by three meaningful exclamation marks. One phrase catches the spirit of the whole, 'Do and Suffer' corrected to 'Love and Suffer'. This, for more than a year, was Cornelia's kind of journey.

Pierce meanwhile continued his travels. Mid-December he arrived in Rome. His petition, he discovered, could not be considered until the pope had seen Cornelia herself about it, and at the end of April he and Robert Berkeley set out for New York. They landed on 1 July; on 8 July (fifteen months since he and Merty left) the letter came calling her to Philadelphia.

The chance to travel with George, on which Pierce had counted for her, had gone, but 'my dear Father Abbadie' was consulted and she decided to 'start off on the first boat'. A flurry of packing followed and in five days she was aboard the *Wm Quack* with Ady and Bun. They would go south to New Orleans 'to arrange our affairs', and then up river. Imploring notes went to John and George. 'Be on the watch for us,' she says to John; and to George, whom she might just catch up with, 'I send a letter to tell you we are off and hope to meet you at Natchez or Vicksburg if you are not gone . . . make a grand effort to meet us.'

Of the reunion in Philadelphia we know nearly nothing. They had about a month before they sailed. At some point they visited Mary Peacock, now a novice at McSherrytown; and Cornelia had a 'sweet little moment' with her own brother George. Harry Connelly hosted Pierce and Robert Berkeley. In New York Pierce and Cornelia tried to see their old friend John McCloskey but he was away. Then the party took ship to England and had arrived by 14 September 1843.

6

Separation

'Here we are for the last week,' Cornelia wrote to Adeline from Alton Towers on 28 September 1843. Merty they had found, according to Pierce, 'now a hearty little Englishman'. Mrs Berkeley had warmly welcomed them all to Spetchley Park and took the children into her own family while Pierce and Cornelia made their expected visit to the Shrewsburys. 'Magnificent Alton,' she told her sister, 'burst upon me as something I had had no idea of', a contrast indeed to her two-room cottage. But her visit was cut short:

> I have just got a note from Mrs Berkeley telling us that Frank has taken a bad cold . . . we must be off at six tomorrow . . . We are too late for the rail train or we should set off at once. I am comparatively easy as I am quite sure that he is taken every care of. She is a most kind, affectionate person.

The brief reunion of the whole family at Spetchley Park was a source of happiness for Cornelia. Pierce, however, had found cause for discontent with Oscott College and, as revealed in a letter of Bishop Walsh, his action characteristically lacked judgment and disregarded consequences for others. In this case his son's education was interrupted yet again and the reputation of the school was blackened. At Christmas Merty left Oscott, spent the vacation at Alton Towers and began school with the Jesuits on 11 January. Bishop Walsh's letter to Pierce in Rome was not written until March. He had made 'a very strict examination' into the state of affairs at the time when Pierce removed his son, and having done so confronted him, giving chapter and verse, for unjustly and 'publickly attacking the College'. He requested 'that you will refrain, Dear Sir, in future from speaking unkindly of Oscott College till you have a better opportunity of examining into the truth of the ill-natured reports you may have heard against it'. The bishop's interest in 'the fair character and prosperity' of Oscott may have warmed his indignation; Wiseman's large-minded presidency was not known for its good administration or discipline, but Pierce appears here as an irresponsible trouble-maker.

The Connellys left England on 29 October. Pierce was still travelling tutor to Robert Berkeley which necessitated leisurely pauses. They passed a month in Paris, often dining, Pierce remarked, with titled acquaintance: then proceeded down the Rhône valley by road, lingered at Avignon, took ship from Marseilles, and stopped at Genoa and Leghorn, from where Cornelia visited Pisa. When the party reached Rome on 7 December they rented an apartment 'just opposite St Peter's' near the busy river Porto Ripetta and the Palazzo Borghese. With bare-faced snobbery Pierce told his brother: 'The Borgheses were almost the first persons we saw on reaching Rome. We were invited to dine there the very day we arrived being not a little magnified in the eyes of the people by the grand carriage and servants the Princess sent for us.'

Their real business in Rome was not generally known, and invitations flowed in. Since their last visit together Mary Talbot, Gwendaline's sister, had married Prince Placido Doria-Pamphilj and lived in the great palazzo on the Corso next door to the Shrewsburys. It was Prince Doria whom Cornelia had to thank for the gift Pierce had brought her in the United States, Ventura's Epiphany discourses, and the Connellys again joined the devout and fashionable Roman society that flocked to hear him. As soon as the week was over the season of *carnevale* began. Invitations to the Austrian ambassador's reception at Palazzo Venezia, to an evening of sacred music at the Colonna, to a masked ball in the Doria have survived in Pierce's souvenir book. The Doria ball was the glittering success of the season. Guests came in costume, there was a buffet supper, an orchestral serenade beneath the stars, a quadrille danced by semi-gods and goddesses. By Shrove Tuesday, rainy that year so that the Corso merry-making among the hosts of lighted tapers was all spoilt, Cornelia may have been very ready to welcome Lent. The seriousness of what had brought her to Rome was no incentive to revelry.

She and Pierce had their all-important audience with Pope Gregory soon after they arrived in Rome, but Pierce's letter of 28 December to Harry, although it refers to the fact, gives no hint of the substance. Nor does Pierce seem to be expecting any immediate action by the pope. They had taken their apartment, he says, only till Easter when he and Berkeley would be visiting Naples and Sicily, then Germany and then England:

It is I believe settled that I shall at once take charge of young Talbot, the future Earl of Shrewsbury, so soon as I have done with Berkeley which will probably be in July or August. Young Talbot will still keep the tutor he now has, but I shall have the general superintendence of him and his studies.

Nelie would be living with the Borghese family and would spend the summer with them at Frascati; and this, he says, would be the state of affairs for maybe two years. If we are to believe what Pierce told his brother (ignorant of why they were in Rome), these were their prospects. In fact things were moving much faster than that. A letter from the Sacred Heart superior at the Trinità, and Cornelia's notebook (no letters of hers have survived), show that within two months this time-frame, if ever true, had shrunk. Upon their return to Rome she and Pierce had placed Ady in school there, in January she herself had become a member of the Sodality of Mary and by March we learn from Mère de Coriolis, the superior, that *already*, with the approval of the cardinal vicar as well as of the general of the Jesuits, arrangements were being made for Mrs Connelly to be received there as a quasi-postulant when the time should come. It was probably with mind and heart focused on no such distant future as two years, that on 4 March Cornelia joined an eight-day retreat for lay women at the convent.

The *Spiritual Exercises* were to have a vital influence on Cornelia's life. In them Ignatius presents three ways of being a Christian and the third is for the person moved to desire suffering, not *per se* but for love of Christ and his mission. This way of love attracted Cornelia from the first. Her director at Grand Coteau said it was her attitude even then. Year by year in the Suscipe, the prayer proposed by Ignatius, she responded with deeper awareness and intention and at her death those around her bed sang it for her:

Take, Lord, and receive all my liberty, my memory, my understanding, and my entire will – all that I have and call my own. You have given it all to me. To you, Lord, I return it. Everything is yours; do with it what you will. Give me only your love and your grace. That is enough for me.[1]

As the years went by Ignatius's Rules for Discernment helped her to make this oblation with increasing fullness. They are a guide for those who believe that God is at work in and around them, and wish to be able to recognise and respond. They lead into the struggle against whatever there is in the self that opposes God's goodness and prevents its overflow to others. Cornelia grew in this kind of self-knowledge and self-determining. Life in a religious community, for her, was to be a place of 'recreation' because all the members were God's children, both recipients and dispensers of God's mercy. But it was also a place where any suffering engendered by the struggle against self-will was to be gratefully accepted, without which one could not see or receive or give that mercy. Her retreat of March 1844, directed by a Jesuit and patterned on the considerations which Ignatius puts before the retreatant, was a milestone on her road.

The convent journal of that date noted that 'A great design' brought the Connellys to Rome and that Madame Connelly came to the retreat in order to obtain the grace necessary for its full accomplishment. She can scarcely not have been aware that consultations with Roothaan were in progress and that while she was away her husband might be preparing the text of his formal petition. In her notebook on the first evening, 5 March, she wrote: 'Make it as the last in one's life.' She reviews the double call of herself and Pierce: 'If our proposition is for the Glory of God then it is his will', and the thought of the glory of God becomes the pole-star of her retreat. How to live for that end only is what she seeks to know. It is, she concludes, to '*Live* for eternity', accepting one day at a time. At the end of the eight days, having offered herself yet again 'to suffer . . . in any manner whatsoever (and without *reserves*)', she writes, 'Actions not *Words*, Gloria Patri. C. Connelly, March 1844'.

Two days after her return home Pierce's petition was formally submitted and the day after, 16 March, granted. The very next day, eight years since he had first petitioned the Holy Office, he wrote to his brother John, 'The Father General & the Pope himself have approved the thing and everything is determined.'

Pierce begins his petition with a reminder of the conversion of husband and wife in 1836, goes on to the fact that they had tested their vocations to the religious life by living for three and a half years in 'perfect chastity' and points out that throughout that time they had had the advice of wise directors who both in America and Rome had encouraged them to believe in their calls. He states that Cornelia is prepared to go as a postulant to the convent of the Sacred Heart and he to become a Jesuit. He outlines the provision made for the children, and cites the example of the Chaudet husband and wife who recently in Rome had been permitted to do as the Connellys wished to. Then he concludes with the proposition, known to the Jesuit superior-general, that he be allowed to become a priest before entering the Society and should therefore not wait for letters dismissory from the bishop of Philadelphia. Instead he should receive minor orders very soon at the hand of the cardinal-vicar of Rome. Before the petition ever got on to paper in this form it would all have been discussed informally among those concerned. Now without further ado the pope officially consented. 'Io farò tutto,' he said. He would do all, Pierce told Bishop Blanc. Letters dismissory from Philadelphia were dispensed with and things began to move with un-Roman speed.

The provision for the children as described in the petition and detailed further in Pierce's letters to his brother John and to Bishop Blanc was, according to the lights of the day, very satisfactory. John was told: 'The children are at once placed as well as any little princes could desire with the best of educations secured to them, with the interest and protection of great and holy people.' This was not merely snobbish satisfaction. Schooling in most of Europe, and particularly in both Italy and England, was what the twentieth century would view as humanly unjust. State systems were non-existent or rudimentary. Provision for the multitudes of poor was grossly inadequate, that for the well-born and wealthy minority both exclusive and expensive. The schools of the latter (for boys) generally boarded their pupils, offered moral and mental education over perhaps seven years, and during that period strictly limited, sometimes even discouraged, holidays at home and visiting by parents: 'In the early nineteenth century the interment of the child . . . far from the world and his family, was considered one of the ideal forms of education.'[2]

Customarily the child left his mother's knee and entered on this long period of schooling at the age of seven or eight. For the less well-to-do like Pierce and Cornelia there was generally no middle way available. They had to rely on patronage or the generosity of some religious order, and the arrangements made for the Connelly children would have excited not critical comment but congratulation. What was largely missing in their milieu was the notion of parental responsibility and the educational significance of the family for the proper maturing of a child. And disregarded was the crisis which mothers had to face when their children, especially their sons, were 'lost' to them at so early an age. Whether or not the Connellys really approved of this state of affairs, they were victims of their milieu as much as anyone else. What they went along with when they separated was what they would have sought to do had there been no separation. Had the earl and Prince Borghese not offered to provide for Mercer and Frank at Stonyhurst, the parents very probably would never have been able to afford it. By April 1844 they were not well off. Although in his petition Pierce makes a large statement to the effect that he will 'assign a capital out of his own private estate for the benefit of the said children', he owed money to Dr Mercer, a debt that he was finding it difficult to meet and which would have to be paid before he could become a Jesuit.

In December when Gregory XVI had seen the Connellys, Frank and Ady were there too. It was a merry and informal occasion. 'As we were coming away,' Pierce wrote about Frank, 'I told him to kneel down and kiss the Pope's foot like Ady, so he jumped forthwith upon Ady's back to kiss it over her shoulder, and finished by giving the foot a crack with his handkerchief.' It was also perhaps a memorable occasion for the genial and ageing pope. He was able to see mother and father and children together. Granted that in view of the purpose of the audience he asked Cornelia directly whether

her consent to the separation was a willing one, it is unlikely that her answer was a monosyllable. She was a straighforward woman, devoted to her family, at the turning point of her life and theirs, and unlikely to leave the vital unsaid. It may well have been that she told Pope Gregory she believed the children should remain with her whilst they were young. For both Pierce and herself, with their experience as minister and wife in the Episcopal church, this must have seemed a *sine qua non*. Although later Cornelia refers to having 'given up' her husband for the work of God, she never spoke of having given up her children. On the contrary, when in regard to them fearful injustice and suffering overtook her, she maintained the opposite, passionately.

Whatever was said at that vital audience, when ultimately the petition was granted Pierce wrote to Blanc that the pope had 'most graciously entered into our desires'. Gregory's active interest showed itself in the speed with which the matter was then carried through but also in ways favourable to Cornelia and the children. Pierce's petition proposed that his wife should enter the Sacred Heart convent and make a solemn vow of chastity at once. The pope ignored this. His rescript made no reference to her becoming a religious and left her free of any vow until her husband was ready to receive the subdiaconate. This would be at least a year later and by then on both counts Cornelia had come to appreciate the pope's wisdom in not binding her to Pierce's offer. Gregory had limited himself to what was strictly necessary, a fact which (later evidence shows) Cornelia did not know at the time. Additionally, the weight of Gregory's authority lay behind Pierce's weekly visits to wife and family, occasions on which the parents could both recreate the spirit of home for the sake of the children. His Holiness had known the Connellys for a long time, the cardinal vicar said, later reassuring the Sacred Heart superior about the irregularities of the situation from the convent's point of view. He 'was taking a most lively interest in this family and during the visit that he had received that morning had been moved to tears'.

On 1 April, Monday of Holy Week 1844, the Promoter Fiscale came to their apartment, 115 Via Ripetta, for the signing of the Deed of Separation. This was not a dissolution of their marriage (it was never dissolved) but a mutual agreement which was to be canonically allowed and blessed by the Catholic church, and they were solemnly interrogated by the Promoter as to their intentions. His essential purpose was to ascertain their mutual determination *'di vivere in perpetuo nello stato di perfetta castità'*. Each gave 'willing consent' to the other, Cornelia to Pierce 'to live for ever in perfect chastity' (in the Society of Jesus) and become a priest; and Pierce to Cornelia 'to live for ever in perfect chastity' (in the Society of the Sacred Heart). Both gave their 'full consent' and both signed the document. Robert

Berkeley, whose tutor Pierce still was, was one of the two witnesses. The intention that both had at that juncture to become religious was not essential to the legality of the separation because the papal rescript ignored it.

For Holy Week and Easter Day they remained at Via Ripetta. On Easter Tuesday, 9 April 1844, Pierce took Cornelia to the Trinità and went himself to the Collegio dei Nobili to begin his studies for the priesthood.

VOW AND ORDINATION, 1845

Cornelia was now thirty-five years old. 'La petite Dame', Mère de Coriolis called her; *'cette charmante et sainte petite femme'*. Behind Cornelia lay a life she had loved and valued, and 'when the gate of the Convent shut upon her . . . she felt the loneliness & the seclusion & the enclosure as a great weight upon her spirits'. Although she was canonically a free person still, a mere quasi-postulant, it was understood that when her little boy was of an age to go away to school her position would be regularised. She came believing that the rest of her life would be spent in the Society of the Sacred Heart and desirous to be considered and treated as a religious at once as far as that was possible. She 'placed herself under obedience in all ordinary matters', followed the convent horarium, joined the community religious exercises and accepted the restriction of enclosure. She also taught English and music in school, and gave spiritual help to other laywomen who came. She handed over her fashionable wardrobe and put on instead, not the postulant dress, but the quiet purple uniform worn by past pupils and friends of the convent who like herself belonged to the Sodality of Mary.

Four days after her arrival Pierce came to see them, the first of the weekly family occasions. Wife and son, and Powell the English nurse, were lodged in what Cornelia described for her brother as 'a large comfortable house, cool & quiet'. It stood within the convent enclosure and was for the use of lay women in retreat. The property was high on a hill, the Pincio. Below lay the city with its domes and tiled roofs, and behind stretched the gardens and vineyards of great villas. Within the enclosure there was a garden and meadowland, farmyard and stables, very pleasant for Ady's school days and a little boy's early years. Ady was subject to school rules but Frank could go down into Rome with Powell, Cornelia's 'treasure of patience', or with his mother's visitors. One occasion when Pierce came Cornelia described for her brother George:

Our little Ady has grown so much that you would scarcely know her I think. She speaks Italian quite as well as French and her English is not neglected. On St Peter's day (dear Papa's feast), she played a little duet on the piano with me and sang some pretty little verses that were suitable for the occasion and little Pierce Frank he had three little verses that he half sang and half repeated for dear Papa who had brought him a little guitar for the occasion. In the evening Papa sent us a treat of ices for all the house and at ten o'clock (to finish the feast) burst forth the Girandola, the fireworks that you know are the most famous in the world.

Papa did not prolong his visit, but that evening, for Cornelia, the children, and the nuns as they gazed across Rome to the Castel Sant'Angelo, there would have been a wonderful sight: fireworks in honour of St Peter leaping into the sky.

The Collegio dei Nobili where Pierce lived was run by the Jesuits. Like other students he wore a cassock, a broad-brimmed three-cornered hat and an ecclesiastical cloak. For their philosophy, scripture and theology they went to the Roman College. There Pierce attended the morning lectures every day for most of the year but spent the summer months at the college villa in cooler Tivoli. Normally these studies took five or six years. As agreed by the pope, however, Pierce received minor orders almost at once. He went for this on 1 May to the convent church where, for Cornelia's sake, each of the rites which led to ordination was to be enacted. The convent journal remarks on the double sacrifice being made and that during the ceremony she sang in the choir. It also describes the way in which Pope Gregory, who liked to express his approval to friends with rather unexpected gifts, showed his great satisfaction at what was being accomplished. After the liturgy a handcart arrived with an enormous fish in it. This big catch, freshly made, was, according to the journal, an allusion to the Holy Father's belief that Pierce Connelly's conversion and vocation to the priesthood was matter for rejoicing in the church.

The months now passed heavily for Cornelia. Increasingly she found herself under strain. At Pentecost, a day of celebration, she upbraided herself for 'misplaced gravity' and promised to 'give to the Holy Ghost many smiles'. There grew in her a doubt, not as to whether she was called to the religious life, but whether she was in the right place. Grand Coteau had led her to love the spirit of the Society of the Sacred Heart, but she arrived in Rome at an unhappy moment in its early history. Through her connection with Adèle Borghese, the dowager Princess, she knew that the regional superior was working from the Villa Lante to establish a separate Society of the Sacred Heart for Italy. Were this successful – which it was not – there would be schism. At the Trinità the superior was loyal to Madeleine Sophie Barat, the living foundress of the Society, and Cornelia with great circumspection evaded enticements to join the other house. She thus carried with her on arrival the dismaying knowledge that stability and harmony

95

were at stake in the Society to which she wished to belong. Nor could it have been reassuring to find that Fr Rozaven SJ – who knew her from 1836 and was still the ordinary confessor and director to the community at the Trinità (and would therefore be hers) – was the moving spirit behind the machinations at the Villa Lante.

This was not an easy beginning and other troubles soon touched her more intimately, barely hinted at in the records. The formation of the early Society of the Sacred Heart was austere, something especially encouraged in its Roman convents by Rozaven.[3] Cornelia arrived disposed by her months with Mme Cutts to welcome 'in good earnest' whatever came her way. But she also believed that the right road to perfect loving was 'by meekness and sweetness & not by fear'. Life at the convent seems gradually to have created conflict for her, in particular between what was expected of her as a would-be religious of the Sacred Heart and what she felt were her duties as a mother. As the months went by this problem weighed more and more heavily and by the time the November 1844 community retreat came she was deeply troubled. During it she wrote: 'I belong all to God. There is nothing in the world that I would not leave to do his holy will.' Then comes the cry for help:

> My God help me to know thy will and give me the grace and the strength to accomplish it. I had some stray thoughts about the children. I am so happy the good Father Villefort[4] thinks Frank ought to stay with me until he is eight years old. I think so too. But I am so much afraid of having any reserve with God . . . and how could I ever refuse to *the love of love*?

This was a profoundly personal crisis and no solution offered itself. The retreat, for some of which she was in bed, was a time of sleepless nights, of struggle to rouse herself during mass and prayer and to survive for eight days on bare faith. But before the end of the year, or soon after, an important clarification came her way. She learned that there existed a way of religious life more suited to her needs and those of her children than that at the Trinità and that she was under no obligation to become a nun where she was, the Deed of Separation notwithstanding. By February she was hopeful enough on this score to warn Mère de Coriolis that she doubted her vocation to their Society.

A second matter was sorted out somewhat later, by June 1845 at the latest. The Connelly proposition was rare in church history. The niceties of canon law had not reached Cornelia at Grand Coteau, where in a community of celibates it was apparently assumed that she had to become a nun.[5] In such a milieu one might say that she breathed it in as the only possibility. Attracted, though not at first for herself, and then pressed by her husband, she eventually gave herself not only to the idea of separation from his bed and their home together which canon law did demand, but also to the prospect of a life of religious obedience, which it did not. The desire to belong all to God grew, nourished by a human error, and in the end outstripped what church law could demand if her husband was to be a priest. The certainty in her heart that she could not 'refuse to the love of love' was, in preparing for religious life first at Grand Coteau and then at the Trinità, brought face to face with love for her children – as if there were opposition where there should be none.

In such a dilemma she could only wait before God for a way forward to open and not till Pierce's ordination was in sight did it appear. According to him, Cornelia was put under some pressure just then to become a nun at the Trinità after all, and she turned to the cardinal vicar for support. The cardinal not only clarified that her forthcoming vow of chastity did not put her under any religious or monastic obligations but added that her primary duty was to her children, which, she told Pierce, made her heart 'palpitate with joy'. By now she knew beyond doubt what she wanted for herself. 'I had no doubts about my vocation to a religious life,' she wrote to her sister concerning this time, 'Oh no, this is the thrice blessed road that our dear Lord has been pleased to place me in.' But she could not accept either for herself or her children the life she found at the Trinità, and the cardinal's words showed her that her vow for Pierce's sake would leave her still free to wait till she found the religious life she felt called to. Her gratitude was great. She told her sister that she had been 'prevented so wonderfully from taking any promise or any obligations' upon herself before she knew this.

As 12 June 1845 approached therefore, when Pierce was expected to begin the time of special prayer before ordination, Cornelia was in possession of facts which, though they did not clarify her future, did relieve her of certain fears about it, chiefly those of the mother. A more profound anxiety however had grown upon her, its source her husband.

Pierce had for long wanted to be a Jesuit. His petition to the pope stated it as his intention, that he felt strongly called to the Society by God and that the general had already accepted him. The pope himself in his rescript assumed that it would be so (though he did not require it as a condition), telling the cardinal vicar to consult with the Jesuit general about timing. Pierce also announced it to the family, via his brother John: 'the Father General & the Pope himself have approved of the thing . . . So soon as I am in priest's orders . . . I shall enter into the Society of Jesus . . . It is a little uncertain if I . . . go into my noviceship here or in England.' In spite of all this, within six months of receiving minor orders Pierce abandoned his Jesuit ambitions. He did so before Cornelia herself had found out that the undertaking to join religious communities, which at the signing of the

Deed of Separation they had both agreed to, was not canonically binding, and his news must have come as painful shock. There is no record of what precisely had happened nor of what he now told her, but there is enough evidence to advance a theory.

In August that year, 1844, he was ill and remained out at Tivoli until late in October. This recalls how at Natchez, overworked and under strain about his resignation, he had not been well. But Pierce was a tenacious man, and there is no sign that health or anything else caused him to waver in his determination to be a priest. Nor, supposing that others advised him against the rigour of Jesuit life, was he the man to take advice unless it suited his scenario. He had described the Society of Jesus as 'beyond doubt the most illustrious association of private individuals the world has ever witnessed' and when he left Grand Coteau the Jesuits there had known his intention to join them in Europe. Yet this plan, so long and publicly professed, was now dropped. It may have been health, but there are two other facts which become significant in the whole story and, if taken together, are possibly clues to why he reversed his decision.

Pierce was not under the restriction of enclosure which his wife had voluntarily accepted. When not at his books he was out and around, in ecclesiastical and Rome society. He continued, as far as the evidence of correspondence goes, to experience himself as a person of importance and influence. In these circumstances, so different from the 'wilderness solitude', as he called remote Louisiana, it could have grown on him that a degree of independence to choose his own roads was of greater value than the obedience and prestige of being a Jesuit. To encourage him in such thinking an invitation came his way. That summer he received via the earl Bishop Walsh's proposal that when ordained he should come to the Central diocese and be stationed at Alton. This was an attractive road on which as a Jesuit he might not be sent to walk. It offered him a field of ministry and a *pied-à-terre* among influential friends.

To turn to the second clue, in 1851 Pierce wrote to Cornelia's brother Ralph that when she was at the Trinità the Jesuit general had told him he was seeing her too often. Whether Roothaan on this occasion also said he could no longer accept him for the Society, or whether Pierce himself withdrew, we cannot be sure. But Pierce must have glimpsed something of what Jesuit obedience would demand, and if he did not like what he saw, realised that it did not matter. Ordination was his goal, not religious life. He did not need to be a Jesuit and very probably knew already or could easily check that the pope's rescript did not make it a condition. The one thing required was separation from his wife.

According to Buckle, he told Cornelia of the change in his plans during October. It was a blow sufficient to account for the great desolation of her retreat. A deeply personal blow. What they had embarked on was 'our proposition' not just his; a matter that demanded mutual, selfless trust, and he had kicked away a cornerstone. 'The sorrows of the heart were many and heavy to bear,' she wrote in her notebook, and quoted Psalm 93, underlining the words, 'Unless the Lord had been my helper, my soul had almost dwelt in hell'.

Cornelia did not have the insights of twentieth-century psychology to tell her how dangerously deep her husband's emotional immaturity reached, and in any case she would have been largely blinded to its seriousness by the effectiveness of the support which her own love had given him unfailingly through thirteen years of marriage. But she was aware of his ups and downs, his 'crotchets' as she later called them, and she had probably counted on the stability of Jesuit life and long formation to hold him steady and channel his gifts for ministry. During the months after his disclosure she must have pondered his chosen future with a new urgency and misgiving. The Deed of Separation would become permanently effective on the day she made her vow of chastity, and eventually, against 'any will and wish of her own', she offered to reverse all that had gone before. She offered Pierce the chance to go back on their proposition and return to family life. We have her solemn testimony that this was so:

> [She] . . . warned him of the difficulties and trials of the state into which he was about to enter . . . represented to him the nature of the obligations to which he was about to bind himself irrevocably, and offered to release him from all such difficulties and trials by returning to their previous mode of life.

There was, if we follow Buckle, about seven months between hearing from Pierce that he was not going to be a Jesuit and making this offer. What line of agonising thought brought Cornelia to this position has to be surmised. A consideration of her circumstances in conjunction with Roothaan's objection to Pierce's visits throws some light on it.

Cornelia had voluntarily submitted herself in obedience to convent enclosure restrictions, but she did not see visits, or letters, between husband and wife as something *per se* to be ruled out. Both Connellys carried the indelible evidence of marriage lived as Episcopalian minister and wife. Their first four years of mutual happiness was grounded in a tradition unlike that of the nineteenth-century Catholic. It was one in which marriage, not religious life, had pride of place. Pierce must have preached this. 'To be married,' as his Episcopalian friend Revd Henry Mason wrote, 'was the first law of nature and the first law of God.' Mason styled himself 'a man who feels no compunction but much congratulation in being a married priest'. A couple coming into the Roman church from such a tradition may well have assumed that they would be able to continue to give each other support as they saw fit in what was in fact a continuing marriage, one flesh in a spiritual matrimony. When Pierce's petition was granted the sympathy of Gregory XVI and his vicar – by then Cardinal Patrizi – allowed freedoms for them which neither Jesuit nor Sacred Heart life could comfortably accommodate, but which to Pierce and Cornelia may have seemed unsurprising. Cornelia certainly considered visits, limited to once a week, as 'consistent' with their situation. That was what she told her brother George.

Both husband and wife also wrote privately to each other, and this was permitted. Other correspondence until November 1843 passed through the hands of the Sacred Heart superior. Part of a letter of Cornelia's has survived, one of excerpts from several published a few years later by Pierce in a pamphlet directed against nunneries. It reveals how personal their relationship had remained:

> You looked so ill yesterday that I am afraid you are worried about me . . .
> It does indeed seem hard, after having sacrificed one's natural happiness
> for what is for the glory of God, to find nothing but vexation, disappoint-
> ment, and opposition. If you are at home write a few consoling lines, for
> I am at moments sick of heart.

Apparently they gave each other support, took it for granted and communicated freely within the limits set. And did this in the context of the life of chastity which they had lived under varying conditions for the past four and a half years.[6]

But it was precisely about visits, their frequency, that Roothaan had spoken. The Jesuit general had been told, Pierce said, that he was 'in company with his wife *"every day all day"*' and that it was giving scandal. Who told the general this Pierce does not say, nor can we be sure of the accuracy of the statement, given its context, his petition against nunneries. But he remembered the interview as a mortifying occasion and we do not know how much he shared with Cornelia. If he admitted to her that Roothaan wanted him to see less of her and gave that as his reason for not becoming a Jesuit after all, he inadvertently betrayed to her the strength of his need of her: he would jettison a religious vocation rather than cut down on visits (something which she on the other hand asked for).

If this hypothesis is correct, then Pierce's decision not to be a Jesuit must have given her very serious pause. It raised doubts, surely not for the first time, about the sheer quality of his love for her. Worse, his capacity to embrace, fully and permanently, the celibate life to which as a priest he would have to commit himself, was called into question. So was his real willingness to obey a bishop, as he would have to. So was the permanence of his agreement in the Deed of Separation that *she* could make a vow of chastity, and ultimately commit herself to obedience in religious life instead of obedience to him in the married state. If even the shadow of such perceptions crossed Cornelia's mind she was indeed in great trouble.

Whatever it was that caused Cornelia's doubts, she had to face and deal with them. Others were certain of her husband's call to the priesthood – bishops in America, cardinals in Rome, and the pope himself whose approval had confirmed him in his unwavering convictions. Cornelia had nothing of substance with which to withstand or move persons of such experience and eminence. She was, as far as we know, alone in her uncertainty and, one suspects, often at the mercy of a single fearful question, 'Could I, should I all along have decided other than I did?' According to Buckle, Pierce's change of plan plunged her into crisis. Always at such times during her Catholic life Cornelia turned to Mary. In the cloister at the Trinità during her first months there she helped paint a fresco, Madonna of the Lily – later to be called Mater Admirabilis – a young and pensive girl, her workbox at her feet, the thread of life in her hand, pondering the future. Cornelia pondered and in the end took what seems to have been the only responsible course open to her, spoke to her husband and made it possible, as we have seen, for him to decide to return to her and to family life.

In view of later events it is helpful to identify exactly what is happening at this moment. The Connellys had entered on a mutual agreement when they signed the Deed of Separation in April 1844. It would become legally and permanently binding only if and when Cornelia vowed the perpetual chastity which at once made possible the ordination which was their shared purpose and his part of the agreement. During the fourteen months before this happened, however, their obligation to each other was moral, not yet legal. The agreement of each had enabled the other to start already on a new life-course, and again the only way back was by mutual agreement. Cornelia understood this and made an offer which left Pierce free to agree or not. When this last opportunity for a mutually agreed reversal had gone, which would be when her vow was made, then they would be canonically bound to separation; and the moral obligation of both, for the good of each other and for the end they had in view, would be to abide by the law. There would be no way back, either moral or lawful.

It seems unreasonable to suppose that Pierce – a well-educated, intelligent man, who had read law as a young man; who had made exhaustive inquiries about procedures for himself to become a priest and talked the matter over with learned ecclesiastics; and who at this moment was actually studying for the priesthood – did not understand as well as his wife that there would be no way back. In particular he must have understood that it was a celibate life to which he was about to commit himself and that this would have to be accepted when he was admitted to the subdiaconate in two or three weeks' time.

The momentous conversation took place between them some time before 18 June. It did not deflect Pierce from his purpose. Her testimony continues, 'He persisted, however, notwithstanding such warnings and representations.' Accordingly she made her solemn vow of perpetual chastity on 18 June 1845, and signed it 'with the full knowledge and approbation (testified by his signature at the foot of such written vow) of her husband'. Four days later he received the orders of subdeacon at the Trinità and a week after that those of deacon in the cardinal vicar's private chapel. On 6 July, again at the Trinità, after only fourteen months of study, he was ordained a priest of the Catholic church, and three days later at the same altar celebrated his first mass. Of this celebration there is an eye-witness account, written by a student at the Propaganda Fide.

This morning about 10 o'clock, Mr P. Connelly sent word to the College for some of the American students to go and assist at his first Mass, which he celebrated in the church of the convent where his former wife lives. We arrived when the Mass had begun, and there were a good many persons there who wished to receive communion from him. Among them was his little daughter, about nine years of age, who made her first communion: she wore a wreath of flowers on her head, and just before giving the communion, Mr Connelly turned round from the altar and addressed her publicly for about 15 minutes, exhorting her to remember this day, and celebrate the anniversary of it, not only here, but in heaven. It was a very affecting scene; the circumstances, the occasion, and manner of the father as he addressed his child, all united to render it one of the most affecting scenes I ever beheld.

Then he describes the effect on husband and wife:

After Mass we went into the sacristy to see him and congratulate him, but he was entirely overcome, and could scarcely speak with us, and invited us in another room to congratulate Mrs Connelly: I have seen so much in the American papers about Mrs Connelly's pining away upon Monte Pincio, that I was almost surprised to see her so joyful: Indeed I never saw any person more so: I am sure it is the happiest day of her life.

There were many causes for this radiance. One was shared at once for all the world to know: 'she expressed her joy at the consummation of her so long cherished wishes, and that were it possible she would see her sons priests as well'.

Cornelia venerated the office of priest in the church. Seeing her husband's weaknesses, loving both him and the church, she had less than a month earlier made herself its warning voice to him. But now when the church itself had authenticated his desire, personal hesitation fell away. Like King David, who when his child died 'anointed himself and put on fresh clothes', she accepted the irrevocable as from God and entrusted all to the future. This was not the moment to think of the pain. Gratitude must have trebly filled her heart, once for her husband, once for her children – they were all baptised Catholics and their education wonderfully provided for – and for herself; she was free to seek a form of religious life which would provide them too with a home which she would make happy.

Behind these immediate and obvious causes lay another of a different kind, whose presence she will have recognised only gradually as life moved on. Here was the moment of closure on years of uncertainty, on the kind of experience which would have led many a woman to breakdown. They had been years marked by prolonged deliberation, prayer and waiting, by great love and extraordinary trust in God. They were also years of confused feelings, of shifting roles and – most of all – of conflict within herself which she had never been able to alleviate, as would a late-twentieth-century wife, by effective decisions of her own. This was a moment of unseen beginning when potential began to stir and action call. She was like one whose life so far had always been in the half-light and who now stood waiting in the wings till the new scene was set. She had learnt to wait and a cue would come.

TOWARDS A NEW FUTURE, 1846

The day after celebrating his first mass Pierce went to visit John Grassi SJ, and the day after that Cornelia too asked to see him at the Trinità. This Jesuit, already her confessor there, now began more particularly to help her shape her future. He was a man of seventy, an Italian, but his experience in the Society had been much wider than Italy – White Russia, England, the United States. On his return from the latter he had written a briefly successful book about America whose way of life and pioneering spirit he wished Europeans to understand better. When the Connellys knew him he was one of Roothaan's assistants, and his experience of the Catholic church and of education in both England (at Stonyhurst) and the United States (as president of Georgetown) made him a providential guide for Cornelia at this juncture.

Grassi came from Bergamo where as recently as 1831 his niece Teresa Verzeri had founded a congregation of religious called Daughters of the Sacred Heart. When he met Cornelia he was helping them to revise their constitutions. Hearing of her reservations about the Trinità he must have told her why, like herself, they had felt they could not join the religious of the Sacred Heart. They had wanted a life unrestricted by enclosure. They believed they were called to bring the spiritual works of mercy – to use the catechism phrase of the day – to the girls and young women of their time, and that for this they had to be able to offer not only merciful, open hearts but also an open house.

This enlightening information came to Cornelia probably not long after her dark retreat of November 1844, the year in which, Pierce told his brother, she 'fell into' Grassi's hands. According to Pierce, Grassi from his vantage point as confessor soon saw God meant her for great things. When in February Cornelia warned the superior that she might not become a Sacred Heart nun it was probably Grassi who encouraged this; and when she was making up her mind about what she should do in regard to Pierce and ordination it could equally well have been he who advised her. As soon as the matter was settled and the ordination had taken place the question of her future was taken up in earnest: 'for nearly a year longer', she later wrote to Ralph, she was 'reflecting on the wants of the day', and at once there was toing and froing between herself, Pierce and Grassi over what alternatives were open to her.

It was a hard summer. Cornelia found Roman heat so debilitating that the doctor said she and the children should not stay another year. Pierce came in from cool Tivoli to visit her and act sometimes as go-between for her and Grassi:

> And now my dear Ady to explain at once why I did not answer your letter immediately. The truth is it would then have passed through the hands of the Superioress here and would probably not have been such as would have pleased her for I considered myself obliged to announce to her nine months ago that I doubted very much that I should ever enter the order of the Sacred Heart, tho' I had no doubts about my vocation to the religious life . . . How good God is, how good, and I am so happy, so happy doing his most holy will and ready for whatever my dear and holy confessor shall direct me to [Grassi]. The nuns here are very good and kind and there is nothing whatever with respect to ourselves that I would wish different . . . [but] this *french* order . . . is not the one for our country. I shall ask your dear brother Pierce to tell you a great secret which you must keep as your heart or you will never be trusted again.

By that date Cornelia was working on 'a sketch or outline of a rule' for religious life. 'By Fr Grassi's orders she put her ideas on paper,' Pierce wrote. Perhaps this was the 'great secret'. In the coming months Grassi advised her but was too busy to attend to detail and Pierce became redactor for his wife, translating and editing what she with Grassi's guidance selected from a variety of sources. The completed sketch she submitted for approval to her director. Pierce, she said, worked 'upon the foundation I gave him', and though it was 'actually drawn up by Mr Connelly' she had 'no idea of accepting anything' that had not been inspected by Fr Grassi. These facts are important later in her story.

Increasingly as the months went by at the Trinità Cornelia became sure that there was 'something more to be done for the glory of God'. It must have been for her a period of steady reading and absorbed thought. She wondered by what name this new community should be called, hoping that the name of Jesus, Saviour, could be part of it, and often she contemplated Mother and Child, the embodiment of God's mercy in the incarnation. One day she seemed to hear the words 'Society of the Holy Child Jesus', and thenceforth 'spoke of it and prayed for it under that name'.

She and Grassi shared educational interest but mercy seems to have been the recurring consideration. Newman heard that a woman was going to found a congregation for 'all spiritual works of mercy'. Wiseman wrote of the Society's 'exercise of spiritual mercies'. To Ralph she wrote of 'the means of spiritual mercy to be exercised' and added that in order to be able to do this the Society would 'enter . . . into the active duties of the world and not be cloistered'. Obviously she owed a great deal to Madeleine Sophie Barat's vision and to Teresa Verzeri's but she captured her own vision of 'something more' out of her life's experience and in the title that came to her during prayer. She trusted to the future for making it real. The rule sketch was based on the rule of St Francis de Sales for the Visitation nuns which had many Ignatian elements and provided an element of security for the early days, but the intention was to develop or discard as experience directed. Grassi meanwhile was in touch with Bishop Fenwick of Boston and Cornelia hoped to begin her religious life there. What her husband, who wanted her on Europe's side of the ocean, thought of this plan history has not recorded.

Until Cornelia left Rome nine months after Pierce's ordination she continued to observe enclosure at the Trinità. This was a matter of choice, perhaps a wisdom in regard to her husband, and perhaps a discretion on behalf of the strict but hospitable convent which still gave her and her children a home. Her days were very full. There was the outline to be finished before summer heat drove her from Rome; there was teaching in school; there was daily prayer and mass. Letters had to be written to Merty and family; and the two children with her had to be given their full share of loving attention and guidance, Frank continuously and Ady when free from the boarding school. 'Our dear little Frank', she wrote to her sister, was doing spelling and Bible story and repetition with her and found it very hard *'to keep still'*. There was a nursemaid and we can be sure that at Christmas Cornelia sent them to see Rome's fantastic cribs and helped them to make one at home; that there were special birthday treats; that the appearance of papa once a week was a high holiday; that Ady visited little Agnes Borghese at the big palazzo by the Tiber; that on wet days, as was the fashion, the nursemaid sometimes walked her charges in the great basilica of St Peter; that every night, as at Gracemere, Cornelia said prayers with her Frank and when he was in bed marked the sign of the cross on his forehead.

Although Cornelia did not leave the enclosure she certainly and increasingly received visitors: the Borghese and Doria families; visitors from the United States, for example Bishop Odin. In December 1845 the Shrewsburys arrived in the city *en route* for Naples and came every day for a week to the Trinità where Pierce said mass for them. Then early in January 1846 the Berkeleys came for a stay of several months, bringing two daughters with them, and they too were in and out of Cornelia's apartment. They stayed nearby in the Piazza di Spagna at the Palazzo Mignanelli where on two occasions Cornelia had to visit them on family business. Pierce often dined with them in their lodging, showed them the sights and celebrated mass in a great variety of places that she knew well, frequently at the Trinità itself. They also often visited Cornelia independently of Pierce, treating her and her children as part of the family. Ady was in school but Frank was taken to a puppet show, went for drives and watched the great horse race from a Corso balcony at carnival time. At one point his mother, who trusted Mrs Berkeley from olden days, even let him stay with them for a week.[7]

'God in his kind providence' had brought such friends to Rome at precisely this moment, for against all Cornelia's expectations England not America had become her destination.

No complete explanation of this fundamental change of plan has come down to us. Buckle makes a general statement, that Cornelia had come from Rome with the pope's full approbation to begin the Society in England and was recommended to found the Mother House there. Cornelia herself wrote that the Society, 'having had the verbal sanction of His Holiness Gregory XVI, 1846, and the Protection of Cardinal Fransoni, Propaganda Fide, began the germ of their future life at the convent in Derby, where they were placed by the Rt Revd Dr Wiseman.'

Bellasis offers an explanation, possibly drawing on information from Cornelia, or perhaps from her own father who was an intimate friend of Cornelia's and had a large circle of friends whose children were one day going to come to Cornelia for their education. She speaks anonymously but repeatedly of 'those who' interested themselves in Cornelia's future and in the end had their way. 'They', she wrote, wanted Cornelia 'for a special work in England,

and their views had been very fully discussed'. Only Lord Shrewsbury is named, but the earl, whether in Rome or at home, was the influential lay leader of Catholics in English society circles. A picture emerges of a group of 'those who' saw an unexpected possibility for their daughters of schooling in England of the kind they wanted. The earl could tell them that she had taught in two Sacred Heart convents. He could have known through Pierce that her future was not yet settled. The idea was perhaps generated by chance among guests at Alton Towers, gathered momentum on the social grapevine and eventually converted into a plan of action. At some point Bishop Wiseman, a personal friend of the earl's, was drawn in, if indeed it was not his vision and his own knowledge of Mrs Connelly that initiated the discussions.

Shrewsbury, visiting Rome, brought the proposal that she should come to England. Fransoni, as Prefect of the Propaganda, concurred and it remained only to win Cornelia's agreement. The combination of such forces, even including the prestige of the Prefect, would not inevitably be sufficient to move her or her director. They could refuse. The proposal, after all, was nothing less than that she should begin a community, for other people's reasons, in a foreign land; and, one might add, without financial resources. But the interested people, Bellasis says, made sure of her agreement: 'Gregory XVI whose fatherly interest had been shown even in small details since he summoned her to Rome, declared to her, in an interview, that she was called to do a great work in God's Church.' And these words of the pope, 'changed her whole outlook'.

By way of parenthesis one may wonder, as did Buckle, what part, if any, Cornelia's husband played in this plan, so convenient to him in its outcome. He was an anglophile and an enthusiast for English élitist education. He had accepted the offer from Bishop Walsh and the earl to go to England, and had always wanted his children and their mother on the same side of the ocean as himself. No one except perhaps Grassi was in a better position than Pierce to know how long his wife might hold out against what she was not sure was right, nor how deeply she would reverence a directive from the pope himself.

Shrewsbury brought the proposal to Rome at the beginning of December and, as Pierce put it to his brother, 'strongly argued' with Grassi, and presumably with Cornelia too for they had the chance to argue after mass every day for a week. At least by the time Lent came the interview with the pope had taken place, and according to Bellasis 'all opposition from Cornelia ceased'. Gregory's 'verbal sanction', precisely as vicar of Christ, must have transformed what had been personal hopes for a suitable way of religious life under a bishop in her own country into a solemn charge given her by God for the universal church. Her project ceased to be hers. She was missioned, taken by the hair like the prophet Habakkuk, and deposited elsewhere. And as on those crisis occasions in the past when suffering was intense – the death of a child, the 'loss' of a husband – when she had not refused belief or trust or love, nor therefore obedience, so now again it was Yes. Many years later she wrote: 'The Society of the Holy Child Jesus is not my work. I have only followed the inspirations of God in obedience to *His* not *my* will.'

For the first time in her life the full responsibility for the management of some large task had been laid on her in her own right as a person. As such it was in retrospect a stepping-stone in her development as woman and as Christian. Meanwhile she was saved from headiness by her enduring sense of being *only* what she was in the sight of God. Bellasis said later that she never claimed the title of foundress and disliked the word. She saw herself as a mere 'tool' in the hands of God.

So Lent 1846 found Cornelia preparing to leave the Trinità, having come there, she had thought, for ever. On 24 March Pierce and Grassi visited her together, perhaps for a final word about the outline of her rule. On Palm Sunday she and Mrs Berkeley had a private visit. Once again she and her children would stay at Spetchley Park, this time for the first few difficult weeks of the vague English future. And 18 April, the Saturday of Easter week, was departure day. At 8 a.m. all the Berkeleys joined Cornelia and Ady and probably Frank for mass in the convent church, and Pierce was the celebrant. After breakfast came the goodbyes, Ady a little tearful, Frank agog to go. The mother, children and nurse were packed into the hired *vettura* for the long, rattling drive to Civitavecchia from where the steamer would take them up coast. With snobbish pseudo-humility Pierce informed his brother that they travelled second class, in 'servants' places'. Three weeks later, with permission granted to be away from the diocese of Rome for three years, he too set out for England – not in servants' quarters but in style with the earl of Shrewsbury.

It was ten years since Cornelia had first come along this road *en route* for Rome. She was then, at twenty-seven, a happy wife, mother and convert, whose horizon was filled with light and hope. Now the way out of Rome was shadowed. It was a road-in-reverse. What had then been barely conceivable was now fact. Separation. From her husband. From all past dreams for the future. She had yet to find that, though a single stroke of the sword had placed her in a new state, life was to be recreated through many severings.

7

Beginnings in England

On 17 August 1846 the Revd Pierce Connelly wrote to his brother John, 'Nelie is expected in England to-morrow.' She and the two children and Powell were coming on the railway to Birmingham *en route* for Spetchley Park. Merty was to join her for the rest of his holidays from Stonyhurst. It was three years since Cornelia had had all three children with her and since she had seen her eldest son.

Spetchley was a spacious and lovely Georgian house set in rural Worcestershire in the middle of England. There were parkland and lake, wood and garden, stables, yards and barns; Mrs Berkeley had a large family and the young Connellys could be happy there. Mercer was a delicate, dreamy lad, now thirteen; Ady was eleven and Frank five, both dark-haired and dark-eyed. This hospitable Catholic home[1] was to be Cornelia's and her children's while she made decisions about the Society's future. The joy during the three summer months in Paris (of which we know little) of having the two younger ones to herself once more was at last crowned by the presence of Merty for at least three weeks. Now that she was in England she would have the consolation of seeing him regularly at holiday times, and the others would remain with her wherever she decided to begin. Frank in about three years' time would join Merty at Stonyhurst, and Ady could be at school in the convent.

Cornelia's experience of England was superficial: brief stays on the way to Rome in the homes of the highly privileged, Spetchley Park and Alton Towers. Unlike Pierce, whose long visit in 1836 had led him to keep up his contacts, she was not intimate with the more general scene, though of the state of the Catholic church there she knew rather more. The 'immense number of converts' made England 'so large a field for Spiritual Mercy', she had told her brother, that it justified beginning there instead of America.

Britain, unlike the United States which had its own hierarchy, was divided into districts governed by vicars apostolic who were the pope's episcopal delegates. The district in which she found herself at Spetchley was the

Central (or Midland). It ran from Derbyshire in the north to Oxfordshire in the south, with Birmingham as its administrative centre and already well served by the new railway. On the city's rural periphery lay Oscott College. Spetchley, which she travelled to and from, was southwards. The Central was a district in which the church was making active progress and where there were people she already knew, or knew of. Bishop Walsh, living in Birmingham, was the vicar apostolic. Wiseman was his coadjutor but also president of the college, and Newman, now a Catholic for almost a year, had settled there for the time being in the old schoolhouse with his convert friends. Faber's Brothers of the Will of God were about to move near Derby. George Spencer, also at Oscott, would very soon be working as a Passionist with Dominic Barberi among the poor of the Stafford Potteries. The Jesuits had a house near Sheffield. Ambrose Phillipps de Lisle's monastic foundation was the first in England since the Reformation. A press set up in Derby by Thomas Richardson was publishing Catholic materials. Pugin's architectural genius had been harnessed for ecclesiastical building, often with the aid of the earl's pocket: for example for Oscott, for St Mary's at Derby, for the monastery and for St Chad's cathedral in Birmingham.

Also within its boundaries was Alton Towers where Pierce Connelly now lived as second chaplain. An appeal of Wiseman's to the Propaganda for money to support Cornelia's foundation says: 'It was the intention of the foundress to begin the Institute in London.' Had providence in the shape of Wiseman and her lack of means not intervened, Cornelia would thus have been well distanced from her husband, both geographically and juridically. As it was she finished up not merely in the same district as Pierce but at a convent in Derby within twenty miles of Alton Towers. Bishop Walsh must have concurred in his coadjutor's proposal, but with a judicious eye on Protestant sensibilities took some precautions. He asked Pierce not to visit her except at a convent and not to go to meet her when she first arrived in the country. Cornelia knew this. It was perhaps the first warning she had of how different things would have to be in England. She had written from Dieppe in August:

> And do you really mean to say that you cannot meet me in the way, even in the presence of all the world? All as God wills, and when he wills, but I think this is going too far, and if I see the good bishop I will tell him so very respectfully.

This and two other extracts from letters to Pierce, written between her arrival and going to Derby, show that both of them had expected the freedom of visits and letters which they had had in Rome. The realistic Cornelia adapted herself to the new situation as soon as she understood it, but Pierce was not able to.

Whether before she left France Cornelia also knew anything of Wiseman's Derby proposal we do not know. But whatever information had reached her, her July letter to her sister shows that she was quite clear that ultimate decisions were now hers to make, not her husband's. They were legally separated. A work for God had been confided to her, and in all important decisions, interested as Pierce would naturally be, she knew she should turn for guidance to those appointed by the church and not personally involved. While at Spetchley it would be Henry Mahon SJ, the house chaplain, whom she would consult, not her priest husband even though she presumed they would be meeting. She wrote: 'We shall not leave Paris before August and then we go to Mrs Berkeley's to stop there until I decide under Father Mahon's direction upon my future movements.'

In the end she had to make decisions which were against her heart and judgment because her freedom of action was so circumscribed. Because the Propaganda had committed the project to Wiseman she owed him obedience; because she had no financial resources she could propose no alternative to what he wanted: and because the pope himself had sanctioned the project and, according to Bellasis, expressed his wishes to her personally, it was not in her view possible to drop the whole thing.

At a crucial point Cornelia had brief dealings with Newman. Pierce had arrived at Alton Towers in July and, with his usual nose for important people, at once invited the famous convert to Alton, 'to tell him about his going to Rome'. While there Newman heard of Cornelia and the reason for which she was coming. He wrote to a friend about:

> . . . a new congregation, under the sanction of Rome, with the object of instructing girls, principally the middle and upper classes: of affording a refuge (for a while) for ladies cast off by their families, and of assisting priests in various things. The works will be all *spiritual* works of mercy, in opposition to corporal . . . The person who begins it is in the truest and best sense an enthusiastic person, of education and great influence in her circle, who has been married, but not elderly I suppose.

When Cornelia arrived she went to see him at Maryvale, and soon a convert friend of his (known also to Pierce), Miss Emily Bowles, decided to join her. She often had to be in Birmingham to consult Wiseman, and the convent of the Sisters of Mercy there became her *pied-à-terre* when necessary. In less than three weeks she contacted Newman again. Already Wiseman was pressing her to go and see the Derby convent he wanted her to take. She thinks she must make the visit as a matter of obedience, but 'it is very doubtful,' she writes, 'whether we should accept the Convent or rather be more retired & nearer the Jesuit Fathers'. She wanted to talk this over with Newman but he was due to depart for Rome and in fact they never met again. Initially Emily was Cornelia's friend with Newman but became her calumniator.

She and Emily visited Derby on 2 September. The convent was new, large and encumbered with debt and she is said to have exclaimed: 'We shall never stay here: this is not Bethlehem.' She had neither money nor yet enough companions to run such an establishment. But by the 6th Wiseman was sweeping aside her objections:

> My dear D[aughte]r in Christ
> I have no hesitation in saying at once, that I will take the whole Convent and its liabilities on myself, and trust to Divine Providence for the means of meeting all . . . In the name of God & of our Blessed Lady let us begin at once courageously, and put our trust on High. On Tuesday, Her Nativity [8 September] the foundation stone of the work may be laid . . .

and on 10 September Emily's brother wrote to Newman, 'It is settled they go to Derby.'

In fact it was not quite settled. Having realised that she was not to be allowed to begin in a small way, that she was going to have to be responsible herself and at once for everything, including the religious formation of those who would join her, Cornelia insisted that the community should have Jesuit guidance. So firm was she that both earl and bishop pressed the Jesuit provincial to allow this. Wiseman wrote: 'It is particularly desired that for some time at least, the spirit of the order should be formed under the Society of Jesus, and that the Director be a member of it . . . the fate of the Establishment seems almost to depend upon this concession.'

For Cornelia one determination of his, the most painful and unacceptable, remained to be obeyed. She had been told after she arrived that while she was a novice Ady could not be with her. Pierce knew this before Cornelia reached England, and on 8 October Ady went from Birmingham to the convent school at New Hall in Essex, apparently chosen by 'Papa or Fr Lythgoe'. The bishop's reason was almost certainly the fear of giving scandal. No one was accustomed to the idea that a nun who was also a mother might keep her children with her, and the ears of Protestants were all too open for fearful rumours of young girls imprisoned in convents. The Catholic church in England, as an Anglican study has recently confirmed, still had to survive in an atmosphere of barely concealed hostility. There existed widespread dislike, even loathing, of the Roman church; 'ignorance of Catholic doctrines [and] a sensationalised popular literature about Catholic practices'; and (most hateful) 'a political tradition of civil liberty which associated Catholicism with autocracy, treason, and intellectual enslavement'.[2]

Ady's going was affliction for Cornelia. A precedent for keeping her children with her even during the novitiate did exist, though not in England. In Georgetown in 1817 Archbishop Neale had permitted Mrs Jerusha Barber to be a novice in the Convent of the Visitation (where Pierce had visited in 1843) and to keep her little girls with her.[3] Grassi knew the Barber story personally and is unlikely not to have told Cornelia this. It was also Grassi who told Pierce that Cornelia would be 'another Mother Seton'. In 1832 in Rome Cornelia had become acquainted with Elizabeth Seton's daughter and almost certainly knew that story too, of how a mother's young children had stayed with her while she established community life at Emmitsburg. There is a strong likelihood that Cornelia arrived in England knowing no reason why Ady and Frank should not remain with her from the beginning, as had the children of these other women.

Not only Ady but also the five-year-old Frank had to go, but it was longer before Cornelia brought herself to give him up. If Wiseman was insisting, it was a question of when, not whether. There were also Miss Bowles' fears and protests echoing in her ear: at first Emily was Cornelia's only prospective companion for the Society, and her attitude, that of a convert English-woman who knew the country and its religious currents, was a warning not to endanger its beginnings in the public eye. There was too, what the sight of the huge Derby convent and the waiting Poor School and all her unexpected responsibilities must have made her realise, that she was in no position as yet to make a home for her children and give her little boy the attention he needed; what her hoped-for small, quiet beginning would have allowed would now be impossible. Perhaps she should find the right kind of school-mistress, and put him with other little boys for a time. Some of this is reflected in a note she wrote to Pierce in September 1846:

> I have waited until now, hoping, if you came in an early train [to Birmingham] you might drive up to the door, to see and kiss little Franky, without getting out, and I have hesitated whether I should go to the train or not: but Emily is so very fearful of a word being said – so much about all the remarks that were made about your coming to England the same time that you knew I was to come etc., etc. I think I have made up my mind to leave the decision about Frank to you and the father [Lythgoe?]. Emily is much too anxious *not* to have him, but I think myself, if he could be with a motherly schoolmistress and little boys that would be better.

This note is a rare survivor in what was probably quite an exchange between Cornelia and Pierce during her first bewildering weeks, and shows something of the psychological confusion she must have been in. It goes on: 'Her proposition [Emily's] not to see you until I am professed is absurd . . . I was so much disappointed in not hearing from you this morning!'

Cornelia was in a complex, culturally strange situation, the target of much advice when she herself knew too little to judge of its wisdom. Yet she was under the necessity of making major practical decisions which would affect the lives of others including those of her own children. She had known herself as wife and mother but now these roles were receding and the community she had been sent to create did not yet exist. She was in a kind of limbo and this note offering her husband support and affection betrays her own present need of both.

AT DERBY CONVENT, 1846–8

The transformation of Derby from a rural little English town of not 10,000 people in the late eighteenth century, to a black and swelling centre of industrialisation was an example of what was happening all across the country. In 1846 when Cornelia arrived the population had leapt to 37,000 and what she met there was in extreme contrast to the only side of English life she had known. The Crown Derby china factory provided jobs for many but the vast majority was employed in lace, silk and cotton mills. Children between nine and thirteen worked nine hours a day, and women and older boys for at least ten. Town improvements were under way but there were untouched slum areas in which living conditions were pitiable: cottages were small, dark and ill-ventilated; the wastes of tanneries, slaughter-houses and chemical works created unplanned cesspools; many streets and alleys were unsewered; in the closed courts of the most wretched there was neither drainage nor water supply. The problems engendered, whether physical or social, educational or religious, were enormous.

This scene was a far cry from Alton Towers and the Palazzo Borghese; from Cornelia's simple home at Grand Coteau; from Whitecottage in wealthy Natchez and the dignity of life as the minister's wife; from her youthful days in fashionable Spruce Street and the securities of a niche in Philadelphia's polite society. She had seen poverty and destitution with Gwendaline Borghese in Rome and probably in the American south, perhaps in Philadelphia. But she had belonged among the privileged. She had never lived in an industrial city such as was then springing up in England, had never been surrounded as now she must be – poorer herself in every way than she had ever been and essentially alone – by the human degradation produced by the ugliness of poverty.

On 13 October, the Feast of St Edward, she and three others, the small Frank still with them, set out for this place. It was six years to the day since Pierce had asked her to agree for his sake to separation. At the Trinità she had copied out a prayer of St Francis of Assisi:

There is nothing on earth that I am not ready to abandon willingly and with my whole heart, nothing, however painful, that I am not willing to endure with joy, nothing that I am not willing to undertake with all the strength of body and soul for the glory of my Lord Jesus Christ.

This still expressed the desire of her deepest will. So did the admonition with which she tried to make real what she had offered in March 1844, 'actions not words'. Pierce, in asking so much of her, had inadvertently fanned in her heart the fire of a far greater love than for himself alone.

The convent, according to one who was a pupil there with Mother Connelly, was among 'slums and narrow dirty streets . . . a sluggish, unhealthy backwater ran on the opposite side of the road the full length of our buildings . . . the basement . . . flooded . . . the sewers of the town emptied themselves at the end of the Convent Garden'. The locality was considered so unhealthy that the imposing new buildings were demolished less than twenty years later.

Sister Aloysia Walker remembered their arrival: except for 'the Parlour & some bedsteads with beds & pillows' the convent was 'quite empty'. A leg of mutton was in the oven and potatoes and carrots on the fire but 'no knives or forks, plates or anything else in the place' and they had to borrow from the priest's sister before they could eat. Because Emily was sick from the journey, making the place habitable fell to the other three, no doubt aided by the five-year-old. The convent chapel, 'of sufficient dimensions for a large community', was not yet completed so the four set up a little brown tabernacle in an empty room, borrowed candlesticks and were somehow ready on 15 October for their first liturgy, the Feast of St Teresa of Avila.

Religious life began in earnest and they plunged into work for the mission. A letter from Wiseman came, a kind of charter for them: 'The field which you have chosen for the exercise of spiritual mercies' was vast but there would be abundant return. The middle classes, till now almost neglected:

. . . form the mass and staple of our society, are the 'higher class' of our great congregations out of the capital, have to provide us with our priesthood, our confraternities, and our working religious. To train the future mothers of this class is to sanctify entire families, and sow the seeds of piety in whole congregations: it is to make friends for the poor of Christ, nurses for the sick and dying, catechists for the little ones, most useful auxiliaries in every good work.

The poor were to have a special place in the community's ministry. They were to take part in 'the most consoling of duties, the education in Catholic piety of the lambs of Christ's flock, his dear poor children'.

This letter set the church's blessing on Cornelia's desires. The sisters were

115

to be women who because they believed, prayed and worshipped together would be empowered to reveal God's love. Opportunities burgeoned on the doorstep. What Cornelia expected them to do was to be simple, to step in and do what they could, obediently trusting the God she taught them to love in action. One who was there wrote, 'we were told that joyful obedience, simplicity and zeal were to be the distinguishing marks & spirit of our little Society'. They caught fire from her. The mission Poor School was waiting for them, Aloysia said, with two hundred children on its books and about sixty turning up each day. The large and daunting schoolroom had six tiers of desks with 'ample space for semi-circles of children in front'. Emily and Cornelia both had teaching experience, but Aloysia's education (and Veronica's, who soon left) had been meagre. Nevertheless 'we each went in in turns'.

There was school on Sunday too. Faced with the choice between no education for poor factory girls and a holy day of rest for the sisters, Cornelia had no hesitation. She wrote to Lord Shrewsbury:

> Sunday is a *very busy* day with 200 girls to lead to Church for the High Mass after an hour's labour in teaching them, and from 2 o'clock until 4 in the afternoon teaching them to read etc., etc. . . . it is the only way to get hold of the working class, the factory girls.

This enthusiasm was fed and sustained from the earliest days by regular attention to the things of the spirit. Wiseman's letter encouraged Cornelia to 'lay foundations deep and solid' and Aloysia wrote that the very day after their first liturgy together regular times for prayer and reading were arranged, and Mother Connelly 'began to give us instructions and teach us all about religious life'. Twice a day they had *'recreation joy'* together – like 'the joyful song of the lark soaring high in the heavens', fun and stitching mixed in with spontaneous prayers.

On 16 December the bishop came, and Cornelia with two others received the white veil of novices. This was the official beginning of their religious life. Cornelia's 'sketch of a rule' described the dress: 'of material strong and lasting and as little as possible differing from the usage of the country', and in the streets, along which they must often have passed on errands of mercy in addition to their work in school, they would have been inconspicuous. By January there were seven of them. The work continued to flourish. She advertised, and lady boarders came to make retreats. Some time in 1847 the night school was begun:

> . . . where we have upward of a hundred girls. They learn the catechism every night besides sewing, cutting-out work, reading, writing and the rudiments of arithmetic, in turn. The school opens at 6 p.m. and closes

at 9 o'clock which gives us almost as much time with the girls as a half-day school would do. We attend to their confessions regularly, and they have instructions two nights in the week from our good chaplain.

Wiseman was very satisfied. He had been broad-minded (and daring) enough to choose a convert who was a wife and a mother to begin this foundation, and in September 1847 he asked for, and brought back from Rome as an encouragement to them while they were still considering their Rule, a letter expressing approval of their efforts. Early in 1848 a small boarding school was opened. A few day girls attended as well and the older pupils helped with catechism classes on Sundays. (Before sending the prospectus to the *Catholic Directory* of 1848 Cornelia passed it to Wiseman, and one item made him nervous, learning French: 'the present French literature is so wicked', he said, but she left it in.) The Poor School was doing so well that it earned a commendation from the visiting government inspector: 'they get an education far superior to the ordinary standard of parochial schools'.

Numbers in the community crept up, and then on 21 December 1847 Cornelia (already vowed to chastity) was allowed to make public profession of poverty and obedience. Wiseman came for the occasion and with his great feeling for church ceremony solemnly installed her as superior-general of the little Society. This had important implications. It constituted Cornelia 'effectively, juridically and (from her side) irrevocably as mother of a new religious family in the Church', and until the day of her death she was 'morally bound to fend for it, keep it in being, to nurture its growth'.[4] What it did not do, which was later the source of great suffering for both Cornelia and her foundation, was to establish her as a *constitutionally elected* superior.

'A seat was placed within the sanctuary to which she was conducted by his Lordship, in whose presence and at the foot of the altar she received the allegiance of the little community God had appointed her to govern.' About half of them were converts, a source of satisfaction to Wiseman. Altogether there were sixteen novices and Cornelia. Maria Buckle remembered her in those days. She had 'the full enjoyment of her genius, her spirits and her beautiful voice, and her beauty was striking. No one could pass her without being struck by her appearance.' She was, Buckle said, 'the life of the whole community'. One of the novices, Maria Cottam, reveals their simple happiness. She wrote to her brother describing her first Christmas as a Holy Child sister:

I cannot express to you the joy I feel at present . . . We had Midnight Mass here very much nicer than it would be in Blackburn for we had the Crib and the Holy Child. On Sunday we had Recreation for the whole day, the Feast of the Holy Innocents, and we all enjoyed ourselves very

117

much. On Monday Tea was given to all the poor children, about a hundred. What a happy thing to be amongst the Poor and they all enjoyed themselves very much.

The community itself was desperately poor. But as that letter shows Cornelia was able to instil into the little group a spirit of joy in the midst of their poverty. Aloysia one day heard her say that all her means had gone, and she remembered how lovingly Cornelia accepted the poverty in which they had to live: 'When the boots she had been wearing from the beginning began to wear out a Sister covered them with one big patch I should call it, for it was a piece of cloth put on all over to cover up the rags. Our dear Mother wore them with joy.' Somehow she kept going. The Derby account books show small grants from the Catholic Poor School Committee (CPSC) and the Catholic Institute (total £202 10s), irregular donations, occasional sales of jewellery or holy cards, retreat offerings and takings from the Poor Box.

Although Cornelia was superior of the community she was also for the first twelve months a novice among novices and, as she put it, they were all learning together. But she was, Buckle says, 'very far advanced in perfection & quite understood practically the science of the saints'. What she instilled was to 'be yourself but make the self just what our Lord wants it to be'. Yet the needs of her very maternal heart could have stifled the personal growth of those around her. She was after all a woman temporarily deprived of her children, the smallest of whom had run about these very rooms for a day or two and had only recently gone away. She was a wife whose love of her husband was often maternal, and of him too she had been deprived. Of the group with her she was by far the eldest and most experienced yet did not expect them to form their spirit on her own. Beginners were to be helped, but not to model themselves on another person or pattern: 'All ought to form themselves to their vocation and *thence* to the spirit of the Society. The ways of God are many, and He knows how to lead to the same and by diverse means.'[5]

And they were a mixed batch. A few could barely read or write, some were highly educated. The former were taught, the latter enabled to use at once the advantages they already had – Emily and Maria were set to translating spiritual books to which Cornelia wrote the prefaces. One of these, *Meditations as a Preparation for Whitsuntide and Other Feasts*, published in 1851, became in the early days the 'textbook' for beginners in the Society. Its preface (written for children) shows what Mother Connelly believed and lived and taught:

    . . . it will be of no use to you to learn a great many things & to like to hear stories of the Saints & holy things unless you practise what they practised & what made them holy. You must take for your pattern the Holy Child Jesus . . . growing as He grew in stature & grace & . . . may you so love & follow the Man Jesus, that you may be one of the number of those 'little ones whom our Blessed Lord will bring into His everlasting kingdom.'

This was the kind of wisdom that made her 'the life of the whole community'.

Were there no more than this to be related of Cornelia's days at Derby it would be a simple story of success, but 'exterior troubles' began to take over, a presage of the kind of road she would have to tread for the next thirty years.

It was when the community had 'been going on for some months' that Aloysia heard her say that 'all her means were gone'. This lack of financial resource levered their departure from Derby. When the convent was built, the mission priest, Thomas Sing, mortgaged it and counted on the community who would use it to pay the interest. Cornelia when she came had Wiseman's written assurance that he would take 'the whole Convent and its liabilities' on himself and Sing had urged her to come. She also understood 'in September 1846' that the property was going to be transferred to the bishop 'for a certain sum' agreed between him and Mr Sing.

Whether Cornelia ever realised there was no deed to this effect we do not know. The bishop evidently found it more difficult to raise funds for the foundation than he had anticipated. Moreover before she completed even her novitiate year he had been moved to London, and the Central District had become secondary in his responsibilities. Nevertheless he remained loyal to her interests. He had contributed out of his private resources £1822, and when he was transferred he 'took steps towards securing the principal & interest of a considerable portion of the Debt yet remaining'. Even so, his very large initial promise made to Cornelia did not take into account the straits to which she would be reduced should funds from him temporarily dry up when her own small resources ran out, when meagre earnings and irregular donations were insufficient, and when Mr Sing, able to get payment from neither her nor the bishop, would no longer wait for his money. In mid-August 1848, though the trouble was brewing much sooner, Sing complained to Bishop Walsh. He had spent '£300 in furnishing the convent here, Dr Wiseman telling me again & again that he would pay me at certain times' but failing to do so. 'In the meanwhile Mrs Connelly not only has all this furniture & linen to use without paying for it, & the house without rent, but I am left to see our very flourishing congregation disorganised because no one will interfere with or inquire into Mrs Connelly's proceedings.'

'Mrs Connelly's proceedings' had increasingly become the object of Mr Sing's anger, with how much justice one cannot say for lack of evidence other than his. Moreover the coming of an Italian chaplain to the convent had created a situation in which a multitude of misunderstandings were possible.

Dr Samuele Asperti, aged twenty-nine, arrived in October 1847. He had studied under the Jesuits in Rome and intended, when it was possible, to join their Society. Grassi, who had warned Cornelia that the English Jesuits would come as confessors to the community only for the time being, knew Asperti and thought well of his appointment. He took up residence in a small separate presbytery and the sisters gave him board and stipend. Soon he was devoted to the community and its works. Necessarily he was involved with the people whom the sisters served, and almost inevitably, given his energetic zeal, his imperfect English and his lack of experience of an English mission, he alienated the priests. Misunderstandings arose. What happened on the day Maria Buckle was to become a novice flared into a crisis. Although the clothing of a novice was the responsibility of the chaplain not of the mission priest, and Wiseman whose concern the convent was had already asked Asperti to preside, Sing was furious. He wrote to his bishop, Walsh:

> Your Lordship sent me word that I was to preside at the clothing this day at the convent: it has taken place however without the slightest consideration of me whether in town or not. I knew nothing of it but from a letter sent to me by Sister Cornelia so insolent that for the sake of peace I would not answer it but sent it to your Lordship.

It was an odd way of seeking peace and unfortunately Cornelia's letter has not survived for judgment. Everything is taking place, he goes on:

> ... as if *we* were not the priests of the town, as if I had not spent thousands on the place ... Nothing shall induce me to let them stay on my property ... I will not allow parties, who do no good, to enter into my house, and then leave me to pay for the very chairs & beds they lie on, & take no notice of any other promises, secure, as they think, of being *in*.

The next day the Italian too took to his pen, also to Walsh:

> To be expelled from a Convent without knowing *why* ... a Community of *22* subjects with their Chaplain to be ruined in the public esteem ... Mr Sing ... *accuses us* without naming any fault in particular & for our *faults* he wants us *driven away* ... My dear Lord, a *Visit* of yours might prevent every further evil. We begged of you this grace; we renew our prayers; do not leave us any more in this anxiety ... *I will only protest before God* ... that our Revd Mother *kept silence too long about all* that has

passed between her & Mr Sing, if she had not borne so patiently we should not be now so much wronged.

Walsh, a sick man, never came. Wiseman was busy in London. Two months dragged by. By the time the new vicar apostolic, Bishop Ullathorne, was due, Mr Sing's anger was focused less on the unpaid debt and more on the power wielded by Cornelia as superior. All the 'missionary inconveniences borne of late', he reported, arose from 'the convent being without [episcopal] control and directing instead of being directed'. In November, by then waiting for the bishop's verdict, the community had become 'these women'; Cornelia had nearly burnt the house down by altering a flue and had upset the insurance arrangements; someone had refused him admission to his Poor Schools 'until the reverend mother had given her consent'; the proper class routine had been suspended for three days while the children prepared a play in honour of the chaplain; but, said Sing, this *'playing at nuns'* no doubt will be stopped whenever they 'come under direct episcopal control'. And there was a sense in which they were playing at being nuns. In this first group there was all the creative fervour of beginning something new. The community's heart was contemplation of the Holy Child, its framework the total loving obedience they saw in him. But the warm flesh and blood of their life through which they related to each other and those they met was joy at being in his 'house of re-creation'. It was not a life of solemnly-kept regulations according to ancient custom but of earnest and delighted discovery and giving.

In all these months there is very little indeed of Cornelia's that gives her point of view. Once, writing to the earl, she remarked incidentally that Mr Sing was continually annoying them and even wrote to both bishops; and in late August her relief at the thought of a visitation after so long appears in her letter to the new bishop, Ullathorne:

> Your Lordship's very kind promise to visit our convent, in our present oppression, is a source of great consolation to us, and we shall pray fervently that . . . nothing may interfere to prevent its fulfilment. We have earnestly solicited the visit during five months without success . . . it is necessary for us for our affairs to be examined into and that we may be judged impartially . . . Our confidence and hope is only in your visit. The Community is going on religiously and in great peace notwithstanding our exterior troubles.

He came on 17 September. No record of his visit to chaplain or mission priests has survived but he saw all the religious community individually and together. There were eighteen novices and four beginners of whom eleven taught with Cornelia in Mr Sing's Poor School. Buckle says that the bishop told them all how much he liked their light-hearted poverty and the 'great charity and union' among them, and Wiseman wrote to Cornelia that he was delighted to have heard it had all gone well. Ullathorne's scanty and almost indecipherable notes show that he had been told that Mr Sing made a habit of ignoring Mother Connelly and showed 'disrespect' to her 'before others, priests and seculars', and that according to Emily Bowles Sing had made it impossible for them to continue with him.

Sing was not the only man, as her life went on in England, who saw Cornelia as a high-handed woman. She was certainly not nor ever had been a merely submissive one: she would stand on a principle and reserved submission for where proper authority lay. Nor, in the sphere that was hers, did she shrink from using her right to make the decisions when necessary. But ecclesiastics, whether high or low, dreamed as little as other men in general of the independence of women (and nuns) or equality between the sexes. She had education and experience beyond what was common. She was self-possessed, socially adept, competent. Her gift for organising was evident in the schools; she was a centre of influence. She was *different*. Finally when the bishop installed her as superior-general she acquired status and a field of authority. Mr Sing, as his letters show, felt forced into second place on his own mission, threatened. To him she seemed insolent.

In this matter the Italian chaplain's presence was no help. He came as a foreigner to a provincial corner of insular England. She too was a foreigner. For each of them there must have been shocks, both social and religious. Cornelia's Catholic contacts, until she came to Derby, had been with cultured, often learned and sometimes saintly people. Her most profound exposure to the church had been in Rome and she had come to England invited by a prelate like Wiseman whose whole desire was to move the English church into Roman ways. Until Asperti arrived she was in this isolated, and his coming must have been a welcome reinforcement. Such an 'alliance' would not have furthered good feeling between herself and the mission priests. It seems fairly safe to say that both as a woman in authority and as a foreigner she was likely to be the object of prejudice not only in Derby but anywhere in England. That she was also a nun later added fuel to the fire.

A day or two after Cornelia had written to Ullathorne she received a letter from Wiseman:

> I have been endeavouring to make such preparations, as would neutralise Mr Sing's violent opposition, and should you be compelled to yield to it, give a harbour and home ... The question is, will you be able ... to remain where you are, and do good *in spite* of the clergy there; or will Mr S forgo his legal hold upon the Property, and allow you to remain.

He then offers her an advantageous property in the south at St Leonards-on-Sea, Sussex, where, he says, they will be 'sure of peace, kindness, co-operation and active assistance'.

One reason for not moving was the offer to Ullathorne from the CPSC. They wished to propose Derby convent, under the direction of Mrs Connelly, for government grant to establish the first Catholic teacher-training centre for women in the country. This was in mid-October. By November Mr Sing was fulminating to Ullathorne about 'these women lingering in the convent' and 'insolence, arrogance & folly running rampant'. He was the legal owner of the property and refused to allow them, the bishop said, to remain any longer. Before the end of the month Cornelia had visited St Leonards and accepted, and by 21 December 1848 the last of the community had departed. Mr Sing pursued her with claims which Wiseman's lawyers said could not be justified. But he did not forget. Ten years later he was writing to Wiseman's successor, Bishop Grant:

> She left this town, & took with her *all the linen* & *all the blankets* I had not long before bought . . . I am quite sure that £150 wouldn't repay me . . . I could easily have compelled restitution, but the Fathers whom I put my case before advised for some time to be silent.

8

Connelly against Connelly

Behind Cornelia's parochial troubles at Derby lay a far deeper source of anxiety.

In July 1846 she had written with happiness to John Connelly about Pierce: 'he is well and deeply engaged in the duties of the ministry, instructing, preaching, hearing confessions etc., etc. So you see it is not for nothing I have given him to God.' His ordination lay behind and her own plans were about to be realised. Cardinal Fransoni, prefect of the Propaganda, was the 'protector of the project'. Since Pierce was to be so near after all, she presumed – at this date – he would still be her messenger 'in many external and distant matters', just as he had been in Rome when she could not herself visit the cardinal to discuss her Rule sketch. To all appearances their shared venture was about to bear good fruit. Pierce too seemed content. He was proud to let people in the United States know that the ideas for the new foundation were hers: 'By F. Grassi's orders she put her ideas on paper', and Bishop Wiseman 'had taken it up very warmly; sees in it a remarkable providence of God . . . says it is just what he was longing for'. Yet in two years time Bishop Walsh had cause to write that 'Poor Mr Connelly must be deranged'. Shrewsbury had heard from Pierce that he believed the atmosphere of the convent was '*worse* than a *brothel*', that his duty was to rescue her '*from the hands of devils*', and that he intended to sue in the courts for restitution of conjugal rights.

Pierce reached England ahead of Cornelia and found himself merely second chaplain at Alton Towers where previously one had been sufficient. His role seems to have been less one of ministry than of aide to the earl and there was ample time to turn his attention to the convent affairs. 'God seems to have called her to a great work,' he wrote to his brother.

In regard to his wife Pierce apparently expected, as a matter of right, to go on seeing her in England with the same degree of freedom as in Rome. He seems also to have assumed that he would continue to have a finger in the making of the Society pie. But Cornelia's obedience was now owed not to her husband, as previously both would have understood it, but to the bishop. This was basic and that Pierce knew it is undeniable. In the Rule sketch with which he assisted Cornelia in Rome, making a fair copy in his own handwriting, come the statements: 'The houses of this little Congregation shall be under the jurisdiction of the Bishop of the Diocese . . . to visit them in person . . . to watch over the observance of the Constitutions . . . nothing shall be done herein but with the express approbation of the Bishop.'

Pierce, in a new kind of wilderness at the Towers, knew the facts: he was canonically separated from his wife, her obedience was due not to him but to the bishop, and the bishop, Wiseman, was opposed to his visiting her. Except in regard to the children about whom there had to be communication between mother and father, he had – legally – no place in Cornelia's life and the consequences of this he does not seem to have envisaged. Nor did Shrewsbury understand. He was confused as to the nature of the separation in Rome, and at first had great sympathy for his chaplain. As the facts grew upon Pierce rising rage blotted out of his consciousness what he had undertaken. Wiseman would explain to the earl (emphases added):

Mr C had given his *full consent to Mrs C's taking vows* (I have it in his writing) and when he took orders, he knew that to be an inevitable consequence. He had by this lost all power to protest against what he had himself accepted as a condition for his own ordination . . . In addition to this Mr C signed at Rome a deed of separation which *made Mrs C completely independent of him,* & in fact, as far as the Church permits, severed them completely. He has *no rights as a husband* whatever before the Church, *yet he assumed all authority over Mrs C as though they were merely living separated in the world by consent.*

The details of the crisis as it developed are now beyond retrieve. Missing pieces of evidence force conjecture. But the main lines of what happened are clear, and because they scarred for ever the hearts and lives of both Connellys and of their children, have their place here.

When Pierce first arrived, there were discussions with both Shrewsbury and Wiseman, ranging over financial provision, noviceship, and the children, about all of which, it would appear, he fell in with what was said. Of these only hints survive. Developments suggest that Wiseman did not then or ever trouble himself with Connelly's human situation. He judged well of Cornelia's capacity to carry through the work he wanted her for in the church, but misjudged her husband catastrophically when he left him disregarded at Alton Towers. At this moment in Pierce's (second) ecclesiastical career he would certainly have been desirous of Wiseman's goodwill. As with Odescalchi, he was ready with agreement. The affairs of the convent,

Walsh agreed, were to be left to Wiseman who thus became Cornelia's superior. Walsh retained the exercise of his authority over Pierce and requested the new recruit to the district not to visit his wife outside a convent. At this stage Connelly agreed. He did not go to meet her on arrival nor did he visit her at Spetchley or in Birmingham. Then, for four and a half months, he did not go even to the convent, his frustration mounting because Wiseman put restrictions on Cornelia.

Wiseman had assumed his proper role in Cornelia's new life. He took over the welfare of her Society, provided it with a home, chartered its service in the church, clothed the sisters in the religious habit. The removal of the children from the convent for the duration of her novitiate removed also the need for husband and wife to meet there, and early on Wiseman told her that she should not allow visits from Pierce. This she adhered to and they only corresponded. No doubt Wiseman's name often figured in what she said about convent affairs, sometimes reflecting her attitude to him, 'the great and good Dr Wiseman', as she told her brother. Very possibly there were those who thought and spoke of him as the ecclesiastical founder of the community. If such comments reached Pierce's ears they would not have pleased him.

The convent was only one of the bishop's many interests. Cornelia consulted him by letter, he responded when he could but seems not to have visited often either. The clothing ceremony on 16 December 1846 was a special occasion, an official moment of beginning, which he endorsed with his presence but from which Pierce was absent; and in a letter to John Connelly on 1 January 1847 Pierce conveys for the first time overtones of discontent:

> The Bishop, Dr Wiseman, clothed them . . . what a consolation to have her in the same country! Though I have not yet been once to see her, it is so different in a Protestant country that I have thought it best. In Rome of course every week or ten days I saw her. I said High Mass and Low Mass in the chapel very often [at the Trinità].

If the early biographers are right, his discontent was showing in another fashion too. It was now, they say, that Pierce, unable himself to visit the convent, conceived the idea that his personal friend of Roman days, Samuel Asperti, could usefully be chaplain there. According to Bellasis who had access to a letter no longer extant, Pierce 'wrote in January 1847' begging him to come. Cornelia was induced to approve the idea (and therefore obtain Wiseman's sanction). Bellasis sees this 'as a step to furthering his wishes to interfere with and oppose . . . arrangements' made by the bishop.

Two months later (before Asperti's arrival) the first crisis was precipitated. Pierce refused to be excluded any longer. On 4 March, accompanying

Dr Winter, the senior chaplain at Alton Towers, he visited without warning. He and Cornelia had not met since she left Rome nearly a year before; but only Winter's name was given and she came into the room not knowing her husband was there. The human reality of her reaction is hidden behind Bellasis' guarded words: she 'remonstrated strongly against this visit and against any repetition of the same'. Put more bluntly, Cornelia was being manipulated and was furious at being thus trapped. Somehow she held back the tide of urgent longing which his sudden presence aroused and angrily rejected the visit. Next morning 'a very violent letter' from Pierce arrived, 'complaining of the injury he had received'. It has not survived but it elicited from Cornelia a response so immediate and agonised that one wonders whether he accused her of no longer loving him. Her answer affords us a rare glimpse of the suffering which separation was costing her:

> I have been so looking and hoping for a letter from you this morning; your letter has just come, and makes me cry so that I can scarcely see what I write. Forget your visit to Derby. I never told you, that I assumed that excitement to hide nature, as I must do sometimes. No! You have not the violent temptation that I have in thinking of the little Bethlehem room [at Gracemere], nor have you perhaps gone through the struggles of a woman's heart. No! you never have.

It was also in his 'very violent letter', that Pierce made another protest. Although Merty, Ady and Frank were all at schools agreed by both parents and although there had been as yet no interference with anyone's correspondence, he claimed that Wiseman (by opposing his visits?) was trying 'to prevent their acting together in regard to the children'. To hear now, as he very soon did, that the bishop disapproved of this, his only visit, would scarcely rid him of such thoughts. Emily, busybodying, first told Wiseman that Pierce had visited and then passed to Pierce what the bishop had said, namely, 'I am sorry, very sorry, for Mr Connelly's visit. I know that Dr Walsh will be exceedingly grieved by it . . . a young house must escape even ill-natured censure as much as possible. It ought not to have been done, without leave at least.'

He made no further attempt as yet to visit Cornelia but continued to correspond. In spite of his claim about the bishop and the children, a letter of Cornelia's to Merty in August shows that through correspondence mother and father did act together in regard to them – and also how unsatisfactory this was. Their son, now nearly fifteen years old, had done badly in his studies at Stonyhurst. Even though at the end-of-year Academy his very indifferent work would be publicly displayed, the boy longed for his father to come for this school occasion and had begged his mother to persuade him:

My dear Merty

I did the best I could to induce your dear Papa to go to the Academy, but it seems that you have been disappointed . . . Oh Merty how you will grieve over the education you have wasted. Five years time and expense, purely wasted! . . . What is to become of you? . . . You know that you will have to depend upon your own efforts for an honourable livelihood and that what we have will neither go to you nor to Frank but to Ady . . . Ah Merty will you yet give me some hope that you may be fitted for something? I fully impressed on you that you would have to depend on your own efforts after leaving college. If you would but try to study. If you would but *do what you are doing* there might yet be time and we might still hope . . . Ah Merty your Papa will not try you beyond a certain point and this may decide your destiny for this life. If you have anything to tell him about the examination & prizes that will be in any way favourable I trust you will communicate it to him at once. May God have pity on you and upon us. Oh if I could tell you what I suffer on your account you would pity me my child and pray for me.

Ever your affectionate mother.

The end of her novitiate would mean seeing all three children again – Merty for holidays, Ady and Frank to live with her at Derby. But separation from them was making darkness in her, as on this occasion. There was nothing she could do for Merty and her appeals to 'dear Papa' were unavailing.

A second crisis had begun to loom. Conceivably Pierce hoped for easier access when the novitiate year ended, and in April when only four months of it had passed he had pressed for her to be allowed to make her profession 'without delay'. Necessarily Wiseman refused. In November, hearing she would do so next month, Pierce protested formally against her taking *any* vows in *any* religious congregation. Her debts would be his responsibility, he said – perhaps a warning by Mr Sing. But this was not the fact. More probably he wanted her not to make a vow of obedience because it would put the seal on Wiseman's authority over her and the foundation. Winter and Asperti between them induced him to withdraw this protest.

Asperti had arrived in October and from then on – now incredible – correspondence between husband and wife was open to the chaplain. Such a thing must have fanned Pierce's rising resentments. So suspicious did he become, for instance, that a teacher living in the convent 'was asked by Mr C to act as spy on Mrs Connelly' – and, as a friend, warned Cornelia and then left. By May 1848 Asperti felt he must report affairs to Fransoni. Of the occasion of Pierce's protest about vows he said: 'I went to see Mr Connelly, I tried hard to pacify him, I assured him of the excellent running

128

of the Convent, in which not even a shadow of those disorders that he imagined, existed.' Pierce had confessed to him:

> ... that he had thought of trying to destroy the Convent, forbidding the Mother Superior to have any communication with her children, and of going himself to Rome to harm the Convent, Dr Wiseman, and the Jesuits, and to obtain the Approval of the Rule in Rome and found other Convents ... When I left Mr Connelly I thought he was appeased.

A good deal was evidently fomenting in Connelly's angry imagination and he was not appeased for very long. What he had owned to Asperti he did. On 21 December Mother Connelly made her vows and became superior-general. No doubt she wrote to her husband about it, a ceremony in which Wiseman was a key figure. No doubt also she rejoiced that now Ady and Frank would be returning and Merty would come for holidays. Eight days after the ceremony, his passport reveals, Pierce started to get visas for Europe. Without telling their mother anything at all he removed Mercer and Ady from their schools and by 14 January had taken them to unrevealed destinations on the continent. What he had done with Frank, now nearly seven years old, we are not certain, but *en route* he visited Protestant friends who probably took the boy into their home. He informed not Cornelia but the chaplain. Asperti's letter continues:

> I received a letter written to me by Mr Connelly from France, in which he tells me that he has the children with him, without giving any indication of where he is going etc. and orders me to forbid the Mother General, in his name, to communicate in any way with the children, and does not wish to let her know the place to which he is taking them, etc. ... I saw carried out one of his threats, to remove the children from their mother.

Pierce, justifying the situation to his brother, said there was 'a plot laid' to take them out of his hands. There is ample evidence in Pierce's own contributions to anti-Catholic literature that his imaginings fed on stories of the fate of daughters held captive and corrupted in convents.[1] The plot theme, however, does not reappear. What emerges is that he meant to prevent the children's imminent return to Cornelia in order to reassert his own control over wife and family, and thence over the convent. When a year later court proceedings were about to begin, Cornelia gave to Wiseman, through whom her defence was to be arranged, letters she had received from her husband. They were never used in court and none has survived, but Wiseman stated to Shrewsbury:

> Mr C's letters show that it was not about his *children* that he quarrelled or feared, but only over his power over the convent. In one letter he tells

Mrs C that he had carried off the children *as the only way to get hold of her through them*. Good Dr Winter thinks it was for their welfare he was so anxious. His letters will set that at rest.

Of the occasion on which Cornelia learned that the children had been taken, there is no record. No word has survived of the mother's tumult of feeling; nor of the bitterness of realising that her husband was trying to use her for his own unjustifiable ends, that she had been wrong in thinking (as she later told Wiseman) that Pierce's demands for authority over her and the convent would gradually give way to 'some other crotchet'. On the contrary, the man whose own demand for separation had lawfully freed her of his dominion wanted dominion so much that it was greater than his love for her, and he was taking the one way left to regain it – through the children, so darling to her as he knew. He had promised that everything done in regard to them should be with her consent. Now, in order to regain them she must be compliant to his will, and his action was a threat that if she was not, she might lose them for ever.

The only evidence of the effect on Cornelia is a vow recorded without comment in her notebook, and written one week after Pierce had abducted the children. Its first sentence places the whole in the context of the sacrifice of the mass. The opening phrase, 'In union with my crucified Lord', is the one sign given of the suffering that lay behind her offering:

> In union with my crucified Lord and by His most precious blood, in adoration, satisfaction, thanksgiving and petition, I, Cornelia, vow to have no future intercourse with my children and their father beyond what is for the Greater Glory of God and His manifest will, known through my director and in case of doubt on his part, through my extraordinary [confessor]. Gloria Patri. Jan. 21 1848. St Mary's Convent, Derby.

Because the subject of this vow is Cornelia's relationship with her husband and children we have to ask what she is really meaning here. It was a private vow, according to church law *revocable*. In addition to that, with her clause beginning 'beyond what', she made it not absolute but conditional. She was not going to regard herself as bound by it when she and her director thought that communication with her family would serve God better.

There is a more fundamental point, its relationship with what she had vowed already.

During the years since Pierce had first asked her to free him it had been through the heart's natural affections that she had chiefly suffered, and in trying to decide and then to accept what God apparently asked of Pierce (the only ground on which she could agree to it), it must have been the dictates of feeling with which most of all she had had to wrestle. Like her husband, and particularly since being in England, she had had to learn what the separation implied.

Experience had eventually brought her, still struggling, to the once never-dreamed-of day when she signed a deed of separation; and more recently to a similarly unforeseen and irrevocable moment, when in obedience a small community accepted her as its leader and she in obedience accepted responsibility for its continuance in the church. Her private vow was made soon after this. It was prompted by Pierce's traitorous removal of the children, a searing moment of truth for the mother: he would do even this to gain his end. The temptation to temporise with God's claims must have hung over her. And she made a special vow to support herself. It was a particular, concrete and costly offering, a way of saying her profession of obedience was indeed a matter of 'actions not words'. In this matter she would temporise no more.

As life went on Cornelia certainly made many such acts on other matters, not all so costly, not enshrined in the form of a vow and not recorded, but all to implement more fully the gift of herself and to identify with God's will for her in the church. There was a prayer she sometimes used: 'Oh Eternal Will, live and reign in my will and over my will now and for ever.' In principle her private vow added nothing to what she had professed on 21 December 1847. It simply said that family claims were not to be put *before* those of God. It was the most recent expression of the silent offering she had made not quite eight years before on that sunny day in Grand Coteau when the desire to love God unconditionally had seized her being.

She thus fortified herself against the desperate longing to give up everything for the sake of the children – which Pierce had probably counted on. But a natural stubbornness helped Cornelia to stand firm. Her husband, one suspects, had not reckoned with this streak in his 'saintly little wife'. Had he been able to see what she had written out with such solemn care he might have had misgivings about his plan of action. The religious priorities so clearly expressed and the evident determination for their sake to set herself beyond his will were not the submission he was after. As he made his hopeful way across the continent with Mercer and Ady he did not know that she had seen through his ploy to use them as pawns. Nor was he aware of what else she had done. She had withdrawn from usual communication not only with the children (as he had ordered), but also with himself. Inconceivable. It was in spirit undeterred and with plans confidently in place that he arrived in Rome.

Pierce's reasons for going to Rome in particular were mixed. On behalf of the earl he was to gain the pope's ear on Irish affairs. It was said in the *Tablet* to be 'commonly believed that Mr Connelly aspired' to be nuncio to Ireland and rumour even had it, according to the editor Lucas, that he hoped also for a cardinal's hat. This is marginal to Cornelia's history, except to tell us she was married to a man whom some saw as very ambitious.

A second purpose was imputed to him, that he hoped to prevent Wiseman's appointment as Archbishop of Westminster. In April the earl received from Rome, and passed on to Wiseman verbatim, Pierce's denial of this rumour: 'The report Lord Arundel and Surrey speaks of as coming from Rome that I was endeavouring to get Doctor Wiseman removed from London, he did quite right to contradict. Since I have been here [Rome], *I have done nothing of the sort, either directly or indirectly.*' But his denial was a camouflaged lie. On 26 December, five days after Cornelia's profession and just *before* going to Rome, he had written to Lord Minto, then on a diplomatic mission to the pope:

> Lord Shrewsbury from an undue confidence in Dr Wiseman has been active in recommending him to Rome for the intended appointment as Archbishop, not that he is the man that he would have wished, but for want of a better . . . Dr Wiseman is the last man to be named to so prominent a position: either for the good of England or Rome. If the formalities of his appointment are not completed, as I believe they are not, a word from your lordship to Cardinal Ferretti . . . or to His Holiness would delay at least if not prevent it . . . I again beg your lordship's pardon for this intrusion. I have no personal interest whatever, I am not even a subject of Her Majesty.[2]

To have spoken *in* Rome against Wiseman would have defeated the third and secret purpose. Pierce took with him a copy, with alterations made by himself, of the 'sketch or outline of a Rule' with which he had helped Cornelia before coming to England. Then he had acted as link between her and the Cardinal Prefect of the Propaganda because she was living an enclosed life at the Trinità. Now he presented himself as founder of the Society, and his wife figures in his introductory statement for the Propaganda merely as the recipient of his inspiration. The rules were prepared, he wrote, for 'a little Congregation which the Good God had long inspired me with the desire to try to found with the help of a holy person who was well known to me, and who was very docile to me [*qui m'était bien docile*]'.

Cornelia's docility to him was probably Pierce's deepest need. He relegated her to nonentity, put himself forward as 'founder' and requested approbation, letting it be assumed that he had Cornelia's assent. Such conduct allows us to suppose that even in Rome in 1846 he had let it be thought he was co-founder at least. Had he not done so Fransoni could not have paid attention to the present request. Cornelia, the moment she heard of it, wrote to the earl: 'Mr Connelly seems to have forgotten that he assisted me with the Rule on the foundation I gave him and that at that moment as well as at this, I had no idea of accepting anything in the Rule but what passed through the inspection of my director [Grassi].'

Meanwhile Pierce had to justify his request. It was Wiseman's beneficent authority that had endowed the Society with a degree of stability, he who had provided a convent and had 'judged it well to receive the Vows and give the habit to the Reverend Mother'. That he had also installed Cornelia as superior-general goes unmentioned. Thus claimed by Pierce as benefactor, Wiseman could not at the same time safely be opposed in Rome for advancement.

The Propaganda fortunately dealt with the matter through its usual channels. Bishops Walsh and Wiseman were consulted. The news reached Cornelia and at once, on 10 May 1848, she wrote to Fransoni:

> I was very surprised to receive a letter, from Alton Towers two days ago, which gave me some important information regarding our Rule, and the approbation of the same. I was equally surprised to hear today the same thing from the Bishops themselves, and they surprised in their turn, that I knew nothing about it.

She then states plainly that the Rule by which the Society was living and on which it was working, was in her possession not Pierce's, and that it was not yet ready for approbation:

> My vows were made on the Rule now in my hand, which had the approval of Your Eminence and that of Dr Wiseman. Any change or addition, which may have been made by Mr Connelly, I can have nothing to do with. We have all the approval which is necessary for us at the present time and we would prefer to practise it under our Bishop & to give it the proof of our experience before anything more is done to it.

The next paragraph reflects her appreciation of the support given her by Wiseman, but also brings out his opposition to Pierce's visiting and her concurrence in his point of view:

> I am very grieved to hear the rumours spread in England by Mr Connelly concerning our Convent and the influence of Dr Wiseman on our Rule. This is in fact false. Dr Wiseman has been truly a great & princely Father to us: he has neither opposed nor changed a single point of our Rule; on the contrary he has left me perfectly free to put it in practice to the best of my power under the direction of my Spiritual Fathers [Jesuits/Asperti]. The only thing, to which he was opposed, was the visit [March 1847] of Mr C to our Convent. I have no need to explain to Your Eminence what would be the harm to our Convent in a Protestant Country if it were supposed that Mr C had anything to do with our Direction, and perhaps

[harm] also with our Bishops if Mr C had anything to do with the approbation of our Rule.

What Fransoni made of the situation with which he was now confronted is not clear. He had Cornelia's statement and Asperti's detailed account of Pierce's conduct, both arriving after Pierce's departure from Rome. What had been credited now had to be questioned. At the request of Cornelia and Wiseman the consideration of approbation was dropped, but Pierce's spurious rule – with a report on it (unfavourable) already initiated by the Propaganda – was put into the files. Whenever in the future she presented her own Constitutions for approval, it sabotaged her efforts.

Meanwhile Pierce was heading homewards. With no reason to suppose that his plans had gone awry, he landed on 1 June. At Alton he asked Winter to get Wiseman's permission for a visit to the convent, but did not wait. Instead, armed with a blessing and a medal from Pius IX, he arrived hot-foot in Derby without warning at 9 a.m. on Saturday, 3 June. Cornelia refused to see him. The consequences were calamitous.

Plaited into Cornelia's refusal there must have been many threads of feeling. It was five months since Mr Connelly had gone. He had doubly and deeply affronted her. He had stolen the children away and had tried to supplant her in the work which was her other 'child'. She now knew for certain that he so wanted power over her that he was willing to go to extreme, cruel and unjust lengths to get it. To refuse to see him would be to assert the independence to which she had the legal right, freed of the manipulation and veerings of her husband.

But there was another and in no way self-gratifying reason for refusal. In Rome it had been for the children's sake, not for the comfort of separated man and wife, that the family had been regularly reconstituted. During her noviceship at Derby there were no children at the convent to justify this. Nor on this occasion were the children there, and Cornelia knew well Wiseman's views in the matter of visits. It had become a matter of obedience. The Connelly history would have been very different had Pierce waited for the bishop's permission.

It is at this moment in Cornelia's early years in England that the rearranging by Rome of vicars apostolic most directly affected her life. Wiseman, later defending himself from blame in the Connelly affair, claimed that he no longer had jurisdiction over the Derby convent in June 1848 because by then he had moved to London. True. But in an earlier letter, *c.* September 1847, he had told the earl that his appointment as pro-vicar apostolic there did not release him from his coadjutorship in the Central although 'it suspends its action for a time, as I cannot possibly attend to both'.[3] Walsh, a sick man, continued to consider the convent 'entirely under the guidance of Bishop Wiseman' and Wiseman continued to be looked to as the community's ecclesiastical superior. From time to time he came to admit candidates to the novitiate and now Winter took for granted that it was he, not Bishop Walsh, who could give Pierce the permission to visit. Being too busy in London to answer Winter's request, Wiseman scribbled a note to Asperti telling him to 'look to the matter', thereby leaving the responsibility to the chaplain. The note could barely have been delivered at the convent when Pierce arrived. There he was, awaiting his wife in the parlour, and a decision had to be made. Asperti opposed the visit.

Of the consultation that went on between him and Cornelia we have only hints. She 'told the nuns afterwards' that the refusal was contrary to the 'wishes and request' which she made known to the chaplain. She feared the effect of opposition on her husband, she said. The community seems to have thought that because the children had been abducted Asperti suspected some attempt on the wife. Whatever his actual reason, in Buckle's opinion he 'presumed on his authority' when he disallowed the interview; which is not quite true. Both Cornelia and Asperti knew that Wiseman was opposed to visits. If she represented to the chaplain that there was good reason on this occasion for making an exception, and if he, her director, maintained that nevertheless obedience to the bishop was the course that must be taken, she would see herself as bound to obey. And she would do so freely and fully. She had after all made a private vow eminently applicable in her present dilemma. Accordingly she would have adopted Asperti's point of view and sent him, as we know she did, with a message to Pierce declining to see him. The turning point in the Connelly drama is this moment of refusal. Its consequences were sensational, prolonged and public. Psychologically their origin is the clash of will and temperament in the scene that ensued. Pierce, beside himself at the refusal, 'threw himself in a passion of tears' on the parlour sofa and lay there, he said, for six hours. Asperti remained with him throughout, offering sympathy but unyielding, and earned for himself defamation at his friend's hands as a secret seducer of women in convents.

Neither did Cornelia yield. Her desire to do God's will and her native stubbornness were yoked, not only for now but for the rest of her life's work. On this crucial occasion they kept her in her room upstairs for those six hours. Love-hate for her husband, anguish for the children, loyalty to her foundation, obedience to her mission must have striven in her heart. But she adhered to the road.

Eventually Pierce left, profoundly humiliated: his wife, it appeared, had defied him; his friend had taken her part; his ruse with their children had failed; what he regarded as his rights over her and the convent had been set aside, and even though he said he came from the pope it had cut no ice. He went away as Cornelia feared, a desperate man. Claims, schemes, expectations, so falsely based and yet so pathetically necessary to his self-esteem, had collapsed like a castle of cards. He knew nothing of the struggle and pain which the refusal was causing her during his own six hours of misery. All he could see was that, through Asperti, she was again preferring the bishop's wishes to his own, and when at last he went away it was under the enraging misapprehension that because Cornelia had refused him she was now Wiseman's tool.

Had Walsh and Wiseman been able to see their way to an arrangement of visits on some regulated basis the road to major misunderstandings such as this would not have been so broad. Nor, in spite of what had been allowed in Rome by the pope himself, might visits have loomed so large in Pierce's expectations had he not lived where he did, so near the convent and with those who maintained such an interest in Cornelia and her Society when he had relatively little to do. On the other hand that is not the whole story. Pierce's present behaviour in the matter of visits bears a certain continuity with the past. Three years earlier Roothaan had queried this prospective Jesuit's need to see his wife so often and the result had been surprising: not a simple cutting down on the number of visits but the abandonment, whether through his initiative or Roothaan's, of the long cherished plan to be a Jesuit. Now in Derby convent his right to visit was more than questioned. It was denied – by his *wife*, and beyond her by the church. His reaction was correspondingly drastic. When about to institute legal proceedings to get his wife back he wrote to Shrewsbury: 'I vowed to God to do what I am now doing if necessary the day I waited 6 hours in vain at the convent in Derby.'

A sequence of ugly events was now irreversibly on the move. It had already begun with what Cornelia, so devoted to her children, described to her brother Ralph. Their father, she said, 'broke his word and his promises and stole them away from me in a moment of excitement and unjust anger'. Her refusal was part of the sequence. Whatever psychological theories or nineteenth-century legal or social assumptions can be adduced on behalf of Pierce's conduct, and however one may compassionate a man so reduced, the fact remains that both she and her children were the victims of his faithlessness, itself servant apparently to a need to dominate. Her obedience, in this century not easily sympathised with, was catalyst not source. Negatively it precipitated Pierce in the direction in which he was already moving: an offensive against the bishop who stood between him and access to the convent.

Only two letters of Cornelia's, both to the earl, have survived. The first went to him very soon after the scene at the convent:

136

I should like to write to you on many things concerning Mr Connelly, and as I know so well your happy & holy influence upon him & your true friendship for us both, it is a comfort to me to do so and I feel it will not offend you. I however wish at this moment to speak only of one subject; and that is, my wish that he should give up any interference with our Convent or our Rule. His visit to Rome has been only time & money thrown away so far as we are concerned, and indeed, as soon as I knew what he was doing at Rome I was obliged to write to the Cardinal, Propaganda, to prevent any thing being done at present.

She wants the earl who hears everything from Pierce's point of view, to know hers:

Had anything been done I should *not* have accepted it since it was not with my knowledge or consent that any thing had been proposed . . . Mr Connelly seems to forget that he assisted me with the Rule on the foundation I gave him and that at that moment, as well as at this, I had no idea of accepting any thing in the Rule but what passed through the inspection of my director.

And she ends with an appeal. Pierce was a priest. Their proposition had called for undeviating dedication from both of them, putting God and the people of God before each other, she in religious life, he in the priestly. Part of her present great sorrow is that she sees he is losing sight of what ordination had committed him to and that his heart is not turning 'all to his flock for the love of God':

Will you then my dear Lord explain all this to him in your own gentle, holy way and induce him to turn his heart all to his flock for the love of God? I have much more that I wish to say to you but I cannot now do any thing more than undeceive Mr Connelly in his hopes *of ever having any thing more to do with our Convent or our Rule.*

Before she wrote the next letter, 'other means' had been tried to calm Pierce and had failed. She speaks of 'a decisive step' which she herself had then taken with her husband: she has told him he can visit her when he brings Ady back to her care but never till then, and only if the bishop commands her to alter this decision will she do so. If he wants to see her he must 'prove his sincerity by sending my little girl to me'.

What part Cornelia's private vow played in all that followed is not clear. When Asperti had gone (Easter 1850) and Grant had become her bishop in place of Wiseman (September 1851), there seems to have been less restriction placed on her in family matters. An invitation in 1852, for example (not accepted), to Ady for Christmas and for her to be brought by Pierce had been allowed. Between Grant and Cornelia there was a certain spiritual affinity and from scattered references to her family sorrows in letters it is evident that she confided in him. Very possibly she told him of her vow. Certainly she remained true to its intentions, not to let family deflect her from God's claims upon her. To the vow itself no further reference has survived. It simply stands upon the page of her notebook, a secret cry to God for help at the most bleak crossroad of her life.

Pierce did not yield. No news of the children reached their mother and by August the Sing affair at the convent was becoming acute. Early in September Wiseman proposed the community's transfer to Sussex, part of his London District. Early in November Ullathorne advised them to pay Sing or leave. They could not pay. By the 25th the move was agreed and on 4 December Pierce's first irruption reached Ullathorne. The fires had been smouldering for six months. Again, as he saw it, Wiseman had come between him and his wife and he would bear it no more.

My dear Lord Bishop

It has pleased Almighty God, more than once, as it appeared to me, to call me to hard trials. If I hesitated for a little, it was only to be certain of my duty. Once satisfied of that, I have never yet shrunk back . . . . I am a man, a husband & a father before I am a priest, & my first duties cannot be abandoned. Faith, fidelity, honour I will never forsake, nor will I forsake the wife I vowed to protect for life, the mother of my children, to those who would make her abandon them.

With Dr Wiseman for her Bishop & Dr Asperti for her Confessor, the principles with which I left that saintly person & gave her up, meaning it for God, have been, I will not say corrupted, but rooted up.

It has only just come to his ears that Cornelia is moving to the London District:

I hear that she is about leaving your lordship's jurisdiction to come again under that of Dr Wiseman. My object in writing is to beg your lordship to prevent this if possible, for the sake of the scandal otherwise inevitable. If the laws of justice & honour cannot be at once enforced by the authorities of the Church, I am determined to apply to those of the country. I have my Dear Lord deliberately counted the cost, & with God's help, will go on & finish.

A second letter to Ullathorne followed hard upon this. Under certain conditions he is willing to go no further: he must have the access to Cornelia he had in Rome; and there must be a 'solemn engagement (private) to have hereafter no communication by word or by writing, direct or indirect, with Bp Wiseman, Dr Asperti, Miss ___ or the Nun whom I saw in Dr Asperti's bedchamber'. This was the first libellous innuendo about Asperti's sexual immorality. It was soon food for public gossip and Cornelia wrote that 'what Mr C has put forth about Dr Asperti is *positively false* and for the truth of what I say I am ready to take my oath'.

Ullathorne answered by return of post, a measured letter. He would do his best to explain Mr Connelly's feelings to the bishop in so delicate a matter; but as to jurisdiction he himself no longer had any over Mrs Connelly's community (some of whom have already gone), having delegated it to Dr Wiseman. Pierce's reply was immediate:

My dear Lord Bishop

Your Lordship's letter leaves me no alternative. I cannot consent to hold any intercourse with Dr Wiseman. The matter will have to go to the laws of the country. I have done nothing without the advice of my Confessor [Winter]. The consequences of attempting to carry out right against wrong I leave without fear & without anxiety to God. They are in his hands & in such a case are no concern of mine.

He sprang into action. The very next day he was in touch with Henry Drummond MP, an anti-Catholic of repute and already known to him, who offered him hospitality at his home in the south, Albury Park. He left Alton Towers and as soon as 21 December wrote to the earl: 'The case is now fairly in legal hands. Unless Dr Wiseman requires her at once to put herself into my hands . . . she will be delivered to me under penal enforcement.'

PRELUDE TO PROCEEDINGS

It was not without good ground that Bishops Walsh and Wiseman had tried to shelter Cornelia and her convent from Protestant hostility. The anti-Catholicism which both Connellys had experienced in America now bore in on their lives again. Eventually Pierce was engulfed by it and Cornelia became an object of national scandal-mongering.

In the years before their arrival Britain's focus on its Roman Catholic citizens had sharpened. With the Act of Union in 1801, agreed with the Irish on a pledge of emancipation for Catholics, Ireland had become part of the United Kingdom and what had been a minority of about 129,000 swelled overnight to one of about six million, too great a proportion of Britain's 15 million to go unnoticed. The movement for emancipation had coincided with the evangelical revival among Protestants. Awareness of difference between Catholic and Protestant belief and practice became more acute, and the Act when it came in 1829 was disliked not only by ultra Tories and Anglican bishops, but by evangelicals everywhere. It increased

Catholic confidence and Protestant fears simultaneously, and bred a conflict situation. Papists now had constitutional rights, the Protestant Association was formed in 1835 and its missionaries toured the land to defend the people of Britain against the evils of Rome. In the thirties and forties fear was aggravated by the sheer number of Catholic Irish who began to pour into the country, and also because the established church itself was felt by many to be teetering on the edge of the Roman abyss. John Henry Newman's thinking had reminded Anglicans of their Catholic roots, followers took to papistical practices, and after 1845 when he went over to Rome conversions increased. In the same year a government action had raised public anger. Sir Robert Peel wished to endow Maynooth, the seminary outside Dublin, with a permanent income instead of arguing the matter every year. Protest swelled. Dissenters could not stomach the idea that Protestant Britain should 'educate a romish priesthood' or 'endow popery', and this was only one year before the Connellys arrived. In Derby there were fifteen dissenters' chapels, eight Anglican churches and one Catholic, and like most places Derby had its Protestant demonstrations. Three weeks after Cornelia had settled there, the Tory newspaper *Mercury* reported a meeting held in the Mechanics' Lecture Hall, 4 November 1846. The meeting viewed 'with alarm the religious efforts and political progress now making by the emissaries of the Church of Rome throughout the United Kingdom', and called on those present to 'unite to stem the torrent of Papacy'.

Among those in the country very ready to stem the torrent was Henry Drummond. It was he who had financed the *Morning Watch*, a paper started by the then Presbyterian Edward Irving to propagate the doctrine of the imminent return of Christ to judge and reign for a thousand years. In 1833 Irving was deprived of his ministry by the Presbyterians whereupon he and Drummond founded their own sect, the Catholic Apostolic Church. Thomas Carlyle gives an engaging portrait of Drummond:

> . . . swimming, if I mistake not, in an element of dandyism . . . well-nigh cracked by an enormous conceit of himself, which, both as pride and vanity . . . seemed to pervade every fibre of him . . . He was by far the richest of the sect, and alone belonged to the aristocratic circles, abundant in speculation as well as in money: a sharp, elastic, haughty kind of man.[4]

Out of his personal wealth he built the Apostles' Chapel at Albury in Sussex and a very complex liturgy developed, ritualistic and sacramental. By 1848 Albury Park was a well-established centre for Protestants of millenarial and apocalyptic leaning, as influential as Alton Towers among Catholics.

What his new church offered was apostolic tradition, sacraments and high ceremony, important elements in Catholic belief; but it also evaded what Pierce no longer cared for, a teaching episcopate which had authority. The only authority acknowledged in Drummond's church was that of the Spirit at work in the individual. One wonders with how much interest Connelly, with discontent already creeping up on him at Alton Towers, listened to this man so 'abundant in speculation' when first they met. Certainly he knew well enough, when he began to protest his treatment at the hands of the Roman church in England, that Albury was a place which would extend its sympathy. Drummond was aggressively anti-Catholic as his parliamentary speeches and his publications show. Clergy, nunneries, the pope, the teachings of the church, all were vilified.[5] The Catholic Shrewsbury spoke truly when he said to Ullathorne that Pierce 'has I fear placed himself in very dangerous hands'.

Pierce's letter to Drummond of 8 December begins – without preamble – on a note of extreme deference:

> The deep and sincere respect I feel for Mr Drummond, my grateful recollection of the delightful hospitality enjoyed by myself and my children at Albury Park and of all I saw there, lead me to take what may seem a strange liberty, but which I hope will not be thought unpardonable.

Then comes his justification for going to law.

> When I had the honour of being at Albury Park I was flying with my children from the wretched moral influence that seemed to me to surround them. It now becomes necessary for me to appeal to the laws of the country against one of the Bishops of the Church [Wiseman] in order to reclaim my blessed wife from his most unholy influence. Since the month of April 1846, when Mrs Connelly left Rome, I have been allowed to see her only once & her correspondence with me, which for some time has been put an end to, was not allowed to be private. Nearly six months ago my Confessor, Dr Winter, wrote to Dr Wiseman, then the administrator of the District, but to this day he has never answered. But it is impossible to tell all in a letter.

Matters have now reached the point, he says, after several paragraphs on the story of his wrongs:

> . . . where I feel some scruples of honour about involving Catholics. I think it wise to seek the best legal advice. Of course this also must be Protestant: but I am without anyone whom, under the circumstances, I can advise with. I venture then to beg you will let me throw myself upon your counsel & support . . .

He encloses his correspondence with Ullathorne and by way of an interesting conclusion at the expense of his wife he hints at the iniquities of Wiseman and Asperti. Finally he bows very low indeed to the man whose support he hopes for:

> And in excuse for the angelic woman who has become a victim to Episcopal & clerical iniquity I must say that the Asperti spoken of is a reality that goes beyond Shakespeare's conception of hypocrisy & villainy in Iago.
>
> May I beg Mr Drummond will be good enough to present me humbly to the Lady Harriet, the Lady Lovaine and Miss Drummond?
>
> > Most respectfully,
> > Most gratefully,
> > I am Sir
> > Pierce Connelly.

Promptly Drummond placed him in the hands of lawyers who, Pierce informed the earl, were very willing to have so 'novel and exciting a case to try when they seem sure of success'.

There is some evidence that Pierce would have been glad enough to settle out of court, but always on the condition that he gets hold of Cornelia. He hoped Wiseman would 'recommend her to submit' in order to avoid the scandal, and that Cornelia could be tricked into returning to him. The Drummonds, he told the earl, 'think a letter to her from your lordship would have great influence in prevailing on her to come here to Albany to settle everything, of course saying nothing about my being here'. Whether or not he was really hesitating, the lawyer Fladgate soon got from him the agreement to go to court. Pierce was told that an action for restitution of conjugal rights 'was the only remedy known to English law' by which he could obtain '*even an interview*' with his wife. He could have had the interview at once by agreeing to Cornelia's condition and returning Ady to the care of her mother. But this was no longer a possibility. Pierce had become a man whose imagination was befouling his perception of convents, bishops, church. Inside the week he was writing again to Shrewsbury:

> *The first of all my duties is to rescue my blessed wife* from the hands of devils, & so help me God . . . I will now never cease till Mrs Connelly is placed absolutely & unreservedly under my control. I will trust none of them [the bishops]. Should I fail in the Court, I will carry it into the House of Commons, & will then make it an affair of the American Government. And in so doing I believe verily I am doing truth & the Church better service than any other way possible, even though I break up every convent in England for fifty years to come.

Meanwhile letters flew thick and fast between Shrewsbury, Ullathorne and Wiseman. The earl, many of whose connections on account of his rank and political interests were not Catholic, feared the scandal in Protestant England. He was humiliated by Pierce's conduct, but also concerned for him and ready at this stage to take his side against both Cornelia and Wiseman. Initially he blamed the bishop for the whole crisis on the grounds that he had opposed visits, mismanaged Cornelia and treated Pierce discourteously. Had Wiseman pursued 'a proper conciliatory course towards him from the beginning', he told Ullathorne, 'all this would have been averted', and he wrote to that effect to the bishop himself. Wiseman thanked him for his 'candid statement' about the 'afflicting case of Mr C' but said he could not bring himself to agree. Referring to letters (not extant) in his possession, namely some of Pierce's both to Cornelia and to others, he said: 'These letters will abundantly disprove every charge & I hope [throw] the whole odium upon the unfortunate man himself, who knowing of their existence, must be mad to go to law.'

Wiseman hopes, at this early stage, that the suit is going to fall through and that the letters will never have to be produced. In the meanwhile he has a word for the earl in friendship's name. The letters reveal Connelly's 'wild fanaticism (always *implied* in what *he* does, & *opposed* by the Devil)' and they will 'make your lordship not regret that Providence has removed a *baleful* influence from the heir of your line'. He feared that 'worse passions than appear on the surface have been at work' in Pierce, meaning presumably physical desire. But Shrewsbury, a married man, in whose home Pierce had lived for two years, would not hear of this:

> I cannot believe it, never having seen the slightest symptoms of it. He has a natural pride which was never I fear properly subdued. But the main passion which has now conquered him is, I believe, jealousy . . . He was jealous first of the influence of the Jesuits, then of Sister Emily Bowles, and Doctor Asperti and Your Lordship. Man or woman made no difference to him, but all who came between him and the influence which he expected to exercise over his wife, tho' she were a nun, were alike the objects of his aversion.

The earl has put his finger on the core of Connelly's problem: he still expected to be the sole arbiter and influence in his wife's life.

Cornelia and her community meanwhile were settling in at St Leonards but she and Wiseman are corresponding about the case. The first letter that has survived, written probably on 7 or 8 January, is an apparently point to point answer to one of his. He has read Pierce's to her and deduced that it is control over the convent that Pierce is after. Her reply to the bishop reveals the rock against which Pierce is now dashing himself. Cornelia is no longer, as she once told her sister, ready to submit to *whatever* her husband believed to be her duty:

My dear Lord
I am truly happy that you take this clear view of the case . . . We have
God & the truth on our side and therefore we need fear nothing. I am
ready for anything that God wills. Do you not see that Mr C has determined to break up our order and ruin and upset the whole? He declared
he would do this and he probably hopes that I may go to another Convent
to begin afresh under him . . . I *never* intended to give Mr C any authority
over me or the convent, and never considered him in *any way* our Superior.

She explains why she had waited till after her profession to assert the
community's necessary dependence in England on the authority of the local
bishop and not directly on Rome:

You have no doubt been astonished at the tenor of Mr C's letters to me.
I allowed him to write all these things *without answering* anything that I
thought would irritate him to have contradicted. Had I told him at first
the whole truth he would have crushed us when he could have done so,
now he cannot crush us. I also thought he would get some other crotchet
that would have caught his inclinations, and thus his thoughts of authority
over us would have gradually died away.

It was the beginning of a long time of trial. In 1846, on the brink of taking
up her mission in the church, she had been able to support herself in
personal suffering by remembering Pierce's priesthood. It had been for this
that she had given up all she most loved. Now, after so brief a time, this
source of consolation was one of affliction. The nineteenth was no ecumenical
century. Amongst churches by then entrenched for generations in their own
histories of conviction and protest, each asserting its own way 'for the
salvation of souls', the Roman Catholic church stood beleaguered, claiming
what she had always claimed, that she alone was the source of salvation.
In the aggressive religious milieu of the day such a claim was generally
understood in its narrowest and most threatening sense. To apostatise was
to reject God and so risk damnation. When friends told Cornelia that Pierce
was sure to 'relapse into Protestantism' she did not despair of God's mercy
for him, but the sword turned in her heart. Their separation, conceived as
a higher way of union, now measured the distance between heaven and hell.
It had become something to be gaped at, its holy purposes mocked, its loved
initiator faithless, her children its victims. And God was crucified in the
betrayal.

She tried to encourage herself with the hope that apostasy was an empty
threat. Others were less sanguine. Lady Shrewsbury, in whose home he had
recently lived, wrote that Mr Connelly was 'so maddened with jealousy, &
hatred towards the dear Bishop & good saintly Père Asperti, that he is

Cornelia at about the time of her marriage in Philadelphia, aged 22

Pierce Connelly (1804–1883), aged 32,
Rome 1836

Mercer (1832–1853), about
9 years old

Tombstone of Mary Magdalene (1839) and John Henry (1837−1840)

Adeline (1835−1900),
portrait by Frank

Frank (1841−1932),
self-portrait

Gregory XVI, Pope 1831–1846

Gracemere, the Connelly home in Grand Coteau, LA

The young Mrs Connelly, Rome 1836

The Trinità dei Monti, Rome

John Grassi SJ

Derby convent and schools, 1846

Bishop Wiseman, coadjutor to Bishop Walsh in the Central District,
patron of the Derby convent, 1846

St Leonards

Louisa Catherine, Duchess of Leeds
(1792−1874), American, benefactress
in USA and England

Gate Street convent and schools,
London 1851

Ruins of the Old Palace, Mayfield, England, 1863

Mother Cornelia Connelly, Blackpool 1860

wound up to *any* desperate act', and she urged Cornelia to leave Wiseman's diocese. But to Cornelia it seemed that she was obliged to act as she did 'in the truth of God': 'Any step that I could take in this matter would be going against the truth and my own conscience, to the injury of the reputation of others without having any good effect upon Mr Connelly: therefore we must let things go on in the hands of God & the law.'

On 24 January 1849 what had been so far a dreaded possibility became fact: Mrs Connelly was served a writ to appear in court, and the correspondence of the next two weeks, what little we have, is full of the tension under which she was living. She wrote to Wiseman:

My dear Lord

I received the enclosed citation this morning. A respectable person brought it, he asked no questions except to know if I was the person cited. Pray let me know what is to be done. I feel that God alone can help me to bear up in this most wretched & afflicting affair – yet I do not fear . . .

I hope you have got rid of your cold and all your other troubles. My dear Lord what shall I say or how can I make you understand all I feel on this occasion? But you are my Father, and the heart of such a Father can understand all.

May Almighty God reward you for all you have done and are still doing for me.

Wiseman replied at once:

Courage and confidence in God! Fear nothing . . . You will be fully instructed what to do; no personal appearance will be requisite in this suit. I will look after everything for you. I never turn my back on anyone whom God has given up to my care; especially in times of anxiety & trial. Pray to our Blessed Lady for her courage at the foot of the Cross. God bless you & the Community.

Again she wrote to him 'with anxiety for some information on these miserable proceedings', and distraught for the children:

Please let me know when next you write, whether there is any certainty of Mr Connelly's having really apostatised & if so what could be done to keep my poor children out of protestant hands? If he is to bear the expenses of this lawsuit he will soon come to the end of his property and reduce the children to beggary.

Meanwhile Dr Winter received 'a most extraordinary letter from Mr Connelly'. The lawyers had written to him, Pierce said, that Cornelia could now lawfully be 'compelled by force to return to my bed', and he asked Winter to go to the convent and bring her to Albury for him. The chaplain was appalled. Pierce must be 'really mad' if he supposed he would 'second him in his diabolical intentions'. A network of clerical gossip was busy: 'All the priests of the district', he wrote to Shrewsbury, then in Torquay, thought Sister Cornelia ought to leave the country. The Shrewsburys were so shaken that they made yet another effort to induce her to go. The earl offered to pay her travelling expenses and his wife to maintain her. But she answered:

> ... a flight like this would be an acknowledgement of some cause for flight which would be contrary to the truth. We have nothing to fear, God and the truth are on our side. I think only of the consequences of such to our convent, a question of twenty persons who are engaged with me in the establishment of this order. You see at once that this would be an unfaithful and cowardly step on my part which would be destructive to the convent and in every sense giving Mr Connelly the advantage over us. *He would then have gained his point* ... his sole object would be to force me to begin a new congregation under his guidance.

She remained in England and the case began.

THE CASE, 1849–50[6]

English matrimonial law in 1849 still served the needs of a people who for centuries had seen the ownership of land as the yardstick of well-being. It looked not to persons but to property. Divorce law, which focuses on the claims of persons but fragments property, was not yet on the statutes. The only 'person' in the marriage was the husband, and his wife and children were viewed as his property. With that as her legal status the wronged married woman had little hope in law on which to ground a petition for separation, but the married man, wronged or not, stood well. His first step would be to plead in court for the return of his 'property', that is, for a decree of restitution of conjugal rights. If this was granted and his wife then disobeyed, both possible outcomes were to his advantage: either she was returned to him by force (and this did sometimes happen) or a judicial separation (not annulment) would follow, in which case, although he lost his wife, he would generally retain her property along with custody of the children *and* whatever they might inherit.

A good example of the way in which the law put property before people was the case of the Nortons. Caroline Sheridan at nineteen had been married off to 'a coarse, shifty cad, pathologically mean about money and subject to fits of brutal ill temper'. From the start, Mrs Norton being a passionate fighter, violence and quarrel marked the marriage. Eventually Norton put her out, and, perhaps hoping for some financial pay-off, petitioned in court for a decree of separation, citing Lord Melbourne as co-respondent. According to Melbourne's biographer[7] she was certainly innocent and in fact Norton lost his suit. But the court left him with the custody of the children and he was able to use his absolute right over them to block her access. The court also allowed him to retain his right to her literary earnings and to receive when her mother died the life-interest of her inheritance from her father. This was in 1836 and the law did not begin to change until 1857.

Matrimonial suits were heard in ecclesiastical courts, in the case of Connelly v. Connelly in the Court of the Arches in the see of Canterbury. Neither husband nor wife had to appear unless the suit later came to trial. Pleas were made by proctors. The statements presented ('Libel' for Pierce, 'Allegation' for Cornelia) were not on oath but if the opposing party challenged the other then in a second stage witnesses were called and cross-examined under oath. Then if the statements proved false the party could be prosecuted for perjury. In Connelly v. Connelly neither side saw fit to challenge the other. Had Pierce's proctors challenged Cornelia's he risked prosecution for perjury. Had Cornelia's challenged his she risked a decree which would bar her irretrievably from the children. As it was, the case never came to a full trial, and since at this stage in a matrimonial suit there was no jury, everything depended on the decision of the judge, on this occasion Sir Herbert Jenner Fust.

Fust was seventy-one, Official Principal of Protestant England's chief ecclesiastical court in which canonical not civil law was applied. When he undertook Connelly v. Connelly he was in process of considering his judgment in the Gorham case which was dividing the established church on whether one who rejected baptismal regeneration had the right to hold a benefice. Protestants everywhere feared a verdict which might drive many into the arms of the pope. The atmosphere of public religious turmoil created by this was the general background against which Connelly v. Connelly would be heard.

Pierce's Libel was heard before Fust on 17 February 1849. In it his lawyers advantaged him by making his petition as an Episcopalian. It points out that Bishop White who married the Connellys had been consecrated by the Archbishop of Canterbury in order to be bishop in America, and that Episcopalian 'rites & ceremonies' were therefore 'identical' with what was 'by law established in this country'. It omitted entirely conversion, Grand Coteau, the separation, ordination and that his wife was now a nun. It pleaded simply the Episcopalian marriage in Pennsylvania, its consummation and the birth of five children and concluded with the statement that from the time they first left Natchez till they left Rome in 1846 'they continued to live & cohabit together'; they came in September to reside in England and then:

> ... the said Cornelia Augusta Connelly not having Fear of God before her Eyes and being unmindful of her conjugal vow without any lawful reason withdrew herself from Bed Board and mutual cohabitation with her said Husband and that she hath ever since refused and that she still doth refuse to return to and to live and cohabit with him and to render him conjugal rights.

The Libel was contrived by lawyers produced by Drummond. Its purpose in his eyes (at a guess) was not the winning of a particular case but to rouse public feeling against the evils of Rome. For that, a prolonged case with much public reporting would be more advantageous than a quick judgment after a single hearing. In a sense Connelly was his dupe and tool. Nevertheless Pierce had to authorise his proctor to present the Libel and in the legal letter by which he did so the purpose is clearly stated, to procure 'a definitive Sentence or final Decree ... requiring the said Cornelia Augusta Connelly to return home to me the said Pierce Connelly and render me conjugal rights'. Pierce may not in his heart, as he later claimed, have wanted precisely that but he put his signature to the statement and it is witnessed by Henry Drummond.

On 20 March Cornelia's proctor responded with an Allegation of fourteen articles – an autobiographical account of events in legal language. On 9 May Fust asked for it to be reformed to include documentary proofs, that is, he challenged her proctor when Pierce's did not. On 19 June the reformed version was submitted, and an article was added describing the laws of Rome and the Catholic church, under which the separation granted had the full force of a judicial sentence. The documents included a mountain of incontrovertible evidence: Pierce's petition for separation to the pope (signed by Pierce and not by Cornelia); the pope's rescript which referred the matter for execution to the cardinal vicar who was Judge Ordinary in Rome; the Deed of Separation; Cornelia's vow of chastity, the record of Pierce's ordination, her religious vows. After five months it was heard before the court, on 13 November, and Fust then considered it for a further four months. The wheels of justice ground slowly.

All that time the Gorham case was simmering and when early in March 1850 the Judicial Committee of the Privy Council reversed Fust's judgment and upheld the Revd Gorham, the public pot boiled over. The reversal rejoiced many but high churchmen saw it as government interference in matters doctrinal, and in the coming months, as had been feared, many seceded to Rome. It was thus amidst fierce religious disagreement that the Protestant public now awaited Fust's judgment in Connelly v. Connelly.

Would England's highest ecclesiastical court uphold the sanctity of marriage and return the wife to the husband? Or would it condone Romish beliefs and allow a separation based on the twin evils of celibacy and religious life.

On 23 March Fust gave judgment. He side-stepped the human and religious issues and dealt with the case on a point of law. Even if 'Mrs Connelly's allegations were in every particular established by evidence' Roman law was not binding in England and the Roman decree was not equivalent to judicial separation in an English court:

> The Court must not look to the law of Rome, nor to the law of the United States of America, but to the law of England for the rights, obligations, and duties which proceeded from the relation of husband and wife . . . One obligation undoubtedly was the cohabitation of the parties. The law would not permit them voluntarily to separate themselves from each other. Separation could only be effected by a judicial sentence.

That Cornelia had made a vow of chastity made no difference. It 'might influence the feelings of the court but could not affect its judicial sentence'. Her Allegation was, in effect, ignored. Pierce's Libel was accepted. Apparently he had won, and Cornelia figured in the columns of the Protestant press as one who abhorred marriage, who had failed to 'love, cherish and obey' her husband and had deserted her children. Fust had given a popular judgment.

Immediately Cornelia's proctor put in an Appeal to the Privy Council. This protected her from what otherwise could have been the effect of the sentence – imprisonment or forcible return to her husband. Fifteen months passed before the case came up by which time the religious temperature of the country had flared into a national cry for 'no popery'.

In October 1850 there had arrived in England a papal brief for the information of Catholics. It announced that the Catholic hierarchy was restored in England and that Wiseman was now Cardinal Archbishop of the diocese of Westminster. The Protestant editor of *The Times* took violent exception to the pope's impertinence, and hard on the heels of his summons to the British public came Wiseman's pastoral from Rome, *From Out the Flaminian Gate*. It was read from the pulpits of his new archdiocese and inevitably reached Protestant ears and appeared in *The Times*. Its trumpeting language acted as petrol on the editor's fire, the rest of the press joined in, the Anglican bishops rushed into print and even the Prime Minister contributed. Wiseman, by his great courage and through his powerful pamphlet, *Appeal to the Reason and Good Feeling of the English People*, was able to moderate the violence of this situation somewhat. Nevertheless the ancient fires of fear and prejudice burned on. In February 1851 a bill was introduced in Parliament to deprive Catholic ecclesiastics of their right to title – in favour of which Pierce's patron, Henry Drummond, spoke. It got through its second reading by 433 to 95 votes. In March the time was nicely ripe for Drummond to introduce his private bill 'to prevent the forcible detention of females in religious houses', and on 30 April 1851 *The Times* also announced that he would be presenting a petition against nunneries by the Revd P. Connelly.

It was a year and a month since Cornelia had lost the case and then appealed, by no means a time of being forgotten behind convent walls. The busy routine of her religious life went its undisturbed way but the sisters were known as Wiseman's Nuns and at the gate when he came to stay there were demonstrations. Under her bed she kept clothes in readiness to escape if the Appeal, as expected, went against her – the notice in *The Times*, just when her Appeal was about to be heard, of Pierce's intended petition, could not have cheered her. Catholic MPs consulted their knowledgeable friends about how to deal with it. Newman replied to Baron Emly:

> You alone will know how to treat it in the House of Commons. As to the public, I suppose the Petition will do Titus Oates' work. The only way I can think of for meeting it, is to *damage Connelly*. I suppose that some of the facts of his Petition are simple *lies* – again, if it is fair and will tell, I suppose there is no doubt that he is a disappointed man.

Pierce's petition is a specious account of the Connelly marriage since their conversion, beginning with the declaration that it was only 'after holding out for many years' that he had at length allowed himself to be pressured into ordination. He misuses excerpts from notes of Cornelia's to prove oppression in convent life. He conveys that their separation in Rome was never meant to deprive him of dominion over his wife, and that Wiseman, dealing 'doubly and tyrannically' had come between him and his rights. He imputes sexual impropriety to his friend the chaplain (who has now returned to Italy), thereby making the convent the 'brothel' which he elsewhere styled it: Asperti he had seen, he said, 'Half dressed with a young nun apparently domesticated in the chamber', a libel which appeared with increasing mendacity in Connelly's pamphlets. The House of Commons Select Committee on Public Relations decided that 'in the circumstances of the day' and because the petition 'contained matter deemed grossly slanderous' it should be printed for members only. No doubt Pierce had hoped for publication (he published it later with 'improvements'). But he had fulfilled his threat to take his case to the House of Commons if he did not win.

The Appeal finally came up nearly two and a half years after Cornelia received the writ to appear in court. Physical fear during much of that time was a daily companion. As Bellasis tells, she dared not venture beyond the convent grounds or walk there alone for fear of being removed by force. She even had to take precautions if she went to meet visitors in the house. And in the midst of all this she wrote to her sister:

> I suppose you know that I know nothing about my dear children. I have several times sent letters to them & to Pierce which have been returned unopened. But an anonymous letter was sent saying he was advised to take a wife. If it could be without sin by his vows being dissolved I should be very glad, but could he ever be happy again? Do pray for him, dear Adie, and my poor little ones.

On 27 June 1851 four judges of the Judicial Committee at last met for the hearing. Her case (fully reported in *The Times*) was presented, as a matter of practical wisdom, by two non-Catholics, Dr Addams, who had represented her in the lower court, and Roundell Palmer, a devout Anglican, later to be Attorney-General and Lord Chancellor. These two men argued that Pierce was not entitled to restitution of conjugal rights because he and his wife had freely chosen separation, and the law of Rome which could not justly be denied, had ratified it. They believed Cornelia's Allegation should have been put to the proof (which would have led to a full trial by jury). Mrs Connelly would then 'be entitled to the answers of her husband on oath; there would therefore be no difficulty in proving her averments'.

They had no high opinion of Mr Connelly. Their written plea on Cornelia's behalf said that his 'whole conduct' towards her, if the Allegation was proved, 'ought to preclude him from obtaining the aid of an Ecclesiastical Court'. Addams trusted that their lordships 'would not enforce the prayer of such as Mr Connelly' and Selborne imputed cruelty to him:

> It would be most extraordinary if the Court Christian of England held that after a husband had led his wife to enter into the most solemn vows of chastity before Almighty God he could compel her to break those vows. That would be cruelty of the highest description, and the Court would not lend its aid to enforce it.

In other words Cornelia's counsel took fully into account the religious aspects of the case and invoked not only the law but the humanity of the court.

Pierce's on the other hand did not. They maintained Fust's legalistic stand, that Cornelia's Allegation was 'insufficient in law' to bar the restitution of conjugal rights; since the reign of Edward VI vows of chastity and rules of celibacy for clergy were not binding in Protestant England; and because Mr and Mrs Connelly were married according to the Anglican service they should 'never . . . depart from cohabitation during their natural lives'. Humanity was 'the second consideration of the Court, justice was the first'. The president of the Committee disagreed; the religious aspects of the case could not be disregarded and since the state tolerated the Roman Catholic religion then it must also tolerate all reasonable consequences.

Next day Pierce's proctor took up precisely that point. 'More especially at the present', he said, the demarcation between a tolerated and an established religion must be kept clear. What was 'contrary to the public policy of the State' could not be entertained and he reminded their lordships of the religious turmoil against which this case was being heard. They 'could not fail to perceive that this was probably the first of a series of cases arising out of the present disturbed state of religious parties in this country'. Their lordships should 'avoid all religious questions'.

Immediately upon this one of the judges, Dr Lushington, delivered without further discussion what must have been an overnight unanimous decision among them: her Allegation was to be admitted and her cause reconsidered in the lower court. To make the evidence complete, statements on the marriage law in Pennsylvania and on the Connelly domicile at the time of the separation should be added.

So far so good. The Privy Council had refused to be party to the injustice of the lower court and Cornelia's Allegation now had to be heard as her defence. But the judges also gave an indirect assurance that they believed her statements and that the law would vindicate her. A significant order was issued, that as a *pre-condition* for re-hearing in the Court of Arches, Pierce Connelly was to pay the costs *to date* of *both* parties, an order which could not have been made were he seen as likely to win his case. This action of the Privy Council, as Dr Hargrove has pointed out, was a way of saying that in their judgment, even with the additional statements Cornelia was required to make, Pierce could not succeed. Their order was a signal to the lawyers (though not to England at large) that the law was in Mrs Connelly's favour. Bowyer, the eminent writer on jurisprudence and a recent convert, who had worked with her preparing the Allegation, wrote, 'I sincerely congratulate you.'

Pierce's road was blocked. But he wanted to go on with the case. If he could win the law would leave him with custody of the children *and* indisputable rights over their property and any further estate that might come through Cornelia's line for them. That he had his eye on wife and children as a source of income we know from his letters to his brother-in-law. A legacy from the English side of Cornelia's family was due to be paid through Ralph in Texas. Pierce, presenting himself to his brother-in-law as one most evilly done by, was in anxious correspondence with him. In March 1851 he was hoping that Ralph would 'secure their mother's share to my children', and a month later he was trying to get him to authorise the lawyers in England to pay the children's share to himself as father. Whether this legacy ever came through, the documentation does not reveal.

When after the judgment he found himself unable to meet the costs he took up pamphlet writing against the Roman Catholic church, with the approval of Drummond, now his patron instead of Shrewsbury. It was a way of raising money and it kept him in the public eye. By 1853 he had attracted enough attention for a committee to be formed to raise money for the case to proceed, and an anti-Catholic association, the National Club, paid for the anonymous publication, *The Case of the Reverend Pierce Connelly*. So mendacious was it that Bowyer took up the cudgels on Cornelia's behalf in *The Times* (to no good effect). Her copy has survived. At the end of it she wrote:

> I am persuaded that Mr Connelly can never in heart cease to love the Holy Catholic Church but his love was always more a love of sentiment than of sacrifice & therefore less to be trusted. His feelings have been wounded & his love turned to hatred *for a time*. When the opposite party gradually let sink [*sic*] into nothingness we may then hope that his eyes will be opened & his heart touched.

Pierce's committee petered out and he was never able to pay. Cornelia eventually paid his costs too and on 24 June 1858 Connelly v. Connelly was dismissed. Then Pierce fell silent. Taking the children with him he left the country.

THE CHILDREN AND THEIR FATHER

On 28 March 1850 Pierce had written to Cornelia's brother on 'the sad state of things which the wretched religion that I sacrificed everything for, has brought us to'. It is an extraordinary letter, written either by a man of very great and clever malice and deliberately filled with what one can only call lying and persuasive misrepresentation; or by one pathologically subject to illusion, in whom paranoia has temporarily loosed his hold upon reality. Its sometimes pathetic plausibility suggests that Pierce believed what he was saying, at least at the moment of writing. He was desperate, he needed money and help. With the picture he painted of his plight and its causes, he set out to justify himself to Cornelia's dear Ralpho – the only member of her family who had not become a Catholic – and revealed the straits, perhaps with exaggeration, to which his actions had reduced the children too.

It was Nelie, he told Ralph – and only Ralph and 'dear Mary' were to know this – who had first proposed the separation. This untruth is the platform on which the rest of the letter and the two following are built. He 'carried out the thing once determined on' but 'never consented' to the kind

153

of separation which she was accepting in England. Nor had the (now dead) pope, he said. She was in the hands of 'diabolical possessors' who forced her to reject his letters and visits. That Nelie, at least twice since the scene in Derby convent, had told him letters and visits could be resumed if he brought back her little girl gets no mention. He was 'indignant' that she submitted to 'pretended holiness' and he had cut off communication between her and the children because he so wanted to 'bring her back to our old dear affectionate correspondence'. He had discovered 'a plan to get possession of Ady as well as of Nelie', and because Merty was at school in the hands of his 'bitter enemies' the Jesuits, Lord Shrewsbury and his confessor Dr Winter had agreed – which was not true – that he ought to remove them out of England into safety. He omits what he was doing in Rome for five months, and simply says that when he returned he dutifully went at once to the convent with a message and gift for her from the pope himself, in spite of which she still would not see him, at which he had indeed broken down and wept. On top of that had come from his 'poor blessed Nelie' such a letter that he almost thought it a forgery. Yet he had continued to submit until to his horror Wiseman, a 'mere devil of selfishness, sensuality and hypocrisy' had taken her off to his new diocese. Even then he only *'threatened'* a lawsuit. But that was 'laughed at' and he and the children were 'threatened with ruin'. Now, having had to go to law and having won his case, it was all going to be tried again 'at an awful expense' because 'these devils' had appealed, even though judgment was in his favour:

> All this dear Ralph has been a heavy trial, has thrown me out of all employment & brought me almost to beggary, but if . . . my children & I beg from door to door I shall never give up till I have delivered Nelie . . . my children, blessed be God, are all three with me in a furnished cottage lent me by Mr Drummond . . . What am I to do with Merty I cannot tell. *What could you do with & for him in Texas?* I ask you seriously?

By March 1851 his own brother has helped and Mercer has been packed off to New Orleans. But, 'What is to become of us God only knows. I have kept out of debt but am unable to educate my children or indeed do anything more than barely *live*, as you may suppose with £80 in England . . .' If Ralph could spare him £20 it would be a 'blessing to my poor little ones'. He was also, Cornelia said, using her dowry 'contrary to his promises'. There is no sign in any of the three letters to Ralph that he acknowledged any responsibility for the situation. It was not *his* demand for separation, *his* removal of the children and *his* lawsuit that had brought it about but Cornelia's wish to separate, Cornelia's 'cursed bondage' and Cornelia's Appeal. The latter he said was made 'apparently with a view to bringing us to beggary'. He may not have known of Cornelia's own financial straits at St Leonards but he described her conveniently as 'in affluence', and her share of the legacy then expected would be most opportune, he told Ralph, for the children, 'poor Adeline and Frank, both of whom I have at home without even the money to buy books necessary for their education'.

Merty, from the age of nine and a half until nearly eighteen, when he was sent to America, was the victim of his father's egotism. He had nine years of a happy family home in Natchez and Gracemere, the last two at day school with the Jesuits – who made no charge for his schooling. Then Pierce, in need of cover for going to Europe and desirous that his son should have the education of English nobility which Lord Shrewsbury had offered to pay for, uprooted the boy from home and country to dump him in a foreign school, Oscott, to hold his own. If we are to believe the surviving miniature of Merty, he was a slight, delicate lad.

Little more than a year later his father decided Oscott was not good enough and the boy was moved yet again. From 1842 to 1846, except for a brief time in the summer of 1843 of which no details have survived, the boy saw neither parent. They were not in the country and he had to cope alone with the insecurities of a very odd background: a dependant who had neither home nor family standing, nor money behind or prospects ahead, among boys who took all that for granted; a boy whose parents never visited and who were, of all things, priest and nun. Vacations at magnificent Alton Towers and a pony there all to himself was no compensation for circumstances of such consuming loneliness. When he began at Stonyhurst his grade for application was 'excellent'. By the time he left he was nearly bottom of the class. When the wonderful summer came at Spetchley (he was 'crazy with joy at the thought') and he again saw his mother and Ady and the baby brother, he was already fourteen, already an anxiety-ridden, very insecure adolescent whom Cornelia tried in vain to coax out of the useless day-dreaming which had taken over. When he had returned to school she often wrote about it – in her anxiety perhaps too often:

> The truth is dear Merty as I told you, while Henry Berkeley & the other boys are labouring hard at the foundations of their buildings like persons of good sense, you are building your Castles in the air that will never be realized in any other way than to bring upon you a few more ferrules [cane-strokes] before the end of the week. This will make you laugh perhaps but if you will only think of the ferrules that are in store it will give you the strength to overcome your imagination.

The subject cropped up continually.

Back at Stonyhurst he had some hope that he was not deserted after all for he treasured the letters he had from his mother and showed them with pride to one of his Jesuit teachers. For the twentieth century they smack

altogether too much of advice, virtue and piety. But she sent him news of
Ady and Frank and things he asked for too (drawing the line at the request
to hide money in a cocoa tin). What she could not do was visit. This was
his father's obligation but not even for the end-of-year programme, which
most parents attended and the boy hoped for, did Pierce come. Later he
was removed yet again, this time to be taken with Ady to the continent
without warning and with no chance to write to his mother. Some time in
1849 Lord Shrewsbury paid his return fare to England and he joined his
father and Ady and Frank in the cottage at Albury. Then in October 1850
he was shipped off to America, ill-prepared for life in his own very different
country or for any work or profession, and his 'kind uncle George' gave him
a home. As to correspondence, although Mercer wrote to his mother through
Pierce, the letters were not forwarded, and Cornelia's letters to her son were
returned.

Ady too suffered from her father's determinations. She had a good start
because for seven years she had the family life that her brother had and for
the next four was in the care of her mother while at school with the Sacred
Heart nuns. But when she came to England in 1846, having had to go away
during Cornelia's novitiate, Pierce then prevented her return to her mother
and took her instead with Merty to the continent. She too was then left to
herself, now aged thirteen, at a convent school in Nice. After fifteen months
the Drummonds paid for her journey back to England and she went to the
Albury cottage. Letters from Cornelia, to her as to the others, were for at
least some time returned unopened and it was many years before mother
and daughter met. Pierce's own letters to her (two have survived from the
Nice period) were written when she was thirteen or fourteen and treat her
as if she were seven.

From Albury onwards, for thirty-five years, her life was spent as his
companion, the fate then of many an unmarried daughter, but not all of
these had been torn from a mother who had intended that her daughter
should grow up able to decide her life for herself. George Connelly sent
Pierce money for her on some regular basis, and when she was twenty-five
she went to visit him in Philadelphia. A letter shows George's opinion of
her father's care for her:

My dear brother

I have come on to see Adie & I confess I am greatly disappointed. At
the age of 25 instead of a dignified lady like woman with some knowledge
of the world I find a gentle affectionate ignorant child with no practical
knowledge & if suddenly left alone in the world not so capable of taking
care of herself as an infant for she would expect everyone to befriend her
and be disappointed . . . I consider you have utterly sacrificed her to your

own selfish enjoyment of her company. I consider it absolutely necessary she should have the society of a sensible practical woman . . . Adie on her arrival had not decent or sufficient clothing. Indeed I may say hardly a family slave in any respectable family but would have a better supply. The money I send her was for this purpose & any other application of it till this neglect is remedied is wrong, to use no stronger term.

It was fortunate that later in life Cornelia's wealthy half-sister Isabella made Ady a major beneficiary in her will.

As to Frank, before he was born life was shadowed by the day when his father asked Cornelia, then pregnant, to agree to their separation. He seems to have been more robust than his brother and sister and was able, encouraged by his father, to carve a place for himself in the sun (he became a well-known sculptor). The separation threw him much sooner than it did the other two into the orbit of the father alone whose magnetism he evidently enjoyed without being overwhelmed by it. Of ordinary family life he knew little. After the first year of babyhood he lived with his mother in semi-conventual situations, at five went to the school for little boys in Hampstead, was fetched away by his father and lived at the Albury cottage for about four years. For the Catholic education which Prince Borghese had undertaken to provide for him with the Jesuits, a strictly Protestant one was substituted in 1852, six years at Marlborough College. During these, the impressionable years of eleven to seventeen, Albury Park was his home background; Pierce was writing pamphlets, and the son grew up a fervent anti-Catholic. The enduring strength of his devotion to his father and against Rome shows when many years later, both parents being dead, he answered Ady's letter that told him she was returning to the Catholic church. He tried to dissuade her: 'Think of your father's memory . . . Think that this step is a stain on his memory and a lie upon his life. Be resolute, show you are your father's child, say you have been deceived . . . fly, arrive here . . . Blacken not your name with this thing.' Until he was beyond youth and had outgrown his mother's influence he too was not allowed to see her, and her letters to him too were returned.

In 1855 Cornelia wrote of the children: 'It is now seven years since Mr Connelly has cruelly kept them away from me and thus alienated as far as possible their affection for me.' How often, one asks, during the years since she had agreed to the separation, had she remembered that her husband 'had promised me before he became a Priest that whatever he did in their regard should be subject to my consent'.

There is little documentation on which to draw but from time to time the children will reappear in this story.

Cornelia at this point, 1858, had another twenty-one years to live, Pierce twenty-five. No correspondence between husband and wife has survived, and their lives were more fully separated than either had ever dreamed. For the next ten years extremely little is known of Pierce's doings and whereabouts. But in 1868 Ady and Frank made their home with him in Florence where he had contrived to become rector of the American Episcopal church. His writings during the seventies reveal the old spirit somewhat quenched but still fixedly opposed to the Roman Catholic church and to the ecumenical approaches which he had once espoused. There is no evidence that he repented his broken promises to his still Catholic wife, and four years after Cornelia, he died an Episcopalian, a peaceful death with Ady at his side.[8] After 1858 Pierce's activities no longer impinged directly on Cornelia but his shadow was long and lay always across her life and will occasionally fall on the following pages.

Part II

1849–1879

Preface

During the St Leonards years, 1848–79, Cornelia's whole effort was to be God's good instrument for the planting of the Society, and it was the hidden life of community that supported her. All that now happens has to be seen against that background. That she and the sisters lived together, in a sense *with* the Holy Child, was what inspired them. A brief attempt to describe this is needed before going on.

For Cornelia, Jesus in his childhood was the humbled God, the *holy* child. He was not only the Word proceeding from the Father to take flesh and grow for nine months in Mary's womb, though that is mystery enough. She also looked back on him from the cross (his, but also her own); saw him destined to be the risen Christ (and herself with him); believing with the theology of the day that from the moment of his incarnation he was consciously united to God who was his Father, and that no shadow whatever darkened the love between them as he trod the hard human road (and on her own road with him she strove never to refuse love to love). She also saw the child as would a mother who knew well both the pain and the incomparable joy of giving birth. In him she thus found the fullness of both human and divine life, the inspiration for living and for giving.

She tells who the Holy Child is for her and the sisters in her preface to the Society's Rule: he was a suffering child; he was the revelation of the Father's mercy and love: one whose life was ordinary, hidden within him, loving, obedient; who showed those who live in his company how to grow as he grew, minister as he did.

In this spirit she and her community at St Leonards sought to live. This was what impregnated life in the convent – its horarium, its relationships, its schools, its prayer times; all jobs whether domestic or scholastic or administrative; welcoming visitors and visiting in the town; recreations, silence, gardening, writing letters, penance and laughter; in all things the apostolic desire to be 'like the Holy Child Jesus'; learning to know him intimately so that they might 'run with ardour' as he did, each becoming 'like' differently.

Cornelia accepted burdens and sufferings as did the humbled God who grew to be a man, but she also accepted with the Holy Child a simple, poor and hidden life, to be lived in a joyful, childlike spirit. The Society annalist who knew her well, shows us this: Cornelia with her little brown basket turning down the hems of cap boarders; dusting the front staircase; serving in the refectory 'with great charity & alacrity'; washing dishes; and when piles of linen had to be ironed making it fun by proposing races; at recreation she and the sisters:

> ... entering heart and soul into playing 'Crazy Jane's dead, how did she die?' ... Notwithstanding all her trials & the anxieties weighing constantly upon her, she retained her youthful spirit of enjoyment whatever pleasure came in her way ... Indeed her character was a wonderful mixture of greatness & simplicity ... Though occupied with such great enterprises she was amused & pleased with the least thing.

This ordinary, unpretentious, hidden life of the community was strength and consolation to her. She once described it for Bishop Grant: it was the Holy Child's family, it was in a humble way that they would become saints, their life was 'Quiet and active as Nazareth.' She was moved by God humbled as child and man. She aspired to make living one continuous act of love going step by step, and ready always – whatever the circumstances – to begin again.

9

Cornelia and Nicholas Wiseman

The little group which arrived from Derby late in the evening of 21 December 1848 were burdened and travel-weary. After sixteen hours *en route*, cluttered with boxes and bundles and blankets, they at last reached a small railway station on the Sussex coast. A cab took them up a steep road and deposited them in the dark at the door of their new home. Supper and beds were ready but one traveller wrote, 'as there were not enough bedsteads, some of us had to sleep on tables . . . or on the tops of sets of drawers'.

The town of St Leonards at that time was still very small and only recently accessible by rail. It had been laid out in 1828 as a high-class watering place for the wealthy and fashionable. The neat line of houses along the front looked out across the English Channel. The convent was on the crest of a hill facing south, its view unimpeded across fields, over cliffs and out to sea. The house was low, a two-storied L-shaped building sheltered by trees against the strong sea winds. Beside it was a half-built church. In front a shady terraced garden stretched downwards to the gate. Behind lay the sixteen-acre farm. This place was to be Cornelia's home for the thirty years until her death.

The Revd Mr Jones, the owner of All Souls, who had invited Cornelia there, lived in the west wing and the community had the east. He was an elderly gentleman. He carried a silver-topped cane and an ear trumpet and addressed the sisters as 'Dame'. He also had ever-changing plans in his head for development. When the community arrived the place was full of scaffolding and he was always tap-tapping his way round their part of the house and ordering the workmen to do something different. Mother Connelly and the sisters had been told the property was eventually to become theirs and were expecting a deed of conveyance to be signed any day. What with that and the unpredictable shifting of Mr Jones's ideas and the very cramped living quarters for the community, life could not have been easy.

In spite of these difficulties they settled down. A week later Bishop

Wiseman's arrival created what might be called an opening occasion. Now was the moment for another profession, the first since Mother Connelly's a year before. Seculars were invited and in full regalia he solemnly conducted the unfamiliar ceremony. Three sisters made their vows and three were clothed in the religious dress. It was all very impressive and encouraging and the presence in St Leonards of a Catholic religious community was publicly established. In the house a school for the poor was started at once and as soon as the sisters had fitted up their own temporary chapel the small mission congregation came for liturgy. Wiseman wished the convent to be a centre where Roman practices prevailed; and Cornelia, artistic, musical and courageous as well as Roman in her tastes, concurred, nothing loth. In spite of shocked warnings even processions on May Day and Corpus Christi became the yearly custom and the garden gates stood invitingly open.

During the first year and for some time longer Cornelia focused her energies on the formation of the youthful and slowly increasing community. Time was needed in their early years for reading and prayer if ministry was to be more than mere activity. Some who came were scarcely educated, which had to be remedied. She was also committed to preparing five for the CPSC as the nucleus of a teacher-training college in the not too distant future. All this, the latter with Emily Bowles' help and that of a lay teacher specially engaged, was afoot in the community. Mr Jones, anxious for more schools to begin at once, had to wait, and Newman, who hoped for novices to work for him in Birmingham, was reluctantly refused.

Meanwhile the community had barely enough to live on. Mr Jones had given them a home and allowed them the produce of farm and garden but nothing else. When they left Derby they had £30, a grant of £125 for two years from the CPSC, an annuity of some kind from a Miss Granville who had moved with them to St Leonards, and something from their two or three boarding pupils. There were also occasional donations and small church collections. The year's total might have been £400. With this they had to provide a stipend for Asperti, equipment for the Poor School (115 children) and chapel; furnishings as more space became available in the convent; and necessities for an increasing community many of whom brought little money with them. This lack of adequate income did not deter Cornelia but it certainly worried her – personally when the court case loomed before her, and for the community when she thought of the number of young women for whom she was now responsible. But somehow she held on. She saw to it that the pupils did not suffer and inspired the sisters to bear privations in the spirit of St Francis. A story survives from the early days of how once, taking her turn round the refectory with the serving dish, she said to each with a cheerful smile, 'Bones! Blessed be God.'

The chaplain in some way was another source of anxiety. According to Bellasis, Asperti had a 'gift for interference', an impression easily made by a zealous Italian who wanted to walk faster than the British ran and did not always judge well how far and hard to push. An example of this appeared very soon after the arrival of St Leonards. The community had come at Mr Jones's request to provide, specifically, 'education for females'. They were also living in cramped quarters. But early in 1849, with walls going up and coming down all round them, Asperti demanded a separate classroom and a dormitory for the local boys. Wiseman wanted it, he said. Asperti insisted and Cornelia had to manage a compromise: schoolroom space only. This kind of demand will have had repercussions in the community. Bellasis wrote that he 'interfered in the matter of Community Observance' and 'became the originator of discord'. The annalist says there was 'schism'. Exactly what happened we cannot be sure, but some climax was reached in January 1850 when Wiseman, on request, promptly removed him.

Asperti's departure will have lessened community tensions. But Cornelia in the light of her experience with him at Derby also had personal cause to sigh with relief. To have as chaplain one whose judgment she could no longer have trusted was hard. A more experienced director, hindsight suggests, would have paid greater attention to what the wife and mother had asked. Later Asperti became a Jesuit and a renowned spiritual director and was guide to the Comboni Fathers when they converted their association into a religious community. Mother Connelly when she died had founded a religious congregation and by many was loved and revered as a most holy woman. Out of such painful beginnings notable wisdom apparently grew. Their paths never crossed again.

MR JONES, 1850

In the matter of dismissing the chaplain Wiseman acted quickly in support of Cornelia. In another he failed to do so, with lasting consequences.

At about this time, January 1850, the long-developing crisis with Mr Jones came to a head. One of the facts that Cornelia probably did not know when she agreed to come to All Souls was that five religious communities had been temporary or prospective residents there before the Society arrived. The history of these predecessors shows that Mr Jones was not an easy man to work with, being both changeable and autocratic, something she had an early opportunity to find out. Jones went up to London leaving her and Asperti and Dr Duke, a leading layman, to settle between them the site for building a girls' Poor School. This they did to the satisfaction of all three, whereupon on his return Mr Jones would have none of it. Lengthy protests went from chaplain and layman to the bishop and the seeds for long future discord were sown.

Difficult incidents multiplied, not all with Mother Connelly. Jones was elderly, ailing and deaf. Adapting to strange ways was beyond him. He and Duke, a cantankerous, self-important man, never agreed; and Asperti was a constant source of outrage. 'These foreign priests,' the old English one wrote shortly before his death, 'there is something so *outré*, so extravagant in their statements of *practice*.' Affairs at All Souls, he said, were full of 'continual disappointments and vexations', and evidently disillusion had set in with Mother Connelly and the sixth community, for he added the old saying: 'There is no mischief but the devil and women must have a finger in the pie.' The annalist records what happened:

> The year 1850 began inauspiciously for the infant Society. The Reverend Mr Jones no longer treated Mother Foundress with the same confidence and kindness as at first. Deafness rendered him suspicious and he mistrusted her intentions. He became unkind and went so far as to forbid the use of the farm to the Sisters who, being very poor, suffered greatly through this, and at times were almost starving.

As Jones's mistrust deepened he began to speak of changing his will. Cornelia envisioned a denouement at All Souls like that at Derby, and for her foundation continuing insecurity. According to her understanding at the time, what was being threatened was the promised deed of conveyance. It had been with this as instrument that she had agreed to carry forward the Society's mission at All Souls.

According to the notes for the draft of this deed the property was to be assigned in trust for ever to the Society. They were to be the owners, with four sisters and Cornelia on the board of trustees, two priests and the local bishop ex officio. Had this plan been adopted all might have gone smoothly. It was what both Cornelia and Wiseman expected. They were in accord, she very willing to identify with his aspirations for the church and ready to use the property (which, after all, his efforts would have acquired for her) in accordance with their mutual hopes. But the deed was left on Jones's shelf. No evidence suggests that the bishop pressed for its completion once the community had settled in and it is more in keeping with his character that he did not. He tended not to carry through on the detail of projects.[1] Chosen friends or collaborators were all too often let down, and Mother Connelly joined an illustrious list of sufferers – Newman, Bishop Grant, Bishop Errington. Wiseman's failure to see to it that Jones did what had been agreed brought lasting detriment to the local church, and 'Mrs Connelly' became the central object of calumny, 'that bold woman.'

Twice this bishop had given Cornelia large assurances for the future which required a more exact fulfilment than he made, the one at Derby financial, the second at St Leonards legal. Now, with Jones threatening to withdraw what he had promised, she found herself yet again at an impasse. This time she called the community together and told them how uncertain the future was and that 'perhaps our Lord meant us to leave St Leonards and seek some other home'. Then she invited them to pray with her for nine days, asking our Lady of Sorrows to intercede for them in their temporal necessities. This began the Society's 'strong novena' for times of desperate need. All the sisters gathered in the community room on 14 February in front of a statue of Mary suitably draped in black as devotion then required. The statue was on a little altar decked with candles and white flowers, and they recited every day the seven mysteries of the Dolour Rosary and sang the Miserere and the Stabat Mater.

Mr Jones was seventy-two years old. He had just returned from his London house and, as far as the sisters knew, was 'in his usual health' when on 21 February 1850 chaplain and doctor were suddenly summoned from early morning mass. Mother Connelly and some of the community came from chapel and gathered round his bed. In the words of the annalist, 'the dying priest held out his hand & asked her to forgive all his unkindness, adding "All is yours; the Will is not changed; the old one is not destroyed".' And a few hours later the lawyer arrived, too late to execute a new one. Cornelia thought 'all is yours' meant that the deed of conveyance stood with legal force. But unbeknown to her Jones had told Wiseman that he was leaving everything to Shrewsbury and Wiseman would soon be acting on the supposition that *this* arrangement stood. In fact neither Cornelia nor Wiseman had the right end of the stick.

However stunned and hesitant to be grateful the community were at this solution to their problems it was as well for them that they did not know the Pandora's box of trouble which now yawned before them. During the month which followed, when the will was being frantically searched for, Cornelia herself must have been prey to mixed feelings: of shock; relief that they had a permanent home after all; hope that that was true; awe at such an answer to prayer; and then great anxiety when the bitter news came two days before she heard the will read, that Pierce had won his case against her. Eventually, if he won the Appeal also, this could destroy them.

Wiseman, however, was her friend and at this moment she knew no reason to fear that he would ever cease to be so. As soon as Jones died and before the will was found he assumed 'rights' over the property. He also assumed Cornelia's co-operation with his wishes in regard to it. He sent his secretary, Mgr Francis Searle, to 'look after everything for you', believing it was 'vested in Lord Shrewsbury . . . who will no doubt do what is right and be guided by my wishes'. Searle duly removed Jones's cash box and deed box to London. But neither contained the will. At this juncture Cornelia was going along with whatever Wiseman wanted. She agreed, for instance, that he should have for his own occasional use the part of the building he wanted and the library it housed. A separating wall would have to be built (about which she apparently wrote to him) and he tells her to treat the whole house pro tem as reserved for the sisters because 'the division can easily be made afterwards'.

Here a rather long aside is called for, on a curious aspect of Wiseman's expectations in this matter: that he so much as considered having a residence at Mrs Connelly's convent. He who was so protective of the Society as to keep Pierce at arm's distance from Derby and have the younger children sent away, was now oblivious to a scandal linking his own name with Cornelia's. Pierce had already made him the object of calumnious insinuations. He would repeat them in his petition to the House of Commons: 'The Roman Catholic Dignitary aforesaid [Wiseman] was removed by the Pope to a distant part of England . . . It was the said Dignitary's extraordinary purpose to . . . carry her [Cornelia] off with him to a place announced publicly as his future "Marine Residence".'

Until the will was found the question of Wiseman's residence was not an issue with Cornelia. What he asked had to be allowed and she was pleased to be able to show her gratitude to him by satisfying his need for a bolt hole. But later she raised the question of propriety and Wiseman ought to have realised that she was right. According to his vicar general he was a man 'utterly indifferent as to what Protestants thought or said of his conduct'.[2] In this case his determination to have his own way at St Leonards must have fed Pierce's motivations: personal jealousy, desire to keep the case going and get his wife back, and an increasing need somehow to tear down the Catholic church.

And the populace seized on the impropriety. Every year since 1605 when the plot to blow up the Houses of Parliament was attributed to Catholics, 5 November in England was by law a day of celebration. Sermons were preached from the nation's pulpits and year after year the conspirator Guy Fawkes was burnt in effigy at the stake. By the nineteenth century the occasion had lost much of its fanaticism but the law was not repealed until 1859, and anti-Catholicism sometimes burst into flame. In either 1851 or 1852 in London there was a procession through Chelsea carting guys to the bonfire, 'Mr and Mrs Wiseman', the latter clad in the religious dress of a Holy Child sister.

WISEMAN AND TOWNELEY, 1850

To return to the unfound will. From surviving documents the following picture emerges.

In 1846 or 1847 Jones told Lord Shrewsbury of his hopes for All Souls and that he planned to will the property to him. In November 1848, however, he wrote to the earl that 'under the sanction of Bishop Wiseman' All Souls was about to be consigned not to him after all but to Mrs Connelly. In May 1849, with no word to anyone, he changed his mind: the estate was willed to Colonel Charles Towneley, nephew of his chief benefactress. Then, six weeks before he died, he changed it again. The will was to be in favour of the earl after all and he told Wiseman so.

Cornelia believed the property was coming to the Society and Wiseman did not enlighten her. He was sure the earl would be 'guided by my wishes' and one of his expectations was that he would have a lifetime possession of the west wing and receive as a personal bequest the extensive library which Jones had collected there.

But the Shrewsbury will was never executed. In fact the lawyer who arrived at St Leonards on the day of Jones's death was probably summoned for the signing. What is more, the will in favour of Towneley made not the faintest reference to Cornelia or Wiseman, nor to any trust or how any of the property was to be used. It said: 'I give and bequeath all and every my estate and effects whatsoever and wheresoever . . . unto Charles Towneley . . . and I nominate him the sole executor and residuary legatee of this my will hereby revoking all former wills . . .' Towneley thus became the legal and absolute owner of All Souls. He could do what he liked with it.

Cornelia accepted this fact when she heard the will, and treated Towneley as the one who had the rights of decision over the property, the one with whom, if the Society was to stay, she must consult and without whose agreement she could not act. Not so Wiseman.

The will was sent at once to him on the day it was found, 22 March. On that day, before the public reading, he wrote to the colonel, 'you are sole executor . . . I know you will concur with me in carrying out . . . your good friend's intentions'. He makes no reference to the fact that Towneley was also sole legatee. If he was assuming that because he was a bishop this layman would automatically fall in with his wishes the hope was vain. Whatever he may have expected of Shrewsbury or Jones, in the colonel he was dealing with a very different personality who, though of a long-established wealthy Catholic family, a member of the CPSC and known for his benefactions for Catholic education, was not one to be merely used even by a bishop.

169

Towneley was a respected public figure, prominent in affairs of county and country: Member of Parliament, Justice of the Peace, High Sheriff of Lancashire. As such he was familiar with the law of the land, accustomed to administering justice and in this case he knew very well the background to Mr Jones's plans for All Souls because initially they had grown from the beneficence of his own family. Furthermore, before drawing up the will, Jones had written about them to him as his 'old and true friend'. His hopes, the old priest said, were now 'brought to a successful termination': Bishop Wiseman had presented him with a community which little by little would establish the training of teachers for Poor Schools, a boarding school, a school for 'the poor female children of the neighbourhood' and perhaps one for female orphans. Probably this was the letter he had in mind when he said on his death-bed, 'All is yours; the Will is not changed'. In it he made no mention of Wiseman's personal expectations. Nor, be it rememebered, did he refer in any way to the rights of the local congregation.

Towneley took his old friend's wishes seriously and thereby became for Mother Connelly a much-needed ally. In that male-dominated and ecclesiastical milieu it is doubtful whether, without Towneley's support, Cornelia and her Society would have survived at St Leonards.

FRIENDSHIP WAVERS, 1850

The colonel intended to establish a trust for the fulfilment of Mr Jones's wishes but was unable to get it settled until June 1852. In the intervening two years, years filled with the miseries of the Connelly case and its aftermath, Cornelia's hitherto good relationship with Wiseman began to deteriorate. He would live for another fifteen years and become one of those who worked against her in Rome. It is important to look now at the beginnings of this.

Emily (then a devoted supporter of Cornelia's) wrote to Newman a few months after the will had been read. They had wished to repay Wiseman's goodness to them by still allowing him the rooms which he continued to expect to be his, but, she said, 'we could not be unaware there was *no right* whatever'. When they offered him the *use* of the walled-off end of the house, they were told 'that it gave great displeasure & that Mr Searle had exclaimed "This is not the thing. We want the right here".' The cardinal himself had 'expressed sorrow at what he called our "Sticking up for rights, and an independent spirit".'

Bellasis too records an incident. The chaplain reported to Wiseman that Cornelia had refused to allow the preparations for his residence to proceed as he had ordered, and she was summoned to London to give an account of herself. What both writers reveal is Wiseman's displeasure that Mother Connelly takes a stand which is not his.

Of Wiseman's early relationship with Cornelia something can be surmised. When Rome had its sights trained on the 'big catch' Pierce had become, it was evidently *Mrs* Connelly whom the bishop noticed, the intelligent and charming convert whom he often met dining with the Shrewsburys. There is little doubt that it was Wiseman rather than the earl (though it was Shrewsbury who pulled the strings in Rome) who identified her as a possible educator: her work would help him promote the union between converts and 'old' Catholics, and the spiritual renewal, Roman style, which he so much desired for England. They had in common a Roman background, Roman friends and Roman aspirations, a natural source of mutual understanding and trust. Beneath the superabundance of confidence which all too often looked like arrogance, Wiseman seems to have been shy and oversensitive, a man destined by his own personality traits and his mistakes, or through the misjudgments and hostility of others, to be more and more isolated as his responsibilities hugely expanded. Visits to St Leonards in the early years, 1849–51, offered him the welcome and encouragement he needed. The unhappy Pierce, one suspects, sensed that the relationship had the potential of a creative friendship and let his jealousy imagine more.

Wiseman's life, however, suggests that one of his misfortunes was that he could not keep the friends he so needed. He was at his best with those dependent on him: the Oscott boys, London's poor, and probably the 'frail daughters of Eve' as he called nineteenth-century women. Cornelia herself he described as one 'given up to my care'. That she either could or would ever stand her ground against him was probably as inconceivable to him as it had been to her husband; and in his career there are other examples of his inability to imagine opposition from one who was a friend. Bishop Grant and Mgr Searle, his secretary, are cases in point, as Schiefen shows, and his adviser of later years, John Morris, wrote of him that his mind was such that 'there was no other side possible in his view except that which presented itself to him in the affairs that concerned him'.[3] Moreover, in the case of Cornelia, Wiseman's expectation (as both man and bishop) of dependence and submission was compounded by his awareness of her very real gratitude. He had provided a home for her Society and then given his support when Pierce's case for the restitution of conjugal rights came up. 'I will look after everything for you,' he wrote protectively when the arrival of the writ overwhelmed her, and she had responded with feeling. He had 'doubly bound' her, she said, 'by a tie of gratitude that must exist for ever, and this far deeper than my poor life on this earth can ever prove to you'. Nor was this the protestation of the moment's emotion. In the coming years of misunderstanding and eventually of hostility on his part, traces remain of efforts made by Cornelia to heal the breach.

APPARENT PEACE, 1850–1

Before the storm broke there was about a year of peace and progress. Wiseman was often at St Leonards with the community, receiving converts in their chapel, presiding at professions. He also granted an earnest request of Mother Connelly's. If the young Society was to continue to draw candidates to itself it needed not only a flourishing apostolate and a degree of temporal stability but also canonical recognition. This Wiseman now gave. Having 'examined the rules' on which Cornelia had been working, and 'being taught by experience the profit reaped by this Institute in the salvation of souls, to a very great degree', he gave his episcopal approbation. English law had recently declared that Mrs Connelly must return to her husband and although her Appeal was before the Privy Council it was public knowledge that this sword of Damocles dangled dangerously over her. Wiseman's episcopal approval was a necessary reassurance to the body of English Catholics and especially those whose daughters might wish to join her or whose children might attend her schools. It was also a reassurance for Cornelia that the Ignatian road according to which she herself walked was also meant for her Society, and in January 1851 she drew on her now approved, Jesuit-based Constitutions for her Epiphany letter to the Society. The bishop's document was formally drawn up on 1 June 1850, in Latin, illuminated, the whole in Wiseman's elegant hand and with his signature and episcopal seal attached.

In the same month the bishop first heard with gloom that he was likely to be made a cardinal and henceforth therefore would have to live in the Eternal City, as cardinals generally did in those far off days. It was from St Leonards that he departed for Rome on 16 August. There, six weeks later, he was named not only Cardinal but also Archbishop of Westminster, and on the very day of the consistory it was to Cornelia and her community that he sent his first blessing. Prospects had evidently been discussed between them and this letter must have confirmed for her that Wiseman would still be the Society's friend.

Rome, Sept. 30, 1850

Dear D[aughte]r in Christ
You have proved a better prophet than I believed as in the course of a few weeks, I hope with the Divine blessing to be once more in England. His Holiness has, in this day's Consistory, re-established the Hierarchy

172

in England, and put me, however unworthy, at its head; naming me at once Cardinal and Archbishop of Westminster. The old District is indeed divided, into two, Westminster & Southwark. But I retain the latter in administration, so that no change (at least at present & probably for a long time) will take place, so that you remain in the same position in my regard.

I must now claim additional prayers for my new and heavy responsibilities; so give you & all the Community (Dr Melia included [chaplain]) my first archiepiscopal blessing, I am ever

> Your affectionate Father in Christ
> N. Card. Wiseman.

Cardinal Patrizi has just sent me a note for you.

It was Patrizi by whom Pierce had been ordained. He and Wiseman had talked together about the case, 'this dreadful affair', believing there was little hope that the issue would be a 'happy one and favourable' to Cornelia. The note was an expression of his sympathy and esteem for her in such grave sorrow, and reached her at about the time when grief had been sharpened by the departure, with no chance to say goodbye, of Merty, now nearly eighteen years old, to New Orleans on 8 October 1850. In such sad circumstances the prospective return of Wiseman, a friend who knew all, was consolation.

During the month of October the new cardinal enjoyed celebrations in his honour in Rome, then proceeded north in leisurely style with continued acclaim. By 1 November he was in Vienna. With the end of his journey in sight and as yet knowing nothing of the uproar created in England by his pastoral *From Out the Flaminian Gate*, he wrote to Cornelia again, with commanding complacency:

> *Vienna, All Saints, 1850*
>
> My dear Child in Christ
> I hope, with God's blessing, which has wonderfully accompanied me throughout my journey, to reach England about the end of next week. I shall go at once by Reigate to St Leonards, & stay quietly with you a few days. As that stove in the bedroom is of no use, I should prefer occupying the room within; and please to have the chapel ready, upstairs. My blessing to all the Community and Fr Melia.
> > Your affectionate Father in Christ.
>
> Keep my *coming quite quiet*.

Two days later there was no question of having quiet at the convent or anywhere else. Wiseman had to hurry back and immediately face a

Protestant public enraged by the establishment of the hierarchy and by his own appointment at its head.

Yet Wiseman did not consider it imprudent to be seen at the convent. A quick note when he arrived in England put off his 'few days' indefinitely, but we hear of him managing to pay 'several friendly visits to St Leonards before Christmas'. And on 8 January 1851 he came officially as cardinal. Bellasis describes the scene in the chapel (it was small and must have been crammed): to the singing of the *Ecce Sacerdos* (certainly rehearsed to perfection by an insistent Cornelia), the figure in billowing scarlet passed up the aisle blessing every single person to right and left. Community and children pulled out all the stops that day – carpets and banners, gifts and odes. Mother Connelly herself was permitted to dedicate a book to him published later that month.[4] On its fly leaf there is the printed statement that by bringing religious communities into his diocese Wiseman had 'made the wilderness to bloom like the rose', and it was in all probability during this visit that the cardinal thought of having Holy Child sisters to run some Poor Schools for him in Westminster.

Gate Street was an area of extreme poverty where indeed few flowers bloomed, and when in a month's time the invitation came from the mission priest, Cornelia in agreeing to this for the Society knew that she was furthering Wiseman's hopes as well as those of her own heart and her own community. His charter letter to her at Derby had identified 'the most consoling of duties' as the Christian education of 'the lambs of Christ's flock, his dear poor children'. When he appealed to the angry nation for a fair hearing about his appointment, he wrote that 'the part of Westminster which alone I covet' was where 'unlit, unsewered labyrinths of slum' lay; where in nests of ignorance, wretchedness and cholera, 'a huge and countless population' swarmed, 'in great measure nominally at least, Catholic'.[5] Gate Street was a lane in one such area, Lincoln's Inn Fields. Here the CPSC had established schools for 'our own poor, street-sweeping, orange-selling, ragged and shoeless boys and girls'. On the evening before the little band of three sisters set off Cornelia spoke to the whole community about the missionary zeal of Francis Xavier and of her own joy that the Society's 'first mission, as she called it, was among the poor and with none of the conveniences or the beautiful surroundings of St Leonards'.

Gate Street set its mark on the spirit of Cornelia's Society and bears out what Bellasis later wrote:

> . . . it was always a joy and satisfaction to Mother Connelly to recall how the Society was founded in actual poverty; and in considering subsequent foundation of houses she looked upon working for the poor as the essential

first step to be taken to secure help from God in all other undertakings.

She went to settle them in at Gate Street and wrote back with her customary lighthearted, practical piety to the community at home:

My dear Children

One word only to say we are *69 steps high* and happy in the love of our poor and lowly Jesus.

I am in penance, having been out shopping all day and am writing this in the middle of our nice little iron four posts. You would be quite charmed with our attics. We shall have a Community room and a reception room with three large and one small cells, a kitchen and refectory below and a larder or pantry big enough for 20. You will have another parting, for Sr Stanislaus and Sister Martha may come on Saturday! But I feel quite sure you have wiped away all naughty tears 'in the *soulstrengthening* flame of love', loving in strength rather than in too much sweetness. Be *one*, in the Heart of our divine Spouse and He will bless us and do all things for us. Let us try to be great in Humility and little in ourselves.

Laus Deo et Mariae.

Yours in Christ,

C.

Characteristically she made light of privations. Other accounts speak of happiness in the midst of hardship but give more facts. 'For many years their breakfast, to be followed by a hard day's work in the Schools, consisted of bread & a little very poor butter or dripping, with a cup of weak tea or coffee, generally the latter as it was cheaper.' This small courageous beginning was the root of what became a flourishing apostolate among the poor in London, and it was the cardinal's invitation which initiated expansion, a historic moment for Cornelia and the sisters. Nor did he confine his interest to what concerned Westminster. By 1851 there were nine children as boarders in the St Leonards convent, the nucleus of a boarding school. Cornelia consulted him and the first prospectus of a Young Ladies' School (to use the nomenclature of the day) appeared 'Under the patronage of His Eminence Cardinal Wiseman'. There is no doubt that whatever went wrong between them he fully believed in Mother Connelly as an educator and continued in after years to welcome her sisters into his diocese and to speak well to Rome of their schools, though not of her or her community at St Leonards. He also planned for the survival of the Society as well as for her safety should the Privy Council judge against her, which according to Buckle everyone expected. However, on 28 June 1851 a three-line note arrived in haste: 'Dear Daughter in Christ, I have only just time to write to you, that the Privy Council has *reversed* the judgement of the lower court; so that at present all is safe.'

This was the last communication that we know of which Cornelia received from Wiseman as her local bishop. The apparently good relationship between them was already strained when on 6 July Thomas Grant, rector of the English College, was consecrated in Rome for Southwark, the new diocese south of the Thames. On 14 September he was installed in its cathedral (St George's in London, fifty miles away from St Leonards) and by then Wiseman's disapproval had broken over her head.

THE FIRST CRISIS, 1851

Before Mr Jones's death there had been confusing local rumours afloat, aggravated by the contradictory things he said and did in old age, as to his intentions in regard to the property of All Souls. The St Leonards mission congregation was too small to be very active (Cornelia in a statement to Rome put it at 250). Fashionable visitors and immigrants swelled it seasonally, but among its resident members the recent convert, Dr William Duke, saw himself as the mission builder, and had been prepared in earlier days to donate money towards a boys' school. Of this man Towneley wrote: 'Mr Jones to the day of his death had repeatedly declared to my family and his friends that his [Duke's] views were a gross misinterpretation of Mr Jones' wishes and intentions & that he [Duke] opposed and thwarted him in all his plans.' As soon as the will had been read Duke, true to this reputation, proceeded to inform the already informed colonel of what had been the old priest's intentions: 'Church, Schools and Cemetery would be secured to us, the Congregation . . . by the building at All Souls.'

The will came as a shock to Duke but also to Cornelia and Wiseman. Each of the three was now unexpectedly dependent on the goodwill of a stranger. Cornelia accepted the situation. Duke fought – being more ignorant than he realised. He was not aware of the closeness of the connections between Towneley and Jones, nor of the history of the family's interest in All Souls and the extent and purpose of its benefactions. Moreover, whatever hopes conversation with the variable Jones may have raised over the years, his estate proved to be less than was supposed and few could be met.

As to Wiseman, he ignored the legality of the will. He maintained, the annalist wrote, 'that as a priest Mr Jones was not entitled to will the property independently of ecclesiastical authority'. Accordingly he expected Towneley to bow to Roman church law as higher than English civil law. But Towneley did not. He contacted Mother Connelly and was frequently at All Souls, the unexpected proprietor and a layman discussing with her as convent incumbent how best to fulfil Jones's intentions. He was, he told the infuriated Duke, 'positively certain that Mr Jones meant his property to be considered *conventual property*' and as such he intended to treat it. Cornelia looked to him as owner for the decisions but the cardinal did not agree. He 'strongly espoused the cause of the congregation'.

There was a link between Duke and Wiseman, established long before the sisters came to St Leonards, and the question arises: why had Wiseman been so satisfied to have them there on the earlier terms agreed, namely community ownership of the property, when now he was so ready to oppose its development by Towneley on the community's behalf?

Talk of the division of the London District was already in the air when Cornelia and the community were first considering the invitation to St Leonards. 'The good Nuns,' Wiseman told Jones, 'fear they would be in one diocese and I in the other.' Probably there was some truth in this. The community was totally dependent on the goodwill of whoever was their bishop and at that date, 1848, Wiseman was their one security. He goes on: the community could get him named their ecclesiastical superior for life, he says, in which case he would take care not to clash with the local bishop; and if Jones – through a declaration to his executors (the earl, he then thought) – would allow him 'the use of that part of the house which you occupy . . . I could be there without exciting jealousy, and without usurpation'. He then protests '*I do not desire for myself either of these things to be done*'. But the old priest ignored or forgot these proposals and, as we have seen, Wiseman was by no means content when the will was read. At a guess he was possessive of Cornelia and her community. Also at a guess, he had always assumed, ultramontane that he was, that were All Souls to belong to the community everything would be decided as he wished through the obedience which Cornelia and the sisters would owe him as bishop, the relationship which in that letter to Jones he wanted to secure for life.

The opening scenes in what was going to be a very long struggle began on 15 May 1851 with a dispute about the boys' schoolroom (segregation being a *sine qua non*). The boys, on the insistence of Dr Melia the chaplain, almost certainly prompted by Wiseman, as Asperti had been, were using needed space in the convent. The new owner objected. Jones had meant his property to be used for the education of girls. He spoke to Melia and then wrote to Duke. He had directed Melia, he said, to inform the congregation that the boys' school could not remain permanently on the property and that they must build elsewhere. He would contribute something to the cost. With that the fat was in the fire and Duke's reams of protest began forthwith. The colonel's reply shows the kind of man he was, conscientious, not unreasonable, autocratic:

May 20th, 1851

My dear Sir

I have duly received your letter, and I assure you I duly appreciate your feeling as regards the Boys' Schools at All Souls, but there is this insuperable difficulty. *It is utterly impossible for me to build* Boys' Schools or a Priest's house as I have not a SINGLE SHILLING to build them with. Poor Mr Jones fretted away so much money that the funds left in my hands will scarcely finish the Convent and perhaps get the roof on to the Church. With what money remains, I mean to make the Convent, the girls' Schools and Infant School as efficient as possible; and this cannot be done without removing the Boys from the room they at present occupy, & therefore if a room can be hired for them at present at Hastings or elsewhere, I should not mind contributing from the building fund a small sum, say £7 or £8 per annum for 3 or 4 years as a temporary substitute. If this cannot be done, the best thing is to give up for the present, till the Congregation are able to re-establish them. But they cannot remain in the Convent, indeed, I am quite convinced that they *ought not to be there*. I am very sorry that there are not the means of supporting the Boys' Schools, but that being the case, we cannot help it.

Pray excuse this hurried note.

After this the cardinal visited St Leonards 'much displeased' and Emily gives Newman a vivid picture of the kind of impossible situation in which Cornelia found herself: 'Dr Melia was exceedingly angry that Reverend Mother had *spoken at all* to Mr Towneley, and called it "taking counsel of lay persons".'

Difficulties increased. The cardinal began to talk about 'suppressing the Community and dispersing the members among other convents'. Early in August he sent another Italian priest, a friend of Melia's, down to St Leonards to give a retreat to the professed sisters. He was to induce them to adopt Wiseman's point of view about the property and its uses. Melia himself 'endeavoured to persuade the religious to put themselves unreservedly with the property into the hands of the Cardinal', and advised them, 'to quit the Society should opposition to the cardinal continue'. This is all reported by Buckle who was one of the professed. Finally Wiseman himself came down on Sunday, 17 August, and having preached on the pharisee and the publican, no doubt rubbing in for Cornelia's benefit the baseness of pride and ingratitude, departed ominously without another word. No longer bishop of the diocese he could do no more – except from behind the scenes. Duke remained on the front line.

We have no word of how Cornelia felt about the cardinal's so publicly expressed disapproval. The issue for her was, What authority in regard to the property was she to acknowledge? Buckle was sorry that she had 'not put herself entirely . . . in the hands of the Cardinal and let him act as he pleased'. But Bellasis tells us that for Cornelia (underlining added), 'it was a case of justice or injustice to the Order and not a personal matter. Before deciding on her course of action she had well reflected, prayed long and fervently, *and taken competent legal and ecclesiastical advice.*' Cornelia was a realistic woman, not given to hasty decision. She must have been well aware that to take this stand was to invite Wiseman's powerful opposition. Nor will she have wished to offend one who had been so good to her. But it could not be ignored that Towneley was owner, and an owner in no way disposed to let even a cardinal tell him what to do with his lawful property. To oppose him would be to deny his rights. It would also court trouble at least as serious as any Wiseman might cause. Towneley could legally turn the community out. It cannot have escaped her thinking as she surveyed the whole subject that in England the law was more effectively operative than the power of the church. In an anti-Catholic country under Protestant government in Protestant courts she herself had barely escaped being returned to her husband like so much baggage. Nor will George Bowyer, her convert friend and legal adviser during the case, have failed to point out how precarious was the legal status of religious communities and therefore of the Society. Men like Drummond and her husband were taking advantage of this when they pressed in Parliament for the inspection of nunneries.

The colonel was unmoved by Wiseman's disapproval of the community's attitude. He asked Melia yet again, pleasantly enough, to remove the boys from the convent. The chaplain sent a three-line reply: 'in such an important matter . . . I must consult my Ecclesiastical Superiors', whereupon in the manner of one who knew very well that in law his ownership was absolute, the autocrat and Justice of the Peace answered:

September 14/51

My dear Sir

I see that you mistake the nature of my demand. The All Souls property is my present property & the Community and School are only in the convent by my permission.

The Cardinal himself could not come there without my leave. I therefore must insist upon your dismissing the [boys'] School without further delay.

Though I have the sincerest regard and esteem for your ecclesiastical Superiors I cannot and *will not* allow them to interfere with my temporal rights and private property, & I don't believe they would think of doing so and therefore I repeat my positive order to you not to allow the School to be carried on within the walls of the Convent any longer.

Yours very truly.

179

A battle which would last for another thirteen years lay ahead, gradually spreading like a slick of oil and eventually reaching Rome. All the people concerned – Wiseman, Grant and Cornelia; Duke and Towneley; chaplains and mission priests – desired the good of the local church and would have claimed this as their motivation. Cornelia herself was caught between two fires: on the one hand wrongly supposed to have an influence over Towneley that amounted to authority over the property but was not; on the other subject to Towneley's decisions when she turned to him; nor if he refused, as he sometimes had to, could she always as an alternative provide from the Society's private but meagre pocket. Given the terms of the will, compromise in a spirit of collaboration was the only way ahead for all and it was the chaplain who was best placed to promote this.

DR PIUS MELIA, 1850–3

Asperti's successor, introduced by Wiseman, first came to the convent at Easter 1850 to give a retreat. Melia was an Italian Jesuit, professor of missiology at the Collegio Romano. Like many Jesuits he was forced by the revolution of 1848 to leave his country, and Wiseman invited him to London to minister to the Italian residents. In particular he served the immigrants of the poverty-stricken district of Lincoln's Inn Fields where his brother, a Pallotine priest, already worked.

In England he proceeded to lead a life increasingly independent of the Society of Jesus to which he belonged, disregarding the superior of the English province and ignoring the superior-general's request not to undertake financial responsibility for building a new London church. There was also at St Leonards rumour of scandal with a rich young widow. This all coincided with his time as convent chaplain. By the end of 1853 he had left there and also, by his own choice he said, was no longer a Jesuit. The only authority he acknowledged by then was that of the cardinal. Significantly for Cornelia's history, when Melia first came to England Wiseman had appointed him his personal confessor, a relationship which presumes trust and intimacy if it is to last. Melia retained this office until the cardinal died.

At St Leonards he made so good a first impression that he was prevailed upon to prolong his stay somewhat. In spite of broken English and a sometimes hilarious vocabulary, such as it being necessary 'to plaster the Congregation', and a little habit he had of jangling the front door-bell continuously until the scurrying sister let him in, the community liked him. They benefited from his clear, theologically-based conferences and from the weekly instructions he gave on the *Spiritual Exercises*. His musical gifts enhanced the liturgy and he was able to help Cornelia herself bring the

Constitutions more fully into conformity with those of Ignatius. Three months appear to have passed harmoniously. Cornelia had always wanted a Jesuit for the community and, Wiseman concurring, she obtained permission from the Jesuit general for Melia to remain on a permanent basis.

This was July 1850. Melia was in a key position to mediate peace in the difficulties that arose in the ensuing year. As convent chaplain he was in direct daily contact with Mother Connelly, and beyond her was the powerful Towneley. As mission priest he was in direct contact with Duke, beyond whom stood the powerful cardinal. But as we have seen he allied himself very positively, as might be expected, with Wiseman's point of view – and also with Duke's. Not long after Wiseman's dramatic disapproval of the community that Sunday in August, the doctor, Duke, enraged about the boys' school, threatened to protest Jones's will in Chancery. This, the colonel said, would injure the community and jeopardise the property, and he appealed earnestly to Melia not 'to join this man [Duke] in his attack upon the nuns. Surely you should be their protector & not their assailant?' The threat faded away but the appeal was ignored: Duke and Melia stood against Towneley as one man.

By then Cornelia knew that she was herself the object of hostility. In October she wrote to her new bishop, Thomas Grant (who had not yet visited the convent), urging him to induce Towneley to give the congregation what Duke and Melia were demanding: access to the church always, and land for the boys' school and burial ground. Then she continues on a personal note:

> There is one matter I have not hitherto alluded to. It is this. I think it necessary that I should leave this place for a time and I may do so quite quietly without loss to the Community. I do not allude to the wretched trial brought before the courts, but to the peculiar position we are now in. . .

and she thinks she will go to London, to work 'in the Poor Schools, and thus some good may grow out of much past evil'.

An important element in the 'peculiar position' created by the will was the relationship between Mother Connelly and Melia. The chaplain was Wiseman's watchdog, so to speak, at St Leonards and a December letter to Grant written not long after the bishop's first visit shows how he mistrusts her.

> Since your visit the private affairs of the nuns as far as can be seen are going much better. It seems that the *Reverend Mother* understands clearly that she had put herself in a false position and that she really wishes to put herself in [illegible]. But we must see what happens before believing in words alone: especially when the words also are not absolutely right.

A year later, asking Grant to give 'Dr Duke and me' authorisations as to the use of the convent chapel, Reverend Mother had been downgraded to the 'lady of the convent'. In July 1853 a serious note is sounded. Grant is considering the removal of Melia, and she writes: 'I want you to know how thoroughly every tie of child-like & prudent friendship is broken and rooted up for ever with Dr Melia. I do not speak of any want of Charity but of the impossibility of confidences', and adds a postscript: 'Please do not forget my dear lord that Dr Melia is not only not under the Provincial [of the Jesuits] but that he is only under the cardinal.'

The situation apparently became so impossible that Grant asked George Bampton SJ to visit All Souls to consider whether Melia should be asked to go. Bampton was 'much pleased with the religious bearing and discipline of the Convent, and I see nothing but what must be consoling and edifying to Your Lordship'. But he thought the differences between the chaplain and Cornelia too acute to be done away with by any regulation the bishop might lay down – 'the feelings of aversion are so strong, and the past associations such, that the covered wound would soon be opened'.

What had brought about this state of affairs, one can only guess. 'Aversion' is a strong word. So is 'wound'. Reports of an amorous intrigue (which Bampton in the same letter reported to Bishop Grant) were reaching the community. Did Cornelia confront Melia with the gossip? Was her own situation flung back in her face? Something of the kind would account for the malevolence with which – as will be seen – Melia pursued her. Whatever it was that made Cornelia his enemy, his placement with the cardinal made it dangerous.

In the same month, August, a pamphlet, *The Case of the Reverend Pierce Connelly*, burst upon the public, and the Connellys again became the subject of newspaper columns and dinner-table gossip. Both Duke and Melia seized the opportunity to try to oust Cornelia from the convent. The doctor (who was also corresponding with the cardinal) wrote to Grant. Sing, Asperti and Jones, he said, had all found her out:

> . . . and now that Dr Melia sees her character she has not ceased the *last year* to try to exasperate him and drive him away. And such is the position we are to be in. Whatever she may be in other respects, she is a very artful and untruthful woman. How far such a person is fit for such a situation as she holds is not for me to say.

Melia took a different tack. Pierce Connelly had publicly renewed his charges of immorality against Asperti (no longer in England) and the convent. The pamphlet claimed that there had been placed over Cornelia as confessor 'an individual known to be most unfit for such an office to any female of character or decency'. Connelly, it said, had been forced 'to leave his wife exposed to those priestly arts of seduction, which, he declares, she had herself avowed to him have ere now been tried upon her'. Melia, himself rumoured to be conducting an intrigue with a woman, was prompted by these falsehoods to demand testimonial letters from the bishop lest he be confused with Asperti. Having said that his own departure was due solely to Mrs Connelly's treatment of him (of which Duke 'knew all the facts from beginning to end'), he concludes with threat and innuendo:

> My Lord, I do not know what would happen if some day or other I should find myself called upon to make known some facts with which I am acquainted in order to preserve my honour. It is true that you have not asked my opinion in any way upon this bad business of the Connellys, but I feel it right (having already some little experience of the consequences) to suggest that some decided measure should be taken about Mrs Connelly.

One man, however, came to Cornelia's defence. Bellasis tells us that Sir George Bowyer, as he later became, was 'a constant and faithful friend' to Mother Connelly. He was one of the little group of just-minded redoubtable men, mostly lawyers, all Catholic, some of them converts, as was Bowyer, who defended her reputation, gave her sound advice and maintained friendship with her. Bowyer was a Justice of the Peace, a Member of Parliament and a well-known barrister, a man of considerable standing respected alike by Catholics and Protestants. He had come to know Cornelia in preparing her Appeal to the Privy Council and had been present at the hearings. When the *Case of the Reverend Pierce Connelly* was published, *The Times*, at Bowyer's request, printed his correspondence with the Duke of Manchester, patron of Pierce's money-raising committee. This was an attempt, agreed to by Cornelia, to clear her good name and that of the convent.

A second edition of the *Case* came out in October 1853, just after Melia left St Leonards to live in London. This issue included Bowyer's letters and her husband's personal answer. Cornelia had a copy and we can imagine her sitting at the small writing desk in her room in the convent, by the window looking west across the sea. To make his points Pierce had used long-forgotten notes of hers, taking them out of context, and as she read she must have realised the futility of public denial even in the hands of Bowyer; it merely fanned the fire. But her private denials lie scattered over the margins of the pamphlet where she wrote[6] as she read. Pierce's declaration that it was she who had told him of 'priestly arts of seduction' practised on her in the convent had now become a claim that she had never denied it. In her clear slightly spiky handwriting there appears beside this: 'I positively deny that I ever charged any Priest, Confessor or otherwise with making such attempts. C.' When the *Herald* described the effect upon 'Mrs Connelly' of the Roman convent system as 'the gradual drying up of the natural affections; the cold-blooded, deliberate severance of nature's holiest ties', her pain and the Christian courage with which she bore it illuminate the page: 'The affections do not so easily *dry up* but they may mount up to Him alone who is capable of filling the heart.'

Such brief scribbles as these on the pamphlet are rare windows into her state of mind at this unhappy time, for while others generously vilified her in print she seldom committed feelings to paper, and even less often defended herself. She once wrote to a sister advice certainly grounded on her own experience of 'turmoil within' on occasions such as this, when what she identifies as 'wounded sentiments' were courageously put aside by her desire to love truly:

> It is in suffering & especially the suffering of the heart that Charity takes root, but it requires always the soul of humility to nourish it. Try to make a good heart . . . 'Sursum Corda'. If you can remember to offer all the turmoil within *at the time* as an act of burning love, & tell our Lord that you *will* to turn it into love . . . instead of the burning of wounded sentiments – if you really *do* try this *at the time, I promise you* that He will quite *fill your heart with love*, & give you with this love, the fortitude & *strength* to keep yourself in His holy peace.

Pierce's *Case*, source of so much intense private suffering to his wife, was a windfall to those who wanted her departure, Melia and Duke. She was shoehorned out of convent and country by a request from Rome in October 1853, engineered, as we shall see, by her bishop and Wiseman. The letter which Bowyer wrote six months after Melia returned to live in London presents him as her bitter enemy with the cardinal and as the one who worked for her removal. Bowyer, a lawyer, speaks of his 'certain knowledge' of the sentiments of both chaplain and cardinal. The latter, at least during his earlier years in office, called on Bowyer for legal advice. Melia had apparently sought him out in order to level scandalous charges about what went on in the convent:

The Temple, 13 March [1854]

Dear Reverend Mother

I have a letter from Monsr. Talbot stating that serious complaints have been made against the conduct[7] of Dr Pio Melia. I have taken the opportunity of saying that he has injured you with the Cardinal, and that he formerly injured you with me, and that I am convinced of the utter groundlessness of all that he has said against you. I have referred him to Lady Georgiana Fullerton for the high character of your school, & stated what I know of the respect & esteem in which you and your community are held among all classes at Hastings. I also mentioned the high commendations bestowed on your school by the Government Inspector; and the high terms in which several protestant friends of mine have spoken to me of your convent, which they visited & heard of during their stay at Hastings. I have said that for the last two years Dr Pio Melia had to my certain knowledge been trying to have you removed from St Leonards, & that the Cardinal's feeling against you (which I have heard him express) is all derived from the conduct of Dr P.M. while at St Leonards. If so you should tell the whole truth. Nothing else can open the eyes of the Cardinal and make him see how much he has been misled about you.

I have said nothing of certain particular charges which Dr Melia made to me against you, for no one could believe them. I refer to matters of the house, which if true would show an utter disregard of decency. I never believed them myself, & indeed they first began to open my eyes as to the real character of the man. But I have said that to my certain knowledge he has been a bitter enemy of yours, with the Cardinal especially. I took great care not to give any idea that I had been in communication with you.

I trust that this will be a favourable turn in your affairs, & that it will show how ill-used you have been, by unmasking your principal enemy. Dr Duke is still entirely under the influence of Dr Pio Melia. He wrote a letter a few months ago which I did not condescend to answer, in which he warned me against you.

Pray let me hear from you & rely upon my friendship and secrecy. Believe me . . .

After this letter Melia's name disappears from the documentation, but his friend Duke was still at St Leonards, and Melia remained in London, well placed to influence the cardinal.

TOWNELEY'S TRUST, 1852

If Melia's hostility to Cornelia and the convent developed from something highly personal, his friend Duke's certainly arose out of Towneley's decisions about the use of the property. Duke's own ambitions for 'chapel, schools & house' belonging to the congregation had been thwarted by Jones when he was still alive. Now the doctor posed as the one person who really knew Jones's intentions, and, supported by the cardinal, he refused to accept that the finality of the old priest's bequest as well as its wealth devolved upon the new owner. His opposition to the colonel grew to include Cornelia, the beneficiary on the spot of Towneley's decisions, and gradually she had to bear the brunt of what later turned into a full 'attack upon the nuns'. Even when a trust was set up that allowed generously for the congregation Duke did not give up, though until 1859 he created only local difficulty. In the end he convinced himself that criminal injustice had been done: that the St Leonard's mission and the diocese of Southwark had been cheated of what it should have inherited because Mother Connelly, with the tacit agreement of Colonel Towneley, had deprived them of the benefits of the All Souls property.

Towneley's Trust, enacted June 1852, was the springboard for misunderstandings and scandal for years ahead. In the background Wiseman played his part. Eventually not only Cornelia, Towneley and Duke on the local scene were involved but also four of the English bishops plus the cardinal, the Propaganda Fide in Rome and the pope himself. The whole affair is closely examined in the *Positio*, but here only detail that highlights the consequences for Mother Connelly has its place. Her problem was how to act justly in the face of mounting injustice and how to preserve her Society. At this juncture some facts about the Trust itself will be useful.

The Trust was the colonel's effort to meet his old friend's wishes. He had to find, he said, 'the *safest* mode of settling the property for the objects of an Educational Religious Community'.

In the politico-religious climate of the day this was not easy. All too many Catholic trusts, having been made in penal times, had not been drawn up according to the civil law of the land. Some were based on wills that were invalid because a bequest was to be applied for what the law of 1852 still called 'superstitious practice', prayers and masses for the dead. In 1853 the first Charitable Trusts Act became law by which all trusts would be registered and examined by government commissioners.[8] The Catholics because of the complexity of their position were not included until 1861, but Towneley as a Member of Parliament probably knew that the 1853 Act was afoot and struggled accordingly to make his Trust as legally foolproof as possible.

Nor was contemporary anti-Catholic feeling, with which Pierce Connelly was so fully identified, advantageous to an undertaking by a women's religious community. The beginnings of even Anglican sisterhoods were made hard in the fifties by the English fear that nuns and monks were a mark of popery.[9] Drummond's bill of March 1851, when Jones's intentions were already Towneley's concern, wanted the registration of Catholic convents. He proposed twice-yearly visitation by Justices who would be bound to see every nun privately and be empowered, if she so wished, to remove her without further inquiry. In the same year Connelly's pamphlets[10] began to appear and such pamphlets did not rest unread on bookstalls. When Towneley's Trust was nearing settlement one Hobart Seymour was earnestly gathering the ladies of Bath together and in April 1852 lectured them about the goings-on in nunneries. He was not content with warning the ladies only. In June he followed up the meeting with one for 1500 gentlemen, mostly clergy, to whom he quoted lengthily from Pierce's *Reasons for Abjuring*, on the subject of a young lady 'seduced into the convent [at Derby] under false pretences' and 'kept there in spite of every effort of her family'. The assembly was so impressed that it passed a resolution in favour of the visitation of nunneries, just as Drummond's bill had proposed. Reflecting the popular belief that convents were full of ill-gotten wealth, they also stipulated 'that all assignments of property to such institutions, by any person who may become the inmate of a nunnery, should be rendered void'. Meanwhile, with Drummond's bill in the public mind, *Punch* carried a cartoon: 'The Kidnapper: A Case for the Police'. It showed an innocent little child-heiress clutching a fat money bag. She was being enticed at the convent door to exchange it for the veil which a leering friar dangled before her.[11]

In this atmosphere, which Towneley had to take into account, Jones's intention of promoting education for Catholic girls through a religious community could be most safely achieved, he thought, if the community itself was given neither possession nor authority. He saw to it that Mother Connelly knew nothing about the terms of the Trust when they were still under discussion; he put aside Jones's idea that sisters should be on the board of trustees; and the property was to be used for what was acceptable in civil law, namely education. He went to great lengths to be sure that his Trust would thus be regular before the law. He sought much legal advice, including that of the future Lord Chancellor, to make sure that his own power was absolute; and with his two friends Henry Stonor, a future judge, and George Bowyer, the cardinal's lawyer, he settled the form the Trust should take. In January 1852 he wrote to Grant, 'I am advised that I am absolutely entitled to this property for my own use and can dispose of it in any manner I think proper.'

Then he proceeded to describe the terms of the Trust for Grant's consideration and asked him to be the one ex officio trustee. The property was to be conveyed not to the community but to seven trustees for the education of female Catholic children and the sisters were to be the administrators for the pupils. This gave the community no ownership but it guaranteed them a base from which to operate as long as they wanted it and which they could improve if they wished to and had the means. The trustees were to be the local bishop, one other priest and five lay persons. They were trustees not on behalf of the community, nor on behalf of Jones, but of the proprietor Charles Towneley who gave them by law the responsibility of seeing to it that All Souls was used only for education. Grant was consulted fully before these matters were settled and possessed a copy of the Trust. Later he acted as if he had not realised what he was a trustee of, in particular that he was trustee for Towneley, not Jones.

The small congregation was going to do well from the benefits which the Trust conferred on them (at the earnest request of the sisters, Towneley said): use of the community chapel until Jones's church was completed; land given for presbytery, cemetery and boys' school; all collections and bench rates to go to their priest, not the convent chaplain. Even Wiseman should have felt faintly gratified: the divinity portion of Jones's library about which he had made so much fuss on his own behalf (and of which Grant did not think much), was to go to the new presbytery when it was ready and where on any future visits he would stay.

Twelve years later, indignant at Duke's false charges to the Holy See (at their height in February 1864), Towneley would complain that the Propaganda was treating 'the Community and me as if we had frustrated the intentions of my Aunt and Mr Jones in favour of the Community, whereas I had in fact departed from these intentions to the detriment of the Community and for the benefit of the Congregation.'

Before the Trust was signed Grant pressed for one important alteration, the inclusion of a clause about Jones's church. There it stood, fifty yards inside the convent gates, its walls about eighteen feet high and ivy beginning to climb over them. Towneley wished it to be known as the convent church from the beginning, he would complete it for the community when money allowed and the public would be allowed access always. The bishop's proposal gave the congregation priority. Duke had already agitated to him that the colonel meant 'to deprive the Mission' of church and schools, and probably the cardinal too had stirred the waters. What Grant wanted was for the unfinished church, as well as the community's temporary chapel, to be declared a public place of worship at once. He proposed a ten-year term for dual occupation of the chapel during which time the Jones church was to be completed. At that point the chapel would revert to the private use of the sisters, the implication being that the church would never revert to the community unless it was not completed within the agreed period.

Towneley later aserted that Grant undertook to finish the Jones church and he may well have intended to do so. But Wiseman's refusal to share justly with Southwark the resources of what had been the old London District must have destroyed many of his hopes, among them conceivably this one. Towneley was reluctant to agree to the clause, believing that it would lead to inevitable dissension, in which he was right, but in the end he accepted it against his better judgment. Grant agreed to be the ex officio trustee and signed the deed. Cornelia was kept in ignorance of the terms. And the failure to finish the Jones church became the chief weapon in Duke's armoury when he made his first appeal to Rome seven years later.

Wiseman, throughout the affair informed by Duke, supported the cause of the congregation against the convent. And against Mother Connelly.

CORNELIA'S PERSONAL TROUBLES, 1851–2

Cornelia's deepest sorrows are easily overlooked in this welter of less personal trouble. When the Privy Council refused to accept Fust's rejection of her Allegation against Pierce's Libel and returned the case to the lower court, one great fear fell from her. George Bowyer wrote reassuringly that there was no need 'to be uneasy as to the ultimate result'. In other words the law was not going to force her to return to Pierce. In spite of the lightening of spirit which this must have engendered, and the rejoicing in community because she need not flee the country after all, a substrata of pain remained. During the next nine months a few documents recall this with some vividness.

It is now that she tells her sister Adeline that she knows nothing as to the whereabouts of her children and that her letters to them are returned unopened. And anonymous letters were to become part of her life. One of them, Towneley later told her, 'my cowman would be ashamed to write'.

Meanwhile her brother Ralpho 'has never written to me once since my troubles began and I do not know why'. She was isolated from the family, but brother, husband and son were corresponding. Mercer was grateful to his uncle Ralph for 'kind offers to Papa on account of me' and wrote:

> I had a letter the other day from Papa in which he tells me of his having been to see the Great Exhibition with Ady & Frank & that they had enjoyed themselves very much; he gives some unpleasant news from Mama. I suppose you heard that Papa's case came on before The Judicial Committee of the Privy Council June the 28. I send you the *Times* Newspaper in which it is all contained, & which I do not doubt you would like to see.

As to the kind of letter Pierce was writing to his son one hint in November 1851 has survived. Only Buckle's meagre summary is extant but it shows enough to make plain by what means the father sought to divide son from mother:

> From Albury Heath, November 24th, 1851 Pierce Connelly writes to Merty that he was pleased with the letter he had written to his poor Mother but that he thought it best not to send it. His own letter to his son is in terms too gross to be repeated here. He talks as if he were out of his right mind and says he will pray for Mother Connelly 'as one given

up to the devil' ... He thanks God for being delivered from that 'cursed Church of Rome'. In the same letter he talks of the devotion of Ady and Frank to himself.

The kind of thing, presumably, which was 'too gross' for Buckle to repeat was published by Pierce and probably read by his wife only a month later in *Reasons for Abjuring*. Here appears for the first time, as the climax of a highly rhetorical paragraph on the immorality of the Roman Catholic church, his statement that in the convent a priest had made 'an attempt upon the chastity of my own wife, the mother of my children'.

There could have been no doubt in Cornelia's mind by this time that her husband had apostatised, if not formally yet in fact. The news, whenever it reached her, that Frank, now just eleven, had started his education at a recently established (1843) Protestant boarding school which provided especially for the sons of clergymen, would have convinced her that the children too were to be uprooted from the ways of faith she had taught them to love.

On 3 February 1852, the month in which Frank began at Marlborough College, she wrote on behalf of her eldest son Merty, with a kind of despairing hope, to the bishop of New Orleans. To contact this friend of former days was to recall the happy years of conversion and of married life in Louisiana when Anthony Blanc had given them such friendship. Her love for Merty and her compassion for Pierce permeate the letter:

> ... with a Christian certainty of your charity for Mr Connelly and my poor children I beg of you to interest yourself in the spiritual welfare of my son ... to tell me what hope or hold there is upon the child, and whether there is any thing I can do or any influence I could make use of to regain him to his faith and duty?

Then she speaks of Pierce:

> It must be as incomprehensible to every Catholic as it is to me that Mr Connelly should have taken the course he has. He has acted at first on the persuasion he was right in his wish to have a certain sort of power over me which was not in accordance with the wish of the Bishop nor with my own sense of propriety in a protestant country and I cannot believe that he had any wrong intention at that time, but since then he has fallen among thieves who have wounded him and robbed him of his faith, and what is to become of him unless our Lord will be himself the good Samaritan and bind up his wounds and heal them?

Even more urgently she goes on:

> My dear Lord I must not dwell on this deep sorrow for I am without the

power of any remedy and can only distress others by my tears, and useless tears unless they move the heart of my Lord to pity. I am sure of your prayers but I want also your influence. Might you not exercise it on Mr Connelly through his brother & my son, and be yourself a father to the poor child while he remains in New Orleans? I am asking with the confidence of a child because I know you to be a father and I know also that you may better understand the delusion Mr Connelly has fallen under than others who never understood his character or comprehended the innocent affections which he seems not to have had the strength & grace to overcome. Ady & Frank are with their father. I have not seen either Mercer or Adeline since I received the religious habit in 1846 and I fear they are not allowed to write to me as my letters remain unanswered.

Bishop Blanc did not fail to reply. In March 1852 he sent a long letter full of warmth. As to Pierce he will 'implore for him' to God but does not believe that to write would any longer be of use. For Cornelia as mother he has sympathy, realising that as possible in her circumstances it is right for her to seek contact with her children. At the same time, divining the doubts that must sometimes have assailed her, he seeks to protect her from a false sense of guilt: 'aided as you are by the consideration that nothing of what has happened around you has so far been under your control, your conscience must be at peace'

Then he turns to news of her son, sad news, hard for her to read. He has seen Mercer and also her convert brother-in-law John, who has been looking into the practicalities of setting the young man up in a Texas farming venture. John Connelly, being now so bitterly and openly opposed to Pierce for all that has happened, has no personal influence whatever, the bishop says, over Merty, whose 'prejudices shall ever be in favour of his father, and rather adverse to you, that is, he will range rather on his father's side, whom he considered *victimised*' (by the Church). He warns her:

> In case it would ever enter into your mind, my dear Madame Connelly, to suppose that in order to save your poor son, you might with a regular dispensation return to this country and win again his former love & thus redeem his faith; I entreat you to guard against the temptation. I have not the least doubt, but so soon as Mr Pierce Connelly would hear of this move on your part, he would be here soon himself and I am equally sure that what he has attempted in vain in England he would obtain in this country. This is the opinion also of Mr John Connelly whom you may continue to consider as a true friend.

He knows nothing of the beleaguered state at All Souls in which Cornelia and her community were surviving, and concludes with unconscious irony:

'No, dear Madam, there is no safer place for you in the world, as the one you now occupy in England.'

When Bishop Blanc warned Cornelia against coming to America (as an individual) her thoughts had most certainly already turned in that direction on behalf of the community. Eight months earlier, on 16 July 1851, she had wondered to her sister Adie about beginning a school in Texas and wanted her to inquire of the bishop there. Three days later, writing to Rome, she had told Cardinal Fransoni, prefect of the Propaganda, *'we* are looking to the West' and begged him to remember *'our sisters'* if a call for religious came to him from any bishop in America. Her 'own dear country' would never have been far from Cornelia's mind but her community at that date had only twelve professed and seven novices and the latter tended to come and go. It was scarcely large enough to undertake what would be a distant and important foundation and it seems likely that she began to consider the possibility so soon chiefly because the immediate circumstances were already calling into question the Society's survival in England. It was not only that the Connelly scandal made people look askance at her convent, nor even the insecurity and local hostility created by the Jones will. A much greater threat than either was the cardinal's active disapproval. By mid-July when she wrote to Fransoni, Wiseman was already threatening to suppress the community, as we have seen, and he had the power to do so.

In the same month the providential news came that Thomas Grant had been consecrated in Rome as bishop of Southwark. The cardinal would no longer have immediate authority over St Leonards. Never one to let the grass grow under her feet Cornelia now seized the opportunity to side-step him and open negotiations with the Propaganda herself. Were the Society to have the pope's approbation of its Rule it would not be dependent for survival on Wiseman's. Fransoni had agreed to be her foundation's 'cardinal protector' when Cornelia left Rome and under this plea she now hopefully wrote. After an account of the good progress made and avoiding all reference to differences with Wiseman, she came to her point: 'we cannot feel satisfied till we are approved by Christ's vicar on earth. What are we to do to obtain this, and who will befriend us, free from the bias of any locality as your Eminence is?'

The 'bias of any locality' diplomatically covers the Connelly scandal, Duke and the property, and also the stance of the English cardinal, in no mood at the moment to befriend them. She had a kind and encouraging reply in September from Fransoni and was told to send the Rule for the

Propaganda's consideration. Meanwhile Wiseman's pointed sermon on the Pharisee and the publican had left the community in no doubt whatever about his disapproval of Cornelia's attitude to the property, and as soon as Grant arrived in London she again seized the moment. He was urged to come at once to settle the All Souls situation, and she sent him, 'packed among the vegetables' in a gift hamper, a copy of 'our Constitutions'.

Communication between convent and cardinal did not quite die and in February 1852 Mother Connelly herself must have written. Judging by Wiseman's answer hers was an attempt to heal the breach between them, and the recent publication of yet another of Pierce's pamphlets had offered her a means of reconciliation. He replied warmly:

Dear Reverend Mother
I need not assure you that your letter has been most welcome and consoling to me. I cannot but feel a lively interest in the prosperity of your house, and especially at this moment that so furious and unjust an attack has been made upon it by the recent pamphlet, I feel not only the greater sympathy, but the absolute importance of your being strongly supported by at least all to whom Catholics will look for an opinion concerning you.

At the end he assures her he has 'no personal feeling in anything that has happened', refers to the responsibility he feels for the convent, and even says he hopes soon to come and stay with them for 'a little quiet'. What may, however, be the real source of this great affability appears in the middle of the letter. Something that Grant had told him about the drawing up of the Trust (whose terms she was ignorant of) had led him to believe that Mother Connelly was no longer a source of opposition. To her probable mystification he 'rejoices' to hear that 'the Trust and other temporal matters are being adjusted with your bishop, so that the Community may be established on a solid ecclesiastical basis'. He is pleased with this submissiveness: 'the more you adhere to the principles of the Church in what regards obedience, direction, and close adherence as between religious and their superiors, the more you will flourish and be blessed'.

Cornelia's reply has not survived but by 16 May when she turned to Wiseman again, his complacence had quite vanished. Melia was about to go to Rome and was willing to take with him the Rule (or Constitutions as it came more often to be called), and Cornelia asked the cardinal to support her application. His reply is cool. She surely knows that he cannot 'take the initiative in any matter originating *out* of my diocese' (but he had influence in Rome), and excuses himself. Only if the bishop of Southwark wishes it can he assist her. And a warning full of displeasure follows.

Its precise cause has to be inferred. The Trust at this date is being closely studied. Lawyers, Towneley, the bishop, Melia, are all into it but Mother Connelly is not. Had nineteenth-century England been less anti-Catholic, less unaware of a woman's rights, less dominated (among Catholics) by ecclesiastics, such a situation could not have occurred. For Towneley's good reasons but also because of the assumptions of her day, she was being ignored when the twentieth century would say she should have been consulted at every turn. That she was not we know for certain. When later on she was still being blamed for the consequences of the Trust, the colonel wrote: 'You had nothing whatever to do in the making of this Trust Deed. I made it without your knowledge or consent except that I consulted you on some minor details – after my decision was taken and the Deed in progress.' A letter to Cornelia from Towneley's solicitor dated March 1852 and a statement by his agent in 1858 confirm this, and there is no evidence that anyone told her more. Yet Wiseman takes the line that Cornelia is being obstructive. His informants can be guessed. It had only to reach his ears through Melia and Duke that Towneley (a layman) was opposing the bishop on the subject of the Jones church (as he was), with Mother Connelly the prime mover (which she was not), for his former satisfaction to be transformed into implacable opposition once more. Beneath what sounds like straightforward and honest warning is the wielding of a power which amounts to moral extortion. Neither he nor Grant, he says, can act in the matter of the Constitutions:

> . . . till a proper settlement is made of the temporal position of the Convent, and [we] have a thorough confidence that the painful relations between it and ecclesiastical superiors will not be renewed. To secure this may require some modification of rules, or the introduction of new guarantees; so that the Constitutions probably could not be passed as they are.

Pierce was not the only manipulator in Cornelia's experience. Indirectly Wiseman seems to be saying she does not obey bishops, and that her support of Towneley's plans for All Souls is a stumbling block to what church authority envisions. Supposing her to have dictated terms to Towneley he is trying to force her into submission before the Trust is signed. In effect he threatens her. The Constitutions (based on the Jesuit Constitutions and canonically approved, as Fransoni knows, by Wiseman himself) will probably not be accepted in Rome because, he says, they do not sufficiently secure obedience to ecclesiastical superiors. For Cornelia, a woman who valued religious obedience to her bishop as the lifeline of her apostolic life and that of her Society, this was a distressing letter to receive. And if it was triggered off by Wiseman's anger about a term in the Trust of which she knew nothing, then bewilderment compounded humiliation.

In the end Towneley gave way to Grant on the ten-year clause; the Trust was signed on 3 June 1852; Melia (Buckle says, giving no reason) congratulated the community on being 'once more united to their ecclesiastical superiors'; and on 4 June Cornelia penned her petition to the pope for approbation and her Constitutions went to Rome in Melia's pocket. At the Propaganda Fransoni took the routine first step of consulting her bishop, and through him Wiseman. To Grant, therefore, for consideration, he sent all documentation in the Propaganda file on the Society. That included Pierce's spurious Rule. It also included the comment of the consultor, who having noticed the discrepancy between his Rule and what Cornelia had now sent, advised that nothing be done until the dust of disagreement over the Institute between 'founder and foundress' had settled. And there for the time being the matter was left.

'SWORD OF STRENGTH', 1853

From several quarters elements now gathered to form a new crisis in Cornelia's life. Taken separately, each came under its own momentum to a painful climax. The coincidence in the autumn of 1853 of several such climaxes brought her to the edge of an abyss.

It was nearly six years since she had become superior-general and definitively given herself for the life of the Society, and it was five and a half years since the scene in the Derby parlour when she had repudiated Pierce's illegal claims on her. One by one allies had gone: Pierce had apostatised; Shrewsbury, whose name alone would have recalled her first days of fervour in Rome had died the year before; Wiseman, initially so great and positive a benefactor, had become at best an ambivalent one. Now this was combined with the hostility of Melia and Duke. Even on behalf of her young community Cornelia, achiever, manager and charmer that she was, found it hard to bear. She wrote to Grant in May 1853, 'I have quite made up my mind to suffer not only personally for the love of God but also in our dear Community. I only wish (just now) that I could *really* love to suffer & not only imagine it while in prayer.' Through August and September there was more to bear. The nation's press had taken the *Case of the Reverend Pierce Connelly* to itself. He was believed, she was declared false, at best the victim of Rome's 'moral jugglery'. She was pictured as a woman 'long debarred from the use of her free will', a subjugated weakling.

These 'miseries', as she named them to Grant, were the warp and woof of daily circumstance. But soon Cornelia was to be invaded by shocking and unquenchable sorrow. On 13 October she heard of the death of Merty. He was not quite twenty-one and had died of yellow fever in New Orleans, the city where, as she knew, the fever-stricken dead were often heaped together in its wet and shallow graves. She had no word from him. As far as she knew he was alienated from her. Worse still, in her view, he was alienated from the Catholic church. She wrote to Grant, 'Of your charity remember his soul in the hope of God's mercy.' According to Buckle she was 'quite overpowered' for several days and could 'only pray to God in secret'. In an attempt to prevent sorrow from engrossing her she made herself work through a book of geometry problems. Perhaps it was now that she put into a little box 'for Ady from her Mother' a curl of fair hair, 'half of all I have of darling Merty's hair'. That we know of, she never received news that might have consoled. No sign of correspondence even between her and Pierce has survived.

The news of Merty's death reached Cornelia on the Feast of St Edward. On this day thirteen years earlier Pierce had asked her to consent to his ordination; on the same day seven years earlier she had arrived at Derby. Now she is forty-four years old and well acquainted with grief. Her sole defence against self-pity and bitterness was her faith in 'the good, good God'. That this faith ran like an always-flowing underground stream, some of her writings within the following months will show.

Meanwhile to understand what happened next we have to step back a month and consider a correspondence that took place behind Cornelia's back.

In September 1853 Grant was thanking Duke for the opinion which he had 'so kindly proposed to the Cardinal and myself'. Duke a week later was informing Grant, 'I have received a satisfactory letter from the Cardinal in reply to mine.' This exchange of letters between bishop and doctor with the cardinal conspiring in the background was prompted by the publication in August of Pierce's *Case*. Duke was urging that this 'artful and untruthful woman' be removed from office and/or sent out of the country. If not, he will speak his mind publicly. Grant, sympathetic to the Congregation and deeply fearful of public scandal, was gradually beaten down. He made a final and most serious appeal to Duke, explaining why 'I cannot adopt your mode of dealing with the present difficulty'. Duke refused to listen. It was very painful for him, he says, to differ with the bishop but he cannot omit to mention:

> . . . one instance of what I meet with. There is a Protestant lady of some station at Brighton whom I have to see once a month or so, who lives in Warwickshire and a friend of Lord Dormer's and who formerly gave me a five or ten pound note for the Church of All Souls and which I gave to Mr Jones. This shows that she is no bigot. After we had finished about her health she said, 'Well Dr Duke, what do you say now about your

convent matters.' I replied, 'I fear Mr Connelly must be a bad man.' She replied, 'Yes, and she is about as bad, but I will not press you upon the matter, only pray Dr Duke do not allow your daughter to go to that Convent. As I told you two years ago, it has a bad name and if she should become a nun let her go to Princethorpe in our county, which is respectable.' I could simply say that I could not defend either Mrs Connelly or Mr Connelly.

Cornelia was not unaware that 'dinner-party talk' buzzed to and fro across the tables of residents and visitors along the south coast. During these days she was reading from cover to cover and annotating Pierce's *Case*, realising that it was being widely circulated and avidly read.

Duke's letter continues. It referred to an unfortunate note of Cornelia's to Pierce, quoted in the *Case* – 'just taking my paper to write what comes into my head', it begins. It had been written seven years earlier, during her first weeks in the industrial Midlands. Among convent and family matters she included a remark about Birmingham Catholics, her first impression of them. 'I am disgusted with the clergy and the grossness of the people – that seems too coarse to understand spiritual things,' she had scribbled. It was the quick judgment of a lonely woman whose whole Catholic experience so far had been with some of the most cultured and distinguished members of the church and who at this moment of writing was probably fearful of what lay before her. Pierce transformed it for the public. It became an 'outburst' against 'the whole body of the Romish clergy', whose impurity made her insist on absolute separation between herself and him.

Duke seized upon this statement of Pierce's: 'a living witness against her in the eyes of both Catholics and Protestants', he tells the bishop. 'This fact *alone*' is sufficient 'to make the Holy Father take decisive measures [against Cornelia] when he hears of it.' And he mocks Grant's appeal for no publicity: 'It is not myself that will expose her faults. She has done that herself before the whole world.' In the sad privacy of the margin of the pamphlet an older Cornelia answered: 'If I wrote this letter it was a confidential expression of momentary feeling and certainly not founded on any facts.'

The conclusion to this epistle of the doctor's shows the cardinal playing safe. He has told Duke that as the convent is not in his diocese 'he can say or do nothing'. But his Eminence had at the least been talking. On the very day on which Duke wrote his galvanising screed, 16 September 1853, Grant sent a carefully considered letter to the Propaganda: 'his Eminence the Archbishop as well as myself and others agree that it is absolutely necessary to find a pretext to remove Mrs Connelly at least for some time & perhaps entirely'. He sent 'a good and just pretext' for consideration:

She has sent [1852] to the Sacred Congregation a request for the revision of their Constitutions . . . The Sacred Congregation could have her written to, that his Eminence the Prefect who showed great love & kindness for the Connelly family, desired much that she would take the Constitutions as soon as possible to Rome. Being an American, later on she could be advised to found a house in America. This is a plan that to His Eminence the Archbishop and to me appears most sure & least capable of exciting the minds of the Protestants.

In due course an invitation reached her in late October: 'nothing now is wanting', it said, 'in the arrangements for the approbation of your Institute, but your personal attendance in Rome'. Cornelia was suffering from the shock of Merty's death and from one of her recurring bouts of gout. By mid-November she has not gone and a second letter came, this time politely peremptory and she guessed its real purpose:

My dear Lord & Father in Christ [Grant]
I enclose a copy of a letter from Rome with the copy of the answer sent by to-day's post. I *beg* of you my Lord not to put off the retreat & clothing. I can keep Mother Alphonsa here in my place if I am to go to Rome which I suppose I must in obedience do. I do not think from the tenour of this last letter that the approbation of our Rules is the object *really* existing. I have rather come to the conclusion it is simply to get me out of England (because of the noise of Mr Connelly) . . .

The transparency of the pretext made this summons the more humiliating. Here was an intelligent and committed woman whose share of responsibility for a religious community had apparently merited no consideration. All she had done was put aside by persons who did not identify themselves. She was excluded from their confidence. It was a moment, we may guess, when she had to say to herself what she taught the sisters, be 'great in Humility, little in Pride'.

It was also an unwise moment at which to absent herself from England. A crisis about the Trust and the Jones church was under way and in her absence Duke's arguments against the rights of the convent might prevail with the bishop. She had young foundations in London, Liverpool and even more recently Preston, and of these Liverpool was in trouble because the superior had rashly taken on more than the community could carry. Most important, before going more work would have to be done on the 1852 version of the Rule. Were she not allowed to return – a fear she must have entertained when she realised why she had been sent for – then it would have to be sufficiently developed to support, inspire and unite the communities without her. Even Wiseman doubted the Society's capacity to survive yet without her leadership. She was, he would write in 1854, 'the only one who possesses any wisdom and the local Superiors and the Nuns themselves would quickly be lost if they were taken away from her care and direction'.

Cornelia continued her letter to Grant upset and seemingly incoherent – perhaps because we do not have his most recent one to her. Trustingly she encloses an unexpected letter from Pierce:

> I had written my answer to Dr Cornthwaite having come to this conclusion [that the summons to Rome was a ruse] & that it also must be the will of God for some other wise end, when by the second post I received the enclosed unintelligible letter from Mr Connelly. What have you to tell me 'is inevitable' my Lord? It nearly upsets me not to see things clearly or not to come at what any body is meaning. As Mr Connelly says that no one knows of his writing this letter, pray do not name my having sent it to you.

But Grant did 'name' it. He sent it to the Propaganda, and if it was true (as was later said) that Rome had decided not to allow approbation to Mother Connelly's Rule while her husband still lived, then that letter provided a reason: in it Pierce begged Cornelia to leave the convent and return to him.

After Cornelia's signature there follows the significant postscript: 'Is not our faith a sword of strength. I *feel* it so My Lord.'

When she realised, having heard again from Rome, that she must continue work on the Constitutions at once, the community asked her to make certain additions. Among these were the introductory paragraphs which her Society has treasured ever since. They spoke of the 'Eternal Wisdom'; of the 'wonderful manner' in which 'the treasures of His Mercy and of His boundless love' are revealed; of running 'with ardour in the way that He has pointed out'; of being 'flung forward from the heart of love'. These are not the words of a woman giving way to personal wretchedness but of one who in the face of it encourages herself and others from the depths of vision and conviction. Similarly, writing to the sisters after fruitless weeks in Rome, she describes 'this miserable, ungrateful, wasteful life' as 'more heavy than the heaviest purgatory can ever be', and the holds out to the community she is founding the vision God has given her to pursue: 'Let us try day by day . . . to love what He loves, and thus make our lives one with Him, being in one continued act of love from night till night and from year to year.'

It is such a passage as this, so brief yet so powerful, written at a time of known suffering, that prompts one to ask whether Cornelia Connelly was a mystic. She was reticent about the ways of God upon herself but one may adduce at least that she had sometimes been given direct and profound knowledge of God, so joyfully sure was her conviction of merciful, saving love always at work – even when only darkness and pain surrounded her.

199

The fact of Christ's passion at work in the world was, it would seem, the source of her confident joy, and she longed that her sisters, and she with them, might 'accomplish that which is wanting in the Passion of Jesus Christ, *your co-operation*'. There is a verbal echo here of what she will have read in the Douay version of Paul's letter to the Colossians: 'I, Paul . . . now rejoice in my sufferings for you and fill up those things that are wanting in the sufferings of Christ, in my flesh, for his body, which is the church.' This is the scriptural passage which justifies those mystics who 'knew' that their suffering was, in God's mercy, life for others and embraced it as such, rejoicing. Such was Francis of Assisi, the saint perhaps most loved by Cornelia. If we attribute this kind of gift from God to her we can believe that her prayer, 'Possess me, rule me, inflame me', was granted, and we can better understand how she can tread her path so unswervingly, and speak with such authority as the years went by of the intense consolation with which it filled those who went the same way: 'that kingdom of peace within, where the soul's whisperings are answered by the King Himself, giving abundantly that jubilee of heart which had not been bargained for in his life of accepted suffering'.

During December she struggled with the Constitutions. Council meetings were held about them. On Grant's advice they were translated into French for the convenience of Rome. His own copy, for reference, reached him in bits at the last minute. She was burdened in spirit and not well. Christmas approached, possibly her last with the community. They began their annual nine-day litany to the Holy Child. On 21 December, the anniversary of her profession and the birthday, so to speak, of the Society, three more sisters made their vows. A crib was set up in the chapel, a task she delighted to do herself. And at midnight mass there was singing.

ROME, 1854

On a wintry evening at St Leonards late in 1853 or early January 1854 Mother Connelly gathered her community round her before leaving for Rome. Her Epiphany letter that year, perhaps written after her feast and a little ahead of time, was to 'My very dear Sisters' – now in not only the quiet of Sussex but also the streets of the poor in London, Liverpool and Preston. She encourages them with love. Above all they were to be faithful because through fidelity they would learn how to love God. It is her characteristic mix of the ideal and the practical, the holistic approach to living:

I thank you, dearly beloved Sisters, for your nice presents, they are more dear to me because of their being marks & fruits of your diligence. 'By their fruits ye shall know them.' Let all be diligent in giving daily proofs of love this year, & as you step on through the muddy streets, love God with your feet, and when your hands toil, love Him with your hands, and when you teach the little children, love Him with His little ones, and thus may you be blessed in each action and in each member with an abundance of Divine Love and purified and prepared in this world, as far as possible, to enjoy an eternity of love.

Pray for your unworthy servant in Christ. C.C.

With the community at St Leonards on her last evening she acted with some solemnity. First she read the Rule aloud to them with the additions for which they had asked and the professed gave her their signatures to it. Sister Lucy Woolley was there, called from Preston to act as superior during Cornelia's absence. So possibly were Emily Bowles and Alphonsa Kay because they too were on the council. Then Mother Connelly knelt down among them all and asked their forgiveness for anything she had done ill 'since she had governed the Society'. Next day, on 'a cold winter's morning' and with two companions, she set out.

They stayed in the heart of Rome just opposite the Gesù, conveniently near the Jesuits and to the new superior-general whom, as plain Fr Beckx, Pierce if not Cornelia as well had met in Vienna. While they awaited the Propaganda's good pleasure they went house-hunting. Cornelia wanted to establish her Society in Rome, and had even arranged Italian classes at St Leonards for the sisters she hoped to send for. She also seized the opportunity to put her artistic gifts to work. An assistant from the school of the master painter Overbeck came to give them lessons and she undertook an ambitious long-term project, a large altar triptych with the Holy Child in the centre, Francis of Assisi on one side and Ignatius on the other. 'We are now painting in oils,' she told her sister-in-law. Perhaps because she was in frequent contact with Jesuits of the Gesù, could pray every day at their founder's tomb just across the piazza, and was working with their Constitutions, she elected to begin with Ignatius. When finished it was six and a half feet high. It now hangs in the convent at Hastings.

The Propaganda took its time dealing with her concerns. A confidential letter of Grant's to Fransoni on 13 February has survived. It begins by highly praising the work done in schools run by the Society, now in three dioceses. Then, although he had himself earlier proposed that she come to Rome to obtain approbation of the Rule, he proceeds to cast doubts on the wisdom of granting such a thing just yet. The Rule had been put together, he points out, by one who had never been trained as a nun, '*non è stat mai educata come Monaca*'. It was of course, strictly speaking, true that Cornelia (like many founders) had never been a canonically accepted novice before beginning her Society. What she had had was three years of formation for the religious life with the Society of the Sacred Heart. The spirit and strictness with which she had then adhered to instruction is evident in her notebooks of the time. What she learnt then reappears in much of what she taught her sisters from the earliest days at Derby, and was clearly reflected in the Rule now being presented. For the first year at Derby she was both novice and superior, directing and forming the community in which technically as a novice she was supposed to be a learner. Bishop Wiseman had rushed her into this situation, and then being consumed by diocesan business left her to the chaplain for any advice she might need. Grant, himself a canon lawyer and a man much less ready than the cardinal to risk such an irregularity, seems to have regarded it with a cautious, more legalistic eye.

Grant is also – consequently – doubtful about the Rule itself. He makes it a convenient excuse for detaining her in Rome. Although he (and Wiseman) knew that it was based on the Jesuit Constitutions, as was the approved rule of the Sacred Heart sisters, yet he asks that its spiritual principles and practices be examined very carefully by a consultor 'versed in ascetic matters . . . so that it will be conformable to spiritual principles and to regular discipline in everything'. The Propaganda, he goes on to suggest, could correct it and praise it and then 'wait a little' so that the bishops would have time to 'observe the practical effect'.

Grant's primary objective was very clearly to keep Mother Connelly out of England, and a letter of Towneley's on 19 February hints at a probable but unacknowledged reason, that with Cornelia away the bishop hoped he could more easily satisfy Duke and establish the congregation's rights over the property. If so he had underestimated the colonel. Towneley wrote: 'I regret that I cannot alter the decision I came to after Mr Jones's death of making whatever remains of Mr Jones's property into an endowment for the Convent. I stated this to you at our meeting when the trust was executed.'

This subject, so closely linked with the reason why Duke wanted her out of the country, goes unremarked; instead Grant relies on the scandalous 'noise of Mr C' and points out to Fransoni that:

> . . . she must travel from time to time to see the houses of the Institute. She is a very talented woman and very capable and the Lord has blessed her hard work. But living in England she is always in the middle of the juridical questions that her husband can arouse. I enclose a letter dated November 22nd 1853 [not extant] written by him to the Superior who sent it to me at once. With this letter he begs her to leave the convent . . . [page torn] better stay in America or elsewhere . . .

While Cornelia painted and prayed she had no idea that such wheels within wheels were at work. She revisited shrines she had loved, had several audiences with Pius IX, and renewed her veneration for the Holy See. As she understood it Rome was indeed a holy city, the core of unity in Christ's church, symbol and visible reminder in the person of the pope of Christ's authority on earth. She had guessed why she had been called there but had no reason to suppose that her Constitutions, given such letters as this of Grant's, had little chance of immediate approbation. After all, the first invitation had said 'nothing now is wanting in the arrangements for the approbation of your Institute, but your own personal attendance in Rome', a statement on which Grant of course, having engineered the invitation, had cast no warning doubts.

While Cornelia's own bishop evaded particular comment on the Rule, Wiseman did no such thing. He was in Rome and on 24 March sent his opinion as requested, some two thousand words of it. Until the final paragraph he has nothing good to say and then it is only of the work the Institute does, not of its Constitutions. At the beginning he briefly noted certain obvious omissions which Cornelia remedied once Fransoni had pointed them out. The rest was written 'confidentially'. Here he provides not comment on the Rule but a context for what is his underlying drift: that these Constitutions reveal a woman greedy for power and who ignores the authority even of bishops. The spirit of the Rule, he says, 'is such as to render absolute, unlimited, and irresponsible the authority of the Superior General'.

As the letter proceeds it becomes clear that criticisms masquerading as objective are in fact coloured by Wiseman's personal attitude to Cornelia. As a statement from the cardinal of England it influenced the Propaganda's thinking through all subsequent revisions of the Rule. Along with Pierce's pseudo Rule and consultors' comments on it, Wiseman's letter was passed on to whoever next had to consider the Society's Constitutions. Not till 1869 would the prejudicial impression be corrected, and then not permanently.

The cardinal's words poured on: 'Elected for life, she alone holds sway . . .'

Election for life for the superior-general was the unanimous decision of the council working with Cornelia on the Rule before she left for Rome. This was a reversal of what Wiseman had insisted on in 1850. He had considered it safer to limit the office to six years in view of 'the weak points in the character of women generally'. But Cornelia and the sisters did not have this view of themselves and wished to follow the Jesuit model. They judged it, presumably, the best source of impetus and union for ministry in the church, and now, in 1854, used their right to ask Rome's higher authority to approve it for their Society. Elsewhere in the letter he does his lengthy utmost to ensure that the Propaganda will put Jones's library out of their reach because women will not realise that it is a tree of knowledge full of danger. The superior is 'certainly a very capable woman, of strong character', but would there be others to succeed her? These Constitutions invest her 'with a power which would need a man of the highest ability, experience, and courage to exercise it; much less should it be entrusted to a woman'.

From there he moves straight into what most outrages him, the Rule's failure to inculcate obedience to bishops. Cornelia (basing herself on the Jesuit Constitutions, which in this matter were no guide) did not know that she should have spelt out espiscopal rights and powers in the community – any more than she had realised till Fransoni asked her for it that a horarium was required. What Cornelia had focused on particularly and which earned no comment whatever from Wiseman, was not the requirements of canon law, of which she knew little, but on what a later consultor described with pleasure, 'a good spirit and beautiful rules to maintain religious discipline, to sanctify the Sisters and to procure the glory of God'.

Wiseman overstated his case. He wrote that 'from beginning to end there is no mention of any account to be rendered to the Bishop, nor of any authority at all that he can exercise', which was not true. Part 1, article 4 lays down the principle clearly and everything that follows in the whole Rule falls under it: 'The houses of this Society are subject to the ordinary jurisdiction of the Bishop'. Nor is this mere window-dressing. A glance back at Cornelia's surviving letter to her current bishop, Grant, in the months before coming to Rome, makes plain the detailed obedience expected in those days *and given*:

June 20, 1853 . . . perhaps your Lordship will at the same time examine the postulants . . .

You know my dear Lord we are only waiting for your orders respecting the loan for the building . . .

July 15 . . . I want *very* much to see you my dear Lord & to ask about many things . . . will you allow me to apply to the [Jesuit] Provincial [for a chaplain] . . . ?

Sept 16 . . . I do not think I ought to leave for my journey on Monday . . . Will your Lordship have the kindness to send me one word of advice . . .?

Wiseman needed examples in support of his argument and turned to the time of his own jurisdiction at St Leonards. The 'hardest nut I had to crack', he says, was the disregard there of the bishop. He was not expected to 'interest himself' in the 'affairs of the house', and 'its absolute independence, as far as temporal administration was concerned, was almost insisted on'.

Any ecclesiastic at that date could have mistaken Cornelia's undeniable independence of mind for irreverence, pride or disobedience, indeed for all three. But when Wiseman goes on to instance his experience of disregard for episcopal authority at St Leonards he has only one thing to say: that he was opposed by Mother Connelly in the affair of the seaside residence and Jones's library. He offers no examples of failure to obey in matters of religious observance. Nor does he make any attempt to present the property dispute – of which residence and library were only a lesser aspect – in the broad context of mission, congregation or church. An egotistical grievance is at work, such as could partly account for the success of Melia's tale-bearing and Duke's representations, and now it overthrows Wiseman's power to speak impartially.

More than half Wiseman's lengthy epistle tells Fransoni the story of the property, selectively and unjustly. It begins by stating that the community was *expelled* from Derby by the bishop there and underplays his own part in persuading them to move to St Leonards. His expectations from Mr Jones are made much of. Doubts are cast upon the finding of the will and on its justice. Towneley is reduced to 'a rich secular' whose correspondence (with Melia?) lacked respect (towards ecclesiastical superiors?) and who 'declared himself absolute, because legal, owner of the property and he wished to deal with the Superior alone'. Then comes the nub of his grievance: 'they both acted without any recognition of any right of the Bishop's to intervene in the affair'.

In the event, he continues, the property was ceded to the community 'without reserve', which was not true. It was never theirs and moreover at Cornelia's desire Towneley had made important concessions for the congregation. It even provided a residence plus housing for the library (which took up several pages of his letter) for the use of the bishop of the diocese. But not to own personally. And Wiseman was not bishop of Southwark.

Towards the end this aggrieved prelate makes an admission. In regard to Pierce, Cornelia 'shows that she is most obedient, and ready to submit to whatever conditions may be imposed on her'. In the context of the body of the letter this particular piece of praise is extraordinary. It stands in the path of his general argument – the disregard of episcopal authority – like some huge, immovable boulder, like truth thrusting through what is false. Their apple of discord was the property. Her consistent stance with Towneley on this (whom many years later the Propaganda confirmed was in the right when at last they had the true facts) was outrageous to him and it elicited this long, destructive response for Fransoni about her unwillingness to obey bishops. Yet her equally firm readiness to obey as required about Pierce is mentioned only in passing, apparently seen as no more than a convenience to the Roman authorities should they wish to lay down

conditions for the cooling of scandal. There is no sign that he has comprehended the depth of obedience willingly offered here, and he gives it the
smallest recognition.

In spite of a foundress rated thus and a Rule of which he speaks only
negatively, the institute she has established is too useful to lose. It has been
blessed 'in a singular manner'. It has increased and spread. Its work is
excellent. He cannot but recommend it and hopes that the Constitutions
can be rendered 'worthy of the approval that is asked for'.

Fortunately for Cornelia, Fransoni thought better of her than did Wiseman and will also have read the cardinal's two thousand words in the light
of what he would have learned from Bowyer's comments to Mgr Talbot.
The examination of the Rule would have to go through the usual long
processes, but in spite of bishop and cardinal he sent Cornelia back to
England, urging Grant 'to try and promote the good of this devout Society'.
Nor is there any reference to 'founder and foundress' now. Cornelia must
have enlightened Fransoni about a great deal because to Grant he now calls
the Society the 'Institute that she founded'. It was one of the misfortunes
of her religious life that this good friend, already an old man, died only two
years later.

The foundation in Rome was put aside and Cornelia returned to England
in April. Eventually Grant received the Constitutions and was told that the
required revisions were to be made by Wiseman who could consult him.
But the cardinal had neither the time nor the goodwill for such a task. He
contented himself with telling Rome that the Society 'did not yet merit
formal approbation', and that he had left it to Grant 'to induce these Ladies
to accept the proposed emendations'. Grant still thought it Wiseman's
responsibility. Some of the points he discussed with Cornelia but did not
give her the comments of the consultor. What he did was to withhold them
for ten years, saying nothing.

10

Cornelia and Emily Bowles

INSUFFICIENT MEANS

The continual lack of financial resource was a major obstacle to the Society's development. What degree of wealth lay in Cornelia's earlier background is not clear. We do not know for instance how large was the dowry which she said Pierce was using against her and 'contrary to his promises'; nor how much 'all we have' was, when she warned Merty that it must go to Ady; nor what were the personal resources she brought to Derby and which Sr Aloysia said were all gone after a few months. We do know that Wiseman had undertaken all remuneration to Mr Sing for the Derby convent because Cornelia could not, and that in the end she had to leave what was a thriving apostolate because she still could not satisfy Sing when Wiseman had failed to do so fully. The prospect of the free gift of the All Souls property with its 'considerable endowment', as Wiseman alluringly but inaccurately described it, must have been a great relief. In the event, as we have seen, the property was never theirs. The income from it was very small and the community, though no longer harrassed by debt to any Sing, for many years had to live as frugal a life as at Derby. The Gate Street sisters were in a much more desperate state of poverty than Cornelia would have permitted had she been able to alleviate it, as Bellasis makes plain.

It is against this background that we should read Pierce's remarks when asking Ralph for money, that Cornelia was trying to 'beggar' him and the children, and was 'living in affluence'. The kind of affluence she found in life was far from Pierce's meaning. Inspired by a God willingly reduced to human dependence in a stable and by Francis of Assisi preaching and praying among the towns and mountain caves of Umbria, she led the sisters to accept cheerfully the unavoidable conditions in which they had to live. For sheer lack of money apostolic works were often crippled or even given up. Providentially she was an excellent businesswoman and wrestled unde-featedly with her financial problems. Generally it was a worried Grant who had to be reassured. 'You must not think we are "going to fail",' she would say to him.

When she returned to England in April 1854 she had great need of that attitude. Emily Bowles presented her with what would prove to be a major financial anxiety for years to come. It was aggravated by the attitudes of both Wiseman and Grant and conglomerate in its circumstances, but at the immediate and practical level the problem was money.

INTRODUCING EMILY

Emily Bowles, like Cornelia, was a convert. She and her twin brother Frederick (there were six boys and five girls in what was a very close-knit and well-to-do family) had been caught up in the Oxford Movement. Two other brothers who enter this story, John and Samuel, of whom Samuel was a clergyman, remained Protestant, but Frederick became a Catholic in 1845 when Newman did and in 1847 joined his Oratory. Emily herself had met Newman in 1840 and throughout her life remained devoted to him. Her conversion to Catholicism preceded both his and her brother's, in 1843 in Rome, and when Cornelia, a foreigner, arrived in England to begin her work Emily, though younger by nine years of life and by eight as a Catholic, knew far more of the English scene in general and of its Catholic and Protestant circles. Through family and confessional contacts she was acquainted with many eminent people including Wiseman, and was in a position to promote the Society's interests. She could also press her opinions on Cornelia, as we have seen when she urged that the five-year-old Frank be sent away for fear of scandal.

'I have united myself with a very distinguished writer of the day, Miss Emily Bowles, to put our work in operation,' Cornelia wrote to Ralph. Emily was twenty-eight, according to Maria Buckle (herself a well-educated woman) 'highly gifted'. She took charge in the Derby Poor School; at St Leonards, when the Highest school began to develop, she was its head-mistress – and at Cornelia's suggestion wrote a children's *School History of England*; she helped to re-edit the Rule and probably assisted with the education of sisters as teachers.

But Buckle had other memories of Emily in the early days. 'I was struck with her over activity,' she wrote, and Emily argued about everything. She and Mother Connelly, Buckle says, did not agree about 'the means most conducive to carrying out the work for the greater glory of God'. When Emily joined the Society everything was in the making. Older than most and in addition very articulate, to direct came more naturally to her than to co-operate, it would seem. Some kind of power struggle was probably at work between her and Mother Connelly from the beginning.

A single letter has survived from Emily to Cornelia (other than one business statement), written before the venture began.

Dearest Friend

I was quietly working with Miss Edmunds to-day when the bell rang, & Dr Wiseman & Mr Sing were announced. I was aghast, for I was dreadfully weak. The Bishop was *radiant with smiles*, and he soon told me that he had explained everything to Mr Sing and Mr Sing had brought all his papers & liabilities (this was *sotto voce* to me) . . . He said that he would return, the end of the week & explain all quietly to me . . . he and Mr Sing would be glad if we could begin as soon as possible. I said that I must remain with the Mission till Michaelmas, & felt quite *odd* to think that everything was *done*, really before one could look round.

After some repetitions she changes gear:

How *much* I have to say to you. How much to hear & learn! Alas! I feel that if you really knew me, you would shrink from me, you cannot in the least imagine (even with all your penetration) how *little* I have done for God, how little I love Him, how little like a child I am. Pray for me . . . May God & Our Lady bless you, dearest Friend . . .

Ten years later Bishop Goss wrote of Emily that she was 'of an excitable temperament, & may sometimes let her feelings too much rule her'. The documentation of the ten years endorses that judgment. What Goss remarked independently, Mother Connelly came to know all too well. The core of her continual advice to Emily was, 'Our feelings are never to *govern* us.'

RUPERT HOUSE, 1852–6

When Emily joined the Society in 1846 she brought no dowry, that is, no money which under canon law would belong to the Society after her death but meanwhile was returnable should she ever leave. On 5 July 1852, however, writing from Liverpool where she had been for four months, she formally made over to Cornelia as superior-general £1300. This was a gift for the Society, conceivably made at this juncture because the terms of Towneley's Trust had recently removed all chance that the community would ever own the Jones property. Emily's document, addressed to Cornelia and the council, specifies that she preferred the money not to be used 'on debts or liabilities belonging to St Leonards'. This transaction is important for what happens later.

In March 1852 Cornelia had been invited to send sisters for schools in the very poorest part of Liverpool. Here was a port crammed with the thousands of Irish fleeing from the potato famine, unable in their destitution to provide for their children, least of all any education. She could spare at once only four: Emily as superior, one other professed sister, a novice and a beginner. Before the end of the year three more sisters were sent and according to the government inspector's report the work, which Emily herself directed, had begun very well indeed.

During 1853 Emily was approached by Mr Scott Nasmyth Stokes, secretary to the CPSC and keenly committed to the establishing of Catholic teacher-training colleges. None for women yet existed but he knew that a core group of teachers were already in training at St Leonards. He and Emily now consulted Mother Connelly who endorsed the idea of running one at Liverpool instead but she made it a condition that the CPSC should arrange grants towards building costs. With this in mind she agreed that Emily, if the need arose, might borrow up to £1300 from her brother Samuel and secure the loan with the £1300 which Emily had already transferred to the Society. This was the only asset Cornelia had with which she could support the project. She knew also, which was fundamental to her attitude and explains much of the trouble to come, that Emily wished to invest her private fortune in the venture.[1] She warned her not to incur any personal debt that exceeded the value of a mortgage, and 'gave her no power to involve our Community'.

Property hunting began forthwith. Then Cornelia, no house yet found or approved by her, was called unexpectedly to Rome on the pretext of the Rule. When she returned Emily, without waiting for the certainty of government grant, had borrowed the £1300 from Samuel and paid the first instalment on a house for a sum beyond what Cornelia had expected or approved. When later the college at St Leonards was built and furnished for sixty students it cost £3700. Emily's purchase was £6600. In April the CPSC allowed a grant but only provisionally. In September 1854 the bill for the rest of the £6600 fell due and Emily sent it to Mother Connelly. Mother Connelly regarded it not as the Society's but Emily's personal responsibility, and believed, which Emily later denied, that she had made this plain.

The sum required was beyond Emily's means. Rashly she had done exactly what Cornelia had warned her against. Next, since Mother Connelly made no offer to meet it, she resorted to independent and secret action. She did so, knowing that the CPSC had not yet 'recognised any Female Training School as their own', and that an essential step towards obtaining that recognition was to be able to offer the use of an actual house. Perhaps it was this knowledge that drove her, and the hope that the CPSC grant would materialise. She turned to a second brother, John, and with him signed a Note of Hand for £5000 from a bank. This she did without consulting or asking or informing Cornelia. When six weeks later Mother Connelly arrived in Liverpool even Emily admits that she 'expressed great apprehension and displeasure at the course that had been taken'. Cornelia also found that Emily had contracted for alterations in the house and had counted on their being paid for out of the £1300 which she had earlier given to Cornelia. She thus left her first Note, on the loan from Samuel, without security. She herself had put the Society into debt to him and now deprived it of its means of paying him, and at this point, December 1854, Cornelia removed her from the office of superior. A note of hers to Grant says: 'I expressed strongly my total disapprobation of the purchase and refused taking any share in the responsibility. I deemed the speculation dishonest and sinful, although I have ever been ready to palliate the intention which instigated it.'

In May 1855 came the really bad news: the CPSC withdrew its agreement to allow a grant to the Society for a training school in Liverpool. Another congregation, the Sisters of Notre Dame de Namur, had offered to establish one at its own expense.

Rupert House, Emily's rash purchase, was now redundant. Without a grant there was no possibility of running a college and Mother Connelly was faced with what to do with an unwanted, large property. The debt of £1300 to the Revd Samuel she acknowledged because she had permitted the borrowing and sisters had signed the Note. In time it would have to be met. But she never admitted responsibility for the debt of £5000 owed to John. It was his money, however, which had mostly paid for the property the Society was using. George Eyston, the Society's solicitor and also a friend of the Bowles family, advised her to give John Bowles a simple mortgage on the house, not as legally due but as a matter of justice. She agreed. To this mortgage we shall have to return.

All attempts to find a use for the house or to sell it failed. More difficult still, *both* Bowles brothers began to press Cornelia for their money and this she had not looked for. Later she told Grant that Emily had assured her John knew the purchase had been made without the community's approbation and was 'her act alone'. When the brothers continued to press she gave up all claim on the house and told John Bowles he could foreclose on the mortgage. At once in November 1856 Emily – who knew the terms of the mortgage – went to Bishop Goss of Liverpool, was dispensed from her vow of obedience and left the Society.

From then onwards Miss Bowles worked through her two brothers John and Samuel to exact full repayment on Rupert House from the Society. Within a week John Bowles was writing to Eyston that his bond for £5000 was *signed* by sisters from Preston and St Leonards, a misinformation which only he or Emily could have perpetrated since it was their own joint Note of Hand, as Cornelia told Eyston and the bank proved. Eyston wrote that he was receiving 'very excitable notes' from Emily and that he feared she was 'doing mischief in her own family'. The mischief grew. The possibility of a lawsuit appeared against the sisters who had signed the Note for £1300 borrowed by Emily from Samuel back in 1853. Grant became confused and Cornelia had to remind him:

> As something was dropped about signing a Bond without the means to meet it I send you a copy of the security I had in hand [Emily's gift to the Society] when I consented to the money being raised. I mentioned this [to] you once but you seemed to have forgotten that I told you our Sisters *never signed any Bond but that one for 1300 pounds* which Miss Bowles' security perfectly covered at the time, as the money was in Consols, but she afterwards insisted on having it, and we could not refuse it as she could not pay the contracts she had made for the repairs of Rupert House.
>
> I hope your Lordship sees clearly that no one signed that bond without a right principle governing.

The larger demands of the other brother loomed ominously. He continued to maintain – and only Emily could have told him such a thing – that the £5000 loan was 'asked for by the advice and with the sanction of the Superior'. He too threatened a lawsuit, and the sisters now discovered the awful fact which Emily knew: the simple mortgage on Rupert House recommended by Eyston turned out to be compound. It required the Society, should John Bowles sell the house for less than his loan, to make up the difference. It had been proposed by Eyston as simple but was drawn up by the Bowles' solicitor under Emily's direction; signed by sisters who evidently neglected to read the small print; and signed at the time by Emily who did not point out the unexpected clause even though at that date she, like them, was a member of the Society.

Eyston said that such a mortgage, 'given under peculiar circumstances for the benefit of Mr Bowles', was a solicitor's 'imprudence' to which he himself 'would not have consented'. He was also of the opinion that although the sisters had no legal defence against Samuel's threatened suit for the £1300, for John's debt for £5000 evidence was lacking and the suit was very unlikely to be granted. In the end both brothers, to their advantage, were settled out of court because the bishop, threatened by Emily with public scandal, insisted on a compromise solution. Both Eyston and Mother Connelly would have preferred to let it go to court, but in deference to the bishop the affair dragged on for ten wearing months.

The evidence on the Rupert House affair provided by Mother Connelly and Miss Bowles and in both cases given in retrospect, is often conflicting, but over the long haul – six years – Emily's contradictions and manipulations fall before the consistency of Cornelia's statements. The solicitor Eyston, who was also a friend of Emily's and who initially tried to smooth differences, maintained steadily that the buying of Rupert House was due to Emily's folly and the imprudence of her brother John who loaned her £5000 without security or even inquiry. Eyston had recorded the financial dealings between Emily and the Society since 1851 and wrote to her in December 1856 to show her that she was owed nothing. He had found, he told Cornelia, 'that her family was under the wrong impression that you had seized and spent all her money which in point of fact she had done herself'. Neither Mother Connelly nor the community, he told Grant, was 'liable for a farthing'.

'WE MUST SUBMIT', 1857–8

In January 1857 for the Epiphany Cornelia as always wrote to the Society. Emily, the first professed sister to leave, one who had belonged since its beginning, was by her own choice no longer one of them and Cornelia speaks to them of constancy and stability. It is the letter of a woman enamoured of God. Life in the Society, she is saying, offers joy to those who love and do what faithfulness to God's continuously offered love demands:

Ever Silent, Tranquil, Immutable, Holy, Holy, Holy Lord God

My very dear Sisters in Jesus Christ
The Eve of our Epiphany feast warns me that you will expect a letter from me, if it contains but three lines. You have made your dear retreat, and we are just finishing ours and preparing for the renewal of vows tomorrow morning . . . What shall I say? Three sweet words . . . Faith, Hope and Charity . . . If you practice these with perfect *constancy*, you will become saints; you are saints already, but not *sealed* till death proves your constancy. May your stability prove true till constancy is sealed by death, and by a death which is quickly to introduce you to the Beatific Vision, where you are to be filled with the joy of heavenly light, and encompassed by the ecstatic delight of loving God without interruption. Now we must delight in Him by our homely actions of Charity, and by our passive co-operation, not resisting the love that would fill our poor hearts. Let us not rest, my dear Sisters, for we are *ourselves* the only obstacle to the overflowing of His Divine Love.
   I must not say more than that I am ever your devoted Servant in Jesus Christ, Cornelia, SHCJ.

A week later Cornelia was writing to Grant. She could never trust herself to meet Emily again and during these years, 1857 and 1858, he was the unhappy go-between. Emily by her own account left the Society in order to secure justice for her brothers, and her methods and Cornelia's struggle now emerge dramatically. On 15 January Cornelia summed up her view for the bishop:

> The only view I take of the subject is this: Miss Bowles *acted privately* and independently of our Community. *Not* as a Religious, but as a secular. *Not* acknowledging any superior authority, not referring her Brother to any Authority. The loan of 5000 pounds was an *unprincipled* act on the part of Miss Bowles, and on the part of her Brother an effect of the *weakness* of human affection. Does justice demand that our Community should be responsible for the unknown deeds of another? Surely not, my Lord, for where there is no power there can be no responsibility.

On her return from Rome in April 1854 Grant himself had said she was 'not answerable for the act of Miss Bowles in this purchase'.

For the first eight months of 1857 Emily contented herself with mild threats to the bishop. She said merely that if the money was not paid to both brothers she could not in justice to them 'exert the least influence' to prevent the matter from going to court. She would never, she said, bring forward her own claims if her brothers were repaid.

Her first real onslaught on Grant, a man whom Ullathorne described as having a conscience 'tremulously delicate', came on 4 August 1857. In it she joins the ranks of Duke and Melia who wanted to oust Mother Connelly from the convent. The onus of 'disgrace to the whole Catholic body' which would ensue if full details of the affair were made public in court, would be Grant's, she insisted, not hers. She would herself perforce have to reveal that the convent was ruled by a despot, through 'double-dealing, deception, *sham, want of principle*'. A bishop should remove such a woman 'from a position so dangerous to the best interests of Religion'. Were they not greater than 'those of one individual or even of one Community?' This had an immediate effect on Grant. Unless the matter was settled out of court, he told Cornelia, he would not come down to clothe or profess sisters – a threat not fulfilled.

On 8 August Miss Bowles struck again. First comes a shrewd reference to the possibility of sisters going to prison; then Cornelia's lawyer (Emily's family friend) is denigrated; then Mother Connelly's style of government is said to ignore the Society's Constitutions – and what *right* has the bishop to countenance such an evil? If the suit gets to court her evidence on St Leonards will be 'complete and implicit' which, she devoutly exclaims, 'may God in His mercy and pity forbid'.

It was not only to Grant that she wrote such things. Newman received a letter. He is told that Mother Connelly is ready to 'quietly strip a family of about £12,000' (*sic*), and that 'everyone is a liar I think who is concerned with her'. During these weeks too a current rumour reached Cornelia. She had obliged someone, it was being said, to burn a business letter in order to conceal the truth: 'If I have not grown in humility my Lord I hope *that charge* has at least made me grow in charity and meekness, by the many acts I have made when unbidden it has returned to my mind.'

Emily's shafts were leaving their mark on the bishop. 'Do try to prevent these lawsuits,' he begged Cornelia, and when she responded that the sands at St Leonards were not gold mines and tells him, 'We have not the means to meet your wishes nor could we honestly promise to raise them,' he still says he would accept any terms from the Bowles brothers rather than allow a suit with costs and publicity. 'If we are to become bankrupt, why not let it happen?' she wrote to Eyston:

> . . . *we have no prospect of paying the sum proposed* . . . If Miss Bowles incites her brothers to bring a suit in Chancery it would bring facts to light that are now glossed over, and no jury could bring forth payment when there is no property to produce it. When the facts are known our innocence will be proved.

The pressure on Grant increased. John Bowles was writing disagreeable letters to the cardinal, the cardinal passed them on to the bishop, and on 11 October Emily attacked again. She has 'no pity when a bishop suffers for *allowing injustice*', she tells him, '& believe me my dear Lord, you *are* suffering much more than you know in the opinion of good and holy men who truly feel (& say) that weakness is not charity & that a bishop is bound *by his office* to punish evil-doers'. This drives him into decision: if by 20 October when the law courts will again be in session Cornelia has not agreed a compromise, it will be his duty to do so. Her answer comes: 'You my Lord are our Superior & I am ready to *second* the responsibility you propose taking to the very utmost of my power. Will you remember this my Lord. But at the same time I repeat that *it is impossible for me to meet your last proposal.*'

What that particular proposal was is not on record but he still insists on compromise. On 3 November she rejects one whereby she would have to raise a large sum at once: 'it is not what is, or will be, best but *what is possible*', she exclaims to the lawyer. Only something to be paid in small instalments over the years would be possible.

On 10 November Emily's patience is 'ebbing fast'. She writes cruelly:

> And now my dear Lord, if I bring upon you the swift vengeance (swift and *bitter*) of the *Times*, and if its malignant wrath falls upon the innocent

215

also, to the injury of religion, remember that you will have brought it upon yourself, that it is a most just & thoroughly equitable judgement, & the consequences of it, whatever they are, rest for ever upon your head.

Eyston sees through this and tells Grant, 'Her threats are only to try & get your Lordship to bring the matter to a Conclusion. Neither Mr Bowles or his Brother would like any legal or newspaper war.' But Grant was not convinced. His next letter to Cornelia begs her to:

> . . . hasten these affairs . . . Miss Bowles has written to say that she will now have recourse to the *Times*. The *Times* will admit no reply, and the public will believe none from Catholics. On some points it will be impossible to convince English readers that a Convent can ever be right.

Advent began. In the first week the bishop came down to St Leonards to give the children a pre-Christmas retreat and to clothe or profess five sisters. Festivities for Cornelia's feast that year and for Christmas, according to Buckle, were 'unusually bright' and the chapel 'a very gorgeous sight'.

In the new year of 1858 Grant, still in dread of opening a newspaper, decides that because 'it would fare badly with us to allow these matters to appear in a Court prejudiced as English courts often are on Catholic subjects', the most recent Bowles terms must be accepted and the affair terminated. A loan will have to be raised, which Cornelia still says she cannot do: 'we have no money in hand except such as meets our monthly bills'. He answers that he will raise it if she will agree to 'many years' of repayment and interest.

In the midst of this, on 12 January, some now obscure news about Pierce has reached her:

> Will your Lordship remember the soul of my poor son, who I fear is still in purgatory, and will you also pray for his father's conversion just at this time? It is asking a great deal, but I think our dear Lord wishes us to pray for them, and I will tell you why when I see you again my Lord.

Pierce, as far as is known, was still living at Albury Park with Adeline who is almost twenty-three. Frank, nearly sixteen, would be leaving Marlborough College in the coming June. Conceivably there was a question of the family leaving the country.

A community triduum of prayer comes and goes and the time of reflection fortified her. 'Kindle your fires. Do not stop to warm yourself,' she scribbled in the corner of a Community Work Book page, full of lists of jobs done and things to remember. The day after with renewed trust in God she wrote to Grant: 'Be assured my Lord, that whatever you decide upon in this settlement, we very willingly *believe to be the very best*, "in Domino".' A point has arrived for her when having done all she can herself there remains but one hope, total trust 'in Domino', the 'humbled God': she will do what the bishop requires.

The children were rehearsing for their annual plays and Cornelia was in the middle of it all, painting scenery, coaching actresses, welcoming visitors. 'Mrs Connelly and the nuns seemed not to have thrown off all common sense with their worldly raiment,' a parent noted.[2] February arrived. She was away visiting communities and the lawyers proceeded with negotiations. At last, on 28 March, nearly a year after saying 'if nothing else can be done we must submit', she was able to tell the bishop, 'Mr Bowles has accepted the offer last made.'

And there the matter should have rested. But Emily pushed on.

On 12 February, five weeks before the compromise was agreed, the father of two of the sisters at St Leonards died. Charles Laprimaudaye before his conversion had been Archdeacon Manning's curate. Manning too had become a Roman, and was now Wiseman's Provost at Westminster. He was also Emily's spiritual director. Through him she could have learned of Laprimaudaye's death and of legacies coming to the convent through his daughters.

On 25 March, the day after the Bowles settlement was agreed (as Cornelia believed), she received a brief, urgent letter from Grant. Emily had told him that John Bowles – according to her – was not satisfied with the settlement because by it he would be losing £600. Secondly, she believed the Laprimaudaye legacies were already in hand. Grant wanted to be able to satisfy her that this was not the case. Next day he wrote again. If there had been a reply from Cornelia to his first it must have said the Laprimaudaye money was not yet in hand (the father's affairs had been left in confusion) and that she had no certain knowledge of how much it would be. She may also have said she could not raise another £600.

Grant was a sick man, doing business against doctor's orders. It looks as if Emily had visited him and overwhelmed his judgment. His second letter begs Cornelia to 'add this 600 pounds to the rest'; Miss Bowles' Protestant brothers are scandalised by the way she had had to leave and she has become an object of reproach in their eyes; she had given 'all her money & her time & zeal for many years to the Institute', and though £600 is a large sum it is 'less than you received with her'. In making these two statements about money the bishop is suddenly saying the opposite of what Cornelia, supported by Eyston, had from the beginning maintained to be true. And he is abandoning his original statement that she was 'not answerable for the act of Miss Bowles in this purchase'. His letter appears to be the desperate effort of a sick man to close what had become for him a 'long & anxious business'. Cornelia is told that she will have 'better wealth than

217

gold and silver in the recollection' of her sacrifice if she gives the £600, and he calls on her to show Emily 'sisterly compassion'.

Her reply is angry and blunt. Her feelings sear the page:

Mr Lord Bishop

I cannot do more than we have already offered to do. We only received 700 pounds with Miss Bowles, and we shall have 1992 pounds to pay on her debts. She squandered her own money my Lord, not in the service of God or our Institute, but to follow her own views solely and *in charity* she deserves the reproaches of her brothers, and far more deeply those of our Society.

She was indeed unhappily long enough with us to sow the seeds of disobedience, cabal and disunion, and to give a lasting example of an ambitious, restless and seditious character, which can never be forgotten or effaced. I wish I could forget that she ever existed, unless it be to pray for her in a general way.

Begging your Lordship's blessing . . .

These two people were often a great trial to one another, Cornelia with her directness of speech and strength in action, Grant with his scrupulous, vacillating disposition, ever conciliatory. But there was understanding and trust between them. She could write him as straight a letter as this one, and yet confidently add a personal request: 'PS. Perhaps I am asking too great a favour from you, my Lord, but still I ask it – will you say the mass on Good Friday for Mr Connelly and my dear children?'

Meanwhile, with lawyers already at work on legal documents for the settlement, Emily decided that because Laprimaudaye money was coming to the Society it was no longer right for her to forgo her own claims. Nor could she, unless repaid, make up to brother John his loss of £600. A jumbled account of moneys owed to her (all claims which Cornelia and Eyston, with documented proof, denied) went to Grant, and requested the withdrawal of her name from the settlement. Her brothers' claims could be settled legally, she told the bishop, but her own by arbitration – with himself, forsooth, as arbitrator. Grant, grateful that as bishop he could not act as umpire, put the proposal to Mother Connelly: would she be willing to meet with Miss Bowles in the presence of someone not a lawyer, to settle Emily's claims 'in a friendly way between yourselves?'

Foreseeably this elicited a refusal. To agree to arbitration would be to admit that there had been a time when she had control over Miss Bowles' property. But another reason headed Cornelia's refusal. She could not trust herself to speak and act with charity if she met Emily. The first draft of her answer runs:

I must decline any interview with Miss Bowles. In all charity and forgiveness, we still feel that she has acted the part of a demon towards us, and the only way to secure charity is to keep apart. The calumnious effects of her many grievous falsehoods can *never* be effaced, nor will it be easy in time to *forget* them, tho I trust Our Lord may remove the Viper of animosity, and help us through the burden of wrongs which must be felt for some years.

Cornelia is on the brink of bitterness here. A sense of injustice burned within her but what she actually sent to the bishop was calmer: 'I must decline any interview with Miss Bowles. I could give very strong reasons for this determination, but I refrain from motives of Charity.' And although she declined to meet Emily she did not wish to block Grant's efforts towards a settlement. She reiterated her promise to second, 'in Domino', whatever he decided: 'we feel every confidence that our dear Lord will help us through the heavy burden of these wrongs . . . Will you pray for us much, my Lord, and bless us.'

Now Cornelia met step by step Grant's final requests as each reached him from Miss Bowles. First she demanded back the two donations she had made, then she increased the total, then she exacted that it be paid to her heirs should she die; then she pushed to be paid interest:

> . . . considering the whole matter, the way in which my whole fortune was spent in the service & support of the community, that my personal clothing even was shared among them, & I myself left almost destitute, I think your Lordship will decide that my request is only reasonable, & that to refuse it would be neither just nor wise.

Her last bid was to demand that in the document to be drawn up Mrs Connelly must state that: 'Miss Bowles' whole available fortune was spent in the service & for the use of the Community.' This Eyston refused to countenance and contrived to evade in the final Letter of Agreement. In October 1858 the Bowles affair was at last settled out of court as the bishop wished. Mother Connelly and the Society were left with a debt of £2850 plus interest and lawyers' fees. It took her till 1866 to pay off the Revd Samuel, and till 1871 to pay Emily and John.

In November Cornelia wrote to her brother:

> How one's thought flies over years long gone, carrying many heart-breaking sorrows . . . Do not be touchy or testy with me. If my letters have offended or annoyed you I am very sorry . . . We are growing old my dear Ralpho and perhaps you are cross and do not know it. I also am getting very old. I shall be very soon at the end of my 50th year.

219

Ady is now twenty-three and Frank seventeen. She has not seen them for ten years: 'I have nothing to tell you about my own darling children except that Pierce has taken them to Brussels without bringing them to see me or even letting me know of their departure. May God forgive him!' She can do 'nothing to help them except by prayer' and has offered to go as a missionary to Japan to win God's blessings on them and their father. 'I so much wish to go if possible.'

These are the private burdens of her heart, but those inflicted by the unjust outcome of the Bowles affair concerned the community too. For them at the end of such a year she wrote with insistent faith, and in the middle of sickness: 'God is good! Good! Good! When shall we understand the extent of his goodness. He has sent us money just when and as we require it not only for ourselves but for others who need our help. He has fed us spiritually as well as bodily.'

REFLECTION ON EMILY

If in 1846 Emily with her relative wealth and her many contacts was well placed to promote the Society's good, she was now equally so to do it damage. Two letters show this happening, one to Newman, the other to Mother Margaret Hallahan, the close friend of Bishop Ullathorne.

Six months after the death of Mr Jones, in her days of devotion to Cornelia and enthusiasm for the Society, Emily had written to Newman about the troubles they were having with the congregation about the property at St Leonards. Among other similar remarks came the statement that Jones 'never would allow that the congregation had any right or authority whatever, nor suffered them to exercise any'; and as to ownership, she said that in her presence Jones had told Mother Connelly that although he had thought of putting the property in trust, 'I advise you my dear to keep things you know in your own hands, as most communities find it the Best way.' Yet by contrast in 1861, five years after she had left the Society, Emily was recalling conversations with Mr Jones to exactly the opposite effect and regaled Mother Margaret accordingly. Jones, she said, had wished all to be 'for the Mission & parish' and it was 'Mrs C who continually advanced in her wishes of overthrowing the congregation'.

Other contradictions emerge. The woman loved and admired in 1851 amidst the St Leonards difficulties, in 1861 is traduced. To Newman Emily wrote: 'Oh if you knew how Rev Mother has been tried & what it is to see her so tried, so tortured as it were & be able to do nothing.' And to Mother Margaret ten years later: 'It seems to me positively monstrous that a whole property should have been taken possession of . . . under false pretences . . .

the total want of truth & integrity . . . the curse of money . . . is an awful thing to weigh upon those given to God . . .'

When Emily wrote this letter to Mother Margaret, Bishops Ullathorne and Grant were in almost daily correspondence about the St Leonards property dispute and her letter finished up in Grant's archives. It portrays Towneley as a tool of Cornelia's manipulation and, were it accepted as true, destroys all confidence in her probity. The letter was a step in a sequence of events and the sequence is revealing.

In April 1860, having in terms of money won the Rupert House affair hands down, another letter went from Emily to Newman concluding with: 'When I look back upon the whole thing – the cost, the political manoevres, the subterfuges, the want of *singleness* altogether, I cannot but bless God for my deliverance.' Yet by June she wanted to return to the Society. She so convinced Thomas Seed SJ of her sincerity that he wrote on her behalf. Cornelia presumably refused.

In October 1861, in the context of possibly becoming a Dominican, she wrote the letter to Mother Margaret. In it Cornelia is slandered and St Leonards described as 'polluted with human passions'. Eighteen months later she swung back once more, this time encouraged by Peter Gallwey SJ. Again she wished to rejoin the Society and wrote to Cornelia. Her letter has not survived but Mother Connelly answered her with good advice about how well, with all her gifts, she could serve God without being a member of a religious congregation. It was an encouraging and kind letter, a wise substitute for any meeting, for as a correspondence (very incomplete) with Gallwey shows, the memory of Emily was still 'extremely painful'.

One whose behaviour so consistently swung between such opposites as Emily's must have been the victim of ungovernable feeling, even of conflicting self-images. What she says of Mother Connelly, the object of the hate which so often prevailed, cannot be taken at its face value however unyielding or difficult Cornelia may sometimes have been. One is left to conjecture what it was that brought things to such a pass.

Emily had given her trustee William Buckle the impression that she was co-foundress of the Society. He speaks of her as having been at one time '*joint head* which she was always so considered'. His daughter Maria, there almost from the beginning, remembered Emily as often arguing with Mother Connelly about Society matters. But other evidence does not suggest that there was solid ground for any such pretension on Emily's part. When Wiseman had to persuade the Jesuits to become confessors to the new foundation he called on the earl to support his request. Shrewsbury did so and wrote: 'I am confident there is no one so capable of carrying out an Institute of this description as good Mrs Connelly so I beg of you not to discourage her by throwing unnecessary obstacles in her way. She may also lose valuable associates by any delay.' Emily was a 'valuable associate' but is not named. Moreover she had no experience of religious life and although Wiseman persuaded her to join Mrs Connelly (against another inclination, according to Luigi Gentili), it was Cornelia with whom he settled affairs and whom he installed as superior-general. And he did not, as in the case of Cornelia, privilege Emily by allowing her to be professed after only one year as a novice, instead of two.

Nevertheless if this extremely intelligent, energetic but emotionally insecure woman began the life with even some sense that she was of notable importance to the foundation, and then gradually found herself unable to move it in directions she wanted; if eventually she lost in the process both the venture in which she believed and the family money she had sunk into it, albeit illicitly; if in consequence she was then deprived of office and status – all this could have generated an emotional conviction and vindictive anger that she had been unjustly dealt with. Eyston, though a family friend, warned Grant: 'she is ready to do every injury possible to the Convent at St Leonards and the inmates thereof'.

The initial yoking of these two women, according to Gentili who said he knew Emily well, was Wiseman's idea. Wiseman's great pastoral concern for the poor made it important for him to find religious who would work with them. In Cornelia he had a woman who wanted an uncloistered but religious life of active mercy. In his enthusiasm he saddled her with a financially impossible convent (in 1859 Sing was still hounding her) and with a companion who though intelligent, zealous, interested in education and quite wealthy, was also irredeemably headstrong. Of the Rupert House affair Mr Buckle, one of her trustees and fond of her, expostulated with her for having purchased a property of which even the rates and taxes would be beyond her means. And he wrote to Grant: 'Miss Bowles neglected her duties at Liverpool in consequence of having but one idea, that of possessing the large house. In point of talents & accomplishments she has not her equal but of common sense, judgement, and now principles she is wanting.' Speaking more generally Cornelia herself wrote: 'I warned her against natural rashness of character as frequently as I thought prudent to do so.'

The 1851 census in England revealed that in the over twenty age group women outnumbered men, and articles and pamphlets in their hundreds appeared on the theme, Why are Women Redundant? What were the 'ladies' not drawn to marriage to be allowed to do? The census figures merely highlighted a long-growing problem. On a voluntary, unprofessional basis women in large numbers had long been committing themselves to Christian social service. But to become a religious was also one of the answers, one which Newman as an Anglican and also Pusey had advocated, and in the forties (when Emily became a Catholic and also joined the Society) Anglican sisterhoods, mostly founded for 'good works', were beginning to proliferate. For the Catholics the new non-monastic congregations, of which the Society was a clear example, had appeared. In either church intelligent and educated women with a religious turn of mind undoubtedly sometimes looked to these as a way of channelling their devotion and energies. Not all, however, were suited to the life, and sometimes – conceivably for Emily – it was perhaps a reaching for independence.[3]

The best side of Emily shows in her unflagging zeal for Christian service, especially to the poor and disadvantaged. Cornelia's letter to her in 1863 recognised this and encouraged it in her. She also had a capacity for faithful devotion to those she admired. Newman's religious genius and great mind were a beacon to her for the whole of her life and Cornelia too evoked this kind of loyalty until she called for an obedience which Emily could not support. Away from Cornelia's positive influence at St Leonards and invested with the freedom and trust of her office in Liverpool, she succumbed to a driving need to realise her own dream, and the values of religious life shifted in its service. She could not be opposed: Cornelia who checked her was trampled underfoot. She was perfidious: to gain her own end she lied to her brothers about Cornelia and to Cornelia about her brothers. She was self-serving: when she wanted to win back the money she had squandered and could not do so as a religious, she secured a dispensation from her vow of obedience, left, suborned Wiseman and intimidated Grant into imposing on Cornelia an unfair settlement with her family, and then asked to return to the Society she had slandered. Blocked once more by Cornelia, she turned to calumny and manipulation of opinion among her many and high-placed acquaintances in order to destroy the former object of her admiration. Like Pierce, Emily Bowles in the long term did great damage to Cornelia and the Society.

THE SOCIETY ENDANGERED, 1857

One consequence of the Bowles affair was Wiseman's intervention with the Propaganda virtually to suppress the Society. Apostolate and community had already been drawn into Emily's destructive orbit. Now, soon after her departure, constitutional matters of first importance were discussed and proposed to Rome with no reference whatever to Mother Connelly. Unjustly represented there, she had no chance to defend herself, and the existence of the Society as she envisioned it was in unseen danger.

Emily's large family circle of Protestant connections buzzed with her account of why she had left: 'the Bishops of Oxford & Chichester & the Knollyses are acquainted with the matter & I should not be at all surprised if it is brought into public by some of them'. And as to Catholics, 'A person high in the Church said to me lately, "I should think Mrs Connelly had had nearly enough 'notoriety' without this".'

These latter remarks were part of Emily's unsuccessful effort to convert the parents of Maria Buckle to her point of view. They sent the correspondence straight to the bishop but her Protestant brothers sent their 'disagreeable letters' to the cardinal; and the cardinal, already for other reasons ill-disposed to Mother Connelly, was a friend of Emily's.

In view of this groundswell of scandal from both within and without England's small Catholic world, it is not surprising to find that soon after Emily had left, and when the spectre of 'going public' in a lawsuit was already faintly looming, Grant requested 'a meeting about St Leonards' with Wiseman and his Eminence graciously concurred. After it Grant told Cornelia that Wiseman, accepting as true the claims of the brothers, presumed that she would settle things as he wished. At once she requested Grant to tell the cardinal what she and Eyston believed were the facts. But Wiseman was already entrenched in his opinion and Grant had told her nothing of the meeting's main outcome. At its conclusion he had sent the bishop of Liverpool a plan which he and Wiseman had made for the life and government of the Society. Before forwarding it to Rome they needed Goss's agreement because there were Holy Child sisters in his diocese. Goss replied with approval.

He did more. He offered for Grant's perusal a lengthy statement written for him by Emily Bowles. Its purpose was to show why she could not remain obedient to so 'wayward & overbearing' a person as Mother Connelly, and why it was urgent there be changes made in the Society's government. It might be 'pertinent to the matter in hand', said Goss to Grant, and could give 'insight into the hidden working of the system'. Emily's thirteen pages of foolscap duly found their way south and finished up not in Grant's archives but in Wiseman's. If the cardinal read them they were no help to Cornelia's cause with him. He had already been outraged by the request to Rome that the superior-general remained in office for life, and accordingly had blocked approval of the Constitutions. The insight now offered of 'hidden working' was more grist to his mill. Mrs Connelly, Emily stated, had reduced the government of the Society to 'irresponsible despotism'.

Having obtained Goss's approval Grant drew up the letter for Rome and sent it to Wiseman to sign. Wiseman replied that he would forward it at once 'with an appendix'. Grant's letter was entirely about the Constitutions, persuasively but dispassionately written and in no way critical of Cornelia. The cardinal's appendix dealt only with the Bowles affair and was full of animus. Cornelia knew nothing of either.

The Bowles affair had thrown into sharp relief the Society's need of

Rome's approbation and it was primarily this need that drew Grant and Wiseman together. Each as bishop of a needy diocese desired the survival of the apostolic work done for them. Here was a useful congregation of scattered sisters held together by Mother Connelly's influence among them, and by their hope that the Rule they wished to continue living by would be approved. Without that they were vulnerable to any destructive criticism that might arise. And it had arisen, through Pierce and Duke and now Emily, none of whom hesitated to spread their falsified information with energy and rhetoric. With Emily's departure the need for approbation became acute. All and sundry heard her account of things, and as one who spoke with inside knowledge she would be easily believed by the credulous. The picture of tyranny which she painted for Goss's benefit could put off both would-be applicants and prospective pupils, make enemies of parents and priests, and encourage discontent among the less settled sisters.

Cornelia was not unaware of the dangers. When Grant wrote to her after the meeting to say that the cardinal considered the community obliged to meet the Bowles' claim, her sense of the injustice and danger of not having approbation poured itself on to paper: 'I *deplore* our Institute not having been approved. Had this been done, proper authority would have been enforced; ourselves secured as a body, acknowledged as responsible, and this scandal prevented.' She is sure that in justice the Society is owed what it asked:

> *We* asked no more than many orders have already obtained, nor have we ever shown any unwillingness to submit, in docility, to the wishes of our Superiors in the smallest point wherein religious discipline might not be destroyed. I am very sure throughout our many troubles we have ever maintained & aimed at that rectitude of intention which ensures us peace & rest while quietly labouring for the souls of Christ's little ones, awaiting the declaration of *His* most Holy Will regarding our Rule.

Emily's conduct will have an evil effect on some sisters:

> But however this may serve those long tried, and for a certain number of years to prove the *stability of the most faithful,* you will see other evils than this *one in question.* The most intelligent and clever are the first to bring up the fact that His Holiness has *not* approved for us the same rule [Jesuit Summarium] which he *has* approved for others. If this was modified for them in minor points, not touching upon religious discipline, why might not the same have been done for us before now?

Approbation is to be desired not as a papal favour but as the essential source of stability. The only question is 'the work of God, and the good of souls, & that we have the means of serving Him, and of *maintaining* a right spirit in those He has given to us, which never can be ensured with stability until the Church blesses us by the seal of her approbation'.

This cry from the heart was never sent to the bishop. Apparently prudence prompted second thoughts and she confined herself to pointing out that Miss Bowles had acted as one who acknowledged no authority. But Grant and Wiseman wanted the Society's stability for their own utilitarian purposes. They came up with what they agreed was 'the quickest and most efficacious way' of providing 'stability and permanence of government'. To amend the present Constitutions would 'require a very long time' but to adopt *in toto* those of some other congregation already approved would not.

Neither cardinal nor bishop had ever lived the religious life. They knew it only at second hand. Nor did they yet have for their guidance a body of church law adapted to this kind of religious group, nor before this the experience of such a one being founded in England. In making their decision they did not consider what today's understanding of religious life would expect: that the identity, the life-giving spirit of a religious community, comes to it primarily through its origins, generally exemplified in the one who founds, and then expressed in a rule of life which characterises the group. It is much more than a disciplinary code, and much more than the description of particular apostolic works – to which both Wiseman and Grant understandably attributed primary importance. But both code and works, adaptable with time, spring from the originating life. This Cornelia Connelly had captured for her congregation in the preliminary and fundamental part she wrote for the 1854 Rule. It was the Society's heart's core, under God its written source of union, and it gave meaning to the disciplinary and governmental sections that followed. These though incomplete were drawn from constitutions already approved, and this is why Cornelia, unaware of confusion with Pierce's pseudo Rule and of episcopal machinations, cried out at the injustice of not being approved. Wiseman, in his so lengthy 1854 response to Fransoni, had paid no attention to her vital paragraphs. Now, in proposing the suppression of the entire Rule, he was advocating, supported by Grant and Goss, what in the long term, if Rome agreed, would deprive the Society of its empowering identity.

A corollary of this solution to the problem of stability was their proposal about government.

In 1854 a key recommendation had come from the consultor in Rome. He did not know Cornelia, was confused by Pierce's pseudo Rule and impressed by the cardinal's portrait of Mother Connelly as a woman who disregarded bishops. He proposed that the houses of her Society should become independent of the superior at St Leonards. Grant knew this. Without showing Cornelia the report, he had discussed with her in 1854 only some aspects of the proposal. It was alien to her understanding of what she had come to establish. The Society had been conceived in Rome. She had been missioned by the pope and the cardinal prefect of the Propaganda, not by a local bishop nor for a particular diocese but to spread to other countries from England. She had brought a sketch of a Rule with her which the prefect had allowed as an experimental basis and which she had not failed to work on. And she knew that since the Society of the Sacred Heart and the Sisters of Notre Dame de Namur, both founded on the continent, had central government there was a precedent for it in her own foundation. She felt deeply on the subject and when in November 1854 Grant had tried to urge contrariwise she wrote:

> Time will surely bring to light His Holy Will in our regard and prove whether we are to be a religious Order in His Holy Church or whether we are to sink into a few scattered houses of pious women without a religious head or strength or discipline within ourselves, and consequently without any comparative, holy religious influence. It seems to me a sort of duty that I should say what we feel & think on the subject and the rest I leave in the hands of God to wait in patience His doings.

To this Grant had responded reassuringly. The cardinal 'quite takes the view which is conveyed in your letter, that you will have the means of effecting greater good if the houses are united as at present'. But this was a diplomatic half-truth. The cardinal had told him he agreed with this *for the present*, that is, until Cornelia resigned or died. And what now, three years later, bishops and cardinal settled for secretly, was exactly what Cornelia did *not* envision, separate religious communities under direct control of individual bishops. The office of superior-general was to cease altogether, but since sisters and pupils were so attached to Cornelia, she was to be allowed to retain until she died the title without power. From the point of view of Goss, Grant and Wiseman it was a very sensible compromise.

Wiseman's appendix was attached to the letter. In it he provides the Propaganda, now headed by Fransoni's successor Cardinal Barnabò, with an account of the Bowles affair. He gives only Emily's point of view. If Grant, as requested by Cornelia, had conveyed to him her grounds for disagreement, Wiseman has ignored them. The Bowles brothers, he says, are 'scandalised by the despotic and dishonest way' in which Mrs Connelly had behaved and are amazed that the church has not 'enough authority to keep her to her duty and to restrain her absolute arbitrariness'. They have given up all thought of becoming Catholics on account of it. Mrs Connelly's obstinacy will probably drive the affair into court or the public press. If Rome decides to adopt the plan now proposed, would the Propaganda please not say it is the suggestion of Wiseman and Grant because that would 'rouse all her antipathy'. And he is giving this additional information only to show 'the urgency of the affair and the need to apply a remedy to the dominant and ungovernable character of that American lady'.

In Rome at that time was Archbishop Errington, Wiseman's auxiliary. The difference between the two men had not yet come to the clash and Barnabò asked him to assess the cardinal's proposal. He did so and condemned it.

It was customary for the church, he pointed out, to leave such an initiative for change to foundress and sisters, and it was not for the Propaganda to take that initiative itself. The proposal, he said, was irregular and extraordinary yet unlikely to secure its purpose, because among other things it was opposed to the ideas of the foundress as already set down in her Constitutions. He implied that since the defects of the said Constitutions arose chiefly from the lack of particular knowledge they could be remedied since the Society's schools had succeeded largely through 'the personal qualities of the Superior and the good spirit of the Community'. It would be better, he said, in spite of the difficulties experienced, to leave the permanence of the Institute of the Holy Child to providence.

His advice was taken. Emily continued her destructive talking, Wiseman's enmity was by no means quenched and reappears later. Cornelia, unaware of the Society's escape, pursued her way. Providence had indeed intervened in the person of Archbishop Errington.

11

'The Only Worth of Education'

One day late in June 1854 Cornelia allowed herself to dream of what the Society might do for the church. The Feast of SS Peter and Paul was coming. Her zealous heart ran away with her and she listed in a notebook prayers from the 'poor beggars of the Holy Child'. There was particular cause at this moment for the exuberance with which her notes bubble.

Cornelia's initial vision was of a community to be engaged in 'the spiritual works of mercy'. One of these could be education but in England there was immediate need for schooling at all levels. True to her inspiration the Society at once received converts, offered instruction and private retreats, and ministered in the parish. But it was education that Wiseman most required of her and over the years the Society was more and more identified with work in schools. Other new congregations, of foreign origin, had already sent communities and Cornelia's English foundation was late in the procession. At the start it was nearly strangled by scandal and lack of means. It survived largely because in a small way it was able to meet a particular social need, the education of the poor. At Derby she tried to set up schools for the middle and upper classes too, but such establishments did not quickly take root whereas schools for the poor flourished from the beginning.

The earliest at Derby had earned high praise from the government inspector, so had the small one at the St Leonards convent gate. So too had the sisters in crowded London classrooms. They ran St Anne's in Soho and the schools in Gate Street, Bunhill Row and Baldwin Gardens, all in areas of squalor and extreme need. Poor themselves, the sisters ministered to the children of the destitute.[1] By 1854 they were also in Preston and Liverpool, and in April of that year came the good news that fired Cornelia's dreaming. The CPSC wrote that a grant might be theirs for a great work in Liverpool, the training of teachers for the poor. It had been resolved 'That the sum of £1200 be granted to the building of the Liverpool Training School under the Nuns of the Holy Child . . . provided that the calls admit it.' With the arrival of this hopeful information lack of money as a major problem

229

temporarily receded. All things, in a moment of enthusiasm and faith-filled fantasy, suddenly appeared possible. The Society's needs danced before Cornelia's eyes, and she listed her longings.

Petitions on behalf of the Society's need

For St Peter's and Paul's
Poor beggars of the Holy Child

1 Election of our General.
2 Church built at St Leonards and two priests. A large and very pious Congregation to glorify God. All loving the convent. One hundred young ladies. One hundred novices, some rich and noble, so that the garden may be the Quadrangle of the Convent & all built round (no need to explain to St Peter because he knows all about it).
3 Large College in London with beautiful chapel and Services to attract all hearts to the Sacred Heart and our Lady.
4 College, Training School and Chapel in Liverpool, with 150 day scholars and 50 boarders. Lecturers etc. 60 students (Novices). House in the country at Gillmoss or Ince Blundell. Jesuit chaplain and confessor. Lamps always burning at the altars of the Sacred Heart and our Lady of Dolours.
5 Preston. Twenty nuns, all filled with fervent zeal for souls. Chapel built on to Convent or Church where Clothing and Professions could take place.
6 Manchester. A college.
7 Edinburgh. A college.
8 *All America* for our own. Ah, St Peter who walked on the waters by faith, take us to America, to California, Texas, Philadelphia, Baltimore, Charleston & Cincinnati.
9 House in Bonn [Rome?] whenever it is time.
10 That we may have real solid virtue & sanctity with true obedience as the marks of our Society.

These are the dreams of a great-hearted and apostolic woman. Opposition and insecurity could not quench her, and her major aspirations at that date emerge clearly: constitutional stability; development at St Leonards; a community in Rome; '*All America*'; and an outstanding desire to train Poor School teachers. In order to understand what brought Cornelia to this level of enthusiasm for teacher-training it is necessary to look back at the situation in which she found herself on arrival in England.

The problems with which the Catholic minority was faced when Cornelia arrived in 1846 were described in the *Rambler* of that year:

> We have first a population of from one to two millions, consisting of a small number of the aristocracy and gentry, a small number of the professional and middle class, a sprinkling of petty shopkeepers, and a gigantic mass of the extreme poor. For the education and spiritual guidance and support of this immense body, we have less than eight hundred priests, including the religious orders . . . Our education, clerical and secular, is universally felt and generally admitted to be still in its infancy, and to present most formidable obstacles in the way of a satisfactory reformation. We have scarcely the shadow of any Catholic organisation of our entire body.[2]

The composition of the body of Catholics posed particular educational difficulties. There were – to speak very generally – the poor Irish who were the majority of the Catholic population; the old English Catholics who through penal times had preserved the faith in its traditional forms and who would not provoke the hidden mistrust of the non-Catholic body; and the increasing number of converts. These were often educated men and women whose personal commitment to Christ had been long and informed before they became Catholics. Often the men had been to Oxford or Cambridge and had held benefices in the Anglican church, and often both men and women lost their living resources when they changed allegiance. They came hoping to share in the rebuilding of the Catholic church in England through their commitment, their education and their experience of civil life. They wanted to build the future rather than cling to the past.

Wiseman was of the same mind. A 'vast movement towards the Catholic Church' had begun, he believed, and he was determined to promote it. Newman's group at Maryvale and Faber's near Alton Towers were encouraged by him in the belief that new converts could be deployed in the work of conversion, and he envisioned Cornelia's congregation for women as something similar. Also he had to unify the disparate groups among the English Catholics. Mrs Connelly, it must have appeared to him – 'must', one says, because why else should she have been so arbitrarily diverted and against all sense from going to her own country – was particularly fitted to create the kind of community needed. She was as well educated as those women of the old Catholic families whose daughters by long tradition had private tutors or were sent abroad. Though American not English she was a friend of Lord Shrewsbury; and would be able to transcend the divisions on the English Catholic scene. Most significantly she was a convert, and her conversion to Rome and her ongoing formation as a Catholic had been essentially European and largely Roman.

The community Cornelia brought into being was, as Wiseman intended, for some time composed largely of converts. It was also not cloistered and the apostolates it undertook reached out to a cross section of the Catholic population. Immigrant Irish joined the English poor in the schools which the sisters ran. Her convents offered home, work and training for some of the country's unwanted orphans, whether Irish or English, as well as hospitality and instruction to converted ladies whose families had rejected them. And the children of both old Catholics and new converts were educated side by side in the boarding and day schools for the better off. Through education in one form or another, and out of Cornelia's gifts of faith and personality and experience which together characterised its particular quality, much of what Wiseman hoped was achieved.

In England when she arrived cheap labour was at a premium. Mounting industrial productivity needed its victims – women and children. A swelling middle class of manufacturers, increasingly affluent and powerful, was ambitious for social status, and schooling for their daughters was oriented to what was needed for social success. Schooling for the poor was contrary to their interests and barely allowed.

The date of her arrival, given what her work was to be, was providential. The country's first Committee of Education had been set up only recently in 1839, and its secretary, James Kay-Shuttleworth, made grants available to certain existing voluntary societies towards building schools. Then on 21 December 1846, one week after Cornelia's little group put on religious dress, he had inaugurated what was to become a national scheme for training teachers for the poor. Till then voluntary societies provided such schools as they could, giving the teachers a brief and narrow training in Normal or Training schools. Generally they used the monitorial system in which, because the teacher taught monitors who then drilled groups, enormous numbers of children could be handled in one school – a cheap system which worked like a machine. But not all the poor could be reached in this way and in the year of Cornelia's arrival Catholic numbers were swelled immensely by the victims of famine in Ireland.

What Kay-Shuttleworth established was an apprenticeship to teaching, the pupil-teacher system. A girl (or boy) of thirteen years would for five years receive seven and a half hours of instruction a week from an approved teacher and in return teach for five and a half hours every day. She could then go (on a Queen's scholarship if she passed one, otherwise privately) to a Training College for at least two, and often three years, at the end of which, having passed the government examinations, she would emerge as a qualified teacher and be able to take charge of a school. To maintain the quality of education given in the schools and colleges, he set up an inspector-ate which he imbued with his own ideals. Stipends to both approved and would-be teachers, whether in Poor School or college, were made only on their recommendation. One of the inspectors became a great supporter of Cornelia.

It was not until she had been at Derby for more than a year that a grant was allowed to Catholics. Till then her sisters could teach the poor but she could not provide for teacher-training. The community was too poor.[3] Yet during those few busy weeks in England *before* she began at the convent the Jesuit provincial superior was told that the new community would be 'educating the poor and middle classes and training schoolmistresses' and when the community had begun this was confirmed. The secretary of the CPSC was told by the sisters that 'the training of Mistresses is their chief desire and the first object of their Institute'. There is no evidence that Cornelia arrived in England with a clear intention of taking up this funda-mental work, though she may well have thought about it. Before she came Newman detailed for a friend the works of the new congregation (informed by Pierce at Alton Towers?) and makes no mention of this. But she appar-ently committed herself immediately and positively to it when there were no social mechanisms as yet in place to rely on. Almost certainly this was the influence of Wiseman.

On her arrival in mid-August 1846 she was at once and often in contact with him. As a bishop, Walsh's coadjutor, there was no important need of the Catholic church in England of which he was ignorant. In 1843 he had roused the Central District to protest injustice to Catholics in a proposed government bill for educational reforms. In 1846 he did the same in the matter of charitable trusts. In the same year the introduction of the pupil-teacher scheme again gave edge to the Catholic sense of injustice, and he was supporting Catholic effort to win a share in available grants. This he continued to do until it was achieved December 1847.[4] He could not have been unaware that whereas there were many (twenty-two) non-Catholic establishments for training teachers of the poor,[5] the Catholics had none. His foundation letter to Cornelia, when in mid-October she settled at Derby, makes no mention of teacher-training, but neither does it refer to promoting the conversion of England which, while still in Rome, she had understood was the basic reason for being sent to England not America.[6] The letter, one suspects, was not intended to define exactly the limits of service, but generally to encourage. She was expected to read it in the context of their conversations, and for her it would have included the teacher-training which they had discussed. With schools for the poor he knew she could begin at once because buildings and children awaited her at Derby. Training their teachers could commence as soon as grant was won.

In the event the grant was allowed very soon, even for Catholics. Cornelia applied at once and it was given for five teachers. The bishops in synod, including Wiseman, by then pro-vicar apostolic in London, 'approved of Derby Convent as a training school' and the CPSC saw it as such. The five to whom grant was given (probably members of the Society) were to become, according to the CPSC, the core staff of a college. Only the difficulties with Mr Sing prevented her from establishing at Derby in 1849 first a pupil-teacher centre in the school, and then a college.

DREAM REALISED, 1854

To return to Cornelia's moment of dreaming in 1854 and to the prospect of teacher-training then. Second sight did not warn her that before the year was out Emily's rash dealings in Liverpool would make it impossible to leave her in charge. Nor that in May 1855 the all-important building grant there would fall through. For a second time the prospect faded away.

Cornelia however pushed on. Prospects of ministry in one city might be lost, but she cut her losses and began again. The sisters in the Poor Schools were withdrawn from Liverpool and the bishop was glad to let them continue in his diocese, at Blackpool. The remainder, with a nucleus of fee-paying children, followed when Rupert House was given up, and began what became a notably successful boarding and day school. For training teachers for the poor, she reverted to her earlier hope that it could be provided for at St Leonards. Towneley and Grant agreed. The inspector T. W. M. Marshall, through whom grant for pupil teachers at Derby had been allowed, now recommended it for college students and teachers, and government through the CPSC agreed to a Catholic college in the south. By 6 February 1856, four days after the Liverpool college began, the one at St Leonards was in operation. By midsummer it was able to accommodate sixty students though in fact its numbers never rose so high.

Cornelia flung herself with great earnestness into every aspect of the project, organising and animating. Sisters now had to pass examinations in order to be college teachers. A government syllabus had to be met. Buckle remembers the daily lectures that were arranged, four every morning, including mathematics. Bellasis remarks on 'the energy and steady active application' poured into launching the college, and indeed Mother Connelly knew exactly what she wanted. When it had been open only a week she wrote to her good friend the inspector, who was anxious on their behalf. He had suggested that an experienced secular teacher should join the college staff for the first year, but no, she now preferred to rely on the group of sisters trained by herself:

My dear Mr Marshall

I hope you will not be dissatisfied when I say that I do not want the certificated lecturer. I really do not want her. Do not be *anxious* about our success. If at midsummer you wish me to have a professor I will certainly follow your advice. At present the Students are not equal to the advantages they already have.

I shall be very glad to see you and to have your opinion upon their present course of lectures & studies. Will you bring your beautiful lecture with you that I may copy it out for the use of the Sisters?

Will you also ask for a grant of books for us?

We shall hope to see you at the beginning of the week as Mother Theresa tells me you are coming very soon. I am sure you will feel better satisfied and have every confidence when your visit has been made.

She was right and later he admitted it fully and officially. Nevertheless Cornelia learned much from Mr Marshall. His perspectives were those of a family man (his little girl Edith came to her school), Cambridge educated and a well-known speaker and writer; once an Anglican in charge of a parish; like herself a convert. In 1847 the government had appointed him as the first inspector of Catholic schools and through him she was able to acquire national horizons and became an informed professional. 'The march of teaching is going on at such a wonderful pace,' she once exclaimed, and sought out the best textbooks, made herself *au fait* with the new government system and visited Poor Schools to learn all she could. In him she had a friend whose knowledge was wide and detailed. Marshall's mandate was to examine but also to encourage local efforts, whether in Poor School or college and he believed wholeheartedly that the poor must be educated. His school reports show compassion for their condition – once he fed a school before examining. For the benefit of those officials who thought the pupil-teacher system an extravagance and grudged the pupil-teachers their pitiable three shillings and tenpence a week, he berated such economy as injudicious. It was, he said, a degradation to be treated so, a reduction to machine level of the young human being and was an obstacle to the progress of real education.[7] He was a source of great encouragement to Mother Connelly. At the end of that first year he reported with satisfaction to the Privy Council's committee that 'the principles which regulate the whole course both of teaching and discipline' were defined by Mrs Connelly, and the effect of her 'prudent counsels and intelligent supervision' was to be seen in 'every department and in every feature of the college'. It was a sad day for Cornelia when Marshall was forced to retire from the educational scene.

MID-CENTURY SCHOOLS FOR GIRLS

The primary purpose of a Training College was to meet the needs of the poor. But its immediate effect was to educate young women for whom, being not very well off, there was little on offer of real use. On the national front a battle was being fought during the middle decades of the century, its prize the right for girls to have an education comparable to that of boys.

Cornelia's Middle and Highest Schools (the nomenclature of the day referred not to age but to social status) began in very small ways, grew slowly and were never in her lifetime many or large. But working undeterred as an educator within what was still an untrusted Catholic minority, she offered an education worthy of the name, a solid preparation for life which most non-Catholic contemporaries lacked. A writer in the *Athenaeum* of 6 May 1848 protested:

> You cannot but be aware that young women and girls in the middle rank of life in England are almost ignored by society in so far as any public provision for their education is concerned . . . If a parent sends his daughter to boarding school, is there any medium between something enormously expensive offering luxuries which he does not covet, and something miserably low which offers only a few paltry and showy accomplishments instead of better instruction?

Whereas Kay-Shuttleworth's pupil-teacher system of 1846 was a long stride down the road of education for the poor, for the girls of better-off homes there was no government provision whatever. Nor was there for boys, but their schools were not accomplishment-ridden; and the daughters of a cultured élite had governesses and tutors at home. In Cornelia's early community Maria Buckle, Emily Bowles, Ignatia Bridges and Theresa Hanson belonged to this privileged group. Not until 1865 was the plight of less well-placed girls considered. A Schools Inquiry Commission was then established to report on the state of boys' secondary education, and, pressured by Dorothea Beale, its members decided to visit girls' schools also. Because none was state-aided, participation was voluntary and no Catholic school for girls figures in the final reports. These furnish a most vivid picture of what schooling (most residential, the custom of the day) was then like for a young girl.

The commissioners visited between them several hundreds of schools scattered throughout the country. They listened to lessons, conducted examinations both written and oral, organised questionnaires and were finally content to give their joint opinion of 'the general deficiency in girls' education' as 'want of thoroughness & foundation; want of system; slovenliness & showy superficiality; inattention to rudiments; undue time given to

236

accomplishments, and those not taught intelligently or in any scientific manner.' The poverty of this schooling was largely due to the intellectual poverty of the governesses who taught in them, many of whom, the reports reveal, knew little even of fundamentals. Rote learning and repetition made up the method. There was no organised course of studies and accomplishments occupied most of the pupils' time. It seemed to the commissioners that in most establishments hours and energies were frittered away on what was of little value. One wrote despondently: 'It is no exaggeration to say, that in the mass [of schools] the intellectual aims are very low, and the attainments are still lower than the aims.'[8]

THE SCHOOL OF THE HOLY CHILD, ST LEONARDS

Cornelia had come to England with a sketch of a Rule which specified 'educating females of all classes' as one of the Society's works. This she tried to do – but 'our poor schools greatly exceed in number the higher schools' she wrote in 1855. On the campus at St Leonards, however, there were by 1856 a Poor School, a Highest School, a Middle School and a Training College, all separate. All of them shared the same educational ideal but it was in the Highest School, the school of the Holy Child, that it was possible to put it most fully into practice. Other schools established for girls at what we would call secondary level (all have not survived) were at Blackpool and Preston, both in Lancashire; Mayfield in Sussex; Sharon Hill and Chestnut Street in Philadelphia; and Neuilly in Paris. She also undertook the management of an orphanage near Mayfield which before she died was converted into a boarding school. All were at least partly residential (as was the custom of the day) and sometimes took very young children as well as older ones. Mayfield began with little ones. In none of these schools would Commissioner Bryce's comment have been applicable, that education in girls' schools was 'for show and not for use, for seeming and not for being'.[9] But in what follows, the Highest School at St Leonards will be the focus. Here Cornelia had the most direct influence. In its day to day life we can see her in action.

In 1855 a child of six joined the school. When she came Cornelia was forty-six and when she left, fifty-eight, and the little Catherine Harper had learned to love her: 'her sweet face rises before me, with that look of loving reproof which I so often saw upon it – for I was a tiresome, wilful child, and had been greatly spoiled by my dear father'. Many years later she wrote an account of her schooldays. Mother Connelly:

. . . had great sympathy for children, and did not try to force upon them

237

wisdom beyond their years. We all loved her and thought her very holy, and would consider ourselves honoured by a smile and a few words from her. Often I came in for rebukes for bad behaviour, and at these times she could be very stern.

But the atmosphere at St Leonards was:

. . . one of joy and contentment. There was no spying on the part of the nuns, but we were greatly trusted, and trained to a high sense of honour, a method that completely achieved its end. There was a sense of freedom and broad-mindedness about the school that was delightful.

They had a lot of fun:

Our lives were made happy by numerous little treats and customs on different occasions, to which we looked forward eagerly. On Holy Innocents day we dressed up as nuns and the best part of this was that we were allowed to go all over the convent and mix with the nuns. On another Feast day we had to hunt for our breakfast which was hidden somewhere in the grounds. At other times, we had long walks or picnics which were pure joy.

She recalled Cornelia as the central influence of the school's life:

Reverend Mother had a very masterful character and a wonderful love of God and great power over others. I thought she showed great good sense in educational matters. She seemed able to imbue the nuns with her own zeal and large-mindedness. Her voice was rather stern and very determined, though her manner was gentle and winning and her face beautiful. We used to go down to the hall on Feast days to wish her a happy feast, and she would speak a few holy, motherly words to us, telling us how we should draw practical help for our own lives from the mystery we were celebrating. She would generally end up playfully and tell us to run away and enjoy ourselves.[10]

Cornelia was a mother and she made school a home. One sister remembered an occasion when two small children had arrived, aged four and two. They stood together at the door, defiant and miserable, and none of the sisters could win a word from them. Then Mother Connelly came in. She sat down quietly and took the little one on to her lap. The child 'looked up astonished, but when she saw the sweet motherly face above her, a change came over her own'. The frown faded away and she 'laid her face on Mother Connelly's shoulder and nestled in her arms'. It is also recorded that sometimes she walked through the children's dormitory at night and pausing by each child's bed did as she had once done for her own children, blessed each and made a little cross on the child's forehead. On one occasion the sister with her asked whether the school's children reminded her of her own and she answered,'The thought of my children never leaves me.' In the school she poured out her affection on these others given into her care. To a parent she would write: 'Your two darling children are quite well and good and they have everything to make them enjoy their sunny sinless childhood.' To another when she was about to be away, she promised that the sisters would 'have a mother's care of your dear children.' The bishop was told: 'we have 40 children this winter, and *such* a happy group to delight one's heart'. And to a pupil who had had to stay at home and was dangerously ill she began a letter:

My sweetest Mary
What a joy it would have been to us if your dear little face had presented itself on Frances' arrival [her sister's]! Our dear Lord did not send us such a favour, therefore we must satisfy ourselves by hearing of you only, and sending you a few lines just to say that we love you very tenderly, and pray for you in all our prayers, and in our thoughts.

But she did not spoil them. The same girl (who recovered) was also when necessary seriously admonished: 'How is it, Mary, that you have spent so much money? Your Papa [a convert] has become a poor man for Our Lord, and you ought to be thinking of saving him as much as possible.' She was, as another remembered, 'always motherly and kind. We fell in with her wishes, not through fear, but through love for her, and we all felt she was just towards us. We could trust her.' According to tradition, when she was too busy to be often in the school she still found time for the 'difficult' children ('Reverend Mother's Gems' as they were called in the community). Essentially the kind of relationship she always had with the whole body of children was maternal.

During Catherine Harper's years, 1855–67, the school grew. Whereas in 1855, apparently, a mere fourteen pupils and the community and the chaplain had to cram themselves into one awkward and inadequate building, by 1863 there were fifty pupils and much more space. A large new hall had been built, and on 18 June there were celebrations. In the morning four sisters were clothed in the religious habit, and a special breakfast was laid on. In the evening the children rejoiced in a fancy-dress party in the hall which Cornelia dubbed their 'Bal Masqué' (and was afterwards criticised for allowing something so improper!). And in the middle of the day, along with children, community and chaplain, she must have been seated at the great long 'banquet' table arranged there to celebrate that now at last they had a school of fifty. Thenceforward Catherine Harper played and studied

239

in the school hall, did examinations there, received prizes and joined in the yearly school plays.

Her reminiscences do not touch on studies but these are well documented in school journals, especially in the 1863 *Book of the Order of Studies*. This was partly the outcome of what Cornelia imbibed from her seven years of working in the Sacred Heart schools at Grand Coteau and the Trinità. At Derby she possessed a copy of the rules of the Society of the Sacred Heart but whether she ever saw its *Règlement des Pensionnats et Plan d'Etude* is open to question: until 1852 it existed only in manuscript versions and John Marmion who has closely examined it and Cornelia's book is convinced she did not. It is certain, however, that she drew consciously on the Jesuit *Ratio Studiorum*, also examined by Marmion.[11] A copy was given her by Peter Gallwey, and by 1855 she had begun to compile a version for her own sisters, 'our Ratio' as Bellasis called it. By the time they printed it for distribution to the scattered communities its contents were familiar to all because Cornelia had been working with the sisters during the whole of the community experience out of which it was born – experiences of noviceship classes, of teaching Poor Schools, of building up the beginnings with boarders, of training teachers, and of dealings with the government inspector. The Society was still small and throughout the fifties she remained in contact with all its members. Even after the printing she continued to recommend to communities recent textbooks they should have, and to provide material for the novices to write in their Ratio notebooks.

The book is too long and detailed to consider closely here but Cornelia's preface is given below *in toto*. It uncovers something of Cornelia's relationship with the sisters, and of their union of purpose in the 'sweetly laborious duty of education'. This was how she taught the sisters and how they should teach the children. There was a tenderness in her for both, and great apostolic desire. Elsewhere she pin-points the calling of her young religious as 'pains-taking for the eagerness of love'. In this preface she encourages them to just that – to accept the pains of tedious hard work because it is a labour of love, and to do it cheerfully:

We have before us the 'Book of Studies', which is simply the same sort of guide as a chart is to the traveller. We must 'use' it in the same way to assist us in the sweetly laborious duty of Education.

Though we so well know, that great things are achieved only by untiring labour and suffering, we sometimes forget that in training and teaching children it is absolutely necessary to walk step by step, to teach line by line, to practise virtue little by little, in 'act' after 'act', and only by such acts of virtue as are suited to the age and stage of moral and intellectual development of those we are guiding. Let us not want 'to fly' by ourselves, lest we leave our pupils behind to be lost in the mist. Line by line and step by step, in all learning and all virtues, form the whole educational system. See the little birds how they carry insect after insect to the nestlings, just so must we give moral and intellectual food to our dear pupils, that from this labour of love may flow the desired result . . . Let us . . . joyfully 'take pains' and 'accept of labour', piece by piece, week by week, and day by day, and thus make sure our victory.

The book itself contains[12] syllabuses, timetables, book lists, all adapted to the ages of children of four to eighteen years; principles and methods in teaching each subject; special directions for the teachers; school rules. School reports, written up regularly by the teaching sisters and remarked on by Cornelia, show that its ideals were pursued in fact as well as theory. Had the commissioners visited St Leonards they could not have deplored (which is not to say there was nothing to criticise) the lack of foundation or thoroughness, or purpose and organisation. In this school education was not allowed to sink into mere learning by rote which left mind and heart unformed: 'the cultivation of the understanding & the judgement rather than the memory have been the pivot', and the immediate aim of every lesson and every course, according to her book, was that meaning be grasped. Towards this she was always pressing. Little ones began with what was familiar and concrete, their lessons full of activity. In the middle years children might be 'backward, timid and careless' or just inattentive, but they were to be helped into using 'conception, imagination, the reasoning powers, reflection'. By the time they were at the top, aged seventeen or eighteen, it was Euclid, the philosophy of history and geography, a little logic, a little geology and the meaning of literature that they were given. The 'accomplishments' of fashionable schools she converted into part of serious education, integral to the programme – 'I never asked the parents about the drawing,' she once wrote to a sister, 'as it is *our course*, whether desired or not. They will soon take to it when enlightened.' Time was allowed for private study and reading. Latin and Greek figured in the syllabus, and the individual with a taste for learning was encouraged. All this, had the commissioners visited, was sufficiently unusual at that date (and would now be thought laughably inadequate) to have earned their praise.

Mr Marshall, describing Cornelia as principal of the college, reported that Mrs Connelly had 'that clearness and lucidity which belongs only to those who thoroughly possess their own knowledge, and can apply it to a definite purpose without confusion or uncertainty'.

This appraisal of Cornelia at forty-eight comes at what seems an immense distance from the days of the young woman who at twenty-seven, in her husband's brief absence up river, wandered tearfully round her home looking for tangible reminders of him and was ready to submit to him in all things. By the time Marshall wrote his report she was no longer a torrent pouring itself out as it did when she decided to marry, but a deep steady stream running between cliffs towards plain and ocean. She had become an outstanding woman, matured by the extraordinary demands of her life, small and still beautiful, but formidable too, because, as Marshall says, she knew and did not lose sight of her purposes. Knowing them she took the means to achieve them. What Mary Allies much later wrote of Cornelia during these years reflects the purposeful energy and influence of a woman who was nevertheless perceived and loved as 'mother':

> The school itself was growing up with the Society itself, and the Society . . . when I arrived at the Convent in 1859, was in the days when the Mother is all-powerful, does everything herself. Whilst Reverend Mother was building up her dynasty, we enjoyed the delights of real monarchy. From the first I felt the impress of that compelling personality. She began at once to be queen and mother to me.[13]

THE 'ONLY WORTH'

For this compelling personality education was not merely a duty or an activity separate from her central preoccupations as a religious. It was a way of loving, the expression of belief. A comment she once made to her brother illuminates this: 'The more deeply we love God the more we love our natural duties and the more deeply we penetrate into the divine mysteries, the more capable we become of fulfilling [our natural duties] perfectly.'

Marmion's investigation of the theology which lay behind the education she gave has shown that life led her into an understanding of, in particular, the mysteries of the incarnation and the redemption. She had grown into a unified and applied comprehension of these two Christian truths. They cast light on the whole of life and gave what she was and did and taught a profound coherence. It was chiefly these mysteries – not as dogma but as revelation of a person – that sustained and fired her love. They were, one might say, her horizon. They directed her decisions and every aspect of her educational work, transforming her into an example of 'love full of action'. Her many natural gifts were harnessed in the service of education, but as Bellasis says:

> However much the natural . . . may have helped the development of her instincts [in education] the supernatural was now [1852] at the root of everything. From God, in God and for God was the mighty crane that

raised the heaviest of weights. For Mother Connelly to realise her ideal of education was an impossibility but she would aim at nothing less.

A recent writer has described well what Cornelia strove for:

> Children were to be given every advantage to grow because only through their full development would God be honoured in that part of creation which was made to be most like himself. Furthermore, the Incarnation had enhanced creation with the presence of the Word in the world. Knowledge, human and divine, therefore, gave access to the mystery of his presence and enabled those with faith to see and reverence it . . . the Holy Child had led the way by growing in knowledge and wisdom. He was Cornelia's exemplar for the developmental process as well as its goal. Because of him, Cornelia could speak of the 'sweetly laborious duty of education'.[14]

This reflects some of Mother Connelly's most considered words. In the *Book of Studies* studies and even amusements are to lead the children 'to view the invisible things of God through the medium of the visible'. In the 1850 Constitutions she set within the context of incarnation and redemption what both sisters and children must learn. When God became a man, she says in effect, it was to show humankind how to live. Jesus accepted the human condition in its fullness and lived justly and lovingly in face of whatever came to him from birth until death. To learn how he lived and how he died was to learn what love and sin really are. Therefore 'so ought all to begin again with the most sweet and holy and loving Child Jesus – a humbled God – walking with Him step by step . . .' And in the preface to a book on prayer:

> May you really so learn of the Holy Child Jesus, my dear children, growing as He grew, in stature and grace; and when you grow up may you so love and follow the Man Jesus that you be of the number of those 'little ones' whom this most Blessed Lord will bring into His everlasting kingdom!

Two ways in which she pursued her end, both detailed in the *Book of Studies*, are worth particular attention.

As long ago as 1844 at the Trinità, when she still had her little boy with her, and Ady in the school, she had made some notes from Urquhart's *Reflections*: 'The education of the child should begin at its birth . . . Affection grows with the *habit of showing* it and it becomes the *mainspring* of the character.' Later in her schools the children were to feel their relationship with God as child with parent. She surrounded them with opportunities to see God's love, to feel it and show it, and thus bound religious lessons and all daily life into one. Even in the lessons on religion, when the sisters were to speak 'impressively' it was also to be 'in an affectionate manner' and outside these periods they were to lead 'by love rather than by fear', helping the children throughout their schooldays to see God lovingly at work.

A corollary to this was the importance which she attached to reverence. She herself, as Buckle says, saw no dividing line between the spiritual and the practical. Religious lessons were to lay the foundation for reverence and were to be different because their subject was God, but rules for external order in school were meant as a reminder that God was present in the whole of their lives. They were God's children and the Holy Child showed the way. Catherine Harper remembered that in school life generally the piety was 'mixed up with our daily life in a happy, loving spirit, which never made devotion tedious or distasteful'. For Cornelia reverence was the sign of living faith and its presence the acid test of a school's success. 'Should the children go forth into the world without reverence they leave us without that which is of the most vital importance for their salvation & the salvation of those for whom they eventually become responsible.' It included 'reverence towards each other, and reverence towards the poor of Christ'; and all relationships because 'Christian politeness should spring from reverence'. It was the reverence of the Holy Child, to be understood not just as awe-inducing 'stiffness and rigour', but as a love-filled, childlike attitude before God from whom all good came. It was to pervade life, a necessity in the world for which the children were being prepared, and where women and men did not see the invisible God at work around them.

The second particular characteristic of her educational programme was the place she gave to the fine arts.

There was evidently an artist's streak in Cornelia's family. Her older brother who died when she was a child had planned to paint in the south of France while recovering his health there. Her son Frank studied art in Paris and Florence, became a well-known sculptor and spent time painting in New Zealand.[15] She herself drew and painted as a girl – Ralph taught her how to prime her canvas for oils. And when she and Pierce arrived in Rome they both took the opportunity to study art there, not confining themselves to visiting fashionable studios or to gallery-gazing. Pierce told his brother he had copied a Guido head. Cornelia took lessons and continued them later when she returned to Rome.

When we examine the *Book of Studies* and the school records at St Leonards it is obvious that her artistic leanings had flowed over into her ideal of education. Needlework is presented almost as an extension of art. Music was to be one of the school's striking features, and all children learnt to sing at sight while the upper classes did harmony and counterpoint. She herself taught the music to be used in church.

Drama, which gathers so many of the arts into itself, was important enough to absorb all school activity and time once every year into what she called the Holy Child Theatre. This was a kind of workshop, three weeks long, when everyone joined forces to produce plays. College students, Young Ladies and Middle School children each put on a 'night' (curtain up at 4.30 p.m., the handbills mostly say) for the enjoyment of the others. Usually there was a Shakespeare, a French or Italian play (in the original language) and something the little ones could act. Victorian families often indulged in amateur theatricals at home and Cornelia used the social custom as an educational form of recreation, conducting it during what in those days was school time. She was herself its chief inspiration. Only one element of drama is referred to in the *Book of Studies* and it is Buckle who tells us that Mother Connelly was 'anxious that declamation should be systematically learnt in our schools'. This Cornelia herself taught in the Highest class, and the educational purpose is clearly stated: to understand a text more fully. A pupil is to 'enter into the spirit of the writer, to seize his ideas . . . test the force of his arguments, the justness of his feelings'; but it is not possible to speak another's thoughts, she says, unless the speaker has placed herself in the other's position, has understood from within. To enter into the meaning, Buckle says, was 'the soul of our education'.

It is when we look at what Mother Connelly believed about art itself that we begin to see that the emphasis on these allied subjects had for her an overall significance. She was doing much more than occupying the children with play-acting or meeting parental demand for accomplishments. She was seeking to imprint wonder and reverence and love of the unseen God and believed that the fine arts were a specially suitable tool for this purpose.

All art classes in the school were directed by Cornelia, and her directions in the *Book of Studies* (seventeen pages) are those of an expert. When, in the college, the bishop told her to cut down the drawing course she did so with the greatest reluctance. The *Book* says:

In our schools we are not to consider Drawing as an extra or superlative Art left to the choice of any one to follow, or leave out, but, on the contrary as a *Christian* Art and one of the most important branches of education second only to the art of speaking and writing, and in some respects even beyond the languages, as it is in itself a universal language, addressing itself to the ignorant as well as to the most refined.

Among the reading books specified for the senior girls was Rio's *Christian Art*. The view she too took of art as Christian made it part of the teaching of religion, more valuable than the rote learning of religious truths and rules then so common, for which Grant was demanding extra study time (to be taken from art). She protested to him that in wishing to keep the drawing, religion was for her too 'the highest and dearest object we have in view'. For the bishop it was of major importance that a large number of hours be spent on directly religious instruction. For her every hour of school life was in some way religious training and those devoted to art particularly so.

Her insistence in school on beauty of surroundings, on order, on proper reverence, seems to have stemmed from her first stay in Rome. She had then taken painting lessons with a teacher[16] of the school of Overbeck; she had often heard the work of the Nazareni discussed at the Shrewsburys' dinner table (where A. F. Rio and his wife were frequent visitors); and if she read Pierce's account of his conversion in the 1836 *Dublin Review* then she probably also read the account of Rio's *De la Poésie chrétienne* in the same volume. She had thus had every opportunity to become convinced with him that whatever was beautiful, in its most perfect expressions, spoke of God and therefore exercised moral influence. When the beautiful was directly related to God, as in sacred music or religious paintings, then the degree of truth, simplicity and reverential feeling in the artist affected the degree of influence. Hence the importance she attached to the quality of all models. Learning to observe these more and more closely, eye and ear were educated 'in all perceptible beauty and order'; knowledge grew, understanding deepened and with it reverence. During lessons, at the liturgy and in all their daily life, they were to be helped to enter into the mystery of God, and art was a powerful aid, an ideal impossible to realise, as Bellasis said, but 'she would aim at nothing less'.

No careful selection process made sure that only the 'naturally rather good' child was admitted. Occasional epithets jotted down against names in the school work records, 1856–76, dispel any such notions:

> . . . rude and bold, idiotic, nonchalant, idle, giddy, weak & bragging, uncharitable, reserved and sly, insolent, boorish, talkative, given to calling names, insubordinate, a greedy bear. But only once the note that she 'wishes to go home'. Clearly the pupil population was very normal, and the convent atmosphere was not stifling the young.[17]

This was fact. The children were to grow into being their true best selves. Therefore they needed both freedom and responsibility. Therefore they were trusted. The school ethos was certainly religious but it was also a very human place, especially so because it was given life by a mother who could put up the following kind of notice: 'Be it known unto you all, my well-beloved little and big darlings, that for *very* excellent reasons, all appertaining to your greater good, the Whit Tuesday Picnic will be transferred to the 21st of June. NB. No grumbling allowed!!! You would not think of such a thing? *Oh No!*'

Many of the children in this large and loved family-by-adoption stayed at the School of the Holy Child for twelve or fourteen years. Unpressured by the constraint of government requirements there was time for growth, and freedom to be different. But the good done by the school was known only to a small group within the Catholic minority. The Training College, to which it is time to turn, functioned under very different conditions and one might think that less of the good which Cornelia sought could be achieved. Yet here – where (as well as all else she had to do) she was herself professionally in charge; where not only a great deal of tedious administration fell to her lot but also the general responsibility for the whole curriculum; where she taught art, took part in teaching practice and found time as well for the individual student, and often to be with them all at recreations – her idea of education, for eight brief years, came into its own. In her own eyes it was a paramount work for the reign of God, 'a work most dear to us, embracing a much larger good than any ordinary Boarding School'.

'A WORK MOST DEAR TO US', 1856–63

The duty of the teacher was to make children happy. This purpose, in Cornelia's philosophy, was appropriate both to the nature of the human person and to the dignity of the child of God. It was rooted in contemplation of the one Child who was God: 'It was not just that happy children work better but rather that love was creative, and all was to be seen in the light of Christ, who was the love of God made visible. He provided the pattern for the person, the school and society at large.'[18] The teacher's task therefore was to create in school a society for children where love was everywhere at work. For the college Cornelia herself had formed the little band of teachers who were to enkindle in the students the love which they themselves had discovered in God. The students received it very largely through being for two busy years part of a happy, purposeful society. Like the children in the school and sometimes with them, they went on picnics with the sisters, had parties with them on feast days, shared in all the serious fun of preparing plays with them, joined the choirs that sang in church, celebrated with sisters on clothing and profession days. Life was not dampened by gloomy Sundays or Victorian surveillance. They sat in summer fields doing their needlework. They relaxed with 'Fancy' drawing over their drawing books. Creative, loving trust was their experience and to it they responded.

This kind of life, whether for children or students, was judged by outsiders as lax. The education given by Mother Connelly consisted in running about the fields, it was said. But the liberty of the children of God into which all were being led was not to be misunderstood as the right to indulge oneself whenever one felt like it. When any student was advised to 'be herself' Cornelia meant more than immediately appeared. She was also to make herself, by her own choices, all that God who loved her would enable her to become. This was something hard to embark on. It often meant renouncing lesser goods, denying an inclination, ignoring a fear. But it was also positive, its focus not sin but the love of God. Cornelia's 'system' directed the whole being to the goodness of God. Hearts were not driven but drawn. Attraction to the Holy Child would mature into love for the Man Jesus, for the Christ and his mission. A willingness to give as he did would become the apostolic desire to speak God's merciful love to others.

In college it was 'the overall responsibility of staff', as Marmion observes, to promote each student's best self, something which 'school spirit and life might sometimes achieve when a lesson might not'. The closeness of association between students and teachers was all-important. In a variety of circumstances the young women learned whether the sisters sincerely tried to be what they taught. Accordingly they took to heart, or not, what they saw.

This element of personal formation was noted by Marshall. His reports to the Privy Council's Committee of Education leave no doubt of his enthusiasm for what the college was doing for its students in general. He sometimes voiced criticism, as that the geography syllabus was too ambitious. And his keenness to attract students to the college did not sweep away his judgment, as when he recommended that Liverpool not St Leonards should begin a special department for infants. Often he elaborated on the excellence of the teaching of the required subjects, and much of what Cornelia added to the curriculum might have been opposed by the committee as unnecessary or innovative but for his comments – on drawing; on the range of needlework; on mathematics, music; on geology, for which he praised the college, where 'they learn that the discoveries of science in this field of knowledge may be accepted without uneasiness by the Christian student'. But what he most admired was the Christian formation of the students as teachers, for which as a body, he said, they could be 'justly distinguished from all others' whose work he knew.[19]

The college, however, had an Achilles heel and an enemy. The heel was the practising school. St Leonards was remote from urban populations, a small place, its local Catholic community correspondingly so. During the early years before Cornelia began the college a huge army of railway workers swarmed in the district, navvies with their families, many of them Irish and very poor. Some of their children must have swelled the ranks of the Catholic Poor School in spite of two railway schools and local agitation against popery, but they were birds of passage and the school was small for a great many years after they had moved on. When Marshall recommended the

Committee of Education to approve a Catholic college for the south, he was presumably taking the long view. A college in the south would one day be an absolute necessity, St Leonards was a healthy place and developing as a resort. Also the practising school seems not to have been, for him, of *primary* importance in teacher-training. Even so St Leonards was vulnerable to criticism on this score. With the reappearance on Cornelia's horizon of Emily Bowles' friend Scott Nasmyth Stokes the fortunes of the college flagged and Cornelia herself came in for yet more injustice and public humiliation.

In 1848 Stokes, as secretary of the CPSC, had apparently visited Derby and wrote confidently:

> That convent . . . possesses all the requisites for a Normal School and its position is perhaps as central & as accessible as any spot in England. It would accommodate sixty young women readily . . . It appears to me that by seizing the opportunity we might secure great advantages to Religion & Education in England. The Nuns at Derby have represented to the CPSC that the training of Mistresses is their chief desire.

The Derby plan fell through but Stokes did not lose sight of his goal. In February 1853 he was appealing in the *Catholic School* for some lady of means to give £5000 to found a college, and to the bishops to name a community to run it. Before the end of the year (by which time he was no longer secretary to the CPSC but inspector for the north), he had approached both Cornelia (via Emily in Liverpool) and the local superior of the Sisters of Notre Dame de Namur there. At first Cornelia's community seemed the more likely to realise his hopes but later circumstances combined to draw him towards Notre Dame.

The Liverpool college was put into the hands of a gifted young Englishwoman, Frances Lescher (Sr Mary of St Philip), who immediately after her profession as a Sister of Notre Dame was sent by her congregation to take up the task of teacher-training. She came from a family Stokes already knew well, and he gave her and her college all possible support. She would write of him in 1870 that 'he had watched over the College with such unflagging interest, his guidance had been so helpful, his counsels so judicious, that to lose him now was like parting with a pilot just as we were launched on an unknown sea'.[20] Through Sr Mary of St Philip, Nasmyth Stokes' dream of Catholic teacher-training in Liverpool was realised.

But enthusiastic determination, however laudable in its object, does not always travel by laudable roads. Stokes, as Marmion indicates, was a dangerous man to have as an enemy, and in 1857 the senior inspector, Marshall, wrote him a letter which could have stirred what was a latent enmity towards the college at St Leonards. Stokes after all, only eight months earlier when Emily Bowles was hoping to join the Notre Dame sisters and that they would buy Rupert House for their college, had facilitated her departure from the Society by being her private postman. This suggests that he knew and sympathised with her views of Cornelia as a despot who had dishonestly thwarted her (and his) first plans for a college. Now Marshall wrote that he had received letters 'complaining bitterly' that Stokes was dissuading pupil teachers who wished to go the St Leonards College. The Liverpool college, he pointed out, would inevitably always have large numbers and he appealed to Stokes to recommend students to St Leonards rather than deflect them. Stokes denied any hostile feeling and explained what he had done. Another remark in the letter he left without comment. The southern college, Marshall had said, offered 'incomparably great' advantages and there was 'a general impression', confirmed even by Allies, the secretary to the all-important CPSC, that St Leonards was 'by far the best Training School in the kingdom'.

Perhaps it is only coincidence that in the summer of 1860 Marshall resigned from the inspectorate on a charge which dates back to some incident 'which occurred two and a half years before'. The relevant correspondence between the CPSC and Lord Granville, president of the Committee for Education, is far from complete and the exact nature of the charge is not clear. It was something to do with 'allowing unfair assistance at an examination'. The CPSC, writing in Marshall's defence, called it 'an error more apparent than real'. Granville saw it as 'a great dereliction of his duty'. M. J. Illing has sifted the evidence and concludes that because of the exclusively denominational nature of Marshall's duties it is nearly certain that the charge was laid by another Roman Catholic and 'a possible explanation of the long delay' was that 'the accusation was a means of expressing a personal grievance and obtaining revenge for it'.[21] This is a guess and Illing names no one. But until 1861 when Stokes took over he was the only government inspector who sometimes accompanied Marshall to the college for examinations, and in the light of events the guess invites consideration.

When Marshall had departed Stokes became pro tem inspector of the college and wrote for 1860 its first negative report: the practising school was the wrong shape and ill-equipped, its children too few, listless and backward; student meals were not being cooked on the college premises (as required) and the food was probably not as fresh as it should be; accounts were not kept separate from those of school and convent, and expenses were with little doubt extravagantly high; he notes pointedly the smallness of the student body, and no comment is made on the remarkably good final examination results at Christmas of the students graduating that year (seven first class and no failure out of sixteen entrants). Even if there had been on Marshall's part (which we do not know) a willingness to ignore the ways in which cooking and accounts were done because he approved the good results for the students, on Stokes' side there appears at the least a much more regulatory attitude. At best his report was ungenerous, replete here and there with unfriendly surmise. It was published by the CPSC, as were all reports, and Cornelia, to ensure that the college would continue to receive grant, must have had to reorganise kitchen arrangements and accounting. 'Mr Stokes is not our friend,' she remarked. During 1861 Allies tried to encourage her. Stokes did not mean to be unfair, he said, 'but he can't help being so sometimes'. Stokes continued as inspector during 1861; and then early in 1862 appeared in Cornelia's secretary's diary the first rumblings of doom:

March 1862

7 Astounding inclosure from Mr Allies containing a cowardly blow made in the dark! . . .

8 . . . Another absurd accusation from our untiring *pecker* [Stokes] – *possible* doom pronounced!

On 3 March 1862 Lingen, secretary to the Privy Council's Committee, had written to Allies, secretary to the CPSC, claiming that at St Leonards a student, Annie McCave, had been presented to Stokes for examination in June under a false name. He concluded the letter: 'My Lords do not doubt that your Committee will agree with them in thinking that the Principal cannot under such circumstances continue to hold any office in the college at St Leonards.' The principal was Cornelia and the CPSC was unwilling to agree without proof. Lingen (the high-handed successor to Kay-Shuttleworth)[22] had made no investigation. The CPSC did, and by late April concluded, on the evidence of witnesses and of the written word and with legal advice, that the allegation was false: 'This Committee trust that My Lords will coincide with the opinion which they have formed that the Principal is exculpated from the charge brought against her.' No answer came. The CPSC felt so strongly about the matter that its chairman, the Hon. Charles Langdale, together with a member, Lord Petre, and Serjeant Bellasis, their legal adviser, sought to confront the president of the Privy Council's Committee. For weeks the correspondence lay before Granville and then for reasons unknown the committee continued to require Cornelia's resignation.

The voluminous details and twists of this affair have to be left aside but not how Cornelia felt and acted. It was yet another occasion for public dishonour. Her first recorded response was a letter to Allies written on the day the news reached her. She is indignant:

It seems to me a very dishonest and wicked thing of Mr Stokes to represent me in this unfair way, or as intending to enter into any fraudulent act. It will be a very easy thing for me to withdraw my name from the Training School, which will no doubt satisfy Mr Stokes, but certainly not on the grounds of any act of deception which I positively deny and which the lists sent to Government will prove. If she wrote any other than her own name on her papers it was unknown to me.

Throughout the course of the affair Allies kept her fully informed, sharing correspondence with her. One of Stokes' letters which came her way accused her of 'levity or folly' as principal, and of having committed a 'gross irregularity'. He added that if 'independent men of judgement' were to conduct 'a thorough inquiry into the state of St Leonards', then 'serious blots' would have to be remedied; and should the college as a result be suspended from training teachers the loss 'would not be great'. Others noted in Stokes' letters a 'pretty little conspiracy', a 'curious animus' towards St Leonards, signs of a 'bad spirit' towards her. Cornelia recalled 'the whole tone of the 1860 Report', and remarked to Allies that Stokes 'came as an enemy and acted out his enmity to the end'.

This conviction about Stokes, and any feelings raised by the Privy Council's demand, did not cloud her practical judgment. She could still consider dispassionately what was best for the future of this work in which she so deeply believed. She wrote to Grant:

It seems to me that it would be much better to withdraw my name (with any amount of injustice) than to risk the loss of the Training School. The one is a personal matter in which the charge has been refuted, while the latter would involve the loss of a great charity.

But Allies took a different point of view. 'To maintain you at the head of the Training School is the point of honour,' he said, 'I hope that we shall succeed'. When the unfavourable decision finally arrived, the CPSC (having made their investigation) turned their guns on Stokes, the sole witness to the charge. Allies informed the Privy Council of the committee's lack of confidence in him as government inspector of Catholic institutions. At the same time Cornelia, knowing he had stigmatised the college as corrupt, counted on the CPSC to be able to exclude him from inspecting them in the future:

... it will give me *much* sincere satisfaction to know that my name is withdrawn if only we can close the matter by excluding Mr S. This is all we can desire; the point of honour lies in the hands of God, and if it makes us more humble and careful we shall gain in his sight more than we shall lose in the eyes of our enemies.

The matter of Cornelia's withdrawal was referred to the bishop. Detained in Rome, he had come late on the scene and now as bishop made his own conscientious detailed investigation. He concluded that a mistake made by Stokes had 'caused Mrs Connelly to be censured for an offence never committed', and invited him as an upright man either to substantiate his facts or retract his statement. Stokes (answering through the bishop's intermediary) ignored the loophole. Grant was brushed aside as uninformed, prejudiced and captious. Yet Grant, a canon lawyer, an exact and scrupulous man if ever there was one, was so sure of his case that he believed it would stand up even in a court of law.

While the bishop was conducting his investigation the correspondence between him, Cornelia and Allies deals more and more often with whether or not it was going to be necessary to withdraw not just Cornelia's name, but the college itself from government, to which neither Grant nor Allies was going to agree willingly. In the end the Privy Council allowed Stokes to remain an inspector, the bishop had to agree to Cornelia's resignation and Annie Laprimaudaye was appointed in her place. She accepted on the condition that Stokes never again darkened the college doors, something Allies could do his best to secure but could not guarantee. The future of the college remained in doubt.

This long dispute between Privy Council and CPSC took place at a moment when government, inspired by Robert Lowe, was devising a scheme to cut down the costs of popular education. Gone was the humane and practical vision of Kay-Shuttleworth and disciples like Marshall. A narrowed and stifling version of his system now threatened. On the principle of paying only for goods delivered there would be, among other entrenchments, no grant for any candidate who had not *already had* two years of college training. This would put a drastic financial pressure on every establishment. Allies wrote to Cornelia after a discussion at a general meeting of all principals and reported how gloomy was the view they took of the future. To some of the Protestant colleges it had been intimated that 'the Privy Council would look with much complacency on their extinction'. He believed that the small Catholic body should fight to keep theirs (two for women, one for men) and that Cornelia should not give up.

Joseph Searle however, the chaplain at St Leonards, thought she should withdraw, not from teacher-training but from government, 'from whom you have derived all the real advantage you can ever get'. More and more Cornelia leaned to this point of view and she wrote to Allies:

You ask me what I feel about the case as it now stands and I answer for the Community, as I am nobody. The general wish of the Community is to withdraw from Government totally. We consider ourselves to have been most unjustly treated and no one who knows the case can have a doubt on the subject.

She went on:

> In many respects we shall heartily rejoice in getting rid of inspections with all their annoyances and excitements . . . The point remaining is to secure our present students for the Xmas Ex[amination]. We must not let them suffer in any way, and rather than inflict any injustice on them, we should run the risk of a visit from Mr S[tokes].

She hoped to be able to build up a Middle School and offer teacher-training independently of government to those older girls who wanted it. The CPSC might allow them grant, she thought.

Allies tried again in December with a proposal to remove the college to London. But the suitable house which he found proved to be far beyond any means Cornelia could raise, and another factor soon defeated his efforts. The news came that Lowe's money-saving scheme was to go into operation in 1864. The Liverpool college was able to survive largely through further benefaction by the SND heiress who had provided for its beginnings. For Cornelia there was no such possibility. She had managed little by little to pay off Pierce's court costs for him by 1859, but the obligation to the Bowles family still hung like a millstone round her neck. She told Searle that it was 'quite certain that we cannot run the risk of supporting the Students under the new minutes', and not long afterwards the final blow fell. Annie Laprimaudaye was informed by the Privy Council office that Stokes would be the inspector for the Christmas examinations. Accordingly on 1 October 1863 she required the CPSC to notify their lordships that after Christmas the college would withdraw from government aid and inspection.

Cornelia did succeed in building up the Middle School but the hope that it could become an independent centre for the training of governesses and teachers gradually faded, and on three more occasions she tried to establish a recognised college in London. A letter written in 1872 speaks volumes – her continuing conviction of the importance of such work; her earnest desire to see it established; and regret and frustration mixed with the hope that always sustained her:

> It seems a great pity that the Training School was not opened in London in 1863 at the time we gave it up at St Leonards. But there was no co-operative spirit to propose or second such a move. It *might* have been done and we could have worked it out ourselves, but up-hill work requires encouragement and cannot resist hostility or prejudice beyond a certain extent, and thus the work of God is lost! Even now it seems that only the Archbishop [Manning] and yourself and the S[panish] P[lace] priests

care about it . . . no doubt there is, if not an apathy, at least a want of spirit *some*where for the general good. We must not say *every* where . . .

And she concludes with a characteristic statement: 'Well, we must be humble and do the best possible, and this at least will be for the honour of God and his Church.'

12

Cornelia and the Duchess

In the winter of 1860 there arrived at the select and fashionable resort of St Leonards Louisa Catherine Osborne, Duchess of Leeds, widow. She and her also widowed sister Lady Stafford took up residence. Their house was on the marina and soon Cornelia and the duchess met. Both were Americans.

The duchess was sixty-seven, getting old, Cornelia fifty-one, getting on. Louisa Catherine Caton was granddaughter of Charles Carroll of Carrollton, Maryland, the only Catholic signatory (still living when she married Leeds) to the Declaration of Independence, a great landowner and one of the richest men in his country. In her youth she thought of joining Elizabeth Seton's institute, founded chiefly for work with the poor and the orphaned, and orphans remained a call to her heart for the rest of her life. She and two of her sisters travelled to Europe in 1811 and, distinguished by great wealth and outstanding beauty, became known as the 'three American Graces'. Courts and palaces were taken by storm and in England they married into high circles. Marianne became Marchioness of Wellesley, Elizabeth married Baron Stafford, and Louisa Catherine (by her second marriage) became in 1828 wife of a duke. The family seat was Hornby Castle in Yorkshire, 14,772 acres.

Both women were also Catholic. The duchess during her married life had made various attempts, beginning in 1846 when Cornelia began the Society, to use her wealth for the Catholic poor. But being, as Cornelia was to discover, unreliable, unrealistic and autocratic, it had generally been others, in particular the Assumption sisters in Yorkshire, who had had to make good what she had initiated. She was by now a childless, lonely and ageing woman. Visits to the convent became frequent, friendship grew, and when in 1862 Lady Stafford died Lousia Catherine went there to live. A small suite of rooms was fitted up for the unusual lady boarder, and downstairs a parlour was set aside for her entertaining. Very soon she asked also to be admitted to the Society, which Cornelia could not allow. To live in a religious atmosphere was to be given needed support but to take on the obligations of religious profession would be beyond her, and eventually her grace contented herself with the semi-seclusion of her 'little cloister'. As far as she could she adapted herself to community ways, sold her carriage and horses for the benefit of the poor, rose an hour before the 6 a.m. Angelus, said it on her knees, attended the 7 a.m. community mass. She also remained an imperious eccentric. She insisted on a private yard for her own chickens to ensure the freshness of her breakfast egg; large bills were paid without a word if made out on large sheets of paper, but small ones were 'growled' over; the lady of fashion's morning toilette continued to take two hours. Autocratic outbursts notwithstanding, duchess and nuns managed to live amicably together.

Certainly there were clashes. Cornelia agreed to Louisa Catherine's request for sisters to accompany her on one of her visits to Hornby Castle, on the condition that there would be daily mass in its chapel. The duchess promised but the condition was not fulfilled and the sisters were recalled. One surviving story, both sad and comic, shows how much she sometimes needed to outwit and triumph over the other queen of the establishment. In 1868 when she was seventy-five both duchess and reverend mother were planning churches. Cornelia was about to complete the Jones church, her grace intended one for her new orphanage. The old lady remarked to some sister: '*I* will build a better church than *hers*. *I* will have marble pillars.'

AMERICA, 1862–7

The greatest thing which the duchess did for Mother Connelly and her Society was to give land in America for its beginnings there. Cornelia's own efforts to this end through Fransoni and then through Ralph had come to nothing, but chance inspired the duchess to act. Before she ever met Mother Connelly a Franciscan friar serving in the village of Towanda on her property in Pennsylvania had begged her to establish a school there. Then early in 1861, herself still only a visitor at the convent, she met a niece of Cornelia's from America who was anxious that sisters go back with her. Enthusiasm was kindled, property offered, plans made. Two sisters would return with Kate Duval at once in order to see the bishop there and choose suitable land.

Bishop Grant foreseeably shared no one's enthusiasm and Cornelia's determined optimism had to pit itself against his equal conviction that no good could come of it. Not till 1862 did six missionaries sail and then into a situation which, had Grant not opposed the exploratory visit, would have been evaded. Her grace's largesse was nearly defeated of its purpose. The dishonest land agent took full advantage of her ignorance of the state of her property, and it was the invincible spirit of the six sisters from England during two near-disastrous years that ultimately saved the American project.

The duchess gave the Society nearly two thousand acres, most of it in Lycoming County. Property in Bradford County was on offer to the Jesuits but the sisters were to have two of its small farms because the mountainous Lycoming area 'was wholly unoccupied & unimproved'. In addition her agent had procured for them a five-acre lot in Towanda, 'suitable for a convent'. Even so, a Jesuit who was exploring the Bradford County offer on behalf of his provincial superior reported privately:

> The Duchess is totally ignorant of the state of persons and things in this part of the country and of the religious wants growing out of them. The Franciscans have . . . all the missions . . . the collections on Sunday . . . barely support 3 or 4 . . . It is a great mistake to introduce Sisters of the Holy Child from England into a little village like this . . . Besides . . . it is determined to introduce Franciscan Sisters to teach their female parish schools.

This information never reached Cornelia, the great mistake was made and deeds were signed by March 1862.

In October 1861, writing to Cornelia for the first time, the duchess's agent Mr W. C. L. Ward had described the proposed convent lot for her benefit:

> . . . a frame or wood mansion, like most of our New England farmhouses of the larger class; it is two stories high, above the cellar or basement room, and has, in all some twelve or fifteen rooms. It has been painted, and there are shutters to the windows; the rooms are mostly plastered and some of them papered. Attached are woodsheds and various out-buildings, one of which is some 140 by 30 feet square upon the ground, wholly unfinished inside, which might possibly be converted into a school-room with dormitories over it. All the buildings would of course require more or less transformation and repairs. There are a number of bearing fruit trees, grape vines, etc., rosebushes, flowers etc. which have been much neglected of late, but could at once be reclaimed.

The place was in a 'retired and beautiful valley'; a 'thousand Catholic families' lived 'in the vicinity'; and 'I will render all the aid in my power, and see that any who come shall be comfortably placed'. Later he told her grace that the Friars were reconciled to having Holy Child sisters there instead of their own, and in February he assured Cornelia and the duchess that the title deed for the convent lot was *'perfect, beyond all doubt or question whatever'*. He congratulated Cornelia on the acquisition of such a property and renewed his offers of 'service and hospitality'.

If doubts ever crossed Cornelia's mind, no sign of them has survived. She grounded her certainty that they were to go at all on Bishop Wood's written invitation to the diocese of Philadelphia ('with house and schools') given early in the sequence of events, and though eager to go she continued to wait upon his decisions. As to uncertainties about the actual conditions at Towanda, one may guess that too many questions could not be pressingly asked of her unmanageable and fitful benefactress. She clung to the opportunity which might never return, knowing also that her grace 'had given so much away and made so many promises' that she had been obliged to sell some of her funds and could not afford, she said, to contribute to the Towanda convent. In Grant's opinion (and he was right) Cornelia would never know 'what next' about the property because the duchess was 'so changeable and so without the slightest precision in business'. That Louisa held to her first purpose and that any deeds at all were eventually signed must have been partly due to Cornelia's patience and tact.

Grant remained an opponent. Cornelia, hoping to send sisters with the American bishops *en route* from Rome via England, was told it was an imprudent venture: 'I have ascertained all the particulars about it from a first rate authority connected with the place, & the sooner you ascertain them, the more speedy will be your decision against the offer. Do not risk a single hour of time or a single sixpence on the undertaking.' Cornelia had kept Grant in the picture. If he had inside information why had he not shared it? The deeds were now signed, which he knew. It was too late to retract and her answer sprang from the heart:

I shall be deeply grieved, and with our Community unanimously, if your Lordship opposes our journey to America. I know the particulars regarding the place thoroughly. There are upwards of a hundred poor children now in the School at Towanda and more than a thousand Catholic families around the neighbourhood. The Convent or frame Mansion with five acres of land together with two farms of 15 acres is our property & not an 'offer' made to us. There are also some hundreds of pounds due to us on this property, which will more than cover the expense incurred. Every preparation is made and all purchases concluded for the outfit of our Sisters & for their Chapel & Schools. The Agent in America is having the Convent repaired & the first immediate furniture is ordered to be ready for us.

She tried to reassure him:

Do you think it reasonable my Lord to doubt the capability of supporting the Community of five Sisters on their own premises with a garden & fruit of five acres, and two farms? . . . All I ask is that you should not a second time oppose our going out . . . boxes are packed and we want only a day's notice to be ready to start.

Grant then sent a letter to be read to the sisters at once: the foundation would have to be entirely independent of St Leonards: sisters who went could not return; relatives must agree in writing to any departure; he was 'wholly opposed to the undertaking'. The sisters were not deterred, and when a meeting with Bishop Wood was in sight Cornelia tried again:

> Will you my Lord give me three words saying that you leave me free to act with him for our future foundation . . . Do give me this consolation my Lord and we shall have additional zeal and courage to go in the midst of the many crosses of this miserable life.

The meeting took place. Having seen Grant first he arrived not disposed to agree to the project. Persuaded by Cornelia he left '*his cordial consent in writing*', on condition that Grant gave his too. Still Grant hesitated. She tried yet again;

> Dr Wood had three or four places he has pointed out to me on the map where he would like to have us should we not wish to remain at Towanda, and indeed he wishes the Sisters to go to Philadelphia first & then visit Towanda . . . before deciding . . . The advantage *there* is security of the house & the endowment, as you will see my Lord by Mr Ward's letter.

Out-argued, Grant at last agreed. On 2 August 1862, with Sr Mary Xavier Noble at their head, the six missionaries sailed. Having arrived in Philadelphia Mary Xavier and Bishop Wood talked before she went on to Towanda. He had agreed to their coming, she wrote to Mother Connelly, '*in spite of himself*' on account of the perseverance shown, which he thought 'perhaps showed the will of God'. He had 'no opinion of Towanda' and did not trust Mr Ward. The sisters were to judge and act for themselves and he would send Carter, his vicar general, with them, 'a man of good judgement'. Wood impressed upon her that, 'If we found we could not succeed at Towanda we were not to hesitate to acknowledge it and come to him for assistance.'

On 19 August the vanguard arrived in Towanda to inspect. They went first to Ward's house ('like a palace', one said) and then in great expectation across the fields to the 'convent'. It stood before them, 'a small wooden building falling into decay'. The path from gate to door 'was overrun with weeds several feet high'. Inside 'paint was covered with dirt', paper 'hung in festoons from the walls', 'rats and spiders had enjoyed themselves for many a year'. One room had six cane chairs. There were two trestle beds with straw matting – lent by Ward. The promised five-acre lot on which the building stood was half that size: the rest was road.

Bishop Wood had placed the responsibility for staying or not squarely on the shoulders of the sisters. They were, as the annalist says, 'heroic women whom difficulties could not turn aside from the mission confided to them'. A letter went back to the other four to come. It began enigmatically: 'We are agreeably disappointed with our convent and have decided to remain.' It concluded warningly: 'Pray, pray, pray very much, the work is difficult and we are only beginning.' The coming days were filled with hardship. There was a single basin to wash in. They tried to make a kitchen table and its legs collapsed. Before the first week was out the middle prop of the house gave way. Workmen had to be brought in. Money was eaten up. Long overdue interest on their farms remained overdue. They counted on rents promised by the duchess and then learned from the bishop that her vacillating grace had changed her mind. The rents were to go to the Jesuits. Ward's 'thousand Catholic families' proved a mirage. About eighty children came to the rudimentary school, the majority paying only a few cents a week. When the academy school opened its doors not a child appeared. The sisters then went from house to house in the vicinity (rafting on the Susequehanna, crossing the Narrows in a buggy) and by Christmas had drummed up twenty-five children, mixed Catholic and Protestant, and only five were boarders. Mostly they paid in kind not cash and the offerings were miscellaneous and unpredictable: pork, potatoes, corn, feathers, hay. The winter that year was unusually severe. 'Some of us used to cry with the cold, our feet being almost useless to us, and the tears forced from our eyes seemed like globules of ice rolling down our cheeks.' Snow came in through the roof, and the unexpected animosity of the Franciscan friar aggravated their miseries. The crowning anxiety was to learn that the Society's title to some of its American property was not secured because the deeds, though signed, were not recorded.

Ward was eventually brought to book by the bishop's lawyer. Grant's doubts had been justified indeed but so was Cornelia's confidence. She had chosen the right sisters. In the cheerful spirit of sacrifice which she had engendered in them and which beginnings in the Society had always challenged, they had made their own choice to remain. They treasured the Rule which they brought with them, and were happy and united, the records say, in spite of the miseries.

They never revealed to Mother Connelly the extremity of their poverty. Sr Mary Xavier's surviving letters are filled with the financial and property problems, complex and new to her. An early one told of the cold attic and how they were going to patch the roof holes with layers of paper as the local people did. But she also says that they will be getting a stove, and a suggestion of Cornelia's that they should buy wool is put aside as too expensive. The feathers they were given made warm coverings, she was told, and 'a furnace in the cellar warms the lower rooms very well indeed'. There is never, then or later in extant letters, a note of appeal or complaint. Nor did Carter's surviving letters, although in one year he visited them four or five times, convey anything to Cornelia of their personal plight. He told her simply that the Towanda house was 'unsuitable' for their purpose and the district not a place for a permanent establishment unless perhaps to 'keep a parish school or for the middling classes'. It would not do 'for the higher classes of society' which was what he wanted the sisters for in Philadelphia. Not till January 1864, fifteen months after their arrival, did she learn the harsh reality of their situation, and then it was Carter, not they, who having suddenly realised it, forced it upon her attention.

Until then Cornelia withstood any suggestion that Towanda should be given up. She did not know what Carter told her much later, that he and the bishop had agreed to the sisters remaining there *only until* something better could be found. When she heard he was hoping to establish them in Philadelphia, she replied that if the *bishop* wanted this she would not oppose it but that she herself thought it premature. When, with the bishop's authority, he asked for more sisters for a second community at Spring Garden Street she agreed and six, plus two who hoped to become novices, sailed in July 1863. When by the end of August he raised the possibility of a boarding school and novitiate, she again agreed in principle but again opposed giving up Towanda. It had been begun, she believed, with the bishop's 'full consent and approbation' and therefore 'we can go on with spirit and untiring determination'.

Her ignorance of the real conditions is apparent:

> There is no doubt they can support themselves in the Schools, the living being low . . . by their own industry they might support a chaplain which would at once make them comfortable and happy in their position. We shall pray very much for the prosperity of the first foundation in America and hope never to part with it.

So for the time being a community continued to live and work in Towanda. By the end of July 1863 there were twelve professed sisters from England in the country. Most of the first group moved to the city and most of the arrivals went to Towanda. The community at Spring Garden Street managed well, better even than Carter expected, running both a parish school and an academy, and though they were overworked, as at Towanda, poverty was less harsh. Then in January 1864 tragedy struck. One of the recent arrivals at Towanda died of consumption and her own sister who was in charge of the parish school in Philadelphia had to go to Towanda to replace her. Roused by anger on behalf of the sisters and anxiety for his schools,

Carter wrote at once to Mother Connelly, a letter that was both accusatory and demanding.

One wonders how she felt when she received it. He begins and ends as from a pulpit, 'Blessed are they that have not seen and have believed.' First, as to the duchess's donation of land: it has hampered more than helped the foundation, it should be sold and Cornelia is to ask her grace 'for at least $2000' to reimburse the sisters for all their expenditure and 'to enable them to furnish the contemplated Noviciate & boarding school'. Cornelia herself must send 'at least eight efficient sisters to carry on the work'. If these two conditions are not fulfilled the duchess's charitable intention will fail of its purpose. The tone is peremptory.

Second, as to Towanda: the '*Mansion*' even though so much has been spent on it is 'nothing more than a *miserable shanty* far inferior to your stables and cow houses in England'. The 'sufferings and deprivations' of the sisters have been 'worthy of the Christians of the first ages of the Church'. Only within the 'last few weeks' has he learned this; 'when I put the plain question to the sisters upon the subject, I got a smiling evasive answer'. Third, as to carrying on the work in the Philadelphia schools: there are too few sisters, the health of some is failing, classes have to be neglected.

He presumed that the sisters had told her much more than they had and finds 'a great deal of incredulity at St Leonards'. She is exhorted, with a mixture of pious reference and what is either heavy humour or sarcasm, to come and see for herself. One in her 'responsible situation' must not allow 'difficulty, trial or temptation' to deter her from promptly fulfilling this obvious duty. Finally, as to property and income, he gives her an order: 'You will please . . . lay the matter clearly and forcibly before the Duchess.'

This letter will have arrived in February 1864 and most unfortunately her answer has not survived. The foundation in America was close to Cornelia's heart. She had longed for it, fought for it. Those she had allowed to go were a loss in England and dear to her. If any of the scales over her eyes were due to her own failure to read between the lines of their letters, or to her own initial, too-willing trust to the opportunity offered, then at this moment they must have fallen. Her first impulse was probably to take the next boat over. But the responsible position to which Carter appealed on behalf of America included England. At this moment the property trouble at St Leonards was causing bitter misunderstanding between her and Grant and had reached such a point that the community might have to move out. She could not possibly leave the country.

Whatever Cornelia's answer to Fr Carter, he wrote that it was 'very kind'; 'we must go ahead', he says – perhaps because of what she had begged, throwing herself on his generosity – 'as I have become an honorary member of the Society & have taken the Sisters under my special care and protection'.

On her part she told Sr Mary Xavier that, should somewhere for boarding school and novitiate be found, Towanda could be closed. In June came the news that he had purchased Sharon House 'the most beautiful place about Philadelphia'. Cornelia was jubilant, promised to send 'three or four' more sisters and in October contrived five, in spite of what she had written to Grant: Carter had asked for more and 'we have not enough for our own work'. Preston, Blackpool and London were all asking for help and 'the work done far exceeds a just proportion to the number of religious employed'. That summer, 1864, the school hall at St Leonards was converted into a practical workshop for sisters 'preparing for the Western Missions'. Very soon at Sharon, novices began to arrive. She knew then that through the sisters from England the Society was fully established in the States and that Gregory XVI's behest to her was fulfilled: '*From England* let your work of catholic education spread to America.' The duchess too was satisfied. She eventually agreed that all the lands could be sold on condition that the fund thus created was available for the Society anywhere within the country.

Cornelia yearned for her own country (even the convent cows were given names such as 'America', 'Towanda'!) and in 1867 she went. A property crisis in Philadelphia had arisen.

The going was shadowed by what should have been joy. Before the crisis arose her son Frank, now twenty-six years old, suddenly appeared. He was *en route* for a 'tour of visits' in Scotland and stayed with his mother for eight days, accompanying her to Mayfield and London and then to Hornby. Ten weeks later, his visits concluded, he returned to St Leonards on 9 October. Meanwhile the need to go to the States had arisen, she was due to depart the next day and had to keep to the plan. Bellasis remembered a moving farewell between mother and son at Victoria station, which probably belongs to this time. They sat together in a railway compartment, she said, talking for half an hour. When the time came to say goodbye the sister who was with her, sitting quietly in a corner of the carriage, saw that 'a pool of tears' had collected in Cornelia's lap. This 1867 visit, as far as is known, was their first meeting since she had taken Frank to the school for little boys in 1846. Before leaving Philadelphia she would have occasion to look to his and Ady's interests. Her half-sister Isabella's multiple wills were soon to be legally sorted out, and anxious for what might possibly come to her son and daughter through herself as a natural heir, she would arrange for a lawyer to act on her behalf.

Cornelia and her companions arrived in Philadelphia on the 28th. At Spring Garden Street she found a flourishing apostolate – 120 children in the parish school and 48 in the academy. She settled the crisis and acquired a new property for a community and school in Chestnut Street (to be called St Leonards). Between house-hunting, arranging mortgages, visiting

Carter's schools, seeing the bishop, giving time to pupils and a great deal to the sisters, and having at the same time so bad a cold that for several days she had to keep to her room, she yet found time in the intervals to see her family.

The diary of the trip conveys an impression of family calling repeatedly and staying for as long as possible. Her sister Adeline's three married daughters all came and so did the Connellys. Twice she herself went visiting, to see her 'angel sister' Mary, Mother Peacock RSCJ, at the convent on Walnut Street. They never met again. Cornelia sailed for England on 27 November, forced by her dangerously heavy cold to leave before the worst weather set in, having hoped to remain until the spring. She took with her Ralph's two daughters Nelie and Bella, to finish their schooling at St Leonards in England, and the knowledge that all was well with the Society in America surely eased the premature parting.

ORPHANS AND RUINS, 1863–8

Five months after the first contingent of sisters left for America, Louisa Catherine removed to live at the convent. She came just in time for the yearly celebration of Cornelia's profession day, 21 December 1862. Gifts as usual poured in and the exhibition was arranged in the duchess's parlour. Her grace presented the sisters with a silver reliquary, and they had made her a rug for her place in chapel. There followed the festivities of Christmas and Epiphany and then came an announcement. She had purchased a house and land at Ore, a mile away, for an orphanage.

This had been secretly in the making between duchess, bishop and chaplain for some time. As the chaplain Joseph Searle (not to be confused with Mgr F. Searle, Wiseman's secretary) had told the bishop, her grace wanted 'something to occupy her attentions' which would 'do some good for poor destitute children'. The 'great difficulty' would be that her grace 'makes such a point of having supreme control'. Eventually they agreed that control of the project should be hers for her lifetime but the orphanage would be 'managed by the Nuns & ultimately belong to them'.

Cornelia now had to be asked. She had long been aware of the plight of destitute orphans. The state made no provision for them beyond boarding them in workhouses and, when old enough to work (at seven years), consigning them to the mercy of mine and factory owners. Since 1851 orphan girls had been educated at St Leonards, trained for domestic work and taught their religion, and she hoped one day to have an Industrial School there for them. The Ore proposal was to be accepted however hard it might prove to drive in tandem with her grace. She provided a community of six,

265

appointed as superior one whom the duchess wanted, and on 8 May 1863 the orphanage for forty girls was opened at Fairlight Hall.

That same spring another great gesture was in the making. It began in April with Searle trying to interest her grace in giving his indigent bishop a property for a seminary. He found one not far from the convent, Mayfield Palace Farm, with which the duchess was at once 'much smitten'. Searle too seems to have been much smitten but the bishop turned it down. At this point chance intervened. The children at St Leonards were planning their annual picnic for Whitsuntide, and Mother Connelly had promised on her feast day before Christmas that she would go with them. The duchess's enthusiasm (or Searle's) for the beauties of Mayfield must have overflowed and it was there they went, Mr Searle accompanying them. A drawing by one of the picnickers has survived. Some were walkers, some went by carriage. Long before they arrived Mayfield was in sight perched on a distant ridge with St Dunstan's ancient little church high in the middle, jabbing into the sky. They climbed the one village street, went under an arch at the top, and there before them, strikingly beautiful, were the ruins of what had once been a palace of the medieval archbishops of Canterbury. A farmhouse was in its shadow; hens and haywains were in possession where once clerks and courtiers trod. The arches of the now roofless synod hall invoked the past. And as far as the eye could see lay the lovely country, quiet and green, a ring of beauty, foil to what was an image-in-little of England's Catholic centuries before the Reformation.

For days afterwards the conversation was of nothing but Mayfield, Searle doing all he could in the following months to persuade Cornelia to buy it. She acquainted herself with its history, its traditions and legends, and made practical inquiries. The price was £5250. There was no money in hand and it could be raised only by borrowing half and reinvesting present funds for the rest. That August she and her council and the superiors from London and the north considered it carefully and on 17 August she wrote to Grant for permission to buy. They believed it could be used at once to supply St Leonards with fresh farm produce and a much needed place for rest and change, and that within a few years it could be readied to receive the novices and the retired or sick. Grant replied by return of post. It was not suitable for a religious house, farming by nuns was an imprudent proposition, and if she had money to spare it must be invested only for the support of the sisters. It was his 'earnest wish and therefore command' that she did not buy. She duly obeyed and by return of post told him so.

The duchess was outraged at such 'unaccountable weakness'. Bellasis tells the story with relish. Grant's command was 'interference' and 'his Lordship could not interfere with *her* and she would make him see it'. She bought it at once and 'now found herself in the position of a lady farmer being called upon for weekly wages, and for instructions regarding livestock and hopgardens! . . . a worry beyond her tackling'. Neither the Jesuits nor the Benedictines would accept it. Finally she offered it to Grant for a seminary, who – ' most unexpectedly' – suggested she gave it to Mother Connelly. Whereupon the duchess did so, 'remarking "A friend in need is a friend indeed! I had intended to benefit you after my death, but I am willing to do so in advance if you would like to accept the Mayfield property" '. And then came the catch, surely her grace's idea, not Grant's, 'on the one condition that you undertake to restore the ruins'.

Cornelia's wish to acquire a property such as Mayfield was far-sighted. Difficulties *vis-à-vis* property rights at St Leonards had mounted through ten years and were approaching a crisis. There were now about a hundred Holy Child sisters scattered in three English dioceses and in one small community in America. If the Society was to remain united in spirit and purpose it had to own a secure home base from which to operate. Needs such as these had justified asking Grant's permission to buy, even though the money could barely be found.

Other less tangible reasons will have moved Cornelia. Here at Mayfield stood a sign in stone of the church at work in the past. What place in England more suitable could she ever find for their home? It would imbue the sisters with a sense of the continuity of the church on earth, with a conviction that wherever they might afterwards go or whatever do, the Society had its place in the stream of the church's life through the centuries. To 'restore the ruins' as the duchess demanded was daunting enough for financial reasons, but not more so than the task of the Christian's life, to restore human faith in the good God. The restoration would be a symbol of all that Cornelia believed in.

Searle was full of approval. Sisters took over the farmhouse at once, scoured it into service as a little convent and rigged up a small oratory. On 17 and 18 November Grant went on an arduous episcopal trip. It began with the confirmation of orphans at Ore. That evening at St Leonards there must have been long conferrings with benefactress, chaplain and reverend mother. Next morning he received the vows of sisters during a sung mass and then, after breakfast in the school hall with the children, he and the newly professed and their guests set out for Mayfield. There he reassumed full ecclesiastical regalia, invoked the Holy Spirit in the little chapel and then processed all round the ruins. With cross borne before and mitre and crozier behind, he sprinkled holy water and blessings right and left. Priests and sisters followed, chanting psalms. Villagers gaped as it all swept by. And at the end, packed back into the chapel, there was a lusty Te Deum. Finally the duchess, 'illustrious lady and noble donor', departed by carriage in glory with the bishop, and the rest trickled quietly away. Mr Searle with

Mother Connelly and a handful of sisters remained and next morning he had the satisfaction of celebrating the first liturgy at Mayfield since the Reformation. On Saturday, 21 November a full account appeared in the *Tablet*. It included an announcement: the Old Palace was to become the mother house and the novitiate of the Society of the Holy Child Jesus.

In May work began under Edward Welby Pugin on the fourteenth-century synod hall, to become the convent church. How to raise the money was the question, and it was Wiseman who encouraged her. He too dreamt of England's Catholic shrines one day restored to their ancient purposes, and knowing that Catholic Europe prayed for England's conversion he suggested the sisters should collect funds on the continent too. He provided a letter of introduction from himself as Cardinal of England to be presented to bishops in whose diocese the sisters wished to beg. Her grace too caught on. Not to be outdone by any cardinal (or by the unenthusiastic Grant, to whom she wrote), she too produced letters of introduction.

For the next two years, generally on foot, sisters begged their way through Belgium, Holland, France, Spain. They went two by two, rarely sure of the next bed or meal. They often lost their way, they survived hunger and winter snow but they did well. On the whole, according to Buckle, it was the poor people who responded most generously. In England there was less welcome. She and her companion once collected only abuse and stones from a gang of boys and had to hide in a shop. Letters streamed back to Cornelia, easing her inevitable anxiety, and when the sisters returned they poured out their stories of consolation and hardship. Bellasis tells how when Mother Connelly listened her eyes would fill with tears because, seeing how thin and weary her poor beggars were, she realised how much their zeal had outstripped all concern for themselves. It was an arduous mission, in its way as demanding as that of the sisters who went to Towanda, and like theirs it resulted in something equally essential for the firm establishing of the Society. In both cases there was at last the security of property owned. More important, it is evident in both that 'the germ of their future life' which Cornelia had planted in 1846 was now a very sturdy plant. Nourished on her spirit of 'no ordinary sacrifice' the sisters were capable, for great apostolic good, of joy-filled perseverance in the midst of hardship. When Mother Connelly died fifteen years later, by which time orphans, young schoolchildren, novices and a community were all housed at the Old Palace, with restoration and new buildings completed, one of the sisters who had never fully recovered her health after the rigours of two years of begging 'freely expressed her joy at having laboured and suffered so much' for Mayfield.

While some of the sisters begged in Europe, communities at home vied with each other to contribute. Bazaars multiplied. In this too the duchess was not to be outdone. Grant was told, '*We* are going to have a bazaar in London'; and she extracted a letter from the Jesuit general warmly recommending all Jesuits in England, France and Spain to support this 'great benefactress of religion'. Mother Connelly organised a gigantic raffle (which nearly fell foul of the law but was saved by the legal ingenuity of Sir George Bowyer). It was put under the patronage of foreign royalty and English aristocracy, and the pope himself sent a gift. His 'Mosaic Brooch Mounted in Fine Gold' headed the list of several hundred prizes ranging from 'An Alderney Cow and Calf' down to books and railway wrappers. Tickets were sixpence each and 80,000 books were printed for distribution in Britain, India, Australia and America. By March 1865 the little convent at Mayfield had a community of five and Cornelia was often there. The drawing of prizes was to be in October and Bellasis, who was one of the community, wrote that Cornelia's correspondence was so heavy that 'the letters had to be delivered by the worthy wife of the postmaster in a wheelbarrow each morning! The writer remembers the good lady remarking, "Is it always going to want a wheelbarrow? It will be the killing of me if it does." '

One of the statements made on the raffle tickets was that the funds raised were for a 'Female Orphanage'. Cornelia sent personal letters on its behalf. The restored ruins at Mayfield were to be appropriated as much to orphans as to the novitiate, she said, 'and it is for the orphans' share I plead'. Whether or not friends responded as she hoped, the five sisters there began their life with twelve orphans to teach and train.

During December 1864 the Ore orphanage had been robbed and the chapel desecrated and just before that her grace's orphanage for boys in Hastings had been broken into. These events determined her to remove them both to a safer location and she seems to have arranged with Cornelia to transfer the girls' orphanage to the Old Palace. But at the very time that Cornelia was printing raffle tickets naming a 'Female Orphanage' as one of the objects of the restoration, the duchess was having a better idea. 'I mean', she wrote to Grant, 'to purchase a farm at Mayfield and remove them both there.' This change of plan might have suited Cornelia if the 'farm' had been conveniently placed close to the Old Palace. But in the duchess's hands one farm became three and the location of the girls' orphanage receded further and further from the Palace. Cornelia knew how difficult it was for Grant to find priests for outlying missions, but her grace disregarded the fact that to people on foot winter and summer as a daily necessity, four miles of muddy cross-country lanes was very different from one mile, and chose for the girls' orphanage, which the sisters would serve, the one furthest from Mayfield village. Cornelia would now have to provide for two separate establishments just too far from each other to be able to share chaplain or any other personnel. Even so, at the Old Palace she still kept the little group of orphans, hoping that in the future provision for an Industrial School could be made.

The duchess's need to have her own way grew with the years. In 1868 the building was in the hands of Pugin and, as he remarked, he had 'no more power at the orphanages than a flea, Her grace alone reigns and that supremely'. He and Cornelia exchanged groans about progress. Although the duchess intended to provide for only forty orphans, saying she could afford no more, it had to be designed grandiosely for a hundred. In 1872 a second architect fared no better. Her grace, now eighty years old, decided on alterations. The 'simple chapel' which the sisters hoped for was to have what Goldie called 'utterly useless' nave, aisle and arches, and as to the covered way from house to church asked for by Cornelia for the use of orphans and sisters alike, he reported that the duchess 'was obdurate as to the *dis*connection of the Church & Orphanage, nor did all my arguments make any effect, except perhaps to confirm her in opposition to the laws of common sense & reason'. Two years later the duchess died. Contrary to her promise she left nothing for the orphanage beyond the little already provided. Society resources were too low just then to be able to maintain even the forty orphans. Later it was possible to do so by receiving fee-paying school pupils but in the end the orphanage ceased altogether.

THE ALL SOULS PROPERTY DISPUTE

'The duchess has been no inattentive observer of matters here,' Searle once told Grant. Through her generosity three vital beginnings were made, two that have endured and one that was a response to a crying need of the day. All three nearly foundered on her unpredictability, but in one situation Louisa Catherine and her chaplain were Cornelia's faithful allies.

When she came to St Leonards in the winter of 1860 the dispute about the All Souls property was nearing its climax. Dr Duke had started sending petitions to the pope. Two had already gone. When Searle arrived as convent chaplain in February 1861 another was simmering, and after that there would be five more until at last in 1864, when he was still there, the affair was settled. Duchess and chaplain played their part, mostly only with comment from the sidelines but finally in at the winning post. Cornelia, loaded with other concerns, had very little support in the struggle. Even her bishop misjudged her:

How your Lordship can suppose that we can love God and not care for the good of souls around us, I have never understood. We have simply kept our ground in the best way we could, and at the same time we have helped all that we could towards the good of the many calumnies and false aspersions thrown upon us.

Searle on arrival stepped into what was an altercation at fever pitch. There stood Jones's church, the ivy thicker than ever on its half-height walls, not completed because Towneley believed that Grant had agreed to do it. But according to the clause in the Trust, unless it was finished by 3 June of the coming year the congregation would lose all legal claim on its use. This was the lever behind Duke's petitions. As far as one can judge they carried weight in Rome for two reasons: the initial appeal conveyed that Grant knew the *contents* of the petition, which he did not; and, it became known there that Duke was supported by Cardinal Wiseman.

Duke was an eloquent misinformer. He overestimated what Jones had to bequeath; he ignored that by Jones's will Towneley became absolute proprietor not a mere trustee; he told the pope (and Wiseman, Grant and Ullathorne) that Towneley knew nothing of Jones's intentions and maintained that, influenced by Mrs Connelly, he was failing to fulfil them. The portrait of Cornelia which he created was that of an avaricious usurper, the immovable beneficiary whom he wanted removed. In February 1862, to Wiseman whose willing ear he filled with long, gossipy and conspiratorial letters, he wrote: 'It is to be devoutly prayed for, that a certain lady be shipped off to America, there to teach the little black slaves their alphabet, practise humility and save herself some purgatory,' and two weeks later off went his fourth petition, authorised, he told the pope, by his eminence. In it for the first time Cornelia is named: the community which has 'entirely absorbed' mission rights and Jones's money, is presided over by the reverend Mother Connelly. From then onwards petitions and memoranda increasingly present her as the source of an infamous situation – her community holds an estate worth '£50,000 sterling' and has expended 'on their own schemes' wealth meant for the mission. She is insincere, false, grasping. Towneley is her tool.

Duke's assistant in all this, apart from Wiseman and Melia in the background, was the easily influenced, neurotic young mission priest John Foy,[1] according to whom Cornelia was determined to 'aggrandise her own community at all costs'. Foy came three years before Searle and had been well infected by Duke. For Bishop Ullathorne, appointed by Rome to arbitrate, one of his statements in a document twenty-nine pages long was that when the Trust was being drawn up (six years before his own arrival, so how could he know) the community had committed 'acts of spoliation with the *greatest stealth*'. And he described Cornelia: the 'well-known determination, self-will, imperiousness and often insolent manner of the present Superioress.

It is not necessary to insist on the peculiarities of her character, for they are known all the world over.'

Cornelia the hot-tempered little girl was now a passionate but self-possessed and compelling woman. Without such qualities her life's mission would have failed. Against their domination of herself, however, she had to struggle interiorly and the years 1862–4 were a time of daily, local trial in the midst of which she was probably sometimes overbearing. But not in her heart. Over the years denigrations of every kind, not only by Foy, were repeated to her. 'She was styled a bold woman,' Bellasis wrote, 'but cruel sayings never disturbed her peace. "Leave them to God," she would say. "We are what we are in God's sight, nothing more or less".'

In these years there was burden and pressure on many counts. Throughout 1862 came the trouble with Stokes and in 1863 the question of whether to close the college. Regular visits to the other communities had to be kept up, especially important since the Bowles affair. Retreats for ladies (about a hundred attended in 1863) were organised at the Harley Street convent in London and she was much in demand for spiritual help. In 1863 the *Book of Studies* was finished and printed. She took an active interest in school, saw the novices, gave conferences to the community. It was at this time that a master was brought to the convent to teach the sisters how to cast and paint figures; and at Epiphany 1863 she sent the other convents a design of her own for a figure of the Holy Child for their chapels.

Behind all that clamoured for attention every day stood the continuing worry that no word (since 1854) had come from Rome about the Rule. Added to this was the certainty that the cardinal was not their friend. On both counts the survival of the Society was not sure, and deeper than any of this lay the hidden ache for husband and children. References to them in surviving records for these years are few. In December 1861 she begged prayers of Bishop Kenrick for Pierce's return to the church. In 1863 crumbs of painful news reached her through Fr Carter about Ady, now a woman of twenty-eight: she is visiting her aunt in Philadelphia, she is a 'strenuous Episcopalian', she is devoted to her father. Of Frank, by 1864 twenty-three years old and living in Florence with Ady and Pierce, there is nothing.

Searle's coming in 1861 was a blessing. Although he and Foy had to share the presbytery he refused to be drawn into the property argument. But he saw what was going on. The effect on the local mission appalled him, and in the dispute his sympathies were with the community. There was 'continual talking about the matter to everyone who comes', he said. The conduct of 'certain parties' was 'reckless' and 'unpardonable'. Rumours were 'industriously propagated'. Duke resorted to 'the weapon of agitation' and was a 'bad and pernicious influence'; Foy was 'completely under his control'. By June 1862 Searle was hoping the bishop would come to 'settle this wretched controversy' and told him that the duchess had several times offered to settle the community elsewhere 'rather than continue to endure the petty & spiteful persecution to which they are subjected here'.

An outline of basic facts during the penultimate years of the case, 1861–3, will be of interest. The whole correspondence exemplifies how the church conducted its affairs at that date when centralisation and the magnifying of ecclesiastical authority was Rome's considered policy; and the corresponding response expected of the laity – not least of a woman – was obedience. Cornelia was caught in a stranglehold. More often than not she was unaware who were pulling the ropes. What she did know all the time was that the property was not the community's, that it belonged to Towneley's trustees and even they could agree only to what was for strictly educational purposes – which the building of a public church for the congregation was not.

In December 1861 Ullathorne recommended to the Propaganda that the trustees be asked to allow another five years for the completion of the Jones church. They refused and in June 1862 therefore the congregation would lose its rights. Grant then identified actively with Duke's point of view. He wanted the church for the mission. At his suggestion Barnabò required Cornelia to finish it for the congregation. This was known as the 'decree'.

Cornelia assured Barnabò of her willingness to obey but added that she would rely on Grant to advise her how best to do so. She presumed her bishop, a trustee, understood and accepted her position *vis-à-vis* the Trust. She wrote to him, 'It is evident that the decision assumes that I have a power I do not possess.' No comment of his is extant.

Towneley reminded her: 'As the property is held . . . *not by you* . . . you cannot apply it to any purpose but the one designated in the Deed.' But Grant expected a 'line by line' obedience to the decree. Her repeated proposals about what might be done within the Trust terms seemed to him an evasion of obedience.

Having consulted Grant, Towneley and Stonor (her lawyer), she sent an appeal in January 1863 on behalf of the Society to Rome, accompanied by a memorandum from the colonel. These gave Barnabò pause. He asked Ullathorne who had already reported to him once (and with whom Duke and Foy communicated) to consider the memorandum. Earlier Ullathorne had said Cornelia was the cause of the trouble; she was 'a person of acute perception' who 'throws all responsibility on the trustees' and 'evades the duty of acting herself'. Now he wrote negatively of Towneley as well: the colonel is a mere trustee, has not the authority of a proprietor which the memorandum assumed, is influenced by Mrs Connelly who wished to 'shut out the congregation', and could if he chose use Trust funds to carry out the decree. This answer was forwarded by Barnabò to Grant in June

1863, 'so that according to your judgement this affair may be brought to a just conclusion'.

Grant then made a proposal which Barnabò adopted, along with Ullathorne's judgment. Writing now to Towneley not as heir but as Jones's trustee, he appealed to conscience: having received Jones's goods the colonel must fulfil Jones's intentions and not allow the community to continue enjoying property and money unless they completed Jones's church for the congregation or provided for them another 'equally beautiful'. Then he inserted Grant's proposal, a veiled threat: the colonel was warned that should the community not agree, it was possible that their bishop would have to place an interdict on the convent. Nor perhaps would anyone be admitted by the bishop to profession without full dowry because such a person would have to be supported out of Jones's funds, which would be a loss to the congregation. This letter of September 1863 Towneley shared and apparently discussed with Cornelia. Everything would turn on his answer.

To return now to events at St Leonards.

Throughout that period much of what reached Cornelia's ears came by the painful route of distorting rumour. A case in point is the Propaganda's response to the trustee's refusal to extend the time limit for the completing of Jones's church. Seventeen days before Cornelia was told about or received the actual 'decree', she wrote to Grant:

> We hear from Dr Duke's reports such wonderful assertions set afloat . . . we do not know what to make of the Cardinal's visit . . . Amongst other facts stated is that I have a letter of censure from Cardinal Barnabò & that if I do not acknowledge it, no doubt the letter is in my pocket. All these wonderful things are announced to the labouring people to bring up to the convent. The first came from Victor Duke [Dr Duke's son] to our Fish boy. Dr Duke states to the Duchess of Leeds and Lady Stafford that *four bishops* have denounced me & my 'sisters' *not only in this but in their general way of going on* so that we are to be dissolved & dispersed etc. etc. etc. I wonder who the four Bishops can be? Dr Errington? the Cardinal? Dr Ullathorne? and who can they have invented for the fourth? These are the diplomatic reports which are unintelligible to us . . .

Searle's comments to Grant on the same occasion fill in the picture. Wiseman had stayed the night at the presbytery:

> I hope I must not connect with the honour of his Eminence's visit a series of rumours immediately put abroad here, & which I heard from the mouth of Victor Duke as well as from others: e.g. That Cardinal Barnabò had written to Reverend Mother – who is always mentioned in these

edifying reports as Mrs Connelly, the principal of an Order not recognised in Rome – commanding her at once to give over the church *completed* to the congregation to whom it belongs; that the trust deed is so much waste paper; that the trustees are not to be treated with; that your Lordship – & you are not spoken of any more respectfully than Reverend Mother – is also commanded to come down at once to see to the prompt fulfilment etc. etc. With very much more besides, as for instance that the Nuns are censured, excommunicated etc. etc.

This is all very stupid no doubt, but it strikes me as strange that the rumours should circulate so immediately upon the arrival of the Cardinal & that they should be actively propagated by one of his Eminence's clergy . . .

It is of course quite possible that the Cardinal would not approve of Dr Duke thus acting, & his Eminence never mentioned the matter to me & is most kind; but he would not visit them at the Convent or say Mass at the church, although I asked him . . .

Earlier in the year Wiseman had written to Manning (then *en route* for Rome), 'I sincerely believe the whole Order to be *rotten*', which Cornelia is very unlikely to have heard, but at this juncture she knew enough of the cardinal to say with some irony to Towneley, 'the view he has taken is not the most favourable to us in this matter'.

On the home front she and her own bishop were advancing steadily into a morass of incomprehension on the subject of obedience. Barnabò's so-called decree demanded that in the finished church there should be separation between community and congregation. Cornelia told Grant on 6 October that she was 'quite in a puzzle' about how to plan for this. She wondered whether separate services instead of separate space might meet what was 'really desired'. Searle too, on 10 October, told Grant, 'decide as we may we must run foul of the Decree'. The misunderstanding is clearly documented. By 13 October 1862 he was writing to her that he would have to withdraw from the Trust 'if it stands in the way of my duty of obedience to the Holy See'. Nor could he adopt any view 'contrary to the justice that obliges the holders of the property to fulfil Mr Jones' obligations'. He hoped she would not delay because 'justice and obedience are stern virtues that will not bear delay'. She answered immediately:

My Lord Bishop
Either your Lordship must have misunderstood my letter or I have very poorly expressed what I intended, as I have never questioned or doubted on the point of obedience, or of the fulfilment of every justice. The question is simply *how* it is to be put into practice, & whether it is to be understood in the true light.

I have had a legal opinion of what can be done to meet the wishes of the Sacred Congregation, and I have no doubt that we shall very soon understand more clearly what we can do & what we cannot do.

He asked for the legal opinion and on 19 October she sent it, reiterating: 'What is to be seen, is, *how* we shall be able to meet the obedience required.' Again she proposed separate services pro tem and offered assistance towards a separate church when numbers later warranted it. She concluded with: 'Whatever I say on this subject my Lord, it is with all submission & deference to your wishes & commands, & I hope that you will understand that I mean to do so always.' But on 21 October he announced that he 'did not intend to have any clothing or profession till the Decree of Rome had been carried out'. This was a threat. Characteristically she had recourse to the Mother of God, her 'alter ego' in the bearing of sorrow:

My Lord Bishop
I took your letter received by the 23[?] October post after having read it twice myself, and read it to Our Lady of Sorrows asking her in her own sweet meekness to listen to it, and the interior answer I got was 'burn the letter & tell the Bishop to forget what he wrote & to come and tell you what more you can do than you have done'. I have burnt it my Lord, & now will you come down & tell me what more I can do than I have done? . . .
PS. Has your Lordship forgotten that you told me to send you the legal opinion that I copied out for you?

Cornelia was desperate. She could not do what was required, but the Society's lifeline was to be cut if she did not. 'I have burnt it my Lord.' Having no other resource she put all her trust in the 'interior answer'. Searle wrote to Grant that he could not 'conceive what new difficulty had arisen for which the Convent is responsible'. Cornelia had assured him that she was '*in your hands, awaiting your orders*'. The bishop neither came nor gave any orders. But the lifeline was not cut. He compromised. Searle was allowed to preside at the clothing ceremony.

The state of affairs continued unabated, and just before Christmas 1862 she begged Searle's intervention with Grant: 'Will you get the Bishop to say what he wants me to do, and state that if his Lordship thinks I have any wish that is contrary to what is right or what he himself would wish *in the end*, it is *not so*.' She was 'at a loss to know how I can act' because the bishop was unwilling to do so. The community had offered to raise the money for the church but 'we are told that we show little disposition to carry out the wishes of the Sacred Congregation! I really need light to understand our own position.'

Eventually she sent her appeal to Rome along with Towneley's memorandum and a formal offer of £1500 towards a church and £30 towards a priest's stipend. A long period of local rumour and agitation ensued. While Towneley and Mother Connelly sought ways of raising the promised sums, Duke and Foy stoked up the opposition. A vivid vignette of the 'partisan warfare' as Searle dubbed it, comes from the duchess. On Sunday, 13 December 1863 she went to high mass in the convent chapel, the celebration for the congregation, and Mr Foy so conducted himself that she wrote three pages to Grant urging his removal.

Foy had put on the convent gate a notice about times of mass and the sisters had taken it down in compliance with the known orders of the police. He seized the chance to denounce the community in his homily. The congregation was told (the duchess there, taking it all in) that the treatment they received from the sisters was insulting, scandalous and abominable because their 'object was to prevent the people from attending church'. Everything he said 'was directed against the Nuns & calculated to make dissension'. Such things had 'gone on much too long', she wrote. 'The poor Nuns do much good. They know *their position*, that everything is in the hands of the trustees. They have no power, and I always hear them say, they *must* and they are *willing* to submit to the decision of the trustees. What more can they do?' She concluded her appeal by wickedly suggesting that the bishop take Foy under his own wing at St George's cathedral: 'Then you would see what he is. He tells people you like him so much that you approve all he does.' But her grace's appeal 'as a *particular favour* to *myself*' was unavailing. Foy remained.

In September 1863 the climax of this long trouble was approaching. Rome's appeal to Towneley's conscience and the threat of an interdict reached him. He wrote to Grant – who had agreed to the Trust, discussed its terms and signed the deed – 'It seems to me most extraordinary that your Lordship did not explain this matter in such a way as to save us all further trouble long ago.' His wife fell ill and they went to warmer climes and not till January 1864 could he answer Barnabò. He referred the cardinal back to the memorandum already received, reiterated – on behalf of Mother Connelly too – the offer already made, and then concluded with a warning which made mincemeat of Grant's proposed interdict. It was his duty to point out, he said, that were the bishop to lay an interdict on the convent the Court of Chancery would step in, because such an act would paralyse the Charity for which the Trust was established. Moreover the trustees would probably decide to sell the whole property and move the Charity elsewhere. Should such a situation arise, he smoothly continued, the community would have 'valid claims for large sums advanced by them out of their dowers with the sanction of the bishop, for the erection of divers buildings'. Having thus demolished Barnabò's supposition that Grant had advised him wisely, a postscript was added. One of the trustees, since he was going to Rome, had agreed to 'give your Eminence every information'. This friend was Bishop Roskell.

Roskell would not be going alone. The duchess, 'no inattentive observer', had reached a conclusion. Her chaplain was not at all well. Would not a trip to Rome do him good? They talked it over in her parlour. She wrote to Grant, 'I am anxious Mr Searle should spend the winter in Rome, for several reasons.' On 3 February 1864 he joined Roskell at Dover and they set out.

Down at St Leonards Mother Connelly and the community had considered their position, and on 2 March a letter went to Towneley Hall. It put on paper some of the points she and the colonel must have discussed and which he had sent to Barnabò, and confirmed that she and sisters wished:

> . . . the property should be sold and the Community transferred elsewhere rather than continue in our present state incurring the dissatisfaction of Rome, subject to constant misrepresentation & most injurious persecution here. We have devoted 16 years to this establishment & we have made it what it is, though with only one object in view, the good of souls amongst our children and Community and God's greater glory therein.

The possession of mere property is not worth the persecution, she says, and continues: 'Pray let me assure you my dear Colonel Towneley that unless our affairs are settled by the Sacred Congregation with you, we shall hail the day that decides our removal from here.'

In Rome matters were moving with uncharacteristic speed. Searle went with Roskell out to Monte Porzio for a few days at the English College villa from where a gleeful letter reached Mother Connelly. Roskell had 'pretty well exploded the Duke bubble', the Propaganda was 'furious to think they had been misled into a decision on ex-parte statements' and those responsible 'will catch it'. To the duchess he wrote that anything Towneley or the community may do for the congregation is now recognised as not of obligation, but he went on with unusually frank indignation: 'how *can* the bishop [Grant] expect them to do anything until the foul charges against them are publicly contradicted'. Duke and Foy ought to be silenced and amends be made to Towneley and Mother Connelly 'for the grievous wrong & injustice which his Lordship has for long allowed . . . his conduct in the matter has been most extraordinary'.

Cornelia heard from Towneley:

> 'Cardinal Barnabò has fully withdrawn the decision given, *& exonerated you & the nuns from any liability to the congregation* beyond what you have so generously offered.'

My dear Mrs Connelly

I have only a minute to say that I think the above extract which I have just received [from Roskell] will be as satisfactory to you as the result of my sale was to me yesterday, so throw up your caps or hoods or whatever you like to call what you wear on your heads & say two acts of thanksgiving, one for the decision & one for the sale!! I'm buried in drainage accounts today with the government inspector, tomorrow I go to London.

> Most sincerely yours
> C.T.

The account of my sale will be in the *Times* of today or tomorrow, so get it & read it – if not against your rules to read an account of a shorthorn breeder's sale!!!

Towneley, angry about the whole affair, now demanded for the twelve years of calumnious misrepresentation of the community and himself public apologies and the removal of Foy; and he refused an extra £500 which Roskell had volunteered he might give. This, during four months, increased the opposition's ill-feeling and it was Mother Connelly (initially she felt as he did) who eventually saved the situation by offering the money for the congregation. Three months later Dr Duke died and with him should have died the controversy. But there was still Mr Foy.

The pope's rescript, dated 17 November 1864, publicly confirmed Barnabò's decision and on Cornelia's feast that year Searle sent her his congratulations:

> May our Lord . . . bless your labours for his glory & amplify your Society by the vocations of many who have the true spirit of the Holy Child. Certainly during the past year you have great reason to bless & adore his goodness. For he has relieved your Society of a stigma thrust upon you by unprincipled men . . .

This was true and Towneley had circulated among friends a copy of Barnabò's letter to him. Many learned that he and the community had been exonerated from all obligation and that the decree was admitted by Rome to have been founded on 'false suppositions'. Nevertheless the rescript was in no way as blunt as that, and the colonel cared not at all for its introductory wording. It accommodated the position of Bishop Grant, not his. It spoke of 'compromise' between community and congregation (a proposal of Grant's) and, amazingly, still spoke of the trustees as those of Jones, thus ignoring that all had been in Towneley's free gift as heir. The colonel was a Justice of the Peace and there is little doubt that the conduct of this case rankled. He did not challenge the rescript but wrote a final letter to Roskell which told him what he thought of the Propaganda:

The evident inability of that body in such a case to obtain proper information, its necessary dependence on ex-parte statements, secondary evidence, private personal communications . . . would certainly prevent any well advised person from troubling the S[acred] C[ongregation] for its advice or opinion under circumstances like the present.

Only three months after the issue of the rescript Cardinal Wiseman died. Mother Connelly owed him a great debt of gratitude. Without his early interest and generous practical support the Society might never have been able even to begin. In a sense he was a co-founder. Bellasis wrote that 'a few years before his death', visiting the convent school and finding himself surrounded by the children of both Old Catholics and converts he was 'quite overcome', and said to Cornelia: 'Reverend Mother, you have realised the desire of my heart.' He had also stood by her in the dark days of Pierce's betrayal, when choice for her was at its most stark and separation at its most cruel. But it is equally certain that he became Cornelia's active enemy, and had his imprecations against her been given full credence at the Propaganda she and her Society would have been destroyed. It is therefore good to be able to record that, according to Buckle, when he heard how Rome had settled the matter of the property he simply said, 'I never understood the question before.' It was possibly Roskell who effected this. He had been a student of Wiseman's at the English College and the first whom Wiseman, newly a bishop, had ordained.[2] He was known among the hierarchy to be a Wiseman supporter and he visited him *en route* for Rome on this affair. By the time of the rescript the cardinal was a very ill man. If there was any reconciliation no record has survived, but the sisters made banners for the requiem and an entry in the diary of community doings for February 1865 runs:

15 The cardinal died. RIP.
23 The magnificent Funeral Solemnities at Moorfields Church.

A new church for the mission was completed with speed on a site outside the convent property. The opening was in May 1866, both occasion and church beautiful enough for even Foy to be pleased. Accord, however, did not last. His persistent demand to Grant had resulted in a directive from Barnabò that when the congregation had its own church the community's must be 'strictly closed', and Mother Connelly was soon caught day by day in a ridiculous and unchristian dilemma. No one at all who was visiting the convent or the schools might attend mass there. There was continual and embarrassing difficulty. When two years later she begged Grant's permission to receive special friends like Towneley and Stonor for the opening of the Jones church, now at last completed for the community, the bishop thought the occasion sufficiently exceptional to agree. Not so Foy. To him the wish to have these 'rich friends' present was yet another proof that all that mattered to Mother Connelly was the raising of money, and her request an example of her reluctance to obey even the pope. He outlived the duchess, Searle, Towneley and Mother Connelly.

The completion of the Jones church in October 1868 was a high moment in Cornelia's religious life. She was nearly sixty. The night before the opening, as the young sister who was with her remembered, she went into the church to see if all was ready. And suddenly in a voice still beautiful she began to sing, hymn after hymn of praise and thanksgiving. Next day at the ceremony of consecration the ageing duchess no doubt sat in her new stall at the back of Cornelia's church and looked around. Four years later she built at Mark Cross the 'better church than *hers*' and two years after that, in 1874, died at the age of eighty-two. Mother Connelly was left with orphanage upkeep and marble pillars. For Louisa Catherine there was an impressive tribute at her requiem, a procession of forty orphans.

13

Cornelia and Bishop Grant

1864, LOOKING BACK

The duchess outlived not only Wiseman but also Bishop Grant. He died in 1870. At the age of thirty-five when Cornelia was forty-two he had become her ecclesiastical superior and remained so for nineteen years. He came, scholar and canonist, from the English College in Rome where he had been rector, and where he had acted as agent to the Holy See for the English vicars apostolic. He would draw on this experience with the Propaganda in the course of his dealings for her Society. His warmest love, after the church, surely because as a child he had been an orphan, was for the orphaned poor. Children were at home with him and he with them. At St Leonards he was a frequent visitor and schools and community loved him. So did Cornelia. She was open with him, looked forward to his visits, told him her personal troubles and turned to him for spiritual encouragement as well as for the multifarious permissions she had to ask. He was a saintly, gentle man full of charity, and eminently peace-loving.

Such qualities do not necessarily qualify one to deal with the hurly-burly of a diocese and there was nothing trenchant in Bishop Grant with which to meet the vindictive campaigns of a Duke or an Emily Bowles. Men like the autocratic Towneley and the forthright Ullathorne thought him timid. The colonel's last word to the Propaganda was a warning that Grant's 'extreme vacillation of mind' was a primary obstacle to the mission's prosperity. Cornelia herself was a woman of decision and Grant's uncertainties an inevitable source of frustration. If her persistence or her ignorance of the 'sacred canons' wore him to a thread, she in turn must have agonised when, seeing the injustice and lack of charity which inaction would create, she could take no step at all because he, overcome by a too scrupulous conscience, could make no firm decision. But he was for a long time, as she became increasingly aware, an ill man. The inability to hold out against the bullying of such as Emily Bowles or Dr Duke must have been due at least in part to the weariness which consuming disease and great pain induce.

In Grant Cornelia could not have had an ecclesiastical superior more different from her first. Wiseman, boundlessly enthusiastic at Derby and initially at St Leonards, vastly busy with great concerns and impatient of administration and detail, had left her to run her own establishment with only a chaplain on hand. But Grant was over-conscientious. As bishop he had to be personally sure that all was as it should be. Even school affairs were under his eye; the accepted proprieties of the day had to be observed: waltzing and the new polka were not to be allowed, a male tutor was to be dismissed without further inquiry, a suspect anthology of non-Catholic poetry was not to be used. Once a Protestant drawing inspector caused a storm in a teacup. The correspondence (incomplete) covers ten pages. To Grant's first enquiry Cornelia replied:

> Yes, we have received notice that the Drawing Inspector is to come on the 17th but we do not know that he is a Catholic, and if he is *not* he will of course have his journey for nothing. What shall we say to him? Sir, are you a Catholic? 'Yes madam but not a Roman Catholic.' Sir, I am sorry you have had the trouble of this long journey, but you will have to be approved by the Bishops' Poor School Committee before we can admit you into our schools. Will this do my Lord? It seems to me very uncivil . . .

The inspector duly came and she duly reported how well things had gone but this was not enough. Grant had forgotten to ask 'whether the Drawing Inspector asked any questions as it was the condition that he was merely to present papers & sit by whilst they were being executed. Your mention of his praise of their "knowledge of the *principles of* drawing" makes me suppose he questioned the pupils.' After a week she told him firmly: 'I think it would be very unreasonable to complain of the Inspector's *speaking* to our girls, and I could not think of doing such a thing.'

The Society's financial insecurity worried Grant. What Cornelia wrote to him once she might well have written often: 'Do, my Lord trust in God, and all will go on well.' Sources of support were meagre. Only if sisters brought full dowries would futures be safe, because dowries would provide for those who left as well as maintain and care for those who grew old or sick. The existing code of canon law required dowries and he appealed to it as a bulwark against the threat of insolvency. Mother Connelly, one of those establishing an uncloistered, active community, saw the dowry question quite differently. She pleaded that vocations were needed for the work of God and should not be refused on the score of money. Nor should what the Society had be saved just to provide for itself:

> I wish you would remember my Lord that we only want to *labour* for our

support as mendicant orders beg, and above all as our Blessed Lord himself laboured for thirty years. If we sink into making provision for our support, *not* imitating our Blessed Lord, we shall not be blessed.

This was the ideal, never completely realised because there were always some who had neither dowry nor earning capacity. For the majority, however, their dowers were the 'value of services', and as numbers increased so would income (from fees or stipends or grants). Eventually she started a fund for the retired; but, generally speaking, money in her view should be made to work. Dowries invested in buildings for the apostolate was 'a change of investiture & not an expenditure', nor did she fear the raising of loans. Her business sense was very good as even Grant acknowledged, but he was fearful of this kind of thinking. With no appropriate canon law to fall back on, anxiety and recurring hesitation took over. In vain she waxed eloquent about America: 'Ah my Lord . . . There religious are valued for their works and they need no dower.' Often building permissions and admittances to the novitiate were delayed.

In another matter, that of the vows taken by the sisters, Grant's cautiousness became a threat to the Society, contributing largely to the crisis which arose after his death. This subject will have to be returned to. But there were two more important areas in which the bishop tenaciously opposed Mother Connelly's vital interests: the attempt to lay hold of the St Leonards property and the attempt to change the character of the Society, in both of which he had worked behind her back, in the latter case entirely so. His letters to Rome on both subjects show him proposing means to achieve his own ends, but he never spoke against Cornelia personally as did Wiseman. Even so, his willingness as her bishop to co-operate with those who did had caused, as Searle said of the property affair, 'grievous wrong & injustice . . . to be perpetrated against them [the community] to the injury of the Schools & their prejudice here in Rome'.

The end of the property dispute in March 1864 brought the bishop a considerable setback because the claims he had supported at St Leonards had been rejected, and the rights of the community confirmed. Roskell met him to talk on the subject during Low Week but there is no record that he, like Wiseman, said, 'I never understood till now'. On the contrary, his comments to the Propaganda were largely protests against the position accepted finally by Barnabò. Where, one asks, was the 'line for line' obedience which he had demanded of Cornelia? His conduct throughout the affair, unless it is attributed to the influence of 'unprincipled men' over one who was sick, remains, as Searle said, 'most extraordinary'.

THE CONSTITUTIONS AGAIN, 1864

The second matter concerned the Rule. A resumé of what Cornelia had done about it since 1854 will be useful here.

In 1854 the version she took to the Propaganda was put in limbo through Grant's inaction and Wiseman's prejudice. During negotiations with the Bowles family she told Grant that she deplored the lack of constitutional safeguards against the débâcle precipitated by Emily. Then in 1856 Grant and Wiseman had secretly proposed to Rome that her Rule be set aside for one already approved and the Society be made diocesan. Errington's opinion had prevented action. By 1861 she had added some clauses on poverty to obviate the kind of financial free-wheeling perpetrated by Emily, and had given a copy of the first part of the Rule to every sister. When the chance of sisters going to America appeared she put in new articles of government for the sustaining of unity in dispersion. Sisters went in August 1862, and in January 1863, writing to Barnabò, she made a heartfelt plea for approval. This she followed up a year later when Searle went to Rome, taking with him her revised text translated into Italian to hand to the English College. And it was at this juncture, and before it could be presented to the Propaganda, that Grant broke his ten-year silence about the Constitutions and pointed her in a new direction. We have no evidence that Barnabò had written favourably to Grant on this subject, but his judgment upholding Towneley's Trust may have induced him to propose steps towards approval, for now the bishop passed to her a summary of the Roman consultor's comments sent to him ten years before. In August 1864, giving no explanation, he told her to begin work on them with a view to approbation.

Increasingly disease gripped Grant. To come and consecrate the new convent altar in 1868 was a problem 'as any hour may witness a return of the inability to stand'. Time was running out and his anxiety for the Society now focused on approbation. Cornelia's reply to the sudden request gives no hint of astonishment at the long delay. She thanked him and promised that 'with the assistance of the most experienced sisters' she would give her 'best attention to the subject'. Notes she made on the consultor's comments show her realising that her Society's fortunes are still dogged by Pierce's action in the past: 'Rule presented in 1848 *Not known to us*'.

By November Grant wanted to know how much progress she had made and for the next four years their letters are littered with proposals about vows, dismissal, elections and so on. She said that she counted on the 'rest and quiet at Mayfield' to be able to make progress, but her letters also leave the impression that she was stalling for time; and indeed she was. Cornelia was a realist, and when the long-term good required it, also a strategist. The Rule so far had been a rule in evolution, developing under her hand in response to the exigencies of real life. But in 1864 she was suddenly told by the bishop to bring it into line with comments from Rome made ten years before, and by a consultor who had confused her 1854 text with Pierce's counterfeit of 1848; and Grant himself required her now to include juridical material that was unfamiliar to the sisters. She must have realised that to do this would be to stir up internal controversy which the Society was not yet strong enough to resolve. So she worked at her task at a walking pace. Later, from the vantage point of 1876 when crisis had overtaken the Society, she would explain this to Xavier Noble:

> Now my dear, how can you who knew the spirit of the Preston Sr [*sic*] in 1860 quite as well as I knew it myself suppose for one instant that I could have acted on Dr Grant's letter of 1864. What hope could I have entertained when surrounded by young and [in]experienced Sisters, of combating with those who had determined to sustain their own School Mistress spirit and even this at the cost of becoming diocesan. Dr Grant's letter gave me advice from Rome of ten years prior to our wants of 1864, so that even if we could have hoped for union of spirit with Preston, we should have been at a great disadvantage in what was advised. Time and patience was needed for patient action . . . What good did my delay of five years do? No other than this, that we have numbers of religious five years older, and more able to combat against the Preston spirit. Then again you may say, why did I not communicate the contents of this letter to all – simply because I should have created a ferment in the minds of all without having the power to act . . .

In December 1868 Grant began pressing her urgently. A woman whose daughter wanted to join the Society was reluctant to agree, as others had been, because of the lack of approbation. 'Do not lose time', he wrote. Finally in April 1869, realising how ill Grant was and that she needed help, she decided to go to Rome herself. In early May she and two sisters set out armed with testimonial letters from all the bishops in whose dioceses there were communities. 'I go with a heavy heart', she told him, 'at the thought of your Lordship's illness.'

ROME AGAIN, 1869

After 'tossing about between Marseilles & Civitavecchia' for four days, Cornelia and her companions arrived in Rome on the eve of Pentecost and settled themselves in a small apartment in the Via San Niccolo di Tolentino – for a longer stay than they had dreamed of, two full months. It was hot and they were going to find themselves 'not able to sleep at night from the irritation of the heat spots over hands & faces – like small pox!' At once they presented their credentials at the Propaganda and were soon afloat on a sea of work. Fr Anselmo Knapen OFM, their appointed consultor, lived at the Franciscan monastery on Ara Coeli and under his guidance they 'worked very hard in doing and undoing' parts of the Rule, rewriting both their manuscripts, English and Italian. Their time was passed very quietly, she tells Grant:

> . . . our days have been spent in the churches, then writing and overlooking various rulebooks, consultations with the Franciscan Father and then a drive out (!) in the Roman cabs to all the magnificent monuments of the Roman Faith . . . What a blessed spot is Rome! . . . We are seeing again everything that is to be seen . . . though the crypts are rather cold for those inclined to stiff knees and Rheumatism.

To be in Rome was a deep joy to Cornelia. Few letters have survived from her time there on this occasion, but her response to all she rediscovered is – she used the word herself – rapturous, whether to its sheer beauty or to its religious significance. A letter to the sisters tells of the first:

> Yesterday we had a delicious drive out on the Via Appia in the midst of the beautiful old tombs & overlooking the ancient acqueducts to the mountains, with Frascati & Albano in view just as you pass the magnificent tomb of Cecelia Metellus . . . all this was our view going out . . . with the sun striking on the objects giving them the hue of reddish gold; then on turning round to come back, we had the very beauty of paradise in the setting sun behind Rome and its exquisite mountains in face of us all the way . . . Never shall I forget the rapturous beauty of the scene . . .

The letter to Grant speaks movingly of her audience with the pope. It was a precious occasion. He sat down with the three of them, 'asking all sorts of questions' while she in secret was 'comparing him with God the Father':

> I could dwell for ever on the remembrance of it! and His Holiness before leaving turned to me and said with his benign smile, 'Propaganda is looking over your rule and doing for you', and when he again blessed all and walked away it was like a vision of a little bit of heaven gradually disappearing.

Such an experience reinforced her belief in Christ's presence and authority in the church and would fortify her during the storm soon to break within the Society.

The whole purpose of Mother Connelly's visit to Rome was to obtain approbation of the Rule. It had seemed to her when appealing to Grant to let her go that it was a question of 'ruin or approval', and being a realist and a woman of faith, she therefore came prepared to do whatever had to be done. What she brought with her, Knapen praised. The good spirit of its rules would 'maintain religious discipline, sanctify the sisters and procure the glory of God'. But the weakness of the Constitutions was in the area of temporalities and government, which Rome expected to be spelt out with great exactness.

Part of the consultor's work was to review all commentaries on the Rule already in the Propaganda's files, including the statements, for example Wiseman's, that Cornelia was a woman who would consider her power as superior-general unlimited and use it in an arbitrary and irresponsible fashion. Knapen went out of his way to contradict this. He praised her to Barnabò for being so ready to do all that was required and added 'Be it said, for the sake of truth, far from pretending to unlimited authority, the Foundress in treating this point would have wished to diminish so much the authority of the superior general that her government would have become too weak.'

In July he recommended for approval the work they had done and Cornelia, about to leave Rome, told Grant Knapen had said 'the rules are now perfect'. The Propaganda might make minor changes but would, it was expected, approve the Rule *ad experimentum* for five years. Approbation would not be delayed, she thought, by any request for the signatures of the sisters and she returned home with jubilant heart.

The first stop on their overland journey was, by chance, 'a night in Lucca'. Pierce had been officially recognised only the year before as rector of the American Episcopal Church not far away in Florence. It was Ady's and Frank's home too. There was no question of visiting but Pierce still mattered to her. She had recently written warningly to a priest inquirer who wished to refute some point in one of Connelly's pamphlets: 'While he lives there is always a *hope* of his conversion.' She could not have travelled through central Italy without remembering him.

They continued through 'enchanting scenery in crossing Mont Cenis' (the bishop should travel that way if he came to the Council in 1870, it would refresh his spirits); 'a day & a night in Paris'; and they were home at St Leonards by 10.30 in the evening on 10 July. The community sang a late night Te Deum.

WAITING AT HYÈRES

Now came suspense. Until the printed Italian text arrived with Barnabò's directions there was little she could do. She shared the English manuscript at once with one of the superiors from Preston who was just then at St Leonards and with another at Preston when she visited in October.

The bishop's health was deteriorating. In July he could not come, as he always had, for Prize Day. Her own health too, long precarious, had been failing for several years. In spring 1867 she had been bed-ridden for two weeks with bronchitis. Later that year she had to return early from America on account of a dangerous chest condition. On and off through 1868 there are light-hearted references to rheumatic gout, to twinges and cramp and to crippling weather, and for three weeks she was ill. As winter approached the need to take care asserted itself. In November 1869, on doctor's orders and with a small group of sisters and children, she set off for the south of France where the climate might do her good. It was at Hyères that the Constitutions would finally reach her from Rome.

Hyères was a health resort with a cosmopolitan flavour in Catholic France. Visitors from England and Ireland, even from Germany and Russia, came for its mild winters. Among the regulars were Serjeant Bellasis and his lawyer friend Hope-Scott, both of whom had bought property there. So had Manning. The infant colony of English Catholics might some day require a school. The Serjeant, who admired Mother Connelly and the education she had given his daughters, kept her informed and when the little group, a would-be school, set out from England, Mary Francis Bellasis was one of the sisters. The enthusiasm and effort which Cornelia summoned for the making of this expedition into a successful venture, has to be wondered at against the background of her health. For nearly the whole of the six months in Hyères she had to be trundled round in a bath chair. For three weeks she was in bed with influenza and erysipelas. Not till five months had gone by does the diary record, with underlining, that she was able to walk to church. The over-exertion of years was taking its toll.

How deeply she had felt at leaving Grant appears in her last two (extant) letters written from England:

> My dear Lord, I so, from the depths of my heart, beg your pardon for all my faults, and thoughtlessness, and for any trouble & anxiety I have ever given you! O that I had never, never given your dear Lordship anything but consolation. You have ever been my most excellent friend and Father and Benefactor. May God himself give you a rich reward, for all your deeds . . .

The Vatican Council which Grant would attend was due to open on 8 December. Cornelia's thoughts too had turned to Rome:

> Do you think my Lord that I might go to Rome after Easter or would there be still so great a crowd that it would be useless to try? The thought

of the Holy Father is like a vision of Heaven to me, and the hope of calling forth the remembrance of the Rule would be worth any sacrifice.

Once in Hyères she characteristically directed all her energies to the good of the present moment. Two nieces, Bella and Nelie, were with her. Lessons began at once with French as the central effort for all. On 21 December, her feast, the first mass was celebrated in the little oratory and to her joy the Blessed Sacrament was allowed to remain. In spite of bath chair and illness, and in spite of anxiety as she waited for the Constitutions, Cornelia had great peace of soul. The Epiphany letter she sent out in January 1870 was full of unction. She had 'discovered' the liturgy of the church in the Divine Office, 'the most delicious task I have enjoyed since wearing the religious habit', she told Grant. She was also using the *Exercises of St Gertrude*, which later in the month she called 'delightfully generous and heart-dilating'. Business and its attendant cares could not dampen her *joie de vivre*. No feast or natural beauty was left uncelebrated: picnics by the Mediterranean, drawing expeditions, visits to local shrines, and nearly always she was with them in her chair. They made friends in the neighbourhood. Other children came for classes. The archpriest of Hyères hoped they would stay. One priest instructed them in the Divine Office. Another became a devoted friend because he so liked the family spirit.

Of correspondence between Hyères and Rome where Grant was attending the council little has survived. Cornelia waited with increasing anxiety, counting on the bishop's influence 'not to forget us or let us be forgotten'. Cardinal Barnabò, Grant replied, had to attend all the council meetings and do his own work at the Propaganda, but was 'willing to do all in his power' for her. She was not to worry.

CRISIS, 1870

The final text reached her at Hyères on 11 February, seven months after she had left Rome. Copies in English had to be printed and circulated for signing. Barnabò's letter explained that his request for signatures was in no way a sign of doubt that the sisters were well disposed but simply part of the customary procedure when approbation was asked for. She was herself to collect and send the signed copies when they were ready. Promptly she obeyed. A printing at Hyères was arranged and she wrote rejoicing to the bishop:

Thanks a thousand times for all your Lordship's thought and care for us. I can quite see the very spot in Group V in the Aula. How shall we sufficiently thank God that you are there. Goodnight my Lord. May Holy Angels guard you and heavenly inspirations be ever near your Lordship.

The Constitutions were sent at once to superiors of the houses for the sisters to sign. To Preston she said:

> I hope there may be no excitement over the Rules, and that all may be thankful if everything be approved in Rome ... and if the Church demands certain changes, I do not see why any of us should demur. I simply say *Fiat, Fiat.* I quite doubted that they would be willing to take over again all the Summary & the common rules, but they have! Every office and every rule just as we left it and it is a splendid Rule, splendid I say, simply splendid.

Grant had impressed on her the need for speed. 'Take your time but do not dally' her next letter says, and the following one: '*Every day* that you keep the Rules is a loss to us . . . Dr Grant may leave Rome before long . . . and there will be nobody . . . to care for us . . . if we dally over anything, therefore do not lose an hour.' News that there is confusion about the vows does not at first disturb her. To a superior in Preston, who Cornelia remarks is in 'a most wonderful puzzle' on the subject, she sends a brief explanation, but adds that of course there must be 'certainty of conscience'. Since she herself still has to wait to hear from Barnabò again and from America, she says there is 'plenty of time' and 'perhaps we may meet'. It is the end of March.

A month later they arrive home, on 7 May. She has heard 'good accounts' of Grant's health and begs him to see Barnabò about a clause inserted in the Constitutions which she does not understand. On 12 May he answers. He has looked up the clause himself and explains it for her. Then on the same day he writes again:

> I am again kept to my room & cannot see Cardinal Barnabò for some time, but you may be quite sure your letter will not be overlooked & will be duly answered whenever he has time to attend to it, with all his other duties. When I can go to Propaganda I will enquire about it.

But Grant was already a very ill man. Going to the Propaganda was soon out of the question. Moreover neither he nor Cornelia was aware of a recent development. Through an intermediary Barnabò had received a confidential request, presented on behalf of unnamed sisters in Preston. It asked that the Constitutions as they stood should not be approved, and begged the right to communicate with Rome without going through Mother Connelly to whom they feared to speak freely.

No correspondence between Cornelia and Bishop Grant later than 12 May has survived. At the end of the month he died in Rome at the English

College, and Cornelia, mourning at St Leonards, wrote in her Commonplace Book: 'He was our friend & Father nineteen years & during that time clothed & professed all our dear sisters . . . Let us pray for him and *to* him . . .'

The sense of urgency which Grant had conveyed to Cornelia seems now to have distorted her judgment. The news of his death had come unexpectedly on 1 June, sweeping away someone she loved and had turned to. It deprived the Society of influence needed in Rome and at home she had no guarantee that a new bishop would support a request for approbation without yet further revision. Her own health and energies, she knew, were now failing. And in the middle of June she wrote over-urgently to the Preston superiors. Her letter has not survived but an offending part was quoted in a protest from Preston to Rome:

> Will you therefore have the rules signed without delay, that all may be forwarded to Rome immediately . . . The Vows stand just as they were made, and under the same conditions as received, until the last Vows. Therefore let there be no further discussion . . . If anyone should turn up whose opinionatedness or obstinacy (or *soi-disant* conscience) will not allow them to sign, leave them to themselves, and to do as they please, sign or not. They are perfectly free, and it will be an excellent test, of how much they prefer their own will and opinions to union with the Society.

Bishop Grant had desired to see the Society firmly established in the church before he died. Within less than a month of his death the approbation process was stopped in its tracks by the response of a small group in Preston to this letter, and it did not move forward again till several years after Mother Connelly too had died. Meanwhile she had to face potential schism, and increasingly for herself apparent failure and rejection.

14

'The Appearance of Irresponsible Control'

Cornelia was accused by Emily Bowles of 'irresponsible despotism'; by Wiseman of being 'ungovernable'; by Sing of 'directing instead of being directed'; by Foy of 'disdaining the salute of the priest'; by Duke of needing to 'practise humility'; by Pierce of being 'high-stomached'.

The impression of her which these people conveyed so effectively to ecclesiastical authorities and to the general public was false, to be attributed chiefly to their ill will. But not entirely. Her natural power of personality invited admiration and sometimes over-identification. It seems that her strength and consistency of character became a reproach to some whom she initially drew into her orbit and whose inconsistency she brought to light. Relationships with her, based on attraction, could turn bitter. Admiration turned to antagonism, identification to rejection. She was too a woman of driving energy. In the past she had known betrayal and terrible loss which often enough creates profound anger and the need to control the present.

In May 1865 when he was about to leave his chaplaincy at St Leonards, Searle wrote to Cornelia:

> As I believe your Society has been raised up for a great work . . . I shall ever be glad to assist in promoting its welfare, & shall pray that the settlement of its Rule by Pontifical authority may very speedily secure its permanence and rescue it from even the appearance of irresponsible control.

This he elaborated in another letter to Grant. The absence of Rome's approbation, he said

> . . . naturally results in an undue amount of power being vested in the Superior & renders the exercise of such power too arbitrary.
>
> Now I have the highest opinion of Reverend Mother, but we all have our natural defects & in a Religious Order subjects should be as much

as possible protected from such: but the absence of the Approbation of Rome deprives them to a great measure of such protection.

The young married woman and new convert who set out from New Orleans to cross the ocean and stay in an unknown world with her growing family was already a competent, singleminded and courageous person. Over the years those qualities had developed in her, strengthened by responsibility and hard circumstance. The love of God moved her to action but it had to be routed through her own imperfect but compelling personality. Given her giftedness and energy it is almost inevitable that accumulated experience made her sometimes too sure and too arbitrary. Her letter to the Preston superiors was to have bitter consequences.

APPROBATION AND GOVERNMENT

Before following her down that path it will be helpful to draw together some of the problems about her Constitutions which bear on this moment of revolt in the Society and which throw light on the difficulties of her position. To obtain approbation was a primary responsibility and probably the greatest burden of her religious life.

Cornelia, arriving in England in 1846, knew relatively little of what constitutions had to encompass if they were to be formally approved. Had Pierce remained faithful to their original proposition, he, a priest known in Rome, could have been the go-between to smooth her way. The 'sketch' she brought with her was *ad experimentum* and originated in Rome, as did the idea of the Society. Had it done so in England for a particular diocese, the responsibility would have been fully the bishop's. As it was, she herself, with what help she could get, had to produce a document belonging to a highly specialised genre of which she was ignorant. From the beginning she knew, for example, that the authority of the bishop had to be stated but not that his powers had to be detailed. Everything that touched the religious life had to be carefully defined according to Rome's long-accumulated norms, some of which did not allow for what she wanted. In community, for instance, her perception of the role of the superior, Grant warned, was 'too human a method of government and regime'. As to the freedom she assumed for her active uncloistered Society, existing canon law did not permit it. What was vital to Cornelia the beginner was not a rule's juridical and governmental elements, but the spiritual and apostolic, that is, what would aid the sisters in their relationship with God and each other, and in the field of ministry. Gradually through hard work and painful vicissitude she learned her lesson. Two versions, 1854 and 1864, had gone to Rome for consideration when in 1869 she took the third. In each the core, known as Part One, was the same. She thought the third an almost finished version and was 'thunderstruck' to find that what she had expected to take only a week to settle would need months, because there was, Fr Knapen said, so much to add and alter.

To turn to a second point, in 1850 Wiseman approved the first evolution of Cornelia's initial sketch. What he approved was in two parts, both drawn extensively from the Jesuit Constitutions. The second was largely on government and used only by the superiors. To the sisters in general 'our Rule' meant Part One alone, to which in 1853 when first about to ask Rome for approbation Cornelia added an introduction on the spirit and mission of the Society. To this, together with the Jesuit Summarium, the sisters were devoted and by 1861 each had her own copy. It was no power-driven idiosyncrasy of Mother Connelly's that Part Two remained unknown to the majority, but customary at that date,[1] and for two decades Holy Child sisters were apparently as content as others of the period with this state of affairs. The practice, as will be seen, was put to each sister before she committed herself to the Society at profession. It was related to freedom for ministry, maintaining union in the Society, and the spirit of obedience. Ignatius's Letter on Obedience was familiar to the sisters and was included in the 1861 printing of the treasured Part One.

When Cornelia went to Rome in 1869 she assumed that since the *superiors* were already acquainted with the English text of what she had with her, approbation would be given by Rome with no further delay. In spite of Grant's warnings to her that all the sisters would have to sign first, she clung hopefully to what had been the practice in the Society. She wrote from Hyères to Grant:

> Regarding the Approbation of the Rule.
> The Italian is a translation of the English which has been read to leading members of our body & two copies left with them. You know my Lord that the Sisters have agreed to leave these matters to the Superiors *before making their Vows.*
> . . . We have *all* now left the decision to the Sacred Congregation and I can easily have a document signed to this effect though I now vouch for all and am quite ready to take the responsibility of answering for all.
> For the sake of others I trust there need not be unnecessary delay, for we have suffered & still suffer from much jealousy and many calumnies. God be praised for ever.

The willingness to assume such a responsibility was consistent with what had stood in the Constitutions ever since Wiseman had approved them, adopted from the Jesuits. The superior-general 'was to take charge of the whole . . . undertake the care of the Society . . . make it her duty to see that the whole Body of the Society be properly governed'. An increasingly important role in that ultramontane century was being assigned by Rome to the superiors of the new congregations. Much more emphasis was placed 'on authority and obedience than on collegial responsibility'.[2] Contrary to Emily Bowles' statement to Goss, however, and contrary to the claims of Lucy Woolley and Alphonsa Kay on whom Emily's mantle fell, this irresponsible despot did consult others, but it was with superiors and her council (and with the bishop and sometimes priests), not with 'the whole Body'.

That is clear in her letter of 16 March to the Preston superiors. They are to read the text of the revised Constitutions to the sisters and before doing so consult a priest on any difficult point by way of preparation for the reading session. This presumes that the superiors are expected to be able to give answers if the sisters ask questions but, she says, they are not to *discuss* with the sisters. The Preston letter said (emphases added): 'The only discussion is that which is necessary for *our own* light, and this you will be helped to by Fr Cobb and *not* by the sisters.' Was Cornelia here anticipating difficulty with these particular superiors? Very possibly. But such a directive could not have been given without acknowledged principle and practice behind it. In an emergency, and anxious, she is pushing too hard.

The letter is worth looking at again from her point of view. She is writing *to superiors*, and therefore frankly and confidentially. She is assuming that their understanding of government is what has been done in the Society for years, taking for granted that they will point out that Part One has not been lost; and that they too will expect the sisters to give their signatures in a spirit of obedience and for the sake of union. That this may be unthinkable now does not make it so then. Except in Preston the English communities apparently did it even though the revision was nowhere popular, and there is no certainty that the majority did it merely out of feeble submissiveness. Their dispositions could have been hers. Her obedience to Barnabò's request that she get the signatures of all had been costly. Though confident that there would be no difficulty (mistakenly as it turned out), it had meant putting aside her own conviction that for the Society in its present critical circumstances it was unnecessary and disadvantageous. She had not herself clung obstinately to her own opinion when her rightful superior required what was different. She had trusted in God and obeyed, and now expected the same trusting, generous obedience from the sisters, not to 'prefer their own will and opinions to union with the Society'.

If we leave Cornelia's idea of government at that we shall have considered only part of the picture. She had learned something else from the Jesuits, that the bulwark of the Constitutions was a personal experience of God encountered in the *Spiritual Exercises*. Cornelia gave conferences on them, the sisters regularly followed them in the annual retreat, and variously used them during the year as a basis for prayer. What Cornelia described as 'being yourself but making that self what God wanted', the *Exercises* furthered, that is, the gradual choosing to be more governed by God than by self-will, which could begin to happen because they focused attention on Christ. It was not just because Cornelia was a nineteenth-century woman that she wrote in the Rule, 'our Divine Master, our Model, our Spouse'. She meant that a living, intimate knowledge of Christ was to be sought in the gospel, in their hearts and in the ordinary round of their daily lives and those they met. That intimacy, the *Exercises* were designed to promote. In contemplating Christ's ministry of compassion, hearts would be enlightened, wills fortified, the meaning of being 'linked' in the 'sweet bonds' of their vows to God would grow on them, and with that the desire to be more and more faithful to the way of life set down for all in the Rule. All were thus disposed, while becoming more truly themselves, to become also more 'one in mind and heart'.

In adopting the *Exercises* Mother Connelly was not intending to create a community of female Jesuits. But her Society needed elasticity, and they would be an instrument to sustain union and at the same time call individuals to personal apostolic growth. The linchpin was the obediential relationship with God concretised in the relationship between sisters and superiors. The Rule staked out the road, the *Exercises* could move individuals to walk it. Whoever was superior was a sister missioned pro tem to minister to her sisters on this journey and in the 1869 Constitutions Cornelia described the superior's role. She was to 'make herself accessible to the Sisters and receive with great kindness any thing they may have upon their hearts to communicate'; she was to instruct, comfort and compassionate, 'doing to all as she would be done by'; above all she was to help them 'to repose generously in Obedience and confidence in God, who never forsakes those who abandon themselves to Him'. This relationship which she wanted was the inner face of government without which the rest was a dead letter. The quality of the relationship mattered and obedience had to be, *for both*, a matter of attention to, and of loving, God.

One more point must be made before continuing with events. The real source of the trouble over Cornelia's Rule was the fact that it had not been approved by Rome and so carried no ultimate authority. By 1869 this was an acute embarrassment. The lack of approbation was publicly known and gossiped about. The foundress was already an object of scandal through her husband and Emily Bowles. Distrust of foundress became distrust of the Society itself. To hold it together in these circumstances Cornelia had only her personal example and influence. She inspired her sisters to live by the

Rule *as if* it was approved, herself continuing as superior-general on the grounds that Wiseman had officially appointed her. But without Constitutions approved by Rome, the office in the eyes of some had no legitimacy. Grant, bishop of only a single diocese, had refused to authorise a general chapter of elections. If over twenty-four years the habit of command grew upon her one cannot be surprised.

The absence of constitutional power served one good purpose however: it accentuated the real source of Cornelia's authority. This lay in her evident and humble dependence on, and love for, God: 'O God of Gods and light of light and joy of joys, fill my poor heart that I too may love thee with an everlasting love, that we may all be one in Thee and live and breathe for Thee alone.'

A sister remembered: 'Once I heard her read aloud the words, "Christ hath loved us with an everlasting love". Her voice and tone made such an impression on me that for weeks afterwards those words were constantly in my mind and heart and I have never forgotten them.' Buckle commented on her serenity in the midst of deep affliction. Always she conducted herself 'with an active quiet and a quiet activity that could only proceed from a soul deeply united with God.'

Such abiding faith undergirding all she saw and thought and did made her to the majority an inspiration and they did not query her right to govern. She exemplified for them the cherished Part One which they too were striving to live and to which they showed their loyalty when they gave their signatures. But the lack of approbation was a great handle for the hostile few. When the Constitutions arrived in 1870 with certain generally unwelcome changes which Cornelia had had to accept in Rome in order to obtain what was so essential, they served as a catalyst for the smouldering discontent of the few and revealed how vulnerable the Society had become.

CABAL, 1870–2

To return to events. The 1869 revision when it arrived looked unfamiliar to the sisters, a fact in its disfavour. Government was suddenly prominent. And although Mother Connelly's introduction still stood at the beginning the rest of Part One was scattered or mostly put at the end. One change in particular caused the trouble.

The church at that date had no code of law adapted to the needs of women's non-monastic religious life, and until 1859 Holy Child sisters, according to the existing canons, still made perpetual vows at the end of the noviceship. In that year Grant, probably because he doubted the Society's survival and because most of its candidates did not bring the usual monastic dower, told Cornelia to remove 'perpetual' from the vow formula for the time being. She was 'not to disturb the sisters' by telling them that canonically this reduced the validity of their vows to a single year. For longer than she anticipated they had to make profession using only the words left to them, 'I promise to live and die in the Society', a phrase which expressed intention but had no canonical force.

Ten years later, in 1869, the unfamiliar revision laid down a period of temporary vows to precede perpetual profession. This, after long experience, Cornelia desired for the Society's stability. But to the sisters it was new. Some now discovered that for years their vows according to church law had not been perpetual; others found the revision did not restore the status quo of 1846–58; and those who viewed Cornelia as a despot took advantage of the confusion. It seems that what they feared – and roused the fear in others – was that the superior-general's power to dismiss was now prolonged beyond the novitiate. In vain would she explain that only in very grave cases could a sister be sent away.

Bellasis was certain that had Mother Connelly waited to take the revision personally to communities and answered questions herself, all would have been well. She 'made a very great mistake in transacting this important business through different Local Superiors', some of whom 'showed little prudence and less tact' in dealing with it, with the result that 'though all signed, not all were united'. But at Hyères urgency had Cornelia in its grip. She and Grant were both ill. Mortality impinged. She would not have forgotten Grant's words to her just before she went to Rome: 'do not lose time as the Institute will break into separate houses if no machinery is approved for the election of a superior general'.

The St Leonards community welcomed her back with great joy (four days of it, the diary says) and one cannot suppose that nothing was said about the changes. But there is no record. She visited also at Mayfield and Mark Cross, and early in June the London houses. All these communities gave their signatures at some time and if there was demur, records have not survived. Late in June she went north. The Blackpool community was taken up with the move to their new, purpose-built convent at Layton Hill. Again there is no record. Then she went to Preston.

Two of the three superiors at Preston were entrenched and locally influential and we have seen that Mother Connelly had known since at least 1860 what she called 'their own Schoolmistress spirit'. The superior at Blackpool too thought the Preston houses were 'too much for work and too little for prayer' and had 'not shown a spirit of charity for years'.

Lucy Woolley, in general charge of the three communities and resident at St Wilfrid's, had been there since 1853 at the age of twenty-four. She had built up a successful apostolate in the Poor Schools and had a network of support and influence in the parishes and with the Jesuits who ran them. In 1858 she had been joined by Alphonsa Kay, a native of Preston, to take over the community at St Ignatius. Both had known Emily Bowles well as beginners at Derby and at St Leonards and all three were in close touch during the Rupert House troubles. Possibly it was Lucy and Alphonsa whom Emily, about to leave, had in mind when she told Bishop Goss that it was 'the experience of the most thinking members of our Society' that 'we have no Constitutions except Mrs Connelly's sole will'. His view of the Society derived from Emily's account, and Lucy and Alphonsa had maintained the relationship with him. It was these two who, basing themselves on the issue of the vows, took the first step in negotiations with the Propaganda against approbation. They did not wait for Cornelia to get back to England although she had said it might be possible to meet.

When she arrived in Preston in June they had received her offending letter from St Leonards about ten days before. In it she had said: 'the Vows stand just as they were made, and under the same conditions as received, until the last Vows.' 'Everyone', according to Alphonsa, 'regarded this answer as equivocal'. With advice from a sympathetic local Jesuit it was decided, Alphonsa continued, 'to sign the rules without remark, and to write at the same time a protest to Cardinal Barnabò, stating that they signed under coercion, and begging that no further steps might be taken until an Apostolical Visitor should inquire into the state of the Congregation.' This some had done. Again they had not waited for the chance to discuss it with Mother Connelly before acting. A formal protest, this time signed, had gone to Rome five days before she was due. Once she was among them no one told her what had been done and, as agreed, the signing was not spoken of. She, supposing them satisfied with her reassurance about the vows, and probably relieved that there need be no argument with those particular superiors, did not raise it either. Having spent a day in each of the three convents, visiting its schools and various Catholic centres – Fernyhalgh, Lea, Cottam Mill – she returned south unaware of the stratagem and believing all was well. It must have been to this occasion she later referred when she said to Buckle they made 'no single objection to *me* but acted secretly'. Alphonsa used Cornelia's silence on the occasion to illustrate for Barnabò her 'want of probity and straightforwardness'. The silence on both sides betrays a long-standing strained relationship.

Mother Connelly left Preston on 1 July. By September she had realised that the confusion about the vows was more general than at Preston only. She wrote to all superiors to help them understand what 'had occupied my mind for many years', and hoping to receive their signatures soon. She wanted to send them all to Rome 'in a few weeks'. She was still unaware of the Preston protest sent to Barnabò and of the decision to send to her acceptances that were false.

Nor was she aware of the hive of industrious letter-writing the Preston convents had become since she left. What Alphonsa next wrote was with Lucy's knowledge and both were in close contact with Goss. At his request she sent to Rome what she called 'the substance' of all she had shared with him. She included her personal criticism of the revised Constitutions and a collection of extracts from Cornelia's recent letters, on which, blind to the evident goodwill in them, she comments only adversely. 'Mrs Connelly' is one who would like to enlarge her own powers rather than acknowledge what is proper to the bishop; and considering 'the arbitrary and unconstitutional' manner in which she uses her 'unlimited' authority, the sisters are afraid to oppose her. Ignorant of Cornelia's efforts to induce Grant to call a chapter of elections, she complains that she has governed since 1846 without ever having been constitutionally elected. Nor does Mrs Connelly consult as much as she should. Alphonsa herself and Lucy as superiors should have been consulted in 1853 about the Rule revision but were not and they have together deduced, she says, that even in those days Mrs Connelly must have been making the changes herself. But surviving records reveal that the council then working with Cornelia on the Rule for Rome had consisted of the three superiors, Emily, Lucy and Alphonsa.

The 'cabal' as Cornelia called it when she knew what was going on, would never have gained the momentum it did had there been no support from their bishop. Goss, who earlier had lent a ready ear to Emily, now became their ally. On 17 September 1870 he wrote to Barnabò outlining their objections to the revision. A few days later Rome fell to Victor Emmanuel's troops, Pio Nono became the prisoner of the Vatican, and the council during which Grant had died had to close. Delays over business with the Propaganda owing to Barnabò's participation in the council were now prolonged. Prompt attention was the remotest of hopes.

In May 1871 Goss moved again. In the course of routine duty he made an official visitation of the three communities and soon afterwards asked his intermediary with the Vatican, Mgr Capel, brother to one of the sisters, to remind Barnabò of his former representation. He passed to Capel what he had imbibed from Alphonsa: 'Mrs Connelly seems to have installed herself permanent superior . . . and to instil a sort of distrust of jurisdiction outside the Congregation.'

Lucy too wrote to Capel, and on 27 May, almost a year after the first protest to Rome, a second went, signed by five sisters. Lucy's signature heads the list, then Alphonsa, then Capel's sister, then Alphonsa's sister and finally a young sister professed only four years who belonged to Alphonsa's community. Capel presented it to Barnabò in June 1871 and on 9 June Goss followed it up with a letter repeating points provided by Lucy, most of which if believed would undermine all confidence in Mother Connelly's government. For example: that the only councillors she had ever had were chosen for 'their personal devotion' to herself and for the 'facility with which they could adapt their ideas to hers'; that her policy seemed to be 'to keep the houses of her body more or less disunited so as to keep more power in her own hands'.

A few days later Goss wrote to Cornelia about the removal of a sister and concluded reassuringly that he was 'well satisfied' with all he had seen during his visitation. The sisters were working 'zealously and harmoniously'. Still unaware of the cabal's activities, she thanked him for his 'consoling words'.

Meanwhile in March 1871 Bishop Grant's successor had been appointed: James Danell. Late in July he went to St Leonards on a first visit as bishop to preside at Prize Day. According to the convent diary it 'went off beautifully'. Cornelia was able to arrange for him to come for a profession on 8 September and on the 2nd wrote to remind him. At the same time she asked if he would be willing to take the signed Constitutions to Rome for her that winter. Preston had sent their signatures and she was still unaware of the continuing ferment. It had been Grant's wish, she told his successor, 'that there should be no delay'. She wrote lightheartedly. And when Danell arrived for the profession she knew the truth.

The efforts of the cabal to win further adherents had – perhaps only recently – spread to Blackpool. Agatha Gray, aged twenty-four, only a year professed and the youngest there, had been won over, but shame overcame her and she wrote to Mother Connelly. She had not understood what the Constitutions were saying about the vows and was therefore reluctant to sign. But neither had she wanted to join those who were deceiving Cornelia by signing the Rule and at the same time protesting to Rome. In the end Alphonsa had talked her round and also extracted from her evidence of coercion by Cornelia: 'it finished by Mother Alphonsa saying that if I should ever be asked why I had signed the Rules that I had to say "because I thought my Superior [Mother Connelly] would be displeased" '. Contritely she ended: 'Really dearest, I feel I shall never get this out of my mind . . . I am ashamed of myself.' By way of reparation she sent Cornelia the original note to 'Mth Alphonsa' [which she must have retrieved] in which she disowned what her signature had effected, her approval of the Rule. It said: 'I don't approve of the rules but I put my signature because I thought my superior would be displeased but I have told Mother Alphonsa my sentiments.' On the outside for Cornelia she wrote, 'Confession'.

Through Agatha Gray Cornelia learned the full story of the deception practised on her. Certainly before she next wrote to Danell on 15 September she had been fully enlightened. What she felt she later shared with Buckle:

> The only complaint that I make is that they had the Rules . . . eighteen months before they signed them and never made a single objection to *me*, but acted secretly against them and *disapproved avowedly* while they signed them to be sent to Propaganda. It is the duplicity with which the one in authority [Lucy Woolley] acted, withholding the truth from me. I have never interfered or objected to their action with Propaganda. It is the want of truth I complain of and the betrayal of all trust in them.

BISHOP DANELL, 1872–3

Mayfield, the ruined synod hall now restored to its original beauty and used as the convent chapel, had become for Cornelia the place of quiet which she often sought. It was the home of the first-year novices – eleven of them in 1871 – a few orphans and a professed community of four. The first group of little schoolchildren would come in 1872 to be boarders until they were old enough to move on to St Leonards. Her summers since 1864 and many briefer visits had been spent here and August 1871 had seen the customary long stay. Now in September she returned. A future faced her very different from what she had anticipated a few days earlier. Then, the signatures were soon to go to Rome, approbation would be given, vows would be approved, government settled, superiors elected. The heavy burden of having to govern without constitutional backing, or perhaps at all, would fall from her and the survival of the Society would be ensured. Now all this had receded. On the Feast of the Exaltation of the Cross she made notes for her new bishop. She began with two important statements. First, that unless the Constitutions are approved 'we may expect nothing but ruin (or division, the next step to ruin)'. Second, that regardless of future legislation there was an 'immediate necessity' for Rome to issue a statement upholding the vows already made. Agatha Gray's letter had brought home to her how dangerous was the anxiety on this subject. Then she described for him how the present legislation on the vows had evolved and her own understanding of the most recent 1869 statements. 'All that has been done,' she wrote, 'has been in obedience & good faith, and we sincerely wish to submit matters to some positive decision through your Lordship.' She hoped he would soon visit again for his canonical visitation '& make things clear to' himself.

Danell, a bishop of only seven months standing, began an attempt to make all things clear to himself by consulting Goss. His own dealings with Mother Connelly and the Society had been slight and now his brother

303

bishop provided a portrait based on the complaints of the Preston malcontents. Danell was warned that Cornelia did not consult; that she was anxious to keep to the minimum 'episcopal interference and supervision'; that she had never held a general chapter; that she had empowered herself to dismiss sisters from the Society; that she did not invest dowers but used them to finance building projects. This was in October. Cornelia meanwhile was worrying, 'Have you forgotten us my Lord and all our anxieties?' She was even thinking of going to Rome again herself. 'We depend totally on your Lordship's advice.' It would be inadvisable, he replied, took the matter into his own hands and for two and a half years produced no solution. For all that time she had to try to hold the Society together against increasing incomprehension and, from some sisters, ill will and opposition.

In February 1872 Cornelia confronted Lucy. Afterwards, since parish priest and one community had requested the change, she took the opportunity to make its new superior independent of the authority which Lucy had previously exercised over all three. Protests from the cabal poured in to Goss: Cornelia's action was arbitrary and punitive. Appealed to by Lucy, he issued a Decree of Visitation by which Mother Connelly could move superiors only with his permission. She promised to comply but explained why the superior had had to be moved, rejected his accusation that she had allowed no liberty of action about the Constitutions, stated she had letters to prove it and asked for an interview. Goss was ill but his vicar was told what answer to give. He thought it 'unnecessary' for them to meet.

Gossip in Preston against Cornelia now ran riot. Fr Cobb SJ, much consulted by Lucy and Alphonsa and who in the end would see through the cabal, wrote: 'The start was bad and uncanonical – a married woman who can find no other order . . . in the Church to suit her, but must found her own.' This was to his provincial who, consulted by Danell, had turned to his men in Preston who had then turned to the sisters there. Thus he too, like Goss, had become a medium through which the cabal's grievances reached Cornelia's own bishop.

Danell's visitation took place first at St Leonards, then at Mayfield and Mark Cross, late in April and early May 1872. Day after day he saw all the sisters one by one. He found that there were some in his diocese too, though fewer than in the north, who had not felt completely free to oppose the 1869 revision. Generally they had adopted the view that since the church required the changes for approbation they should be accepted, but on the whole they disliked it. He and his Italian canonist, Philip Bosio OSM, had put together a detailed questionnaire prompted by the Preston complaints and the sisters were not allowed to speak to each other about the interviews, nor might superiors ask them questions.

Before ending the visitation in June he arranged for the house sisters, who according to canon law and the revised Constitutions now had to recreate separately, to rejoin the choir sisters on certain days. This was a compromise effected by Cornelia's own readiness to return to the old custom but he insisted that in the future new house sisters must be told when they first came that there was separation and that for them it would begin at once. Even now all of them were to have their own community room. Inevitably this was the cause of much ill feeling and Danell did not make plain that the decision was his. Mother Connelly was blamed. One called her a stepmother.

One good came of this gruelling visitation: Danell agreed to the long-needed general chapter. With relief Cornelia set the wheels rolling, but at once a disastrous misunderstanding arose between her and the bishop about who should be called to the chapter to do the electing. Cornelia, writing on 15 July and following the plan outlined by Bosio during the visitation, proposed one delegate for every ten sisters plus local superiors present ex officio. No reply came. At Prize Day she asked him personally and he told her to call superiors only. She sent out a notice to that effect, and there came:

> . . . an immediate outpouring of negative reactions from members of the Preston cabal. They enlist Mgr Capel as mouthpiece and themselves write to Bishops Danell and Goss accusing Cornelia of wanting to control the chapter by 'packing' it with her own 'creatures', the local superiors. Some plead for Cornelia's disqualification from office, some for elimination of superiors ex officio, some for postponement of the chapter, and all for fuller representation of the body. Goss writes to Danell to say that Cornelia rules like 'a clever woman of the world'. He adds that the sisters live in fear of her power of dismissal or of being 'sent for to St Leonards and ground into submission not to the rule but to the will of Mrs Connelly'.[3]

Danell then proposed to Cornelia that each Preston house be allowed to send a delegate of its own, but her sense of what was just to the whole body was greater than his:

> I send a copy of my letter of the 15th July which your Lordship must either have mislaid or forgotten when you advised me to send (on the day of the Prizes) for the *Superiors only* of each convent. Will you now kindly read it and give me your answer?
>
> We cannot in justice to the whole Order make particular exceptions at Preston. We are all quite willing to have an Electrice chosen out of every ten sisters by *all the professed* but we cannot call upon the Superior of each little Community of from five to seven or eight sisters to have an election without giving to all the same ratio of privilege.

The chapter had to be put off. Danell went north to consult Goss and told her he would settle the date as soon as he had seen the bishop. But he also saw the Preston sisters and encouraged them to write, which they did, Lucy in particular. She even requested his word that Cornelia should not know they corresponded. Goss died, Danell visited again and from then on letters flowed to Southwark. Cornelia's bishop became their father and confidant and information of every kind travelled south, very largely indeed through Lucy. Once she even sent for his inspection the envelope of a letter from him to her. She did not trust the superior who passed it to her and suspected that it had first 'gone on a journey to St Leonards'.

Meanwhile time had slid by. At every opportunity Mother Connelly had reminded him of his promise to settle the date of the chapter. The end of 1872 was in sight and 'we are still held in suspense as to the time of the Election, the necessity of which having been once suggested, incurs the absolute obligation of being carried out'. Only because there is 'an almost unlimited elasticity & simplicity of spirit' in the community have they survived. It has been 'a singular year', which God alone knows 'how we have sustained without breaking down totally'. In the new year of 1873, three years since she sent the Constitutions from Hyères to the communities, she took up the subject with increasing urgency: 'Is the time to be left indefinitely? And ourselves in uncertainty? It will be a happy day for me my Lord when I can say that I have no other responsibility than that of preparing for death, for death may be very near.' She was sixty-four and serious illness would overtake her for a time that summer.

Incomprehensibly there was still no response and in mid-May Cornelia decided that as a matter of duty she must press the subject on Danell with all possible seriousness. She knew from the experience of criticism in the north of anything she tried to do, and of the ill feeling of some of the house sisters in her own community, that her authority was crumbling, and that if it did the Society would fall to pieces:

> I beg of you my Lord for the love of God to act promptly. We have gone on nearly a year in a state of doubtful authority, ever since I wrote the first Circular Letter for the meeting of the Chapter. This cannot be allowed to go on, and it is an *absolute necessity* to hold the chapter this summer, otherwise ruin or annihilation must ensue.

She explains why:

> However gentleness, kindness & great patience may keep the peace exter-nally as at present, nevertheless religious discipline must gradually be utterly destroyed when gentleness is *forced* into weakness. At present while the Mother House is held responsible for the Branch Houses we are

divested of the smallest Authority over those in the North, yet surely where there is no authority there can be no responsibility, and we cannot hold ourselves responsible for them in any manner, nor do we think our Lord asks this of us unless the elections are duly made & confirmed.

I now enclose a form of the proposed circular for your Lordship's correction and approbation, and I shall act upon it as soon as I have your Lordship's sanction.

The bishop replied with a kind word and a vague promise but on 22 June, having lightly reminded him four times since that serious appeal in mid-May, she had to try again:

Will your Lordship kindly say whether the circular I sent for your approval will do? And if not, will your Lordship frankly explain to me what you wish changed? The schools in America cannot be left except during the holidays & by deferring the time now we shall be forced to wait another year!

This wrung a date out of him: 8 September 1873. On 20 August it was again put off and when she said she did not understand, no explanation was offered.

Bearing her situation as best she might during that year, she unintentionally crossed the will of Bishop O'Reilly, successor to Goss and heir to his prejudices against her. Her lack of authority in Preston was brought home sharply to her when for the sake of the health of two sisters she had agreed to the requests of local superiors that they be moved. This O'Reilly thought was against Goss's Decree of Visitation and she had to write very humbly to him, explaining that the removal had not been on her initiative and that she had not 'the smallest intention' of acting against his wishes.

Towards the end of the year she took steps to try to heal the relationship between herself and Lucy. She was willing to forgive and 'let bygones be bygones', she wrote. 'When matters will not bear discussion the only safe way is to put them in the hands of God.' But Lucy, ignoring the duplicity with which she had tried to undermine Cornelia's government, maintained that she had done nothing that needed forgiveness. On the contrary it was Mother Connelly who was entirely in the wrong. Cornelia persevered with an invitation to her to come to Mayfield for a special gathering 'en famille' to celebrate the completion of the buildings, but this too was rejected. Cornelia knew enough about pain at this time to write in December to a sister who was in trouble:

Do not allow your heart to be wounded, & if it is wounded in spite of your efforts, stitch up the wound with the love of God. A stitch *in time* saves nine! I very often have to remember this & then resign myself to endure more. *Very* often, of late years more than ever, not to allow ones poor heart to drop blood till it withers!

Eventually in May 1874 the good news came. The chapter was to be held in the coming August. The delegates were to be any nineteen professed sisters. Danell specified the number to be elected in each community and defined the chapter's purposes: to elect a superior-general and four assistants and to 'deliberate on the Form of Rule'.

THE FIRST GENERAL CHAPTER, 1874

The general chapter in the life of a religious community is an instrument for the renewal of life. This was the task of those who came together in 1874. They were the duly elected delegates of the whole body with the obligation to propose, deliberate and decide on matters of vital interest to the continuing and fruitful life in the church of their Society. They were, in a sense, a re-founding chapter because it was the first in twenty-eight years of the Society's existence. They had to confirm or not that what Mother Connelly had set out to create in 1846 and had been leading them in ever since was still what they desired. The major questions before them were whether or not she should continue to govern the Society, and, even more important, whether the Constitutions of 1869 which she had brought back from Rome ready for the approbation they needed conveyed well enough what they believed their life in the church was meant to be.

The nineteen came together as equals, none by right of office. Even Cornelia had had to be elected. They came from very different backgrounds – England, America, France – and, seminally, were already an international group. Not all were teachers though most had been at some time. Present were the headmistresses of several Poor Schools and one of a Young Ladies' School; one who cared for orphans, another who directed the novices; several administrators; some who worked in parishes. Several were hostile to Cornelia, certainly Lucy and Alphonsa. Bishop Danell who was to preside throughout hoped, if Buckle is to be believed, that Alphonsa would be elected superior-general.

The elections took place on the opening day, 17 August, and in spite of the hopes of the few, Cornelia, on the first ballot by fifteen votes out of nineteen, became the Society's constitutionally elected superior-general. She was given four councillors and in the ten scrutinies that had to be conducted to decide these, Alphonsa's name appeared once with one vote and Lucy's four times, each time with one vote. The chapter then turned to the business of the Rule.

It was presumed by the majority that the Constitutions to be considered were those of 1869. The Preston few had grounds to hope otherwise and the long delay in calling the chapter was now accounted for. In the words of Bellasis, who was there:

> . . . his Lordship announced that in his great interest for the welfare of the Order he was going to present us with an entirely new Rule, on the compiling of which he and Fr Bosio had been engaged for many months. That it was a Rule which met all the requirements of the Sacred Congregation, and that in our accepting it, he felt sure that all the uncertainty of the past, and our many trials, would be at an end; that it had been a great consolation to him to do this for the Society. He wished us now to go through the Rule, with deliberation, feeling ourselves quite free to propose any amendments.

Nevertheless he concluded by handing out nineteen already handsomely bound volumes.

A religious rule is much more than a code of regulations, which is what now appeared before them. More essentially it is an expression of the group's understanding of its apostolic personality in the church. To impose a rule was not only arrogance (full of good intention as Danell undoubtedly was) but also in the end self-defeating. For two and a half weeks day by day the sisters worked through the text with the bishop and his canonist, and only to the very few was it to their liking. It lacked all that was distinctive of the Society and most valued. Cornelia's introductory paragraphs on the incarnation and the Child Jesus, treasured since 1854, had disappeared; titles such as 'the All-Seeing God' had displaced 'Holy Child'; the rules borrowed from Ignatius were banished to a directory; there were new prohibitions which would engender not trust between superiors and sisters but suspicion; a demand for reverence to priests merited an article by itself; government and the obligations of vows had primary importance and, amazingly, Danell had named the Bishop of Southwark, himself, as 'Bishop Superior of the Institute'. This meant that anything of consequence had to go through his hands and that he rather than the superior-general, who could be by-passed by those who chose to, would also be the recipient of lesser requests, suggestions and complaints. Inevitably it would be divisive. Here was a rule, Bellasis wrote, which 'tended entirely to change the spirit of the Society'.

The sisters spoke up with the straightforwardness and simplicity which Cornelia had always encouraged, and eventually it became apparent to the disappointed bishop, 'by the astonishment shown on hearing some of the paragraphs and by the numerous amendments which in vital points were overruled', that the proposed rule was not acceptable. Even so they were not at liberty to refuse to give it trial. For three years, he said, they were to use it and consider whether to ask for its approbation. And the chapter ended.

Mother Connelly sat listening day after day, 'singularly reticent regarding her own opinions', and when individually the sisters sought her out for advice she only answered, 'Go to the chapel and pray, pray.' Her election as superior-general, and by so large a majority in spite of current troubles, had surely been a moment of affirmation for her, a brief light in gathering dark. One might say that it was like the coming of Luke's angel to the Lord in Gethsemane. But with the bishop's announcement about the Rule the very next morning the nature of the angel's chalice appeared. She listened, Bellasis said, 'pale as death'. Only in private jottings made later was there any other sign of her anguish:

> After being 28 years at work for the poor . . . we are told we have done nothing . . . After building three Churches in the Diocese of Southwark we are told we have done nothing . . . After having suffered the trials, anxieties & responsibilities of the beginning of a religious order for twenty-eight years and these under most unusual sufferings, which Faith and trust in God alone could bear, we are now told by the Bishop that we have no Novitiate and that we are to start afresh on a New Rule!

Cornelia had long ago chosen for herself to be poor with Christ poor in the many meanings of that word. Humiliation had often come her way and especially since the cabal, and was always to be accepted as suffering for and with Christ, 'He whom I love'. At the chapter, as a sister recalled, a public humiliation was inflicted on her by the bishop himself in the presence of those she had served. It was an Ecce Homo moment indicative of the road ahead. She was painfully crippled with gout. At some point she should have knelt to kiss the bishop's ring and did not. Instead she made an inclination. Danell, said the sister, thought this insufficiently submissive and showed his displeasure. Whereupon she made no excuse but at once knelt at his feet and apologised before all: 'the Bishop made no reply, but left her kneeling there, until some of the sisters who knew her suffering state helped her to rise'.[4]

Cornelia believed that even as it was Christ's life-long, love-filled obedience that gave life to the world, so she too and her community, if they were to convey his love to others, must live in a spirit of obeying. She had had three bishops in particular to obey, Wiseman, Grant, Danell, three very different men, bishops in the ultramontane Roman church which expected unquestioning submission from such as herself. And it was nineteenth-century England, a time when newly appointed bishops in newly created dioceses carved and blundered their hard way, having no precedents by which to guide a foundation such as Cornelia's, and being no less immune

than their fellows to the assumption that women were the lesser sex. As the
years passed it was the things she suffered especially at their hands that
taught her more and more deeply how obedience with Christ could be life-
giving. She was on the final stretch of her road into the heart of the paschal
mystery. The flag she followed through the dark valley would also signal
her vindication: '*Whose* standard have we chosen my dear Sisters? . . . learn
the value of a suffering and hidden life . . . it is to this life you are especially
called by the very name you bear.'

15

'Laden with the Fruits of Life'

In the days at Grand Coteau when Pierce had left for Rome and when separation and religious life seemed inevitably ahead, Cornelia's notebook reflected her soul's convictions. One passage, copied in French, reads:

> Yes, you must die and be buried in the ground. You must disappear in abasement of self and in abnegation, and then afterwards you will revive . . . You will appear laden with the fruits of life. By death you will become the salt that preserves, the light that enlightens, the food of souls, and the wheat of Jesus Christ.

Abasement, exaltation, abasement – this was to be the consciously accepted pattern of her life. Twenty years before that general chapter at which her life's work was set aside, she had put into simple words of her own how the sisters could find nourishment for apostolic ministry: 'It is in suffering & especially the suffering of the *heart* that Charity takes root, but it requires always the soil of *humility* to nourish it. Try to make a good heart, full of this most fruitful sod.' Her life's real work was the effort to make that good heart through whatever suffering came her way. Out of accepted humiliation sprang an amazing apostolic energy, the fruit of her rooted charity. This spiritual resilience is never so apparent as during the time of the cabal and its aftermath. The 1870s were for her years of felt failure and rejection. Yet ardour burned in her as steadily as ever and before she died one bright new fire had been lit.

SUSTAINING THE SISTERS

The steady burning appeared variously. Many were the letters she wrote, informally, which sustained individual courage and perseverance and the Society's *cor unum*. An early instance occurred only six weeks after Agatha Gray's confession. It was the twenty-fifth anniversary of the Society's beginning, an occasion particularly full of meaning given that Cornelia thought the Society now in danger of 'ruin or division'. At St Leonards there were

312

the usual celebrations. The day after, she went to stay at Mayfield, and from there wrote to the sisters at St Anne's in London, and probably to others:

> I hope you enjoyed your Feast of St Theresa yesterday as much as we did. We thought of you all & wished you a happy feast . . . The gifts were made the evening before & the Refectory decorated & we had games in the Evening after reading & walking in the day which was most lovely. I am now sitting in the Donkey chair up at the pond to get the sweet air & take advantage of our pocket Book & pencil to send you all dearest love & blessings.

A sister in Blackpool felt she had been forgotten with nobody to care for her. Mother Connelly wrote bracingly and kindly:

> You must learn to judge of yourself and others and of all things as *God judges of them*, and *value them as you will have to do at the moment of death*. We shall very soon have to give our account to God, and this life is only a little dream that will pass away as a shadow! Oh what folly to tease oneself about human affections! We are here today and gone tomorrow. What makes it who is for us or who against us! . . . Try now to make yourself useful and happy as if you knew you were to remain at Blackpool for the remainder of your life. We all pray for you & care for you in the love of God & for his sake, so make yourself happy & get ready for heaven.

A not very experienced superior was worried about all the money she was having to spend on the community. A clear and human answer arrived: as to food, no faddiness, but '*all* that is *necessary* for *health & strength*'; cloth for cloaks should be waterproof; nightgowns warm, flannel and long. But she adds, 'and now I leave you to do as you please. I have given you my advice, but not to enforce any obedience in such a matter'.

To a sister full of affection (called Anastasia and whose feast day fell at Christmas) she answered with her own warmth:

> You know you are never forgotten on Christmas and this year doubly remembered because of your dear & affectionate letter. However we may crush our feelings they are sure to live brightly for the affectionate and grateful hearts that are not shut up! I sent you my heart's affectionate love in the little picture that you choose out of my little Xmas package [for the community], and beg our dear little Lord and St Anastasia to protect and to help you in that life to which '*He calls you*'. Warm your feet well on the fender when they are cold & take a good rest when you

are tired & say, *yes Lord you call me to be tired in Thy service with Thy little ones*. Deo gratias.

Goodbye dear. I am sure you are very happy with dear Mother Catherine & with such dear & nice Sisters all. I could live with them all till death & then for eternity.

Her letters always showed personal concern and always somehow directed each to 'make a good heart'. They were one of the ways in which Mother Connelly's own trust in the good God overflowed. Those who had less she thus bore along. She also assiduously maintained welcome for the sisters to return to St Leonards for holiday times and occasions. Those from London or nearer were frequently invited to 'run down' to refresh themselves in the country, and at Christmas and for the long summer sisters came from the north as well. This was not new but it had a new value. It helped to reforge union when she feared division. Recreation, discussion, walks, common worship, prayer: these things experienced together would strengthen the sense of belonging.

SUSTAINING MINISTRIES

The same steady burning of active love showed in her pursuit of apostolate. She told Danell: 'I am as full of business & eagerness for the schools as if I were only 30 years of age instead of 64', and it was true. It was during these years that the possibility of opening a training college in London reappeared. We are 'as ready as ever', she wrote to the CPSC at the time of Forster's Education Act in 1870. In 1872 when the Sisters of Notre Dame decided against running one in Southwark her hopes and efforts rose yet again. In the end she could not find a sufficient down payment on the house she wanted. In 1873 the CPSC officially offered her the running of a college for them and with it the necessary funds, but with no explanation it was given to another religious congregation desirous of it – someone had informed the CPSC that Mother Connelly's authority as superior-general had so weakened that she could no longer command the services of her sisters for such an undertaking.

Other needs stirred her. St Anne's was a very poor mission, the house was too small, and continual difficulties arose because there was no church attached to the school. 'After Mayfield,' she wrote to the superior, 'this must be our next good work please God'. She dreamed of buying the little houses beside the community's to convert the whole into school, convent and pupil-teacher centre. All schools continued to command her efforts. The one for Young Ladies at St Leonards was growing fast. She had handed

314

over its direction to another, but continued to attend Prize Days, go to recreation sometimes with the children, and take a share in preparing the school plays. When some wanted to abolish these she argued in favour of their formative value. For the Poor Schools she appointed sisters to visit for the yearly examination and sometimes managed to go herself. When Danell wanted her to take on an Industrial School just outside London she considered it seriously and took time to study government rulings. She made sure that the sisters still working for a teacher's certificate were given enough time by their superiors and she still asked for some of their papers to be sent to her. She worried that sisters in Preston sometimes had to teach in the Night Schools as well as during the day and demanded that it was not to be so. A letter written by her at the end of 1877 describes how much it all meant to her:

> It is sunshine to me to think of you on my sick bed as being again happy and sharing the chance to do well with the dear children, who are always on my heart though there are very few that I know. If I had never seen them it is always the same. That they may learn the joy of loving the God who died for us & of being happy in the Convent where he dwells in his most loving form of Holy Childhood. Stiffness and rigour will not bring forth love and these are *not* the spirit of the Holy Child. But *painstaking* for the eagerness of love will always bring forth delicious fruit.

By late 1871 a translation by sisters of Père Medaille's *Meditations* was ready for the convent press and she was asking Danell's permission to print. A would-be convert wrote, hesitating because of family opposition, and in a letter full of a kind of surging joy Cornelia upheld the morality of the Catholic priesthood which her correspondent's husband doubted: 'God forbid that you should be delayed by any human motives, which can bear no comparison with the Grace of God now moving your heart.' Perhaps she was thinking of a day long before in New Orleans when all human motive gave way before that grace.

SUFFERING OF THE HEART

Throughout Cornelia's life as religious and foundress the one suffering always with her was the apostacy of her husband and the loss of her children. Details in this last decade are few but we know from letters and the recollections of others that family concerns weighed upon her.

In June 1872 Frank came to St Leonards for three days – at a time of stress. His mother was expecting to hear the conclusion of Danell's long and wearing visitation. The house sisters were agitated by their recent separation from the others, and she would be obliged to accept whatever ruling for this the bishop decided to impose. The eye witness who reports the scene between mother and son gives no hint of what lay behind Frank's anger. He was just thirty and endeavouring to establish himself as artist and sculptor. She could give him no money, and perhaps – more painful – not enough time. The account sets the scene 'on the landing over the front stairs':

> He was talking very angrily to Reverend Mother. She heard him say, 'Mother, you love those [sisters] more than you do me.' 'O Frank, Frank, I do not.' He came down, kicking his bag down the stairs in front of him. His Mother said (in such a sad and pleading voice, Sister said), 'Oh Frank, come back, *come back*' but he did not, he went away.

It was during these years that one day a young sister found her weeping at her desk.

Three months later Cornelia was writing to Bella Bowen, one of the two nieces who spent two years in school at St Leonards and went with her to Hyères. Bella had sent her from America a sombre photograph of herself which provoked in Cornelia remarks that lift the veil from over the pain in her heart so recently freshened by Frank's visit. With Bella's picture before her she writes:

> Where has all your joy gone my darling? Surely the thought of Paradise is enough to give you joy under all the pains & sorrows of this life. This is only a dream of sorrow & we must never forget the happiness that is in store for all those who walk with faith & courage in the Pilgrimage of life. We are on *our way home* my darling and the trials & thorns must just be gently brushed aside so as not to interrupt us on our way . . . Ah what is life! To marry & die and leave children for others to be unkind to or something like this . . . do not give yourself to be any man's slave to die and leave a family.

Her dear brother Ralph had died in 1867. Now came other family news of Mary Peacock. In January 1873 she wrote to Danell that 'my best beloved Sister & sweetest friend of my youthful days' had died, and owns to him how deeply religious sisters continue to love their family, cheering herself with the thought that 'in heaven we shall know our own and love God the more'. Early in the following year she would be begging prayers for Frank and Ady: 'they are very gay & Frank is a great man in his art but oh that they were true Catholics!'

To family sorrows were added the deaths of old friends who had stood by her in hard times. Serjeant Bellasis and Charles Towneley were two such men. With Bellasis, three of whose daughters were members of her Society,

316

she kept vigil throughout his illness. Retrospectively, his daughter wrote of this relationship:

> From his first introduction until his death – a period of eighteen years, he was a true and faithful friend and benefactor, ever ready to aid her at any personal cost or inconvenience. Let her express a mere wish to see him, he thought nothing of spending a night with his Briefs in order to find himself free on the following morning to run down to St Leonards.

Cornelia referred to him as 'Brother Bellasis'. She took his legal advice as trustworthy and always in keeping with the integrity she so valued. Newman described him as 'one of the finest men I ever knew', and perhaps it was the Serjeant who had caused Newman to write in 1864, in spite of Emily and other calumniators, that Mrs Connelly having become a religious 'is still a very good one'.[1] Bellasis' admiration of her was very great: 'If I had fifty daughters instead of five', he was quoted as saying, 'I would entrust them all to her.' As his end approached (he died in 1873) it was Mother Connelly to whom he confided the most personal attitudes of his soul: 'I hope you will pray for me, not that I may be relieved from pain, for I willingly suffer that, but that I may be confirmed in the love of God, so as to use that as my motive in obtaining true contrition and perseverance.'[2]

In 1876 Charles Towneley died. If he had not had the perspicacity to create irrevocably a charitable Trust with what he inherited from Jones, he would have been for ever harrassed by Grant's and Wiseman's manipulations on behalf of the mission. Had he given the property outright to the Society Cornelia would have had no defence against Wiseman's incursions and the pressures of her own bishop. It was to Towneley that she owed the preservation of St Leonards for the Society and his death deprived her of a friend and her most redoubtable champion.

By all ordinary human measure these years of Mother Connelly's life should have been characterised by darkness and decline. But in the good heart long since in the making the fires were banked and still aglow. At last a burst of energy caught fire in France.

CORNELIA AND FRANCE

From its beginning and thenceforth, Cornelia's life as a Catholic had been touched and deepened by contact with the French church. Nicollet's faith had led both Connellys to question their Protestant beliefs. French missionary bishops had helped shape her path: Blanc of New Orleans, Flaget of Kentucky, Bruté of Vincennes. In Louisiana she had entertained in her own home the French bishop Forbin-Janson of Nancy, founder of the Association of the Holy Childhood. For five years she lived at Grand Coteau in daily contact with French missionary Jesuits and Sacred Heart sisters, and learned among them what it meant to be called to religious life in the church. Nicolas Point directed her at the time of her spiritual awakening. On her return to Rome she had lived again with Sacred Heart sisters at the Trinità for another three years, this time virtually on French soil in an almost entirely French community. Her confessors there were French, and the library to which she had access gave her the opportunity to imbibe French spirituality and something of French history.

'I want to hear a great deal about Paris,' she wrote when Pierce was *en route* for his first visit to England in 1836, and a year later she and Merty and Ady and the baby John Henry were there with him for two whole months, waiting for a boat to take them back to America. One cannot suppose that she, who in Rome for the first time had exclaimed that there was so much to see and study, let slip similar opportunities in Paris. On this occasion she was a young and happy wife and mother. They had arrived by coach along the Route Royale from Vienna, long days of travel by diligence through countryside and history. They came in via Vincennes, took an apartment in central Paris, in Rue St Dominique, and the beautiful city lay open before them. No record of their doings has survived but their departure route for Le Havre lay past La Malmaison, the residence of Napoleon's first wife Josephine, and when the Connellys first lived at Grand Coteau in a cramped little cabin, happy memories dubbed it 'our Château of Malmaison'.

Cornelia's second and third visits to Paris had a very different tone. In 1843 *en route* for Rome to ask for the separation, Pierce elected to stay there for a month while he introduced Robert Berkeley to the sights. Two of Cornelia's children were left behind, buried at Grand Coteau; her eldest son was at school in England; only Ady and the toddler Frank were with her. It was autumn. They resumed their journey at the end of November, travelling a route new to her: by train to Orléans, Joan of Arc's battleground; by coach to Lyons which the ancient Romans had built, where Christianity had early flourished and martyrs had died; by steamer down the Rhône for ten hours to Avignon, city of the Great Schism and the Palais de Papes. Such journeys fed Cornelia's knowledge and love of France.

The third visit was for three months in summer 1846 on the way to England to begin the Society, waiting for the unknown. She and Ady and Frank stayed with the religious of the Assumption.[3] Little is known of this visit but a book she then acquired and kept all her life has survived, one of the many of French spirituality on which she drew for the ongoing formation of her Society and a few of which sisters translated for publication. One passage in it she marked. It describes well how she lived the rest of her life:

Think well on two points: First, in whatever state, within or exteriorly, God places us He does so only for His glory and our good. Second, if we accept this with a generous heart, His glory and our peace are secured, and always His grace makes it possible for us to accept willingly. Without doubt we shall suffer but we must not let go; inwardly, revolt and struggle will try us: nature does not die without crying out and resisting. But if in the midst of this involuntary tumult the soul refuses to be moved, God's glory loses nothing and peace remains. These principles are simple and clear. We must hold fast to them and let that be our rule of conduct.[4]

A NEW FOUNDATION, 1869-77

Very many years later, having established the Society in both England and America, she told Buckle and others that she wanted it to be in a Catholic country also. Her initial hope had been Rome where she dreamed of a novitiate, so that 'the true Roman spirit' might pervade the Society. But France was never far from her thoughts.

The first attempt was a proposed stay at Pau for the winter of 1867. Grant did not approve it. Two years later the doctor again urged rest and change and November 1869 found Cornelia with three sisters and five children at Hyères on the French Riviera. But here for a school there was to be no abiding city, and on 25 April, temporarily renewed in health, hopeful of approbation and as yet unaware of any cabal, Cornelia set out again, this time for Toul in Lorraine.

The school in view had eighty pupils of whom forty were boarders, some German, some French (a small international school, one might say), advantageous educationally for the sisters as much as for the children. Purchase terms were favourable, Grant with customary caveats agreed, prospects were good and six weeks after Cornelia had returned to England the deed of sale was signed. On 14 July the Hôtel de Rigny became a Society convent and three days later France declared war on Germany.

Toul was in Alsace-Lorraine, within twenty-five miles of Vionville where on 16 August the Germans would begin to drive a French army back to base in Metz. Before that time Toul's citizens seemed not to have expected that war would reach their doorsteps. On the very day of the declaration one of the sisters, herself a Frenchwoman, wrote (in French) to Mother Connelly:

We have arrived in France Reverend Mother at a very bad time. We have nothing to fear from the War, for Toul is not near enough to the frontiers for there to be danger, but everything will be frightfully dear this year: there will be almost a famine. The husbandmen, obliged to go away for the year, cannot get in the harvest . . . Water is lacking in the country and also hay and the grains needed by the cattle; the peasants having nothing to give them are obliged to kill them . . . this winter it will be difficult to find food to eat.

How Cornelia was feeling we know only from a letter in French which she wrote to an unidentified 'Monsieur':

> Our good Sisters have chosen to remain at Toul in order to devote themselves to the poor wounded in this frightful war. I have sent them money for their journey in order to tempt them to return, but I have had no answer. They have great courage and they assure me in their last letter that they are in no danger in the ambulances. Nevertheless, we are very anxious as we have no idea what might happen in Toul and its neighbourhood. Every day we hope for good news but in vain. Our prayers are all for our dear France.

Five days later on 16 August the first shells hit the cathedral to which the convent was adjacent. Then the sisters decided. The military let down the drawbridge for women and children to escape before the enemy laid seige to the town, and the community with its English and German pupils took to the road, six days of rough going across enemy lines. Upon the party's arrival in Paris the German girls were committed to the care of the Swiss consul who saw them safely home and the rest reached St Leonards on 25 August. The war continued. When it ended in May 1871 the revolt of the communards in Paris was not yet put down and we find Cornelia still praying for France: 'I hope you are all praying for the Archbishop of Paris [Georges Darboy] and for the curés. One of them has been murdered and the others imprisoned, also 30 Jesuits. God have mercy on us. Pray hard.'

This was not an auspicious beginning for a foundation. Nevertheless neither she nor the sisters wished to give up. In June 1871, a month after peace was agreed, they went back by taking a route through Belgium, not Paris. The Hôtel de Rigny was a shambles but in October, somehow, they opened school in skeleton circumstances. Pupils arrived, armed with their bedding, jugs and basins. Studies commenced. A fierce winter set in and a sister remembered details: an inner courtyard staircase was open on three sides to wind, snow and sleet and the place began to look like a salt-mine. In the town fires were kept burning beside the fountains lest the water supply freeze up. In bed their breath made flakes of ice on the sheets. To wash became impossible. Cooking was a pain because hands were covered with split chilblains. Yet – for the time being – they survived, making merry in the tradition of the Society's usual hard beginnings. It was as at Towanda where 'no one thought of grumbling', and at Gate Street whose 'courageous souls . . . abounded with joy in the midst of privations of every kind'. They battled on for four years, but it was a war-torn locality. There was poverty in the district among the French families and German and English parents did not send their children. The war had made Toul the wrong place for such a venture.

During these years, 1871–3 Mother Connelly dared not leave England. They were the years in which she was pursuing the possibility of a training college while withstanding the work of the cabal. In the summer of 1873 she was again very ill. Then the duchess, sick and difficult for many months, died in April 1874. The general chapter, at last agreed to, lay ahead. Not till the end of April could Cornelia visit her French foundation. She remained for a whole month and in spite of her heavy anxieties, a sister there wrote, her readiness to enjoy the present moment was uncrushable: 'Great was her delight, when at a picnic with the children . . . she rowed on the Moselle in a boat. It recalled, she said, the days of her youth in America.'

During 1875 and early 1876 Cornelia and her council debated the fate of Toul. In the event the convent was sold and footing sought elsewhere, first in Cambrai, then Versailles. Cornelia was confident that all would be well. A house became available in Paris at 51 Rue de Théâtre, Grenelle. She went to help with the move, the community and children followed and everyone realised very soon that this too could be only temporary. It was, Cornelia said, 'most miserably situated, & cramped even for *six* children'.

Pau, Hyères, Toul, Grenelle – none had realised Cornelia's hope. But she wanted to remain in Paris and made herself 'very occupied in looking for a proper house', invigorating the community in the intervals. With them she was reading a French history of the church, so good, it seemed to her, that she recommended it to the sisters in America, telling them at the same time how deeply she admired the French clergy and the thoroughness of the formation they received – perhaps in contrast to some of her experience in England.

The house-hunting dragged on. Things looked hopeless when one day, stuck in the letter-box, there appeared a notice: 'Property for Sale. Suitable for a convent or a big-boarding school'. It was the Petit Château of the Duc d'Orléans, Neuilly-sur-Seine. At once she went to see it, and decided. 'Our being in Paris at this moment is one of the wonders of God, arranged by the Angels and settled by St Joseph. Do not think I had anything to do with it . . . The only thing I had determined on was *not to leave France*.'

They moved in January 1877. The château had been most beautiful and still through the dilapidation glimmered the ancient splendour and fallen glory of France's royal family. Cornelia, Bellasis points out, took pleasure in its history. Initially it was leased for three years, years of doubt, poverty

and hard work. There were in the district already thirty-three other educational establishments, and everyone was not convinced when Cornelia
dreamed aloud of a noviceship there one day:

> I see a great future for this house . . . It is not so much the good we shall
> do to the children here though that will be not small by introducing our
> school and teaching the gentle spirit of the Society of the Holy Child. But
> I look forward to great benefit from the contact with the French Church
> & we shall gain far more than we can give.

So at last Cornelia had her 'house in France where the blood of Martyrs
has been so lately shed and where the Church is so full of fervour and zeal
for souls'.[5]

There is an amazing bouyancy here. Cornelia was sixty-eight and failing
in strength. She won the reverence as well as the support of the parochial
clergy; gave a happy time to the little band of pupils – 'I give nice singing
lessons to the children [one remembered long after how lovely her voice still
was], and often go to night recreation with them.' She saw to a prospectus
and to advertising and arranged for goods to come from England. As the
future annalist [then superior in France] wrote, Cornelia was 'expending
her latest energies on the Neuilly foundation', and full of hope she inspired
the sisters in France to begin and go on like every other community in the
Society:

> 'Let there be no waiting to begin our usual practices. We have started;
> our boat has pushed off from the shore, & now we must row' . . . She
> ever encouraged all to rise above difficulties; to meet inconveniences,
> disappointments, contradictions, bravely, cheerfully. 'Sacrifice! Sacrifice'
> was her constant aspiration & her spirit was contagious.

During the community retreat at the end of March she had to endure the
freezing cold of an unheated French house with enormous windows where
it was impossible to get warm anywhere, and when at the end of the eight
days sisters and children made a pilgrimage to Montmartre where the
basilica in honour of the Sacred Heart was being raised, she was too ill to
go. Nevertheless as soon as possible she went herself to pray for the French
foundation. Then on the day of her departure for England, ready and
dressed for travelling and with the carriage at the door, she earnestly gave
them her last words:

> I have done all in my power to leave things here on a good foundation,
> & now I recommend three practices to you in parting. First, *Obedience*.
> All have to obey, the Pope, the Bishops, all Superiors. There is no such
> thing as freedom from the yoke of authority, & the *self-will* course must

be abandoned in our conduct & in our hearts. Nothing must be done because *it is our wish to do it*: but simply because it is the Will of God.

To that she added the need to be faithful to the spirit of Ignatius' *Exercises*, and to be generous in acknowledging and making reparation for faults. Then, amid the tears of the sisters who thought they might never see her again, she departed, trusting that all would be well: 'We only need energy and prudence with prayer to be certain of success for the schools here, and for every success. Paris is full of life and energy and the most beautiful place in the world even in winter.'

There was, however, the other side to this picture of fountaining zeal which Cornelia's 'good heart' was generating. 'How full of sorrow is this passing world,' she wrote from France, 'and yet how full of joy in the depths of sorrow.' When Maria Joseph Buckle arrived to join the community in Paris, not having seen Mother Connelly for several years, she recognised the marks of sorrow upon her:

> I shall never forget how touched I was by seeing the change that had taken place . . . She seemed quite broken down by sorrow & though calm and dignified as usual there was a humility & sadness in her manner that made me grieve for all that she had gone through . . . Her eyes especially had lost their fire though their expression was very gentle & she was most kind & thoughtful . . . I happened in getting down from the carriage to tear my cloak. She took if from me & said no one but herself should mend it.

16

Love Knows No Measure

'Anxiety,' Cornelia wrote to Bishop Danell a few months after the first general chapter, 'kills its victims by inches,' and a little later in 1875, having made every effort to clear a sister suffering an extraordinary injustice, the only comfort Mother Connelly could offer was a reflection of the way in which she herself kept going:

> I feel sure that you will try to do your best to be in charity and peace with all, casting aside all remembrances that might wound . . . We are all united in the work of God & toiling for the same end, and 'the night cometh in which no man can work' [Jn. 9:4] . . . your sickness goes on . . . The worry no doubt keeps it up . . . Pray for me.

The next general chapter was due in 1877. With the imposition of Danell's rule and of himself as the Society's superior, he had roused the opposition of other bishops, and schism had become a real possibility. 'Bishops prefer Diocesan Orders,' Cornelia wrote, 'where their power is without . . . appeal', but she was certain that this was not the true character of the congregation which Rome had sent her to found in 1846. Weary but now constitutionally elected and with the strength of an elected council to work with her, she had three years in which to retrieve the situation. The threat of disintegration into diocesan groups had to be fended off and the union of hearts revivified.

THE NORTH AGAIN, 1874–6

The trouble in the north did not cease with the chapter and Mother Connelly's election. Nor was this simply because a few sisters, now that Danell was superior of the whole Society, complained to him endlessly. A greater threat was the intransigence of the Bishop of Liverpool.

Very early in his time as bishop O'Reilly did what Ullathorne would warn him against, that is, he accepted statements from individuals without testing the evidence. Cornelia wrote ruefully to Fr Whitty, the new rector of the Jesuits in Preston and one of her few supporters there: 'The bishop of Liverpool has been misinformed on more than one point! but there is no use in trying to clear up matters that are all one sided and without any just redress.'

The troubles had begun, as we have seen, when he thought Mother Connelly had disobeyed his predecessor's Decree of Visitation. He next became convinced, again wrongly, that one sister and her community were the source of scandal in the town. The thought of court cases and the national press focused on his diocese appalled him, and he decided that the amalgamation of the Preston communities into one would be effective as a means of general reform. By the time Danell consulted him about the approaching chapter he was so unfavourably disposed towards Mother Connelly and her government that he would allow sisters from his diocese (where he was determined to root out all trouble) to attend it only on three conditions: that the superior-general's term of office be limited to three years; that 'no changes by removal or otherwise' of sisters in his diocese should take place without his previous approval; that the three Preston communities be amalgamated. Such terms, Ullathorne afterwards told him, a bishop had no right to lay down for a congregation that had general government over houses in several dioceses. But O'Reilly justified his poaching on the grounds that the Society's Constitutions were not yet approved. Holy Child sisters in his diocese were fair game.

When at the chapter Danell imposed his own Rule and made himself bishop-superior, Cornelia had no recourse but to accept. She was thus brought under direct obedience to him, and O'Reilly's three conditions passed into his hands to deal with. Danell's actions, however, indicate that he considered the conditions superseded by his own legislation and authority. Cornelia may have wondered about meeting them but the responsibility was no longer hers. Danell told her he would inform the bishop of Liverpool about the outcomes of the chapter and would deal with his reactions. In the event, he neglected to do either and this oversight had consequences that were nearly disastrous for the Society.

Only by chance did O'Reilly hear of the chapter elections and appointments. Two of the northern superiors called on him, one to say goodbye, the other to ask a blessing on her charge, whereupon he ordered them to stay where they were. Cornelia, hearing of it, appealed to Danell to make things right with him. But Danell failed to do so. More confusion followed and eventually O'Reilly informed him that rather than alter his determinations all the sisters could be withdrawn from the diocese. He had to go to Rome and was entirely unmollified by a letter from Cornelia which reached him later:

My dear Lord and Father in Christ

I beg to express to your Lordship my extreme regret that the full note of
the elections held at St Leonards was not immediately forwarded to your
Lordship . . . The Bishop of Southwark . . . intended immediately to go
to Liverpool with the Revised Rule and to give your Lordship all the
results of our Chapter. I now enclose a second Note of all the Elections . . .
I humbly beg of you my Lord to forgive any apparent fault that might
offend your Lordship & attribute it to a mistake that originated not in
any want of obedience on our part but solely from the fact of our having
understood that the Bishop of Southwark would treat immediately with
your Lordship and that it would have been rather assuming on our part
to act of ourselves.

These are not the words of a woman greedy for power or refusing obedience
due to a bishop. Rather, the struggle for power was between the two bishops,
and Cornelia was caught between them. Danell's negligence had left her
vulnerable to O'Reilly's accusation of disobedience.

Meanwhile for several reasons tension in the north increased. The prospect of amalgamation was unpopular and it became clear to Cornelia that
it was being required on the grounds of imagined abuses in the one community. But there was no redress. The bishop would neither name the
offence and allow those accused to defend themselves nor investigate further.
Even Danell thought the demand for amalgamation severe. A few were loud
also against Lucy Woolley's loss of office (the council had not reappointed
her); and since Cornelia had obediently refrained from putting moves into
operation until she could see O'Reilly, all superiors whether coming or going
waited in a state of rising frustration for three and a half months. On 17
December an interview at last took place and he was adamant. After it
Mother Connelly and her council knew without doubt that should any
'sisters in the North' second O'Reilly's wishes to have sole control, 'there
must be a schism'. To avert it they had to persuade Danell to bend his
dignity far enough to meet O'Reilly's demands.

O'Reilly had had plenty of encouragement to think ill of Mother Connelly:
from Goss, from Preston sisters and Danell, from Ullathorne. Very soon
after the chapter it came also from a member of Cornelia's new council,
Gertrude Day. Gertrude's real stance about the future of the Society – which
she had been elected to help Mother Connelly govern – is, for lack of
evidence, difficult to judge. Maybe she wished it to become diocesan, perhaps envisaging the communities of the north as a separated unit under its
own superior-general accountable only to the bishop. Or she thought that
by allying herself with the Bishop of Liverpool union of the whole would in

the end be achieved. Or perhaps she was simply a very naïve person acting out of experience that was narrow.

Gertrude had been for fifteen years at Blackpool, ever since leaving the novitiate at twenty. Her community loved her, the school which she established prospered and endured. She had not joined the little group in Preston which in 1870 sent Mother Connelly false signatures but the statement which she now wrote for O'Reilly, like theirs to Barnabò, betrays the same readiness to judge ill and sweepingly of her. Lucy, Alphonsa and Gertrude, one might argue, had all been big fishes in their own distant ponds for too long. They had developed fixed attitudes and reacted almost automatically to whatever Cornelia did in their regard. When she exercised authority she was accused of arbitrary despotism and her motives were suspected. When she refrained from acting she was accused of indifference and neglect. Her human mistakes and failings were routinely magnified. It became almost impossible for them to see her side of the picture or to acknowledge that she ever acted in their best interests.

On 26 September Gertrude, elected only six weeks earlier to general government and called to St Leonards as local superior, saw her bishop, spoke freely to him and felt happier, she said, than she had done for years. She liked the rule Danell had imposed and said to O'Reilly later that she hoped he would allow its use in his diocese. Next day she wrote to Danell and Cornelia that she would be remaining in Blackpool 'until I receive orders from him to leave', and began to prepare the statement she had promised him.

In the first section of it she concentrates on Mother Connelly and life in the St Leonards community. As superior-general Cornelia emerges as a managing, interfering, inconsiderate woman with whom anyone, and in particular a local superior, would find it difficult to live. The community is ill-regulated and lax, schools were more important than keeping the Rule, there is a worldly spirit, charity and union are absent. No alleviating word appears. Most of this picture Gertrude, who had not lived there since 1859, probably derived from her recent conversations with embittered house sisters at St Leonards, all of whom she had seen personally after the chapter as local superior-elect.[1] When she moves on to Mother Connelly's general government she reflects what were the feelings also of the Preston superiors: Mother Connelly has been unkind and unhelpful to superiors, she has encouraged criticism and tale-bearing, she has not promoted charity. Ill motives are imputed: Mother Connelly missioned sisters 'never considering whether such persons were fit for the places they were sent to, but only considering her own personal convenience'. She has been deaf to all conscientious representation. She evades lawful authority, sometimes disobeys the bishop, is not only averse to the new Rule but 'will not lead the sisters to its observance'. Throughout the thirty articles of its eight pages there are only two approving comments, that the 'Mistress of Novices is all that could be desired' (that is, Mary Francis Bellasis), and that at St Anne's convent in London there are 'Good religious & devoted in the service of the poor'. It is a censorious document. Coming from a member of Mother Cornelia's council, it must have confirmed O'Reilly in his opposition.

Gertrude sent it to O'Reilly before she went, permitted by him, to the first council meeting after the chapter. Her accompanying letter hoped he would not give it weight unless he found it supported the opinions of others, and it was given only 'under the seal of confession'. It would be 'ruinous to my happiness for life', she wrote, 'if it were known to the Society that I had put matters before your Lordship', and she concluded, 'I am in your hands my Lord and I intend to be perfectly obedient.' At this date Gertrude had never worked with Cornelia and even as a novice much of her time had been spent with Theresa Hanson in London. The Society did not learn of her statement to O'Reilly till a great many years later and it was never known to Cornelia – who loved and trusted her councillor.

The amalgamation was finally agreed to in council on 13 January 1875. The minutes read:

Reasons for the Amalgamation
A   To meet the Bishop of Liverpool's express wishes.
B   To increase the religious spirit.
C   To secure unity of action.
D   Tis easier to find one Superior than three.

Danell gave way to O'Reilly. He allowed Gertrude to remain in the north and become superior, not of St Leonards but of the new amalgamated community in Preston. Many obstacles had to be overcome and much frustration transcended before this could be put into operation. The three convents belonged to the Jesuits and were attached to their schools. They now had to be replaced with a property to be owned by the sisters, large enough and so placed as to enable them to reach their scattered schools. It also had to include accommodation for pupil-teachers. The Jesuits, naturally enough, were not all too pleased because their schools, both Day and Night, might suffer and Mother Connelly could not provide extra sisters to meet needs created by distance. The shortage of personnel everywhere was becoming chronic, an anxiety for Cornelia quite unthought of as such by her malcontents. At one point when amalgamation was under consideration one of them wrote to Danell that Mother Connelly was 'utterly indifferent' to Preston's needs and 'we may as well be silent and work on till our spirits fail us', when only the day before Cornelia herself had voiced her worries to him. She had said how harrassed she was by demands everywhere for help beyond what she could supply. Her concern was that 'On all sides the work increases, & the health of the sisters is giving way.'

However, in February 1875 the majority of the sisters moved into a house in Winckley Square. Gertrude took over, 'fully determined to use every endeavour', the council told their bishop-superior, 'to bring things round'.

The change meant that other superiors were superseded. Alphonsa Kay protested at her loss of office, saying that it was unjust. She even sent her protest to Rome, and supported by Danell clung to her right as a superior to attend the next general chapter.. Her general unhappiness was such that at one point she intended to leave but was persuaded by him to remain. Lucy Woolley, on the bishop's orders, had to be removed from the town and Cornelia sent her to Blackpool as less strange than the south. But change of status and occupation quite disorientated her. Cornelia, with a mixture of firmness and sympathy, tried to help her to pull herself together but in vain, and in October 1875 Lucy left the Society. Meanwhile at Winckley Square Gertrude made herself as much loved as at Blackpool, and established yet another prosperous school destined to endure. It was a shock and sorrow to everyone when on 6 March 1876, after a very brief illness at St Leonards and aged only thirty-seven, she died. Conceivably the experience of working with Cornelia on the general council for the good of the whole Society had changed her feelings. Mother Connelly, though ill herself, was with others at her bedside during her last hours and wrote a long letter to the Blackpool community about her happy death. Affectionately she described Gertrude as full of loving gratitude, 'for each and all'.

Out of this great upheaval in the north, good came. Submission eventually appeased the bishop. A happy spirit began to prevail among the Preston sisters and on 28 April 1876 Mother Connelly, 'casting aside all remembrance that might wound', wrote to Danell from the new convent:

> I had a very kind letter from the Bishop of Liverpool yesterday appointing Monday for us to go and see his Lordship. I am sure we owe his Lordship a debt of gratitude for the benefits of the amalgamation of the three Convents & for his most kind protection of the work here, which is very prosperous.

But the killing by inches was in process. Ever since the chapter she had been, not continuously but increasingly ill. In November 1874 she could not, for a period, conduct all her own business and one of the council, Angelica Croft, took over correspondence and visits. This would happen more and more often. In February 1875 she said she had been very poorly for the last six months and was 'still an invalid with Bronchitis and general debility'. At Mayfield in July: 'Today I have had our bed for a painting table . . . so that I could bear the penance of the bed with more patience than for the last few days . . . Ah, what are we worth when pain tries us a little.' In September she was still 'very unfit to knock about'. When Gertrude died in March 1876 she had to send the news to the communities, 'writing to all from my bed'. The burden of what had to be done could never be forgotten, but physical strength and energy could no longer be counted on. It came and went in patches. From after the 1874 chapter until her death four and a half years later, weakness and pain came more often and lasted longer, inescapably conditioning all that she strove to do or did.

THE STRUGGLE FOR THE RULE, 1874–7

Danell's imposition at the chapter of a Rule so alien in spirit to what the sisters had been used to had an effect quite opposite to what he had anticipated. The contrast sharpened appreciation of what had been taken from them. Although the new Rule had to be observed to the letter, the spirit of the old was not lost. Gradually ranks closed behind Mother Connelly in the effort she was making, fully supported by her council (Gertrude was replaced by Catherine Tracey), to re-establish the core of the Society's life and win back its own Rule. In this crisis it is the correspondence with America that reveals what were the chief problems and the council's policy for dealing with them.

For some time past Bishop Wood and Carter had wanted the Society in America (now numbering forty-seven) to separate from England. But the sisters were loyal. They treasured the old Rule in the form they had known since they left England. No alternative would be welcome. After the chapter Wood received a copy of Danell's. Seeing no reason why another bishop should impose his authority on sisters not in his diocese, he rejected it and also refused to admit new members until Rome had decided what Rule to approve. Thus the survival of the communities in America as part of the whole Society was imperilled. But it was Danell who sent it whereas the superiors there took for granted it was Cornelia. They assumed she had sent the new Rule to the bishop and thought she herself was responsible for the changes found in the 1869 revision which Mary Xavier had put 'on the shelf' and which Danell's had replaced. Letters of protest poured in. The possibility of schism with her own country could not have lessened her killing anxieties.

One of the council, writing in her defence, first gave a careful account of all that had led to this moment, and then said:

> I hope that you now understand that Reverend Mother is not to be blamed in any way for your present suffering, for indeed she is not. She

herself has suffered . . . more than all of us put together . . . & now you turn & blame her as if *she* had caused the destruction of your peace and happiness. It has been very much against her will that any change has been made in the Rule for she holds heart & soul to the Rule of St Ignatius but she *submits* herself & all her inclinations to the Church, & when she is told at Propaganda that the *old* Rule *cannot* be approved *as it stands* but must have certain changes made in it, she is willing & ready to obey. In fact we *must* obey if we wish to exist as a Religious Order.

Cornèlia's own letters are full of urgency and practical advice. She told Mary Xavier: 'The point to work at now is to examine & to object to whatever *changes* our work [of God] by these alterations in the Rule. To sift them in all their bearings, & to make notes upon them. If you do this the Sacred Congregation will weigh them well.' She sent documents and a book by the Abbé Craisson on recent canon law for religious communities with simple vows.[2] She wanted Mary Xavier to study it so that she would know what Rome would demand, and she insisted that Rome's approval alone would protect them from diocesan rule: 'Your safety is in *union*' – which only Rome could defend and ratify.

In this crisis it was essential to pull together. To a superior in America who had been at the chapter she wrote:

Prayer, thought, confidence in God & a certain amount of *knowledge* are all necessary for us in this anxious crisis. We are bound to the *three years* trial of the rule but object to many points as destructive of the work [of God], but we are advised to obey for the term & then to claim exemption from the power of the Bishop. I do not feel that we should get it unless by a miracle of God's mercy & the death of all we know who would oppose it!!! I heard that Fr Cobb was heart-broken over the Preston rebellion!! Too late when the mischief is done. We shall come to nothing unless we meet & decide unanimously on certain points & a certain mode of procedure. Matters lie with the Community now more than with the Bishops who would make us Diocesan. Now I recommend this:

1. Draw out first your greatest objections to a change of [from the old] Rule.

2. Then take the details [in the new rule] & object with reasons for each objection: Craisson will help you.

3. Then write out an appeal with which we may agree or not, to send to Rome. You have a perfect right to do it yourselves, but it will be better if we can agree on the same arrangements or as nearly as possible . . .

If a concerted reaction to Danell's rule coming from the whole Society were to be sent to Rome, then the old Rule might be retrieved at the next chapter.

Cornelia, speaking from the depths of experience both of the Society and of the Propaganda was 'quite certain that the new Rule *cannot* work & as convinced that it will *not be approved without change*'.

In this great trial she had the very real support of her council. At last they and the sisters at large understood and were of one mind about the style of government which she had so long asked for: 'We are quite united in our decisions and determined to hold together. Our position is most trying under present circumstances and we all feel a heavy weight of responsibility, casting aside all personal considerations as we are bound to do.' She herself did not wish to be spared, whatever Mary Xavier wanted to say: 'Do not think for a moment about giving me pain personally. I must make myself happy in having my heart pierced and broken. A broken heart is love's cradle "when our love is crucified". Let us bless and thank God for every stroke.' Then, having written the long account (already quoted in the context of the cabal) of actions of hers which Mary Xavier has 'stormed against', she adds – with the affection of long friendship and as yet unaware of Mary Xavier's state of health: 'Try to be just in your judgements my dear one, and do not fancy that I act without advice or that I would encourage anyone to do so. I shall rejoice in the day when I shall hold no office whatever.'

Two of the council went to America, their mission to do what they could to smooth matters with Bishop Wood about the Rule and to forestall schism. Before they returned the bishop was sufficiently mollified to revoke his decision not to receive new members; and they had agreed to the appointment of a successor to Mary Xavier who, because of 'an infirmity which more or less affects her mind', he wrote, was to return with them. Although the letter to Cornelia which her councillors brought back with them conveys that all the decisions had been his to make, he also adds that he does not thereby intend 'to prejudice any decision of the Holy See'. Cornelia followed up on her councillors' successful mission with a letter to him:

I wish sincerely to humble myself & to beg pardon for past deficiencies observed in myself or in others . . . and I beg of your Grace to look with a favourable eye upon all faults of inexperience and not to attribute faults of this nature to any premeditated will or to false principles of independence.

Mary Xavier was a sick woman, which seems not to have been realised in England. She had a brain tumour, the effects of which would account for any recent strangeness in her ways of meeting the troubles about the Rule. She had not wished to leave America and there were those who blamed Mother Connelly for the departure enforced by the bishop. In England she died within six months of her return, much loved by but estranged from Cornelia.

By October the council had its plans on behalf of the Rule well laid. They had America's objections to Danell's and also those of the north and could now protest against it confident that their stance would be representative of the whole body. Two councillors were to go to Rome for Cornelia, taking with them the imposed Rule modified 'according to the remarks & experiences . . . gained upon it in the different dioceses'. With the aid of a Roman consultor they hoped to ready themselves for discussion about it at the coming chapter. Their purpose, they told Danell in a diplomatic letter signed by them all, was 'to act in concert with your Lordship in procuring the general good', which carefully worded statement the bishop apparently took to mean that they would be asking, with modifications, for its approval. He agreed to their going, gave them a letter of introduction to the new prefect of the Propaganda, Cardinal Franchi, and sent his Rule off to Rome ahead of them requesting its approbation.

On its behalf Danell argued to Franchi that it met the demands of all earlier commentators (this included Ullathorne's adverse report and that of the consultor on Pierce's pseudo Rule); and that he had remedied all defects referred to by Wiseman. Because Mother Connelly, he added, had had no proper noviceship, she lacked 'thorough knowledge of the order & organisation of the religious state'. Neither had she 'a sufficiently clear idea of her duties & her dependence on . . . the Ecclesiastical Hierarchy'. Therefore he had recommended a 'direct Superior near at hand', and the sisters in chapter having heard this statement on the subject, 'chose', he said, 'to have as Superior of the Mother General the Bishop of Southwark'. They had moreover, all except one, given their signatures to the rule. This is not as the delegates would have described what happened.

According to the notes which Cornelia gave her councillors for use in the meeting at Rome, they had *not been allowed to discuss at all* the articles in which came the statement 'The Bishop of the Mother House is the Superior of the Institute', which they had since learnt from Craisson was not allowed by canon law. A result was that other bishops were already denying the authority of the Bishop of Southwark and to avoid schisms they wished for a cardinal protector in Rome, and at the coming chapter an apostolic delegate. Other points to be made were: this new Rule had been entirely unexpected; they were willing to accept modifications of their own Rule but not its total loss; they had had no theologian of their own to speak to them at the chapter; they had had *no choice but to sign* and had accepted it for three years only.

No record exists of any interview with Franchi but by March 1877 they were back from Rome, meeting in council with Cornelia back from Neuilly. The visit had apparently achieved nothing but in fact it ensured that Danell's rule would not be approved, at least at this time. Cornelia turned to Fr Knapen, so helpful in Rome in 1869, but so did Franchi and then Danell. Knapen proposed to the Propaganda that the chapter should be spent going over the bishop's Rule objection by objection and then continue *ad experimentum* for the next three years, which depressing information reached Cornelia in mid-June. She begged Knapen to come to St Leonards for two weeks before the chapter, feeling that without such preparatory assistance the second chapter would get them no further than the first. But he never came. Maybe so much noise from cabal and bishops had changed his attitude. Maybe it would have been too difficult to wear three hats. Meanwhile one partisan of free speech, Theophila Laprimaudaye, had vivid memories of how much in 1874 their freedom of expression had been limited by the canonist Bosio. The delegates, she said, had been 'over-persuaded, talked-over and talked down' by him. She took advantage of her family connection of Anglican days with Cardinal Manning and begged him to intervene and prevent Bosio from coming again. But Manning was ill. Nothing was done except that, incomprehensibly and after the chapter, her letter was passed on to the bishop. When the delegates assembled in August 1877 the same triumvirate faced them: Danell, Bosio and the chaplain Hogan.

THE SECOND GENERAL CHAPTER, 1877

The five months since Cornelia's return from Paris had been hard. Her health was breaking down. In April, writing to the superior at Neuilly, she admitted:

> I too have been very ill, much more ill than I thought when I exercised myself yesterday morning to get to Mass. The gout flies through me. The foot & ankle would be but nothing if it would stop there, but when your heart is either palpitating or stopping (!) you do not know where you may be the next half hour!

A month later there was 'great prostration' again and she joked about her efforts to keep her correspondence going: 'You see, I am not quite made of iron, and though I force myself to do the utmost possible in the way of writing, still the pen will not go quite like the needle of the sewing machine!'

As August drew near anxiety must have mounted. No theologian. No apostolic delegate. And her right hand councillor, Angelica Croft, had had a breakdown through overwork in April. For three months Angelica had been unable to transact any business and by August was recuperating in France, still not well enough to attend the chapter.

In the end Cornelia presided alone over the week-long meeting with the delegates required by the bishop before he was to arrive. There were nineteen of them as before, but nine were newly elected. Their work was to make a special study of what they considered should be changed in his rule. There is no record of this meeting and for Mother Connelly whose energies were failing it must have been both a strain and a challenge. But it gave her an opportunity which, if one is to judge by events during the rest of the chapter, she must have seized: to describe for the delegates the policy which she and the council had been following in regard to the bishop's Rule; to introduce them to relevant canonical points made by Craisson; and to acquaint them with the work of Pierre Cotel SJ. For another congregation which focused on the spirit 'du Saint-Enfant Jésus' Cotel had composed constitutions which, since the 1874 chapter, Cornelia and the council had been working with.[3]

Except for discussion with her council this would also have been the first chance she had had to present the merits and demerits of the 1870 version of their own Rule for the consideration of a representative body of sisters. During that preliminary week, with what may have been heroic effort, she would have put all her experience and knowledge at their disposal. At the end, delegates, council and superior-general were of one mind, namely to avert if possible what Danell had already informed Cornelia would be the probable outcome, another three years of his rule *ad experimentum*. For this unanimity Cornelia paid a price: absence from some of the chapter deliberations on the score of health.

On the morning of 3 August the bishop and his entourage opened proceedings. The chapter proper began, and he invited the free comment of the sisters on his Rule. What came he could not have been entirely unprepared for. He knew through Knapen, at the Propaganda's request, what had been the objections made by Cornelia and her two assistants to his Rule, and had wondered what they meant by writing that it was '*offensive*'. This he had attributed to Cornelia's influence and inexperience, and her autocratic attitude. His invitation to 'free comment' elicited that it was not just Cornelia nor even just her council who thought this, but an elected group from all over the Society. Bellasis recorded the scene:

> His Lordship turned first to the youngest nun for her opinion. The reply truly came as by inspiration, without any previous thought. 'My Lord,' she answered, 'it seems to me that the new rule has been drawn up to correct abuses that do not exist.' There was dead silence for a few seconds, then the Bishop replied: 'If that is what you think you have done no harm in saying so. I wish everyone to feel quite free.'

According to another, the speaker had also said: 'it does not lead us to love

& obey our superiors', which, probably, was what led them to think it 'offensive'.

One after the other the sisters spoke up. All disapproved and the bishop decided to leave them with the unpopular Bosio for the next six days to work through the whole of the Rule yet again, but with him. With the aid of Craisson they were better able to argue with him than in 1874, and there was a unanimity of votes which could not be ignored. Discussions were 'painful' and the strain 'intense'. Nevertheless, should the bishop continue to insist that his own Rule be retained, at least with Bosio they now won important points. Most especially, Cornelia's original introduction might be restored and with it the expression of the Society's contemplative roots in the incarnation which Danell had set aside. It was also agreed that a section from Cotel could be incorporated, a passage which would help to clarify for the Society that Holy Child sisters were not moved by a 'schoolmistress' spirit but by a loving, zealous identification with the mission of Christ. Some rules for the superior-general and local superiors were also retrieved, and at one point in the meetings a provisional plan of government for the American communities was drawn up. They awaited the bishop, dependent on his decisions.

Danell returned on 9 August and while the sisters had a day of prayer he interviewed them one by one about the elections to be held next day. Bosio had drawn up a questionnaire for him, and some extremely brief notes by the bishop show that he used it. At the bottom of the page is the statement, 'make them sign their answers', and it is a pleasure to record that at least one sister objected and at least one other evaded the required reply by saying she had 'not decided'. The questions included the direct one, 'Whom are you going to elect?' and are largely based on the supposition of misgovernment by Mother Connelly. For example: '4. Has Reverend Mother really and truly endeavoured to promote the observance of the rule or has she rather relaxed it, or prevented in some way its observance?'

One may well ask at this point, knowing the state of her health and the view taken of her by the English bishops, why Mother Connelly did not voluntarily step down. Such an initiative, it seems to the present writer, would have been to violate her life-long habit of soul. This was a moment like many others in Cornelia's life when she co-operated as did Christ, 'Thy will, not mine', believing that by so doing she was co-operating in the 'salvation of souls', for which alone the Society existed. Having done all she could to help the delegates in other ways, she must now accept whatever came, not intervening to tip the scale one way or another. She must not manipulate the situation by forcing her own judgment, her own will upon them. She must be open to the discernment. They knew as well as herself the attitude of the bishops (and others); that she was an exhausted and sick woman. For her personally re-election would be no satisfaction. It would mean indeed carrying a cross until death. But in the mystery of Christ it was that that gave life. In the mystery of God, doing God's will, not one's own, gave life. If she was chosen so be it. If she was not, so be it. In either case she would love to the end.

At the elections next day Cornelia was voted in yet again as superior-general, this time almost unanimously – to Danell's chagrin. What she had wanted when she sent her assistants to Rome, what she and they had written to Knapen, delegates from all over the Society now believed in. Even Danell could not attribute their unanimity to her despotism and autocratic demand. More evident was her power to convince and unite.

It remained for the bishop to conclude the chapter. The hopes of all the preceding days were summed up by Bellasis: 'First, that the new rule should be dismissed. Second, that the old Rule accepted by the Propaganda in 1870, together with the additions relating to the government of the Society, should be the one recognised.' They also wanted two matters cleared up; the misunderstandings with Rome that had arisen through the cabal's appeal, and those with the bishops because Danell had been named superior of the whole Institute. For this purpose they wished Rome to be asked to send an apostolic visitor to investigate everything that had taken place. All this is what had been represented in Rome. None of it was news to Danell. He knew of it already and had turned a deaf ear. Cornelia's 1869–70 version of the Rule was not restored to them. His was not dismissed. It was to stand trial for another three years. He merely accepted the insertions and amendments to which Bosio had agreed. It was, Bellasis says, a severe blow. But Cornelia remained calm and obedient, a pillar of conviction. During the days of trial before and during the chapter she had often been heard to say: 'The foundation of the Society is not my work. If it is God's work it will stand; if it is not, the sooner it is brought to naught the better.'

There was now no question of approbation of the 1870 Rule. The final restoration of all they valued would not occur during her lifetime and meanwhile one thing in particular was almost entirely lost: the texts touching personal government designed by Cornelia to promote what had character-ised her perception of what life in the Society should be like, mutual trust and shared obedience between sisters and superiors. This was what neither Danell nor Bosio had understood at all.

One outstanding matter remained after the chapter for resolution between Danell and Rome, the degree of authority to be held by the bishop over the superior-general's government within the Society. Presumably, with the aid of Craisson, bishop and Bosio had been challenged on the subject. Before the rule could be reprinted this had to be settled and Danell wrote to the Propaganda. He claimed that this superior-general ought to be directly subjected to some higher authority such as himself, and by late October he had learned from Knapen that though unusual it could be done. So the bishop took his stand. The foundress of this Institute, he said, being a convert from Protestantism had always feared and was jealous of the intervention of bishops. She had 'tried as much as she could to be independent of them' and had even infused this spirit into the sisters. Indeed this had been observed by the eminent Cardinal Wiseman of happy memory and by the bishop of Birmingham too, Mgr Ullathorne. It would be dangerous should she depend only on the distant Holy See which could not closely supervise her government. He hoped the Propaganda would agree that her dependency should be stated in his Rule. Fortunately the Propaganda took the advice of Cardinal Manning on the subject. When the rule was printed the sisters found no reference to such dependency and no mention of the 'Bishop Superior of the Institute'.

Throughout her religious life Mother Connelly had shown and inculcated the deepest respect for bishops and for the Holy See. The great sadness, not only as humiliation for her but also as an obstacle to the growth of her Society's work in the church, was that neither they nor Rome realised this. Speaking very generally Cornelia in nineteenth-century insular England must have been looked upon with doubt: as a foreign convert, as a separated woman, as a focus for scandal. For a religious superior any of these was extraordinary, irregular, unsuitable. Quite apart from any aspect of personality her position was likely, especially from bishops, to evoke disapproval and opposition. As long as she had Wiseman's powerful support all was well, but without that and when the Society had expanded, inevitable confusion and collision arose over her understanding and theirs about what authority she had. When she stood up for what Rome had missioned her to establish, it looked to them like resentment at their intervention, independence of their authority and a lack of reverence for their office. Any reports of malcontent sisters, justified or not, fed their fears and determination. Goss believed that she had 'installed herself as permanent supervisor' and was 'anxious to keep out episcopal interference'; O'Reilly that she was disobedient; Danell that she 'tried to be independent'. They all, except Grant, said in one way or another that she was autocratic and ungovernable. Yet when Danell with his imposition of a new Rule had deprived the Society of what she knew was its fundamental right, what she wrote for Rome gives a different picture. It was not that she wished to defy, ignore, challenge their authority:

> We are very grateful to all the bishops . . . & we only wish for the same religious government and privileges of Constitutions and Rule granted

to other approved orders without which schisms must be a necessary consequence . . . We should be grieved to shew the least want of confidence in our Bishop but we need union and we do not see how to attain this unless through an apostolic delegate *from Rome*.

Nor was the respect for bishops expressed here mere sugar for Rome. When a sister protested to her against the amalgamation of the Preston communities which O'Reilly had demanded, Cornelia's answer had been: 'You must really look upon the command of the Bishop as the expression of God's will, & this is not to be doubted . . . We have done what lies in our power & in obedience . . . We can but leave the future in faith to His All-Wise Providence.'

As to her relationship with the Holy See: her attitude sprang not from formulas but from living faith experienced in Rome. As the newest possible convert she had fallen in love with the church, rejoicing in the beauty of Christ's mystical body and not blaming the institution for the weakness of some of its members. What she wrote to her husband in those early days shows what was already the nature of her love: 'give it [your heart] all to the Church – all, all and then I shall have it too for I am not one of its children without a wish that is connected with it'. Later it was the *beauty* 'of the morality, charity and truth of the one, apostolic, Holy, Roman Catholic Church' that she wanted Holy Child teachers to convey to their pupils. Later still with something like horror she exclaimed to Mary Xavier: 'Surely you would never be happy in the thought of going on without the final approbation of Rome!' And in spite of so much suffering at the hands of bishops in England and high ecclesiastics in Rome, she still insisted that her council remembered 'There is but one principle to act upon – *the vicar of Christ* and his flock.'

Examples of this too could be multiplied. She desired the Society, as she was herself, to be totally at the disposal of the church, seeing its obedience as a reflection of the 'absolute obedience' of Jesus the Child in Bethlehem and Jesus the Man on Calvary: 'if the Church demands certain changes [constitutional]', she said, 'I do not see why we should demur. I simply say *Fiat Fiat*', and the reason for such an attitude was that no temporal advantage whatever could 'compensate for any want of peace and union with that authority which we shall ever hold sacred'.

It was exactly the opposite of this attitude which was conveyed to Rome and in her lifetime the Society was not given its approbation. Beyond her own certainty that it was God's work not hers, there was no indication that approbation would ever come. Before the next general chapter she would die, without that which would have put the seal on her life's effort.[4]

ACCEPTED SUFFERING, 1874–7

The three years between chapters gave Cornelia every opportunity to make the good heart she so desired.

A spirit critical of her had been unleashed in Preston and fanned into life elsewhere. Danell had accepted and encouraged it, deprived the Society of the Rule she had given and imposed his own, based on the views of the dissident few. He had taken for himself the authority which should now have been hers over the Society, and lent his ear to all that undermined even the shreds of what she retained. There were both clergy and laity who spoke of the Society's suppression and believed that 'Rome was only waiting for Mother Connelly's death' for it to be disbanded. Their prejudice influenced some of its members. Some thought she ought to resign. Others believed she was authoritarian, and as Bellasis remembered, 'a party was beginning to form'. In the life history of the Society these were the growing pains of the inevitable change from a family-like foundress-directed life into an organisation more democratically governed. It was to be expected that as individuals brought into the Society new ideas and understandings of the world from which they came, and then gained experience of religious life, they should want scope to express themselves and to put their own stamp on the group they had joined. But that did not lessen the pain for Cornelia. At St Leonards itself the officious chaplain with no judgment and a great deal of indiscretion credited everything told him against Mother Connelly, encouraged complaints by his self-important listening and passed on to the bishop every scrap of fact, fiction or rumour that came his way. In the house where for many years nothing had been done without her participation or approval, a local superior was now in charge and as one house sister remembered, there were sisters who told Mother Connelly with rudeness that she 'was not superior now and they were not obeying her orders'. A St Leonards tradition has it that at one point there were those who even wanted her to live not in the main house, but at the bottom of the field in the unused presbytery. Another tradition points to a shady path where she walked weeping.

Today we know the dynamics of any group with a strong leader; however wise her wants, its instinct is to challenge and overthrow her. Then such behaviour was inexplicable: it looked like perverse rejection. It is Buckle who tells us in what spirit Cornelia accepted her situation, so humiliating in many of its aspects. When the cabal's work was at its most destructive she had written to Mother Connelly with sympathy and the answer came: 'Pray for me . . . that this trial may be blessed to my sanctification and that I may learn humility from what is calculated to humble my pride.' Elsewhere Buckle amplified this:

The last sacrifice was the most painful and Mother Connelly's character underwent its last transformation. Crushed and annihilated before men she annihilated herself more profoundly before God, and in a letter she wrote to me at the time . . . she expressed herself as receiving only what she deserved, and begged me to pray for her that her pride might be forgiven by God & that He would spare the Society & accept her as its victim.

Cornelia also told Buckle that because she was 'convinced that the thought of founding the Society was not my own but God's' she could not give up 'what he has given me to do'. She wrote in a similar vein to Danell when he was endlessly deferring the first general chapter: 'I am ready at any moment to give up every responsibility but not to shirk it while it still hangs on me from the beginning.' In earlier days she had thrown all her strength and gifts into the effort of founding. Now she seems to have feared the extent to which pride in her had claimed the achieving. Cornelia's pride was not inordinate. It did not characterise her, and those who shouted about her insolence and arrogance were really saying more about their own inability to brook opposition, and about their own pride than about hers. Like all humankind she had her share, but unlike the majority she could monitor its insidious workings in her own heart. The cabal and its consequences seem to have shocked her into a deeper understanding of her relationship with God. She had once written that we are told many things often enough, but apply them to ourselves 'only when the Holy Spirit gives us the light to see and the humility necessary to acknowledge when we really do see, and the fidelity to practice what he shows us!' Now, having seen, she knew she was summoned to a final separation. Not from husband and children but from self-will. Its annihilation. The Society was God's not hers, and unavoidable circumstances now pointed her allotted road. *Per se* they were a clear invitation to accept not reject humiliation. For love she would do this, in and with Christ.

Cornelia's few surviving spiritual notes of this period confirm the high seriousness with which she desired to 'annihilate herself more profoundly before God'. In June 1872 when Danell's long and painful visitation of the community was over, leaving discontent in at least some hearts, she made what look like notes for a conference. Where do my difficulties come from? she asked rhetorically on behalf of each sister:

From thinking too much of self, weighing every little slighting word & act of others, yielding to wounded feelings and anger, compassionating myself, giving way to sadness & tears. The remedy for this is meditation on the suffering of Our Lord & a generous desire to accept suffering for

His sake, rejecting all thoughts of self love & self compassion . . . Walk on steadfastly in your sorrows to meet Jesus at Jerusalem.

By the time Danell had imposed his Rule she was further along this road of the passion. She listed her personal intentions for the retreat of 1875: 'When forgotten, passed over & neglected . . . When corrected or disapproved . . . When wounded or snubbed . . . What did I promise . . . ? To go in for Humiliations.' In April 1876 she examined herself on the same theme: had she cherished humility, seeing herself as the last and the least? Had she obliged herself to put aside wounded feelings? Had she accepted the arrangements of superiors without murmuring? Had she been the first to apologise? A month later she was reminding herself always to take God's view: How should I view this in Eternity? And in the retreat of that year she renewed her oblation: 'When creatures trouble or neglect me, to turn to God to whom alone I ought to give my heart. God alone. For Thy sake my God.'

TILL THE END, 1879

It was after the last meeting with his disciples that Christ set out for Gethsemane and the final stretch of the road to death. After the 1877 chapter, eighteen months remained for Cornelia.

Her assisting council was not expected to be complete 'for some months to come' because Angelica Croft was still not well. Immediately, in August, there came a demand on strength that Cornelia no longer had. Sr Frances Kenworthy had died earlier in the year leaving a substantial part of her fortune of £40,000 to the Society. Her relatives decided to challenge the will in court on the grounds of undue influence. For two years Parliament had again been entertaining petitions against nunneries, and the public was ripe for yet another convent trial as sensational as Saurin v. Star.[5] The notorious and grasping Mrs Connelly's reappearance would be equally rewarding. This must have induced immense strain, prolonged over many months because the trial did not come on until the following March.

Until November Cornelia kept going, then fell very ill. Writing Christmas letters in December she said, 'the gout has taken to run all over my system'. What she termed gout medical opinion now judges was chronic nephritis.[6] From her bed she wrote to the sisters in America. The 'cross of this suit' was 'still hanging upon us', and the thought of life after death was with her: 'Let us all pray fervently for each other, not forgetting that we have a Community in heaven waiting for us to join them there. Ah when shall this be! Before very long for us all.' At Epiphany her expected letter to the whole

Society was a bare few lines because there were 'hours of great prostration'. She thought herself that she was dying, old friends were sent for, a letter went out to all the Society, she received the Last Sacraments, and Danell visited her.

But she rallied. No one believed that she was really better, and when the law required that she attend the Kenworthy trial as a witness, the doctor refused to allow it. Sometimes she was wheeled into the council room on a couch and she did what she could of business. The trial was to be on 6 March, Ash Wednesday, in Westminster Hall. For many days beforehand the Society prayed its strong novena and many other novenas too, and altars glowed with votive candles. 'Be instant in prayer,' Mother Connelly had said. Lawyers were in and out of the London convent, discussing evidence. Sisters had to come from St Leonards to be available as witnesses and the house was not large enough to accommodate them. They had to lodge elsewhere and placards appeared announcing that at 'The Great Convent Case' forty nuns would be in court. When the day itself the mere sixteen arrived at Westminster – brought discreetly in carriages by friends – the court had been 'crammed to excess' for hours. Had the defendants not unexpectedly withdrawn their plea, the notoriety with which Pierce had smeared Cornelia and the beginnings of St Leonards twenty-eight years before would again have damaged the Society. A telegram of thanksgiving went to her but the anxieties of a lifetime were now taking their toll and respites would be brief and shallow. Not for another month did she get to church (for the Easter liturgy), and it was another two before she could bear the journey by carriage to Mayfield and went for the long summer – not yet well enough, she told Danell, 'to be of any use'.

She was returning to Mayfield for the last time. Earlier stays had been different. A house sister remembered Mother Connelly and herself cutting potatoes for the planting: 'Now & then we used to cook our food on a wood fire & sit at a table close by the fire & eat a poor fare just like poor cottage people & dear Mother seemed to enjoy it & was so bright & pleasant.' The same sister had another memory too, possibly of Mayfield days:

> I had begged for a Bath chair . . . to take Reverend Mother round the grounds . . . & I got knocked up myself. A Sister told her that I *fancied* a Mutton chop. Reverend Mother made answer, if she wanted a dozen she should have them, but I was too ill to eat any – and Mother sent me a half of a peach that was given to her, & half of her bottle of Soda Water & came to me when she was able.

Ill though she was she still endeared herself to those close to her. The novices by now were well settled at Mayfield. Often they sat with her in the garden or down by the pond, delighting in her company, listening to her stories, drinking in her spirit. She wanted the Old Palace to be the Mother House of the Society and one day, standing by the little convent cemetery, said to them, 'It is here I wish to be buried.' When they looked depressed she at once 'raised our spirits & was herself the brightest of us all'.

Two dear friends accompanied her to Mayfield, Theresa Hanson and Ignatia Bridges, Theresa acting as her nurse. Cornelia's relationship with her predated their friendship in the Society. When Pierce Connelly used to visit his wife and children at the Trinità in 1844–6, she had come to Cornelia to be instructed as a Catholic and had learned then to love her. Later she joined her Society at Derby. When Pierce disavowed all he had committed himself to, it was Theresa whom Grant allowed to act as go-between. She saw Pierce several times, trying to conciliate him, and after he had left England she kept in touch with Ady and Frank. Buckle records these facts but says no more. Cornelia, with what inner turmoil one cannot guess, must sometimes have received news of the children through Theresa. Eventually, by 1875, she and Ady were corresponding (a single letter of Cornelia's has survived), and in 1877, a little time after the chapter, her daughter at last came to see her. Only a postscript to a sister tells us anything: 'Yes . . . I did quite enjoy dear Ady's visit & feel very much more happy about her being in good faith at heart and really deceived into error.' This was a crumb for which to be grateful. After Pierce's death it would be Theresa's patient influence at Neuilly that brought Ady back to the church and to devote herself to works of charity – she would die peacefully, holding her mother's crucifix.[7] Now Theresa was a loved link with the first and deepest source of suffering in Cornelia's suffering life. Her company was eminently appropriate.

Ignatia Bridges also was a convert; she too came to the Society at Derby and she too had spent most of her religious life in Cornelia's community. Whereas Theresa had been at one time a superior in London and for many years the infirmarian at St Leonards, Ignatia had been Cornelia's faithful secretary, even to accompanying her on the many journeys round the Society. In her spare time she translated French spiritual books, cared for the garden, enthralled the children by her dramatic reading, and was as enraptured as Cornelia herself by all natural beauty. When Mother Connelly was presumed dying in January 1878, she and Maria Buckle, at Cornelia's own request, had been summoned back from Neuilly. Now to have Ignatia still with her after all, and at Mayfield in its most lovely season, was an unexpected consolation. For all three there had been happy occasions together: the Derby days; community life in the poky little Grenelle house; the cheerful busyness of readying the new convent in Nottingham Place. There was also a bond of accepted suffering. The friendship which both

Theresa and Ignatia had for Cornelia had roused hostility in some quarters. It was to these two that Lucy Woolley probably referred when she said Mother Connelly confined herself to consulting people of no ability except that they would always agree with her.

The three months, therefore, had their quiet joys – drives in the pony trap; the knowledge that here saints had lived; talking with the small children in the school; friendship; prayer in the novices' oratory – the old minstrels' gallery that looked down into the ancient synod hall, now so beautiful a church. But her strength came and went. In August she was dangerously ill again. When at last she returned to St Leonards, in Buckle's words: 'she was much changed . . . she embraced us with tears in the community room, saying as she looked round, "I never thought to see you all here again".' Once more she braced herself for business with the council but her strength could not last. By the end of October she admitted that 'the least worry tells upon my system & nerves from which I never suffered until this year'.

December came. Her thoughts turned to her own country:

A very happy Christmas to you all, and many of them each more holy than the last. You must know that I think I am oftener with you in Spirit than you can well imagine. You know our window looks to the West and the Sunset takes me directly across the great ocean, when you are no doubt fast asleep & not thinking of us.

The Society's great feasts came and went. She wrote to Neuilly from where news had come about the children in its now prospering school, 'I love them each & all as if they were my own.' At Epiphany it had to be holy pictures that she sent everywhere, not a letter. To France she said tenderly, 'My love to *each* Sister.' To America, longingly: 'if *God wills* me to be of any use I may regain my strength & go to America to see you all, for which I must get leave being now nearly seventy years of age'. Her seventieth birthday fell on 15 January. The day before as a gift from heaven came news that must have overwhelmed her with relief on behalf of the Society. Danell gave permission for vows once more to be perpetual. Accordingly on 2 February, the thirty-ninth anniversary of John Henry's scalding death, five sisters made perpetual profession and Mother Connelly signed their vows, one of her last known official acts.

The occasion was a sign for the Society's future, but in community the sisters now knew that Cornelia's life was coming to its end. The feasts of February and March came and went with the whisper, 'it will be her last'. By the middle of Lent the hideous, painful disease was taking over. Inflammation of the skin appeared accompanied by violent internal and external irritation. Sometimes she was unconscious, sometimes lucid. Her physical sufferings even at their most extreme could not quite crush her bright spirit, and nearly to the last, Bellasis says, she kept her 'childlike gaiety'. By April the nerves of spine and brain were affected but she could still sometimes receive Communion. Those who then knelt by her bedside saw 'the sweet smile which seemed almost to transform her' as the Sacrament was brought into the room. Others lingered outside the door to catch the sound of her fading voice as afterwards she sang to God. It seemed to them that she was then 'pouring out' her soul, 'in an ecstasy of joy'. Bellasis records the words of one particular hymn which she sang to music they had never heard before:

> O Jesus, hidden God I cry to Thee,
> O Jesus, hidden Light I turn to Thee,
> O Jesus, hidden love I run to Thee,
> With all the love I have I cling to Thee,
> With all the strength I have I worship Thee,
> With all my soul I long to be with Thee,
> And fear no more to fail or fall from Thee.

By 11 April, Good Friday, Cornelia was in the last days of agony. She was to experience in her own flesh a dying like that of her small son so long ago. She whom Buckle had once described as having 'a face of Paradise' was now disfigured. The burning redness had 'spread over her whole body not sparing even her face and giving her the appearance of one scalded from head to foot'. For long periods she was sunk in coma, yet even as from the depths of a mother's grief she had placed John Henry's death in the context of the paschal mystery, now too she retained some consciousness of the great mysteries of Christ in the midst of which she was sinking. To the amazement of those by her bedside, when the bells rang for the resurrection she suddenly, in a strong voice, intoned the Easter antiphon which tells Mary to rejoice, 'Regina Caeli'.

During Easter week agony intensified. The sisters sang her favourite hymns for her. The day before her death, when one of them was trying to ease the suffering which the skin condition caused, her faith in the for ever incarnate Christ broke through. 'In this flesh', she cried, 'I shall see my God.' This she repeated three times, each time striking one hand with the other. That night in great pain and at death's edge, she often cried out: 'My Jesus have mercy on me. Oh God, have pity upon me.' Next day before going to mass all the sisters gathered round her bed. They prayed, and they sang for her, including Ignatius' Suscipe. Throughout the morning she lingered, unconscious. Only prayers from time to time and her laborious breathing, more and more inaudible, broke the silence of the room. In the final moments she was given the last absolution and at ten to one the bell tolled that she had gone to God. It was thirty-three years to the day since she had set out for Rome on her mission, the reputed lifespan of Jesus whose years on earth she had so unreservedly and strikingly recapitulated.

The sisters were awed by her death. Desolated they nevertheless described it as splendid, holy. It vivified their love and their faith. Ignatia Bridges had watched the sufferings of her months of dying, and wrote:

> . . . you can never know by my poor words how bravely her strong and bright spirit has fought against them all [sufferings] and with what a saintly resignation she accepted them all because it was the Will of God. Often and often has she said, 'Doing the Will of God is the only happiness & the only thing worth living for'.

In that very spring, by then confined to her room, Cornelia had 'applied her fresh & vigorous mind' for the community's sake to the thoughts of plants for the kitchen garden. Unable to move about, she sat 'hour after hour' choosing from nursery lists and then planting cuttings. Tenderly she watched over them 'because as she said again & again they seemed as they shot up in all their variety to be the very last image of the beauty of God'. It reflected the solicitude that she had carried in her heart for the growth of each member of the Society. There in front of Ignatia as she wrote were the little plants, set out with the 'same beauty of Order' with which everything Cornelia's 'little hands produced was done'.

Her requiem on the 22nd was sung with splendour in the Jones church, a great crowd of children, friends, sisters and priests attending. Searle gave the homily. Blazing with candles before black hangings stood the statue of the Holy Child which Cornelia herself had designed. That same day her body was taken to Mayfield and lay all night, with the community and the novices keeping vigil, under the arches of the church she had created out of hallowed ruins. Next morning, escorted by a long procession of perhaps forty sisters, she was taken down to the little convent cemetery. It was spring time. Mayfield was at its most beautiful, its hedges and meadows green and fragrant, the trees in leaf. The graves had been decked with flowers by the novices. The path was primrose-lined and the air sweet. A robin perched on a railing and reminded them of how in winter Cornelia had loved to feed the birds. Round the grave the professed sisters and the novices made a double circle, and at the end of the prayers, each before she left the cemetery dropped in upon her a little bunch of wild violets. Many years later Cornelia's body was removed to an alcove in the church where she still lies – beneath words taken from the *Imitation of Christ*, a book she often read with her husband and every day of her religious life: 'Love knoweth no measure, feareth no labour, maketh sweet all that is bitter, findeth rest in God alone.'

Notes

CHAPTER 1   CHILDHOOD AND YOUTH

1   See E. Oberholtzer, *Philadelphia: A History of the City and its People* (Phila, 1912), pp. 2, 74.
2   See A. Gilchrist, 'The Philadelphia Exchange: William Strickland, architect', *Historic Philadelphia*, 87 (Phila, n.d.).
3   For the life and personality of Connelly see D. G. Paz, *The Priesthoods and Apostasies of Pierce Connelly*, NY, 1986; also C. McCarthy, 'Cornelia and Pierce Connelly: new perspectives on their early lives', *Records of the American Catholic Historical Society of Philadelphia*, 71 (Phila, 1961).
4   See E. Eastmead, 'Nunnington', *Historia Rievallensis*, 175 (London, 1824).
5   See C. and J. Bridenbaugh, *Rebels and Gentlemen: Philadelphia in the age of Franklin*, 51, 65 (NY, 1942); M. Schiffer, *Historical Needlework of Pennsylvania*, 55–67 (NY, 1968); R. Wood, *The Pennsylvania Germans*, 109 (Princeton, 1942).
6   See C. McCarthy, 'Introducing the Rev. James Montgomery', *The Pylon*, XXVII, 2, 27 (1965).
7   No evidence shows that Pierce attended a seminary. For the course, see W. W. Manross, 'Bishop White and theological education', in *Life and Letters of Bishop William White*, ed. Stowe, 196–201 (NY, 1937); P. M. Dawley, *The Story of the General Theological Seminary 1817–1967*, 18–22 (NY, 1979).
8   Vestrymen's Minutes 1773–1840, Trinity Church, Wilmington, DE.

CHAPTER 2   THE MINISTER AND HIS WIFE

1   See P. Butler, *The Unhurried Years*, Louisiana State University Press, 1948; J. Ingraham, *The South-West by a Yankee* (NY, 1835); T. Marshall and G. Evans, *They Found it in Natchez* (New Orleans, 1939); J. Register, ed., *Views of Old Natchez* (Shreveport, LA, 1969).
2   H. Huntington to N. Mercer, 14 February 1837. Mercer Papers, Tulane University, New Orleans.
3   N. Oliver, *This Too is Natchez*, 33 (NY, 1953).
4   L. Beecher, *A Plea for the West*, 54 (Cincinnati, 1835); S. Morse, *Foreign Conspiracies Against the Liberties of the United States . . .* vol. I, 96, 97 (NY, 1835).

5 Schoolcraft Papers, vol. 87, MSS 8391, 8401, in French. Library of Congress, MSS Division, Washington DC.

6 Vestry Minutes 1821–99, Holy Trinity Church, Natchez MS; cf. Bishop Brownell, ed., Beardsley, 'Journal of Missionary Tours, 1829 and 1834', *Historical Magazine of the Protestant Episcopal Church*, VII, 4, 320.

7 See W. Perry, *The History of the American Episcopal Church*, vol. I, 215 (Boston, 1885); and W. H. Stowe, 'A turning point: the General Convention of 1835', *Historical Magazine*, IV, 3, 154.

CHAPTER 3   CONVERSION

1 See W. Chanler, *Roman Spring*, 12–17 (Boston, 1934).

2 See J. M. Farley, *Life of Cardinal McCloskey*, 176 (NY, 1902).

3 Documents preserved at the Congregation for the Doctrine of the Faith, Rome, March 1836. Extracts, *Positio*, 99–101.

4 As pope Capellari reissued his book *Il Trionfo della Santa Sede* (1799). See H. Jedin, ed., *History of the Church*, vol. VII, *The Church between Revolution and Restoration*, 261–8; vol. VIII, *The Church in the Age of Liberalism*, 3 (London, 1981).

5 N. Wiseman, *Recollections of the Four Last Popes*, 325, 332, 335 (London, n.d.).

CHAPTER 4   INTERIM

1 See O. Chadwick, *The Victorian Church*, vol. I, 279–81 (London, 1971).

2 Quoted in D. Gwynn, *Lord Shrewsbury, Pugin and the Catholic Revival*, 28 (London, 1946).

3 cf. F. M. L. Thompson, *English Landed Society in the Nineteenth Century*, 97 (London, 1963).

CHAPTER 5   TIME OF TRIAL

1 See C. M. Buckley, *Nicolas Point SJ: his life and north-west chronicles*, 133–76 (Chicago, 1988).

2 Quoted in L. Callan, *Society of the Sacred Heart*, 119 (London, 1937).

3 See Callan, IV, and the house diaries of the convent of the Sacred Heart at Grand Coteau.

4 J. P. Roothaan SJ to P. Connelly, 24 June 1839; Connelly to Roothaan, 28 February 1839, 29 June 1841, in French, Rome SJ Archives.

5 See Buckley, op. cit. 156.

6 J. Soller SJ to J. P. Roothaan SJ, 20 May 1842, in French, Rome SJ Archives.

7 J. Harrison, *Early Victorian Britain 1832–1851*, 131 (London, 1971).

Notes

CHAPTER 6   SEPARATION

1   D. Fleming, *A Contemporary Reading of the Spiritual Exercises*, 167, 234. Institute of Jesuit Resources, St Louis, 1980.
2   P. Aries, *Centuries of Childhood*, 279–83, 413 (NY, 1962).
3   On Rozaven's recommendation Princess Galitzin entered the Society 'as the most austere educational Order that he could find for her'. *Positio* 1270, N55.
4   For Villefort, see Buckley, op. cit. 29.
5   This was popular thinking, e.g. a contributor to *Dolman's Magazine*, VII, 11, 192, wanted to know why Pierce's ordination had been allowed 'before his wife had positively taken the vows'.
6   For Cornelia's strict observance of the rule of enclosure see 'Statement of Facts' written for her lawyer. SHCJ/R.
7   Agnes Berkeley, 'European Tour, 1845–46', Spetchley Park Archives.

CHAPTER 7   BEGINNINGS IN ENGLAND

1   See W. Elwes, *The Feilding Album*, 80–5 (London, 1950).
2   E. Norman, *The English Catholic Church in the Nineteenth Century*, 15–24 (Oxford, 1984).
3   See E. C. Sullivan, *Georgetown Visitation Since 1799*, 64, 65.
4   J. Walsh SJ, 'The Vocation of Cornelia Connelly 11', MS. SHCJ/R.
5   Cornelia's Customal (*c.* 1860). Taken from the Constitutions of the Daughters of the Sacred Heart at Bergamo.

CHAPTER 8   CONNELLY AGAINST CONNELLY

1   e.g. P. Connelly [Pen Cler Jocelyn], *Five Letters to Sir William Broadlands*, 111, 21 (London, 1853).
2   Quoted in Paz, 130.
3   R. J. Schiefen, *Nicholas Wiseman and the Transformation of English Catholicism*, 149 (Shepherdstown, 1984).
4   Quoted in R. E. Shaw, *The Catholic Apostolic Church: A Historical Study*, 74 (NY, 1946).
5   See H. Drummond, *Remarks on Dr Wiseman's Sermon on the Gorham Case*, 28 (London, 1850); *Second Reading of the Ecclesiastical Titles Bill*, 26 (London, 1851); *A Plea for the Rights and Liberties of Women Imprisoned for Life under the Power of Priests*, 65 (London, 1851).
6   See Bernard Hargrove, *Positio* 111, A35–47; Paz, 135–50.
7   See D. Cecil, *Melbourne*, 230 (NY, 1954); C. Norton, *Caroline Norton's Defence*, introd. J. Huddleston, *passim* (Chicago, 1982); J. Perkin, *Women and Marriage in Nineteenth-Century England*, 26–7 (London, 1989).
8   For Connelly's life and writings during the Florence years, see Paz, 186–216;

and C. W. Welsh, 'The Episcopal Church in Florence; a tale of two beginnings', *Anglican and Episcopal History*, 423 (1987). For Connelly's personality problems, see Georges Cruchon SJ, 'The case of Pierce Connelly: a study relating to the psychological development and affective disorders', *Positio*, 111, A22–34; and Paz, 218–27.

CHAPTER 9   CORNELIA AND NICHOLAS WISEMAN

1   See Schiefen, op. cit. 115; also 197, 201, 219.
2   R. Whitty, quoted in Schiefen, 198.
3   Quoted in Schiefen, 199.
4   P. Nepveu SJ, tr. SHCJ, *Higher Paths in the Spiritual Life* (Derby, 1851).
5   Quoted in Schiefen, 190.
6   Probably for Bertram Talbot, seventeenth earl since November 1852. In 1853 he published Connelly's address given as a Catholic in Baltimore cathedral 1842, and prefaced it with an attack on him and a defence of Cornelia.
7   Melia mismanaged the financial resources of the new Italian church in London.
8   See Schiefen, 138, 308; and C. Butler, *Life and Times of Bishop Ullathorne 1806–1889*, vol. I, 217 (London, 1926).
9   See O. Chadwick, op. cit. vol. I, 507–9.
10   e.g. *Cases of Conscience: or, lessons in morals: for the use of the laity*. Extracted from the moral theology of the Romish clergy. By Pascal the younger [pseud.] (London, 1851); *The Coming Struggle with Rome, not Religious but Political* . . . (London, 1852); *Domestic Emancipation from Roman Rule in England: A Petittion to the Honourable House of Commons* (London, 1852); *Reasons for Abjuring Allegiance to the See of Rome: A Letter to the Earl of Shrewsbury* (London, 1852).
11   B. Bogan, *The Great Link: A History of St George's Southwark, 1786–1948* (London, 1948).

CHAPTER 10   CORNELIA AND EMILY BOWLES

1   Emily's simple vow of poverty allowed her to retain the ownership of property but not the personal use or administration of it. At this point it was administered by trustees. It is not clear how large her fortune was, nor how much Cornelia knew about it.
2   L. Charlton, *Recollections of a Northumbrian Lady 1811–66, being the Memoirs of Barbara Charlton*, 231 (London, 1949).
3   See S. P. Casteras, 'Virgin vows': the early Victorian artists' portrayal of nuns and novices'; and C. M. Prelinger, 'The female diaconate in the Anglican Church: what kind of ministry for women?' in *Religion in the Lives of English Women, 1760–1930*, ed. G. Malgreen, 129, 161 (London, 1986); H. E. Roberts, 'Marriage, redundancy or sin: the painter's view of women in the first twenty-five years of Victoria's reign' in *Suffer and Be Still*, ed. Vicinus, 45 (Indiana, 1973).

Notes

1   For reference to Gate Street schools, see H. Mayhew, *Mayhew's London* [1851], ed. Quennell, 409 (London, 1949).

2   *Rambler*, 1846, 11, pref. iv.

3   Poor Schools were usually attached to missions. At Derby Sing provided living accommodation but paid no stipends. The sisters were allowed the voluntary offerings from the school and church Poor Box. In two years the combined total was £36 3s 11d.

4   See Schiefen, op. cit. 137, 171; also B. Ward, *Sequel to Catholic Emancipation*, vol. 2, 148–52 (London, 1915).

5   E. Midwinter, *Nineteenth-Century Education*, 19, 28–36 (London, 1970); John Marmion, 'Cornelia Connelly's work in education 1846–1879', 309–11 (University of Manchester, Ph.D 1984).

6   This plan of Wiseman's faded as he realised that the conversion of England was not imminent. See *Tablet*, 31 October 1846; and J. Walsh, 'Why an American foundress in England in 1846?', *Pylon*, XXII, 3, 3.

7   See M. J. Illing, 'An early HMI, Thomas William Marshall: in the light of new evidence', *British Journal of Educational Studies*, 1972, XX, 58–69.

8   D. Beale, Preface to *Reports Issued by the Schools Inquiry Commission on the Education of Girls*, 3.32 (London, 1869).

9   D. Beale, 79.

10 For this and recollections below, see C. Gompertz, *Life of Cornelia Connelly 1809–1879*, 301–9 (London, 1922).

11 See Marmion, op. cit. 217–28.

12 It gives also government requirements for Poor Schools, for training pupil-teachers in schools and for further training in colleges.

13 Gompertz, op. cit. 302.

14 *Informatio*, 207.

15 'I am now painting most of the time. I do not think it well to allude to it much – it may be too valuable to talk about. Such as they are the paintings will I think leave here [Auckland] a little after I do', Frank Connelly to his father Pierce, 3 March c. 1880. As sculptor, see Paz, 189.

16 Gebhard Flatz (1800–1881), Viennese painter living in Rome 1836 and associated with the religious fraternity of the Nazareni, *Positio* 1254, N45. For Rio, see Jedin, op. cit. VIII, 52; *Dublin Review*, 1, 1836, VI, 441–5; and W. Vaughan, *German Romanticism and English Art*, 41, 42, 90–2 (Yale, 1979).

17 Marmion, 298–300.

18 ibid. 375.

19 *Reports of HMI of Schools: T. Marshall Esq on the Roman Catholic training College of All Souls at St Leonards-on-Sea for Schoolmistresses*, MCCE 1856–9. House of Lords Archives.

20 SND, *Sister Mary of St Philip (Frances Mary Lescher) 1825–1904*, 128 (London, 1922). For Marmion on Stokes, 341–4.

21 See Illing, op. cit. 66–9.

22   Marmion, vol. 2, 18, N91.

CHAPTER 12   CORNELIA AND THE DUCHESS

1   On Foy, see *Positio*, 979.
2   See Schiefen, op. cit. 240.

CHAPTER 14   'THE APPEARANCE OF IRRESPONSIBLE CONTROL'

1   See C. McCarthy, *The Spirituality of Cornelia Connelly: In God, For God, With God*, 129–33 (NY, 1986).
2   See H. Jedin, op. cit. VIII, 13.
3   *Informatio*, 77.
4   See C. Gompertz, op. cit. 439.

CHAPTER 15   'LADEN WITH THE FRUITS OF LIFE'

1   J. H. Newman to R. E. Froude, 3 August 1864; C. S. Dessain, ed., *Letters and Diaries of John Henry Newman*, XXI, 180 (London, 1961).
2   E. Bellasis, *Memorials of Mr Serjeant Bellasis 1800–1873*, 193 (London, 1895).
3   Mère Eugénie Milleret de Brou whose community (founded for education) was only in its seventh year, and whose guest Cornelia was, wrote to her director Père d'Alzon discussing whether to encourage Cornelia to join her congregation. She concluded that she was 'trop jésuite dans ses idées'. *Positio*, 237, 242.
4   J. N. Grou, *L'intérieur de Jèsus et de Marie*, vol. I, 58 (Paris, 1843).
5   The foundation at Neuilly began to do well in October 1878 and flourished until the Combes Law, 1904, forced teaching congregations to leave France.

CHAPTER 16   LOVE KNOWS NO MEASURE

1   Theresa Hanson, to be replaced as local superior by Gertrude Day, was much disliked by the house sisters and also devoted to Cornelia.
2   Abbé Craisson, *Des communautés religieuses a voeux simple: législation canonique et civile* (Paris, 1869).
3   See C. McCarthy, op. cit. 201, N93.
4   Her Rule was substantially and finally approved in 1893 and its core texts are retained as the foundation of twentieth-century constitutions, approved 1983.
5   See W. Arnstein, *Protestant versus Catholic in Mid-Victorian England: Mr Newdigate and the Nuns*, 82–3, 200–4 (Columbia and London, 1982).
6   *Positio*, 111, A73.
7   Frank was never reconciled to the church or his mother. His relationship with

Theresa was still good in 1898. At Ady's death he asked for the crucifix. He died in 1932 leaving a natural daughter who had married into the Borghese family. There are living descendants.

Index

Catholic Church 49; in
England 51–5; financial losses
59–62; second request for
ordination granted 91; no
longer to be a Jesuit 97–8;
ordination 102; ministry in
England and interference with
SHCJ 137; abducted children
129; suit to regain Cornelia
and her property 139; apostacy
144; pamphleteering 158, 186,
351; Episcopalian ministry in
Florence and death 158
Connelly children, provision for
91–3, 112–13
Constitutions and Rules SHCJ,
struggle for 104, 105, 133, 137,
193–5, 199, 203–6, 225–7,
285–8, 290–2, 294–8, 309,
330–1, 335–6, 387
Cotel, Pierre SJ 335, 386
Craisson, Abbé 331, 336, 337, 354
Croft, M. M. Angelica SHCJ 329,
334, 342
Cruchon, G. SJ 351
Cutts, M. Maria RSCJ 85, 96

Danell, James, Bishop of Southwark
302–10, 314–16, 324–9, 330,
333, 335–8, 340, 341, 343, 345
Dawley, P. M. 349
Day, M. M. Gertrude SHCJ 326–9
Derby (St Mary's convent and
schools) 106, 112, 114–18, 344
Doria Pamphilj, Prince Placido 59,
89
Dower 283–4, 304
Drummond, Henry MP (Albury
Park) 139–42, 148, 150, 179,
186–7, 351

Dublin Review 22, 23, 25, 26, 34, 52,
55
Duke, Dr William 165, 176, 181,
185, 188, 196–7, 220–9
Duval, Adeline Peacock 9, 11, 14,
27–9, 31–4, 56, 104, 189
Duval, Lewis 9, 14, 31

Eastmead, E. 349
education 229–55 *passim*; place of
fine arts 244–6
Education Committee of Privy
Council 248–54
English College, Rome 47, 282, 285,
291
Epiphany, Feast of 59, 89, 213, 290,
342, 345
Errington, George, Bishop 228
Eyston, George 211–13, 215,
217–19, 222

Farley, J. M. 350
Fenwick, Benedict Joseph, Bishop
105
Flaget, Benedict Joseph, Bishop 317
Fleming, D. SJ 351
Florence, American Episcopal
Church 158, 288
Foy, Fr John 271–7, 280
Forbin-Janson, Charles de, Bishop
317
France 317–23, 344, 345
Franchi, Alessandro, Cardinal
333–4
Francis of Assisi, St 86, 114, 200,
201, 207
Francis de Sales, St 105
Francis Xavier, St 174
Fransoni, Giacomo, Cardinal 42,